Learning Democracy

Learning
Democracy

Citizen Engagement and Electoral
Choice in Nicaragua, 1990–2001

Leslie E. Anderson and Lawrence C. Dodd

The University of Chicago Press
Chicago & London

Leslie E. Anderson is associate professor in the Department of Political Science at the University of Florida.
Lawrence C. Dodd holds the Manning J. Dauer Eminent Scholar Chair in Political Science at the University of Florida.

The University of Chicago Press, Chicago 60637
The University of Chicago Press, Ltd., London
© 2005 by The University of Chicago
All rights reserved. Published 2005
Printed in the United States of America
14 13 12 11 10 09 08 07 06 05   1 2 3 4 5

ISBN: 0-226-01971-3 (cloth)
ISBN: 0-226-01972-1 (paper)

Library of Congress Cataloging-in-Publication Data

Anderson, Leslie (Leslie E.)
    Learning democracy : citizen engagement and electoral choice in Nicaragua, 1990–2001 / Leslie E. Anderson and Lawrence C. Dodd.
      p. cm.
    Includes bibliographical reference and index.
    ISBN 0-226-01971-3 (cloth : alk. paper)—ISBN 0-226-01972-1 (pbk. : alk. paper)
    1. Nicaragua—Politics and government—1990—Public opinion. 2. Democrati-
zation—Nicaragua. 3. Elections—Nicaragua. 4. Elections—Nicaragua—Public
opinion. 5. Political participation—Nicaragua. 6. Frente Sandinista de Liberación
Nacional—History—20th century. 7. Public opinion—Nicaragua. I. Dodd,
Lawrence C., 1946– II. Title.

JL1616.A53 2005
324.97285'054-dc22   2004024387

For Thornton H. Anderson
and
Cloyd Dodd

Contents

Preface

Nicaragua is a tiny tropical country on the isthmus of Central America, nestled between two continents and two seas. In precolonial times it lay between the Aztec and Inca empires; today it lies between democratic Costa Rica and nondemocratic Honduras. Its geographical position portends the turbulence of a crossroads, and it is here that the traditions of revolution and the traditions of democracy have come together to create a unique political experiment. This experiment revolves around an intriguing and timely puzzle: Can a powerless, illiterate, and impoverished nation with a long tradition of authoritarian rule and foreign domination democratize? Can such a nation use socialist revolution to break free of authoritarianism and foreign subjugation and then employ free elections to move beyond revolutionary socialism and create an effective, sustainable democracy?

The purpose of this book is to explore this puzzle and to chart the coming of democracy in such an unexpected setting through analysis of the 1990, 1996, and 2001 Nicaraguan elections. In the first of those elections, to the surprise of observers, Nicaragua's citizens rejected the presidential candidate of its socialist-revolutionary government and embraced his more conservative opponent. In doing so, they moved the nation into a more full-fledged electoral democracy characterized by government alternation and regime transformation through free, competitive elections. Thereafter, the citizens twice voted to reaffirm their selection of democratic conservatism. Why would impoverished citizens in such a setting turn against the government they had installed through revolution and affirmed in the 1984 elections and move toward a more conservative democratic regime? And what conditions could prepare voters for such a daring use of electoral process? These are among the most intriguing questions confronting students of democratization in the developing world. The answers can help us grasp how postauthoritarian and postsocialist societies can succeed in moving toward stable, electoral democracy.

We will address the issues raised by Nicaraguans' turn away from the Sandinistas and their sustained move to democratic conservatism through close examination of citizen attitudes and vote intent in the 1990, 1996, and 2001 election campaigns. Access to a unique set of public opinion surveys for these elections allows us to trace the evolution of vote intent during each election, thereby clarifying why citizens voted as they did. It also provides us a distinctive window into the evolution of voting behavior by third world citizens across elections during the early years of democratization. As to the broader issues raised by Nicaragua's electoral experience, we will address them by placing the electoral outcomes in a historical and interpretive context that clarifies how inexperienced voters could embrace electoral procedure and engage in difficult regime choice. This interpretive and historical perspective derives from a reading of the scholarly literature on Nicaragua and on democratization processes worldwide, from the content analysis of newspaper coverage of the campaigns, from fieldwork by Leslie Anderson beginning in the mid-1980s through 2001, and from briefer visits by both authors before and during the election campaigns.

As the reader will soon learn, this book is a union of unlikely traditions in scholarship. It brings substantial training about the politics of the poor, marginalized, disadvantaged, and undereducated in developing agrarian societies together with extensive study of public opinion, democratic elections, and governing institutions in advanced, industrial societies. The first, including a large component of "peasant studies," concentrates on the politics of actors and nations largely outside the mainstream currents of power, affluence, privilege, and world dominance. The second privileges mainstream politics and middle-class electorates in the North Atlantic nations that dominate the world. It is an unusual combination of scholarly concerns, particularly in the study of Latin American politics. And yet our joint training and experience in these two vastly different traditions have made this book possible, and only this unlikely combination could have produced the analysis and interpretations we share here. It is appropriate, therefore, to acknowledge both the fields and the individuals that have taught and mentored us in learning these traditions.

Anderson acknowledges two decades of training and learning in the field of peasant studies and in the politics of the poor, including the vast literature that teaches a deep respect for the political capacities of the poor despite their underprivileged status. In addition to the field itself, five individuals have played central roles in Anderson's training, understanding, and ongoing intellectual development. These individuals watched over her from her earliest years of graduate study, and some continue to do so today. They include Daniel Levine, her dissertation chair, and James C. Scott, second reader on the dissertation committee. Levine provided invaluable insight into popular perceptions and the role of cultural values in shaping those perceptions. He also gave guidance in understanding the politics of Latin America and small Central American nations. Scott offered sensitive attentiveness to the savvy intelligence and moral integrity evident amidst the poor in peasant societies. He also furnished invaluable training in the observation of the politics of the poor. Anderson was able to put such training into practice through eighteen months spent living among the poor of Nicaragua and Costa Rica during the mid-1980s and repeated visits there since. In addition to the central and continuing role of these two, three other individuals watched, guided, and encouraged Anderson for more than a decade: Teodor Shanin, E. P. Thompson, and Eric Wolf. Shanin continues to be a source of support and inspiration. We regret that Thompson and Wolf are not with us now to see this book. They might have challenged us on some particulars. But we believe they would have welcomed this book, if not all of the vote results it reports, and been cheered by its implications about the democratic capacities of citizens in the developing world.

Beyond the study of the rural poor, this book has also demanded serious contemporary and ongoing study of Nicaragua's political processes and institutions. After the 1979 revolution and throughout the 1980s, many scholars from the United States converged upon Nicaragua, impassioned by the Sandinista effort to revolutionize Nicaraguan society. Among that group, Anderson began studying Nicaragua in 1983, with numerous trips there during the 1980s, including eighteen months of sustained fieldwork.

With the 1990 election, so central to this book, scholarly interest in Nicaragua faded greatly. This is an unfortunate development since it is precisely in 1990, when Nicaragua developed a viable electoral opposition, that its politics became most relevant for understanding the development of democracy in new settings. The next eleven years would test just how effectively the revolutionary reforms had transformed Nicaragua and prepared its citizens to control their own lives, moving the nation and its people beyond the legacy of the Somoza dictatorship.

Concerned to understand the long-term effects of the revolution and to observe regime transition firsthand, Anderson has continued to do extensive fieldwork in Nicaragua, visiting there in 1991, 1992, 1995, 1996, 2000, and 2001. During those visits she interviewed various presidential candidates, several former vice-presidents, many members of the National Assembly, every secretary of the National Assembly (equivalent to the Speaker of the House) to serve since 1990, numerous Supreme Court judges, magistrates, and members of the Supreme Electoral Council, and multiple other political leaders and activists from all three major parties. This book draws on that extensive fieldwork as well as on survey data collected from citizens. Anderson gratefully acknowledges the time given by these Nicaraguan leaders for multiple and often repeat interviews during these twenty years. The book could not have been written without their support. She also thanks Ricardo Chavarria and Marvin Ortega for helping to arrange these interviews.

Dodd acknowledges with continuing gratitude his training at the University of Minnesota more than thirty years ago that introduced him to the emerging literature on empirical democratic theory and to the systematic study of democratic politics in industrialized nations. At the heart of Dodd's training were the guidance and inspiration he received from his two mentors at Minnesota, William Flanigan and Edwin Fogelman. Their support of his early interest in the ways parties, coalition governments, and legislatures facilitate or inhibit democratic governance led him to embrace these topics as the central concerns of his scholarly career. In addition, their study of the multiple pathways by which nations democratize, decades ahead of its time, laid seeds of curiosity within him that blossomed forth when the opportunity to study democratization in Nicaragua presented itself. Also central to Dodd's scholarly development was their yearlong course on contemporary political theory. It introduced him to the range of empirical theories relevant to social science inquiry, from rational choice theory to social structure analysis to social psychology to social learning. His subsequent work on parliamentary and congressional politics would have been inconceivable without this training. His graduate seminar at the University of Florida "Empirical Theories of Politics" is a direct outgrowth of his experience in their course, as is his ongoing focus on crafting and applying empirical theory in the analysis of real-world political settings such as Nicaragua.

Additionally, Dodd extends deep appreciation to John Pierce (then at Tulane University), David RePass (at Minnesota), and Philip Converse (at Michigan's ICPSR summer consortium) for the instruction they gave him in public opinion and survey analysis, thereby laying critical foundations for our analysis of elections in contemporary Nicaragua. His appreciation as well goes to Frank Sorauf, Samuel Krislov, W. Philips Shively, Robert Holt, George Bornstadt, and the late L. Earl Shaw for their training across the diverse fields of American party politics, law and society, European politics, comparative political analysis, social statistics, and democratic theory. He acknowledges with deep gratitude the influence of the late Brownie Tanner, who fostered his early fascination with Latin America. Dodd also has benefited greatly from his interplay with Bruce Oppenheimer, who always reminds him that national elections and institutional politics do really matter; with Morris Fiorina, who highlights the capacity of citizens to pursue self-interest through electoral participation and vote choice; with Bryan Jones, whose work on the complex character of citizen decision making in democratic politics proves a continuing inspiration; and with Rodney Hero, who constantly pushes him to remain attentive to the presence and power of the underprivileged and poor even amidst affluent democracies.

Finally, Anderson and Dodd together express appreciation to the sizable group of scholars who have concentrated on Nicaragua and Central America over the past quarter century. This group, cited extensively throughout the book, has generated an impressive and even unique documentation of the struggle of a small third world nation to come to terms with its difficult history of mass exploitation and empower its citizens to shape the political and social forces governing their lives. This book would not have been possible, certainly not with the attentiveness to history and context to which it aspires, without the work of these scholars.

We have many other acknowledgments as well. We would like to thank Gustavo Mendez and the staff at the DOXA Public Opinion firm in Caracas, Venezuela. Mendez began his support for this book by releasing 1990 data that he had collected to Anderson in 1992. We admire his willingness to do so and are deeply indebted to him for his confidence in this work. Mendez subsequently worked with Anderson to gather the 1996 data. That second study was funded by the National Science Foundation. In collecting the 1996 data Mendez again displayed a high level of precision and professionalism.

We also acknowledge Sergio Alberto Santamaria, the director of CINASE, and all of his polling staff who worked so diligently with us to collect the 2001 data. CINASE (Centro de Investigacion Social y Economica), as an affiliate of the larger Nicaraguan nongovernmental organization INPRU (Instituto para la Promoción Humana), has a long and noble history of work with the Nicaraguan public, dating back even to the Somoza years. INPRU is a collection of activists and development workers, while CINASE represents the more scholarly element of the organization. It is good to see Nicaragua develop such professionals who, like DOXA in Venezuela, are devoted to learning the truth about what the public has to say, regardless of whether or not we like what we hear.

During the academic year 1995–96 we constructed a data set based upon content analysis of Nicaraguan newspapers reporting on the 1990 election. The analysis of those data appears in chapter 3 and provides a contextual understanding of the election that would never have been possible with public opinion data alone. We would like to thank the University of Florida for the generous financial support that made that data collection possible. In particular we acknowledge the research support provided to Anderson by the Department of Political Science and the Center for Latin American Studies of the University of Florida and the resources provided to Dodd by the endowment of the Manning Dauer Chair. Together these resources funded the work necessary to collect, construct, and perfect the newspaper data set.

We have benefited immeasurably from the assistance of a series of research assistants who worked on the project at various stages in our research. During the beginning stages of the research at the University of Colorado, Todd Landman converted the 1990 public opinion data set to ASCI format, readied it for analysis, and conducted early statistical analysis; Michael Zarkin did the same at the University of Florida for the 1996 data set and also worked on the content analysis study mentioned above. In addition to Zarkin, Edward Greaves and Christina Reid joined us in doing content analysis. Leonard Tipton of the Department of Journalism at the University of Florida, drawing upon his extensive experience with content analysis, oversaw the beginning of the content analysis project. A fourth excellent graduate student at the University of Florida, Emilia Gioreva, undertook a broad range of tasks in the latter stages of the writing and proved invaluable in preparing the manuscript for final review. We likewise benefited from the diligence of yet another Florida graduate student, Jamie Pimlott, as we prepared the text for final production, and from the skillful preparation of tables and figures by Erin Johnson of Erin Johnson Design/Englewood, Colorado. Finally, we have benefited immensely from research assistance in Nicaragua provided by the late Ricardo Chavarria and from the gracious hospitality extended to us by his family during research trips to Managua. We deeply miss Ricardo's presence and regret that fate has deprived us of the opportunity to share the final manuscript with him.

In all aspects of library and archival research, particularly in accessing the newspapers for content analysis, we are deeply indebted to two outstanding research librarians: Richard Phillips of the University of Florida Latin America Collection and César Rodriguez of the Yale Latin American Collection.

Anderson acknowledges the generous support of the National Science Foundation for a grant to study the 1996 Nicaraguan election. Her thanks as well to John McIver of the University of Colorado, then Political Science Director at the NSF, for his assistance in making that grant possible. Such a study would never have been possible without NSF support, and the comparison of electoral outcomes in part III of this book would never have been possible without this second body of data. Anderson's fieldwork for this book was supported by research assistance from the University of Colorado and the University of Florida. The primary writing stage of this book was made possible by a spring semester of halftime teaching leave for Anderson. Anderson is grateful to Kenneth Wald of the University of Florida for making that writing time available for her. Support for work on the manuscript also was made possible by a fellowship awarded to Anderson from the George and Eliza Gardner Howard Foundation of Brown University. She also acknowledges the assistance of Willard Harrison and John Lombardi in making that fellowship leave possible.

Dodd acknowledges with appreciation the generous support provided to him by the University of Florida Foundation and the Manning Dauer Chair that helped facilitate his participation in this project. These funds provided for critical research assistance and support for a range of supplementary data collection, for field visits to Nicaragua during the 1996 elections, and for the precious time to work on drafting and revising the manuscript. In addition, the Dauer Chair provided the funds for the 2001 surveys by CINASE and thus made possible the extension of our analysis into that election. Dodd also acknowledges support from the University of Colorado in the spring of 1994 that facilitated his participation during the early stages of project design and data analysis, and support from the Woodrow Wilson International Center for Scholars, which awarded him a research fellowship in 2003–4 that enabled the completion of final revisions to the book. Finally, Dodd expresses great appreciation to Leslie Anderson for sharing with him the 1990 and 1996 DOXA data sets on which this project is based and for so warmly embracing the joint analysis of electoral choice, democratization, and learning in Nicaragua.

Several people have read all or parts of this manuscript at various stages in its preparation. We appreciate the comments of Thornton Anderson, John Booth, Ricardo Chavarria, Margaret Conway, Joseph Cooper, Michael Coppedge, Robert Dahl, Sharon Damoff, Emilia Gioreva, Erwina Godfrey, Lewis Grow, Bryan Jones, Terry Karl, Daniel Levine, Scott Mainwaring, Terry McCoy, David Mayhew, Anne Pitcher, Robert Putnam, Mitchell Seligson, Susan Tarcov, and Thomas Walker. Each of these individuals made an invaluable contribution to this book, giving us feedback, criticism, challenges, and detailed support. We are fortunate to be a part of such a supportive and interested scholarly community. The book is better as a result of their input. Additionally, it has taken an extraordinary level of vision, courage, and balance to see this book through the review process and into print. For that we thank John Tryneski, two anonymous reviewers, and the highly professional production staff at the University of Chicago Press. We also acknowledge the cheering section that included but was not confined to Thornton Anderson, Mary Lou Anderson, Joseph Cooper, Richard Conley, Margaret Conway, Christopher Dodd, Meredith Dodd, Michael Dodd, Joan Fiore, Erwina Godfrey, Aimee and Bill Hagerty, Renee Johnson, Jennifer Knerr, Fred and Mary Munson, Cathy Rudder, Randy and Cheryl Winter, Freda Willatts, Mildred and Jack Woodruff, Jon Wotman, and many of our graduate students at the University of Florida.

In the final analysis this book is about democracy. It is about the process and limitations, hopes and disappointments of democratic development and of democratic learning in a setting where political freedom is still new. As we seek to understand that process and as we become deeply involved in the data about that process, let us not forget that both the chance for democratic development worldwide and the opportunity to study it are owing to a generation of young men who went to war for democracy and against tyranny in World War II. Whatever might have happened in the Cold War years since then and however those years may have shaped the democratic process we study here, none of this would ever have been possible without the sacrifice that their generation made then for our generation now. It therefore seems appropriate to remember and acknowledge, in the words of former president Clinton, that "these men saved the world." This book is dedicated to our fathers who have nurtured us and supported us and listened to us and who, before we were even a gleam in their eyes, went to war to save this world for us and with it the opportunity for generations yet to come to learn democracy.

Boulder County, Colorado
July 19, 2004

Chapter 1

The Democratic Experiment in Nicaragua: An Introduction

In 1989 the politics of the world changed. In the future we may compare that year to 1789, 1848, 1917, or 1939 in the effect it had on world politics and democratic development. The changes that have come since 1989—the fall of the Berlin Wall, the end of the Cold War, the demise of Soviet Europe, democratization there and worldwide—are so enormous that we are still struggling to understand their full magnitude. The threat of another and final war was reduced. The Cold War division that had shaped the world for most of the twentieth century suddenly ended, allowing considerations about political democracy and human rights to assume an importance they had long been denied. The contours of Europe changed.

Yet the story of 1989 is not just a story of Europe. The animosity between the two world systems had generated repercussions in every corner of the world. Cold War perceptions, the intense hostilities between communism and capitalism, and local desires to emulate or divorce from one system or the other had shaped politics in Asia, Africa, and the Americas from 1917 onward, particularly after World War II. Now the implications of the new configuration reverberated globally, threatening to disturb domestic politics everywhere.

One place where the new international developments seemed most immediately relevant was Central America, where Cold War politics had dominated the scene throughout the postwar years. The right-wing dictatorship of the Somoza family in Nicaragua gave an authoritarian cast to regional politics and received strong U.S. support in part because of the dictator's Cold War loyalties to the United States. Then in the 1970s a social revolution in Nicaragua looked to Cuba and the USSR for assistance and inspired

official U.S. hostility.[1] Now, as if to dare fate, the socialist Sandinistas who
had led the revolution and then sought popular support at the polls launched
their second electoral campaign in November 1989.

The Sandinistas asked the electorate to choose socialism again precisely
when much of the world was rushing away from it. Yet it was not an unreasonable request. Unlike other socialist regimes, the Sandinistas had already
won an election in 1984, becoming the first socialist regime ever to hold revolutionary and electoral legitimacy.[2] They won that election after instituting
popular social reforms in one of the world's poorest nations, including land
redistribution and improvements in health, education, welfare, and employment. Now, seeking support to continue these reforms, they were the first
socialist regime ever to stand for reelection.

Despite continuing conflict with the United States and its debilitating
domestic consequences, the Sandinistas fully expected the citizens to stand
with them again. In defeating the violent Somoza dictatorship, in surviving a
decade, in defying the United States, the Sandinistas had won unlikely victories
before. If defeatism had been their motto, they would never have achieved as
much as they had. Undaunted, they launched an electoral campaign to reelect
Daniel Ortega as president, again offering a socialist polity and semisocialist
economy. Nor did most observers think the Sandinista quest for reelection
unreasonable. Both supporters and opponents expected the Sandinistas to win.
Scholars, revolutionaries, and counterrevolutionaries alike were surprised by
an electoral choice in which voters selected the nonsocialist Violeta Chamorro
and her offer of a new regime committed to democratic conservatism.[3]

The first goal of this book is to explain the 1990 electoral decision. In our
effort to do so we describe the 1990 campaign and its election outcome in
detail. We then ask why voters made the decision they did, whether it was a

---

1. Walker (1982) and Booth (1985) give the history of the revolution. Anderson (1994b) and
Ruchwarger (1987) discuss the role of citizen participation in the revolution and its aftermath.

2. The 1984 election was monitored by a range of international observers, most of whom
concluded that the election was a free and fair expression of popular sentiment. Following the
election, the Sandinista government was accepted as legitimate by the international community.
The major exception was the Reagan White House, which repeatedly challenged the election
results and supported overthrow of the regime by the Contra rebels. See Walker (1985, 521–32;
1991, 26–28); Booth (1985, 215–23).

3. By democratic conservatism we mean a government that fulfills three basic conditions:
(1) support of free market capitalism combined with limited reliance on a social welfare state,
(2) attention to and delivery of basic civil liberties and human rights within a liberal democratic
model committed to free, competitive, and meaningful elections, constitutionalism, and power
sharing across parties, and (3) a commitment to amiable political relations and economic trade with
other free market nations, particularly including the United States. Democratic conservatism resists
explicit commitment to economic democracy, a large welfare state, or extensive social services.

deliberate move or some accidental or reactive misstep that failed to convey their true sentiments. We also consider why so few visible observers, regardless of political color, anticipated the 1990 Sandinista defeat. Our investigation of these queries takes us into the academic literature on vote choice and requires us to modify the arguments of that literature to fit the reality of new democracies in contemporary third world settings. Guided by our modifications, we provide an in-depth analysis of survey data on the 1990 election. Parts I and II present our resulting answers.[4]

In focusing on 1990, we are forced to consider whether the electoral outcome that year was a product of such unique circumstances that such a focus distorts our understanding of Nicaraguan politics. To address this issue we examine Nicaragua's subsequent experience with democratic conservatism and analyze the decision processes citizens employed in the 1996 and 2001 national elections. We ask whether the basic political perceptions and reasoning processes that characterized citizens in 1990 were reaffirmed by them in 1996 and 2001. Our concern is to explain why citizens have stayed the course with democratic conservatism and to highlight the issues and conditions that might lead them to reconsider their support of it. This analysis is found in part III.

Our second goal is to understand the democratization process in Nicaragua. As we step back from the elections to view Nicaraguan history across the past quarter century, we conclude that a democratic transition is under way there. Moreover, this is true in a context where history and theory conclude that the odds were and are definitively against democracy and democratic development. Nicaragua possesses none of the classic requisites of democracy stressed by theorists, such as affluence, a cohesive elite guiding it to democracy, a long-standing civic culture, or a history of gradualist evolution in liberal institutions and free market economics. Instead, its

---

4. These answers build on a well-established body of literature devoted to the study of elections through the use of public opinion surveys. This work first emerged in the United States and has generated a long list of classic studies of U.S. elections, including Lazarsfeld, Berelson, and Gaudet (1944); Berelson, Lazarsfeld, and McPhee (1954); Campbell, Converse, Miller, and Stokes (1960); Nie, Verba, and Petrocik (1976); Page (1978); Fiorina (1981); Popkin (1991); Green, Palmquist, and Schickler (2002); and Abramson, Aldrich, and Rohde (multiple editions from 1982 to 2003). The study of public opinion and elections has spread more slowly elsewhere, with classic foundation work including Butler and Stokes (1969) on Britain; Converse and Pierce (1986) on France; and Dalton (1996) on the general character and role of public opinion in advanced industrial democracies; see also LeDuc, Niemi, and Norris (1996, 2002) and Michelet and Simon (1975, 1977). Within the Latin American context see the pioneering work on Mexico by Dominguez and McCann (1996) and the essays in Dominguez and Lawson (2004). For compendia of academic survey studies around the world, see Guchteneire, LeDuc, and Niemi (1985, 1991).

modern history is overshadowed by severe poverty and widespread illiteracy, violent clashes among elites, regime repression of civic engagement, and a social revolution seeking to rectify the nation's dire straits through rapid political transformation and socialist restructuring.

The classic requisites of democracy are said to be essential in large part because they provide citizens with vital preparation for democratic citizenship. Without such preparation citizens lack the capacity to comprehend the nature and value of democratic elections, to reason and choose among contending parties and regimes in a responsible and sensible manner, and to honor the outcomes. Yet Nicaragua not only lacked such requisites; it seemed decades if not centuries away from their realization, with a citizenry so poor and poorly educated as to appear incapable of meaningful democratic participation according to the classic literature on democracy. Why then were the citizens of Nicaragua able to participate in the "high stakes" elections of the contemporary era, abide by their outcomes, and embrace a process of regime change and democratization?

Nicaragua's quarter-century journey from right-wing dictatorship to socialist revolutionary government to electoral democracy—all amidst extreme poverty and limited education—is one of the more extraordinary and puzzling developments in a remarkable era of global change and democratization.[5] And it is made even more remarkable by the success of the Sandinistas in capturing control of most major municipalities in the 2000 local elections, while conservatives maintained control over the national government then and even after 2001. The movement from extensive human rights violations and political repression in the 1970s to competitive democratic elections and partisan power sharing today clearly constitutes an improved way of doing politics. It points toward the possibility that Nicaraguans are learning to engage in democratic politics and to use such politics in skillful and nuanced ways. But if democracy is developing and Nicaraguans are learning to resolve political differences democratically, how did they get there from so unlikely a start? And what might the answer to this question tell us about the citizen capacity for democratic learning and political participation elsewhere?[6]

To answer these questions we look closely at the ways Nicaraguan his-

5. P. J. Williams (1994); Robinson (1997, 23–47).

6. Our answers to these questions stress the capacity of citizens to engage in a kind of "fast-forward" learning when confronted with severe crises of the sort enveloping Nicaragua from the late 1970s through the early 1990s. For relevant background discussion that informs our analysis of this issue, see Dodd's argument (1994) that common citizens are more capable of political learning and change than is generally recognized. He proposes that they can engage in transformative conceptual change when severe crisis and anxiety convince them to look for new ways of understanding personal and collective interest. See also Marcus, Neuman, and MacKuen (2000).

tory prepared citizens to engage in electoral politics despite their adverse circumstances. We then utilize this experience and the democratization process it fostered to reassess much of the classic literature on democratic requisites. Our historical argument is presented in chapter 2, and our reassessment of the requisites of democratization is developed most fully in chapter 9. The remainder of this introduction elaborates on the two questions that lie at the heart of the book: why the sudden and unforeseen vote against the Sandinistas, followed by its subsequent electoral reiteration, and why the transition to democracy in so unlikely a setting?

Why the Electoral Revolution?

Students of Nicaraguan politics, focused on the nation's extreme poverty and the Sandinista efforts to alleviate it, had viewed the 1990 electoral result as a virtual impossibility. They saw citizens of Nicaragua as remarkably courageous, cognizant of the social ills of their nation, and prepared to take the steps necessary to address them. Citizens who had risked their lives and lost loved ones to institute social revolution would now stand with Ortega and the Sandinistas to protect it. Certainly they would not embrace Chamorro's offer of democratic conservatism, replacing hard-earned social reform and mass political mobilization with austere conservative policies and procedural democracy. Similarly, there were widespread expectations that voters would reembrace Ortega in 1996 and in 2001 to redress the deteriorating social conditions that came with austerity.

From this perspective, the voters' sustained embrace of democratic conservatism has deeply puzzled observers. How could such a disconcerting realignment in the partisan attachments of citizens occur,[7] generating "electoral revolution"?[8] Why would citizens who had supported the Sandinistas in social revolution, reaffirmed them in 1984, and appeared as revolutionary loyalists vote them out of office in 1990 and then reiterate that vote in

7. The concept of partisan realignment, as first developed by V. O. Key (1955), refers to circumstances in which a substantial segment of a voting population shifts away from its traditional political loyalties and to a new party, faction, or regime in a committed and sustained manner. Walter Dean Burnham (1970) subsequently developed the concept into a broader theory of American politics, in which periodic critical elections realign partisan loyalties and thereby continually reshape institutional politics and public policy.

8. We derive the concept of "electoral revolution" from Burnham's (1976, 149) argument that critical partisan realignments, and the elections that generate them, can be surrogates for social revolution and violent overthrow of government. We note that the idea of electoral revolution traces back to Thomas Jefferson's celebration of "The Revolution of 1800" in his 1801 Inaugural Address as president, where he used "revolution" to describe the defeat of the nationalist Federalist Party by his states-rights Republicans in the U.S. national elections of 1800. See Bernstein (2003, 136–37).

1996 and 2001? Why did social revolutionaries vote like conservatives?

Scholarly literature and journalistic observations suggest five answers: (1) it was an accident resulting from voter confusion; (2) it was a pent-up, over-due repudiation of Sandinismo by a population that had never really sup-ported the socialist revolution; (3) it was a paradoxical choice of the right (to bring peace, reconciliation, and national reconstruction) by a population that preferred leftist social policies on many everyday matters; (4) it was a mis-calculation by a cynical but leftist electorate who overestimated Sandinista strength and voted against them to restrain them, not to defeat them; or (5) it was a capitulation by Nicaraguans to U.S. policies, a decision simply to give up the revolution and accept external domination. A plausible argument exists for each scenario.

An Accident

The first answer explains the electoral outcome as an accident born of Nicaragua's historic poverty and authoritarianism. In this view, citizens were so poor, uneducated, and inexperienced with democracy that they did not understand what they were doing when they went to the polls. This possibil-ity draws upon research in established democracies suggesting that even privileged citizens have only modest levels of refined knowledge about poli-tics and a limited grasp of issues and vote consequences.[9] They demonstrate disconcerting fluidity in attitudes and contradictions between beliefs and behavior across or within elections. They even can misread ballots and elect the wrong candidates. While electoral politics in older democracies reflect considerable order and stability anyway, such patterns result from enduring partisan structures supported by ingrained social alignments, from a profes-sionalized political elite committed to democracy, and from economic afflu-ence that induces citizen satisfaction rather than from sophisticated voters.[10]

If limited sophistication prevails among literate publics, how much more would that be true among less-educated, inexperienced Nicaraguans? If citi-zens in older democracies can be misled by easy promises and well-polished candidates, could not Nicaraguans be led even further astray, embracing can-didates and a new regime based on a glitzy campaign and misleading slogans rather than comprehension of the real issues?[11] Such an interpretation sug-

---

9. Classic statements include Berelson, Lazarsfeld, and McPhee (1954); Campbell, Converse, Miller, and Stokes (1960, chap. 8); and Converse (1964).

10. Lipset and Rokkan (1967); Schumpeter (1950); and Powell (1982, chap. 3).

11. This perspective could be found in leftist observations arguing that "the people" had

gests that the 1990 outcome was a random result made even more problematic by public incomprehension of political reality. The public might even have misunderstood the meaning of Chamorro's candidacy. Perhaps they did not realize that Violeta Chamorro, widow of the courageous newspaper editor Pedro Joaquin Chamorro, whose assassination in 1978 helped spark the final insurrection against Somoza, was now a candidate of the conservative UNO coalition including some former Somoza supporters.[12]

While genuinely supporting the Sandinistas, citizens inexperienced in electoral democracy may have voted in a confused manner, showing little pattern or reason and inadvertently removing Ortega from office. This first interpretation suggests that the 1990 vote was simply a fluke resulting from misunderstanding of the electoral process by a naive electorate willing to die for the Sandinistas but unable to grasp the relationship between electoral choice and governing power.

A Repudiation

A second and opposing explanation is that the vast majority of the public had never supported Sandinista socialism and now repudiated it at the first true opportunity.[13] This interpretation is consistent with the view that the 1979 rebellion against Somoza was spontaneous and momentary, broadly supported by all segments of society, rather than an organized, coordinated revolution in which Sandinista activists provided the necessary leadership and ideals and received deep popular support.[14] In this view the Sandinistas merely exploited the vacuum created by Somoza's fall and used military force to gain power and impose themselves in government. Instead of being courageous heroes and patriots, they were usurpers of the true revolution in behalf

---

not fully understood that this was an election about the illegitimacy of U.S. policy toward Nicaragua, providing an opportunity to end American intervention, rather than about domestic politics and policy. If they had understood, they would obviously have voted for the Sandinistas. See *Boston Globe*, 2/27/90, 9; 2/28/90, 11.

12. See *Los Angeles Times*, 2/28/90, A15.

13. Journalistic reports offering a repudiation explanation took care to emphasize that the population had never supported Sandinismo. Such reports used words like "totalitarian" to describe Sandinismo. The implication or direct statement was that 1990 was the first opportunity citizens had had to express their "real" opinion. See, for example, *Chicago Tribune*, 2/27/90, 1; 3/1/90, sec. 1, p. 25; *Miami Herald*, 2/28/90, 13A. The French newspaper *Le Monde* (2/28/90) likened the Sandinista defeat to the Chilean "vote for the no," repudiating the Pinochet dictatorship.

14. While this effort to downplay the role of Sandinista-style popular socialism and to stress spontaneous insurrection was clearly the approach taken by right-of-center observers and policy makers, it also appears in the recent effort by Paige (1997, 32, 272) to illustrate how coffee elites in Central America constructed the various pathways toward democracy.

of freedom, not socialism. Instead of caring about the people, they were power aggrandizers seeking personal privilege and control. This view challenges the belief among academics and observers that the Sandinistas had extensive popular support. It suggests that the revolution was a romantic illusion of the left unsupported by data on popular attitudes.

This second interpretation accepts Ronald Reagan's view that the 1984 election lacked legitimacy and that the Sandinistas had governed by intimidation ever since.[15] It sees the public as intelligent and informed but highly strategic, secretive, and self-protective.[16] It suggests that most citizens knew what the election was about and understood what they were doing as they voted. They were anxious to end the indefensible conscription of their sons to fight the Contra War that Ortega's hostility to the United States had provoked, exhausted by the economic devastation his reckless socialist experiments had generated, and desirous of a freer daily life less dominated by the controlling arm of the Sandinista state. They felt little confusion or ambivalence but bided their time, keeping their true beliefs and vote intentions to themselves until it became clear that international conditions would force the Sandinistas to honor a negative vote.

With the Cold War ending and Soviet support for the Sandinistas waning, and with international attention focused on the elections, the timing finally seemed right. The public then delivered an "unexpected" defeat that was, in fact, a foregone conclusion once international events and domestic developments together assured the popular will would be honored.

A Choice

Between these two opposing views, one seeing the electoral revolution as a fluke and the other seeing it as a foregone conclusion, lies a third possibility: the voters closely considered both major candidates and regime alternatives and consciously chose Chamorro and democratic conservatism through rea-

---

15. An excellent example of this perspective from within the U.S. media is a *San Diego Union Tribute* editorial beginning, "Nicaragua: the Central American nation with a troubled past turns away from the sorry legacy of the Sandinistas" (11/24/96, G4).

16. See, for example, the argument by two U.S. pollsters, Schuman and Bischoping, that the Nicaraguan electorate was so negative toward the Sandinistas and so eager to throw them out of office that deliberate bias was needed in the design of survey techniques in order to uncover the public's true sentiments. Their results were published in an editorial by Schuman in the *New York Times*, "Three Different Pens Help Tell the Story," 3/7/90, A25. See also Bischoping and Schuman (1992). For analysis questioning the design of their study, see Anderson (1994a).

soned decision making.[17] Confronting severe crisis under the government they had freely affirmed six years earlier, the citizens nonetheless approached the 1990 election willing to reconsider the governing strategy best suited to the nation's current situation, much like informed, attentive electorates elsewhere.[18] Most were supporters of Sandinista revolutionary idealism, including wealth redistribution and social progress. But in assessing the immediate circumstances they concluded that their priorities lay with a new president and a moderate regime that could end the nation's crisis, foster national reconciliation, and generate reconstruction, whereas the Sandinistas' very idealism might lead them away from compromise and forward movement.[19] After a decade of widely supported experimentation and struggle to implement ideals, citizens opted for pragmatism, political stability, and national renewal.[20] In doing so, along lines that Hirschman (1982), B. D. Jones (1994), and Stimson (1999) attribute to voters in other democracies, they shifted their issue focus. They looked away from expanded social justice, which they certainly wanted, and toward the prioritization of democratic liberties and economic stabilization, which they also clearly desired.

In this third view citizens were duped neither by the Sandinistas during the revolution nor by the conservatives in the election. Rather, voters were observant, thoughtful pragmatists who engaged in the campaign, grasped the

17. For journalistic coverage granting that Nicaraguan voters approached the election in a thoughtful, serious manner, see *New York Times*, 3/4/90, C6; *Los Angeles Times*, 3/4/90, M1.

18. Key (1961, 1966); Page (1978); Fiorina (1981); (Popkin, 1991); Sniderman, Brody, and Tetlock (1991); B. D. Jones (2001, 78–81); Dalton (2002).

19. The *Miami Herald* (2/27/90, A10) quoted Paul Reichler, the Sandinistas' American attorney, as taking this position: "The vote was more a reflection of Nicaraguans' exhaustion with the war and inflation than a signal of their dislike for the Sandinistas." See *Boston Globe*, 2/26/90, 10, for similar views from a Masaya schoolteacher, Martinez (no first name given), who granted that "Daniel might have good intentions" but voted against him because "we want a change."

20. Explanations indicating that the electoral outcome was a choice saw the population as having supported the Sandinista regime early on and turning away from it over time in response to crisis or FSLN policies. See, for example, *Los Angeles Times*, 3/4/90, A1, A12; *Miami Herald*, 2/26/90, 1A, 8A. In particular see Haynes Johnson, "The Lessons of Nicaragua," *Washington Post*, 3/2/90, A2. Johnson presents a particularly strong statement of the "choice" perspective. He sees the Nicaraguans as having "strongly opposed the right-wing Somoza dictatorship and welcomed the Sandinistas," turning against the FSLN slowly "after that regime also proved repressive and inefficient." Faced with growing domestic and international problems, "it was the people of Nicaragua who won this victory. . . . Now through their ballots they have presented the United States with yet another opportunity to play a positive role in reshaping the future in their hemisphere—if the United States is up to it, and that's a big if."

In the effort to explain the vote outcome, Marvin Ortega, a well-known Sandinista pollster, argues, "The people were tired of repression and attempts to control their lives." He stresses the voters' seriousness and treats their choice as a deliberate one, even though it was not the one he preferred. See *Los Angeles Times*, 3/4/90, A12.

issues at stake, reasoned their way to their preferred choice, and voted in ways that best served their priorities and the nation's need to move forward.[21] While perhaps not sophisticated in their refined knowledge of politics, they were capable of engaging in a sophisticated process of judgment and choice between two widely respected candidates and two clearly etched regime directions.

This third view depicts citizens who learned rapidly to participate in electoral democracy, despite poor education, poverty, and democratic inexperience.[22] Moreover, it allows for the possibility that highly engaged citizens saw positive dimensions to Chamorro and her vision that more distant observers missed. It also allows for the possibility that they saw limits to Ortega and his leadership, distinct from issues of ideology and policy. It treats the election as offering citizens a moment of genuine choice and sees citizens as autonomous agents using their best judgment in making that choice.[23]

The election proved unexpected because observers assumed that poorer citizens would naturally stay with the Sandinistas, analyzing them less closely than the urban middle class. In failing to recognize the capacity of citizens in rural villages and impoverished barrios to change political loyalties, analysts missed the potential for electoral upheaval in 1990.

A Miscalculation

A fourth answer is that Nicaraguans were not only politically savvy actors but also cynics who believed the election a charade.[24] Everyone in Nicaragua knew that the government enjoyed massive support. If the outcome went against Ortega, he held sufficient strength to retain power anyway. Citizens thus calculated that the election was simply a Sandinista exercise to gain international acceptance, one they would ignore if they lost. The issue was whether to use the election to send Ortega a message. Seeing the election as a game, citizens played their own sort of game, casting a negative vote they never imagined would change the government, only soften it.

---

21. This perspective parallels the view of those scholars of older democracies who argue that voters are fully capable of making serious election judgments in times of crisis as well as in periods of normalcy. See, for example, Key (1961); Schattsneider (1960); and Marcus and MacKuen (1993).

22. *Boston Globe*, 2/25/90, 12.

23. Moreover, voters also could have had good reason to vote for the Sandinistas. Thus an article in the *Miami Herald* (2/26/90, A8) found Virginia Torres de Blandon of Esteli voting for the Sandinistas because they had given her husband "a plot of land to farm for a living."

24. The *Miami Herald*, for example, found such skepticism among the electorate and quoted one voter as saying, "the better bet is that the dictatorial face [of Sandinismo] will emerge no matter what the vote is and how it proceeds." See 2/25/90, 6C; 2/27/90, 12A; *Chicago Tribune*, 2/26/90, sec. 1, p. 6; 2/27/90, 1A.

This possibility is supported by the fact that many observers believed that Ortega enjoyed broad support. Citizens may have believed likewise, so that an individual negative vote would not appear likely to defeat him, just limit his mandate. Similarly, some observers seriously doubted whether the Sandinistas would honor a negative vote.[25] After all, they had come to power through revolution and military force, they controlled the military and state bureaucracy, and they had access to an extensive party militia spread nationwide that could enforce their dominance. They faced no prospect of a military coup and little chance of being toppled by the Contras. The continuing U.S. intervention offered a ready excuse for maintaining that any electoral defeat was illegitimate because it reflected the undue influence of an international power upon a small neighbor.

An intelligent, informed public might have concluded that the Sandinistas would remain in office, most likely by popular decision but even in the face of defeat, so that the issue in the election was how to moderate Sandinista policies. Such voters would have approached the polling booth intending to express grievances to a permanently entrenched yet popular government rather than to choose a regime. This view depicts citizens who supported the Sandinistas' broad social ideals and most social policies but desired a less dogmatic and overbearing pursuit of them. They saw the vote as a chance to send this message.

In doing so, citizens were not naive innocents, unsophisticated in their political understanding or irrational in their actions, as the first view implies. Rather, they were overly cynical in their political interpretation of both the election and the incumbent, too sophisticated and strategic in their calculations.[26] They thus cast "insincere" votes against the incumbents to constrain

25. For examples of cynicism and skepticism in the U.S. media along these lines, see *Chicago Tribune*, 2/25/90, sec. 1, p. 4; 2/27/90, 1A and sec. 1, p. 5; *Miami Herald*, 2/25/90, 1, 12A; *Los Angeles Times*, 2/27/90, 1; *New York Times*, 2/4/90, A3, 6; 2/6/90, A11; 2/11/90, A28; 2/14/90, A3; 2/24/90, A5; and *Washington Post*, 1/22/90, A11. This type of cynicism continued even after Ortega had conceded the election to Chamorro. See *Christian Science Monitor*, 3/2/90, 3, 5. The reporter in this article reports: "I don't see any moves by the Sandinistas to preempt the transition . . . but I hear a lot of people say it will happen."

26. The study of such "sophisticated" or "strategic" voting is a growing topic in analysis of elections in established democracies. Such voting is said to exist when voters do not vote for their first preference in an election but support some other candidate in an effort to accomplish some special political outcome, such as blocking the election of the candidate that they like least. Here we are suggesting that sophisticated or strategic voting may also be said to apply when voters are trying to generate other types of special outcomes, such as constraining the size of the mandate of their preferred candidate, by voting for a second or even undesirable choice. On sophisticated or strategic voting, see Abramson, Aldrich, Paolino, and Rohde (1992, 55–69); and Abramson, Aldrich, and Rohde (2002, 122–28). For a broad-ranging explication and test of sophisticated voting, see Cox (1997).

but not remove them. What such voters did not foresee was the large-scale negative vote against the Sandinistas and the strength of international pressure upon them, such that remaining in office after defeat was impossible. The vote outcome thus was a miscalculation by a citizenry who supported the Sandinistas but preferred to limit their mandate, a miscalculation that also caught off guard observers who had not expected a Sandinista defeat.

A Capitulation

The final explanation suggests that Nicaraguans simply gave up, capitulating to the United States and voting for the candidate it preferred.[27] This perspective explains Nicaraguan politics in terms of the success of U.S. foreign policy in defeating and subjugating the nation's citizens. In this view, the United States is the dominant actor shaping contemporary Nicaraguan history and politics. The 1979 revolution was a revolt as much against U.S. hegemony as against the Somoza regime, and as such was inherently unacceptable to the United States. Thereafter the might of the United States was devoted to sabotaging the success of the revolution.[28]

Certainly the Sandinistas made mistakes, those holding this view concede, as any government does. But in opposing the Sandinistas, the United States was attacking an authentic, broadly supported social revolution, one with the potential to demonstrate the viability of socialist democracy. In one decade the Sandinistas had dramatically improved the lives of most citizens and engaged them in political participation to a degree never before witnessed in Nicaragua.[29] Their supporters argue that, given time and freedom to act, the Sandinistas would have fully reconstructed society along egalitarian lines and engaged its citizens in a truly civic politics, crafting Nicaragua into an example of what the future could be worldwide. By opposing this experiment, the United States showed its true imperialist and antidemocratic character. It also demonstrated the ability of a powerful hegemon to break the spirit of a courageous and revolutionary people.

---

27. See Walker (1997a, 13–14). See also John Carlin, "Why Nicaragua Voted with Its Stomach," *Independent* (London), 2/28/90, 21. Carlin explains how, thanks to Washington, hunger overcame idealism. He provides a particularly poignant statement of this argument: "The Americans blotted out the sun. They made it absolutely clear to the Nicaraguan people, holding a gun to their head in a species of super-power blackmail, that to vote Sandinista in Sunday's election was to perpetuate fighting and to accelerate poverty. That was the Sandinistas' problem. . . . It is a pity, a tragedy, [that] the gods could not have been more benevolent."

28. Walker (1997c, 1991a; Prevost and Vanden (1997); Robinson (1992).

29. Vanden and Prevost (1993)

By 1990, worn down by the U.S. embargo and Contra War, a demoralized citizenry looked fearfully outward as they contemplated the upcoming election. They respected Ortega and what he had accomplished, trusted his leadership, and preferred him as president. Similarly, they embraced Sandinista policies, preferred the FSLN regime, and shared its ideals.[30] Yet in the years following the 1984 election they had tired of the revolutionary struggle, particularly the battle with the United States, and had come to fear that the Sandinistas' goals lay beyond their grasp. This awareness came starkly into focus in mid-December 1989, when the United States invaded Panama, an invasion whose timing seemed designed to send a veiled threat to Nicaragua. Thereafter, however willing citizens may have seemed to stand by Ortega previously, their will collapsed. The U.S. willingness to use its military to intervene in the domestic policies of a neighbor insured that the citizens, fearing a similar fate, would turn to Chamorro and away from Ortega.[31]

This explanation is found particularly among supporters of Sandinismo who believe that Ortega's defeat and the embrace of Chamorro could not possibly have been choices that reflected reasonable political assessments and personal desires of Nicaraguans. It dismisses Chamorro's offer of democratic conservatism as a legitimate and viable alternative to the Sandinista regime. It sees citizens as having little reason to support Chamorro and oppose Ortega, other than U.S. pressure. This pressure so battered the citizens that they simply lost perspective and crumbled. Regrettably, according to some, they gave up the fight just when the lessening of the Cold War would have allowed the international community to force the United States to honor a second free and fair vote for Ortega and accept the legitimacy of Sandinista rule.

Citizen capitulation went unseen and unexpected, even among those who later embraced the capitulation argument, because observers expected a bravery and commitment from citizens that were no longer present. A once

---

30. The initials FSLN refer to the formal Spanish name of the Sandinistas, Frente Sandinista de Liberación Nacional. In English the Frente is called the Sandinista National Liberation Front.

31. This perspective is seen in Robinson (1992, 140): "When the United States invaded Panama in December, 1989, most Nicaraguans were genuinely repulsed. . . . Conventional logic would suggest that the UNO's identification with the U.S. intervention would therefore have damaged the coalition electorally in the wake of the invasion. But the invasion showed that the United States was ready and willing to invade Central America, to unleash its bombs and cannons on the Nicaraguans just as it was doing in neighboring Panama. The invasion reinforced the message to the electorate that the U.S. backed candidates could avoid such a repeat in Nicaragua. Over ten years Washington had been putting out the message to Nicaraguans that they could not challenge the United States and get away with it. The invasion of Panama made this threat more real in people's minds."

defiant, courageous, revolutionary people, willing to seize the moment and speak truth to power, was now a defeated people willing to accept United States dominance.

Exploring the Explanations

These alternative explanations of the electoral revolution are subject to empirical investigation. Evidence of an *accident* in 1990 would be found in strong public support for Sandinista revolutionary goals and continued governance, combined with erratic, contradictory assessments of candidates, weak linkages between political attitudes and vote intent, and little comprehension of the potential for a Sandinista defeat. Such widespread confusion would decrease in subsequent elections, as citizens became more experienced with democracy, but even in later years poorly educated voters might be so unprepared for electoral participation that randomness and accident could greatly influence vote outcome. *Repudiation* by the public would be supported by citizen hostility toward the revolution's ideals and highly negative evaluations of Sandinista candidates and issue positions. Support of Ortega would appear to come largely out of intimidation and fear inspired by the Sandinista militia, with Ortega's vote support in 1996 and 2001 explained by the militia's continued dominance in selected urban and rural areas.

Evidence of deliberate *choice* would appear in support by citizens for the Sandinistas' social goals, combined with widespread frustration over their governing performance and greater public confidence in the problem-solving capacities of the right. From this perspective, citizens' comparative assessments of the future governing capacities of the right and left would closely shape their vote intent, largely irrespective of appreciation for the early accomplishments of the FSLN. Across the three elections voters could be expected to reassess such views and to shift somewhat in partisan loyalties based on their distinctive experiences with particular conservative administrations, but nevertheless to continue relying on systematic, reflective choice in reaching final vote decisions. *Miscalculation* would be evident in widespread support for the Sandinistas, combined with frustration about elements of their performance, belief that they could win a massive victory but that they would hold onto power even if they failed to do so, and a desire to deny them a landslide mandate so as to restrain their overbearing qualities. This explanation would be most appropriate to the 1990 election.

Finally, *capitulation* would be evident in citizen apathy, resentment toward the United States, and little expectation that the new regime would address fundamental governing problems or truly improve their lives. Yet citizens would also see little recourse other than opposing Ortega and supporting Chamorro, particularly following the Panama invasion. Citizens would then continue to elect rightist candidates out of resignation to U.S. domination, despite continuing support for Sandinista policies and ideals and with little appreciation for conservative candidates or the accomplishments of their administrations.

In-depth analysis of public opinion surveys allows us to explore the validity of these alternative scenarios. For this analysis we have constructed a unique data base that includes five nationwide surveys taken during the 1990 presidential campaign, four surveys from 1996, and three for 2001. The creation and general content of the data base are described in the appendix. These data allow us to examine citizen attitudes in contemporary Nicaragua and subject these alternative explanations to empirical scrutiny. In doing so we draw on prominent theories of voting behavior to guide us in modeling the statistical relationship between citizen attitudes and vote decisions. These models help us understand how the reasoning processes of voters evolved during each campaign and also across the three campaigns. In addition, these established theories and modeling processes allow us to compare the voting behavior of Nicaraguan citizens and citizens in established democracies. Finally, we bring to our investigation considerable attentiveness to the history of Nicaragua and extensive field research into its contemporary politics.[32] We draw on this historical awareness and observational fieldwork to interpret the meaning of our voting models.

Citizen surveys, the modeling of citizen decision processes, close attention to the historical and contemporary record—all of these together help explain voters' rejection of Ortega and the sustained turn to democratic conservatism. In examining the data at hand, we see some evidence for all five explanations, and will present that evidence as clearly and completely as we can. Such evidence indicates that Nicaragua is a very real political world, subject to the complexities that one expects in a nation not only struggling with its own traumatic past but also confronting international pressures and upheavals well beyond its control. Yet amidst these complexities, our concern is to determine which perspective best characterizes the voting behavior of Nicaragua's citizens. What stands out most clearly, we believe, is the conscious, reasoned, and decisive role that the citizens played in moving Nicaragua away from the Sandinistas and toward democratic conservatism.

---

32. We refer here to Anderson's two decades of fieldwork in Nicaragua. The early phases of her field research are discussed in Anderson (1994b). Her repeated trips to Nicaragua following its subsequent democratization process are discussed in Anderson (2005).

Voters made their decisions within a constrained context. U.S. hostility to the Sandinistas confronted them with a problematic future should they have stayed with Ortega in 1990 or returned him to power later. The repeated decision of the FSLN to run Ortega instead of offering a fresh candidate deprived voters of the ability to move beyond his troubled presidency while affirming the Sandinistas. Chamorro's inexperience and the fractious coalition she headed made her election an enormous gamble. And the embittered calls on the extreme right for retaliation against the Sandinistas and reversal of social reforms meant that voters risked continued domestic turmoil and the loss of egalitarian gains by embracing and sustaining democratic conservatism.

Within the constraints they faced, the citizens engaged in an attentive, deliberative process of decision making and took the path of democratic conservatism not primarily as a result of accident, miscalculation, repudiation, or capitulation. They did so through reasoned and reflective choice.

The Case for Citizen Choice

While still adhering to Sandinista social ideals, citizens voted conservatively in 1990 because they had come to doubt Ortega's governing capacity in the immediate context of crisis, a crisis they believed Chamorro could not only end but move beyond. This decision was not based primarily on blame of the United States for the crisis, followed by resigned capitulation to it, or on blame of the FSLN, followed by its repudiation, though significant portions of the citizenry did hold one or the other primarily responsible for the nation's circumstances. Rather, it was based on nuanced assessments of the candidates and their alternative regime offers.

While seeing Ortega as an experienced president and patriot who cared about the people, citizens also distrusted him and consistently doubted whether he was up to the presidency. Moreover, while giving him high marks in contrast to Somoza, whom they continued to detest, they were increasingly aware that life amidst perpetual revolution and international conflict had its drawbacks when compared with the stability and order of the previous era. On the other hand, while seeing Chamorro as inexperienced and poorly prepared for the presidency, they saw her as caring about the people and as more honest and more of a patriot than was Ortega. And they saw her not simply as someone who would be acceptable to the United States and whose election would end U.S. hostilities, but as a potential leader capable of generating reconciliation and national restructuring. Weighing these various considerations, a majority of the voters chose Chamorro, setting in motion regime transformation.

Citizens again voted conservatively in 1996 and 2001—despite serious concerns about social and economic reversals during conservative administrations—because they again concluded that the rightist candidates were more reliable in the presidency than was Ortega. They also did so because of what they saw as the successes of democratic conservatism. Thus they concluded that national reconciliation and reconstruction were going forward and that the new regime was honoring democratic procedures and civil liberties to an extent that no previous government had done. They also gradually came to the view that the neoliberal program of democratic conservatism was generating economic improvements in the nation.

Yet the sustained shift to the right was not preordained. While the Chamorro presidency ended the immediate crisis and fostered a sense of national renewal, leaving Chamorro popular personally, its social austerity generated greatly increased hardships for citizens, hardships only modestly reversed by Chamorro's successor. Both in 1996 and 2001 citizens looked nostalgically back to aspects of Sandinista rule, particularly their commitment to social reform, and in both campaigns there were moments when an Ortega resurgence appeared underway. It is possible that a new and attractive Sandinista candidate, free to point toward the future without having to defend his past presidential record, could have built on popular support for the Sandinistas' social ideals and engineered a victory. But with the choice being between Ortega and successive conservative candidates endorsed by Chamorro, most citizens chose the latter.

The electorate's shift to the right was made possible, paradoxically, by the success of the Sandinistas' social revolution during the 1980s, a success greatly aided by Ortega's determined efforts at social restructuring. Sandinismo in power had dismantled the most dangerous aspects of Somocismo, created a more egalitarian society, and introduced a participatory political system. Those changes had made conservative elite government less dangerous than in the past, since much of its ingrained wealth and political power base was now gone. After more than a decade of popular mobilization and wealth redistribution, and amidst the lessening of Cold War tensions, citizens were willing to risk that a conservative government would not lead to authoritarian rule. Moreover, with the continuing post-election influence that the Sandinistas would have in the state bureaucracy, the military, and the legislature, citizens gambled that the party and its leaders could protect advances toward social justice and popular power whether or not they held the presidency.

Adam Przeworski has argued that democratic transitions are necessarily conservatizing moments because only conservative progress will protect the interests of elites who alone have the power to halt the transition.[33] Our study of Nicaragua suggests that democratic transitions may also be conservatizing moments because the masses, or significant elements of them, see conservative democratic governance as necessary to their own interests even when some elites do not. In Nicaragua, the choice of Chamorro, and the transition toward conservative democracy her offer entailed, occurred because much of the nonelite public came to believe that conservative progress protected their interests better than did the efforts at rapid progress that had been so problematic for more than a decade. While significant portions of the mass public supported Sandinismo in 1990, particularly men and young people from the employed ranks, a larger segment, composed especially of women, the unemployed, and older voters, chose the conservative challenger. These last groups were society's weakest members, closer to the edge in crisis, having fewer resources and reserves, more worn down by household scarcity and the death of loved ones. Assumed by most analysts to be ironclad Sandinistas and thus generally taken for granted by the Sandinistas and observers alike, these voters, with their shift to Chamorro, generated the surprising Ortega defeat, a shift evident in surveys that closely probed the vote decisions of the nation's poorest citizens. Ironically, these groups, for whom the revolution had been fought, now found voting allies among the traditional conservative elite, against whom the revolution had been directed. These latter were actually slower to embrace Chamorro in 1990 than the masses but eventually concluded that she, and later Alemán and Bolaños, best served their class interests.

Behind the broad social divisions and conservative electoral tilt lay a serious process of citizen choice. In pioneering electoral studies of the United States, V. O. Key (1966) and Morris Fiorina (1981) have argued that when citizens engage in retrospective voting, making a decision based on overall incumbent performance, they are making reasoned, rational choices about whom to support. Other scholars have expanded the retrospective argument, maintaining that voters consider the past political performance of all candidates and give special attention to the economy of an incumbent government when making vote decisions.[34] We will marshal substantial public opinion data showing that in 1990, 1996, and 2001 Nicaraguan citizens engaged in broad-gauged retrospective assessments, looking both at

---

33. Cited in Mainwaring, O'Donnell, and Valenzuela (1992, 13) in their introductory summary of Przeworski's argument in the same volume. For Przeworski's argument, see Przeworski (1992).

34. Tufte (1978); Lewis-Beck (1988, chap. 8).

candidates' previous political performance and at the performance of the economy. They then voted partially on the basis of these retrospective assessments. These patterns alone would demonstrate reasoned choice at the heart of the electoral revolution. Yet these patterns are not our only, or even primary, evidence of choice in these elections.

Nicaraguans not only cast votes based on assessments of the past performance of candidates or the economy but also voted based on their evaluation of regime performance. In doing so, citizens assessed past experiences under rightist and socialist regimes and used those assessments in reaching their final candidate choice. These considerations of regime performance shaped vote choice more between 1990 and 2001 than did retrospective evaluations of candidate image or the economy. This evidence points toward a process of reasoning that includes a broader and more consequential array of considerations than those normally present among more experienced electorates and further demonstrates that serious electoral choice was under way.

But our case for choice goes beyond citizen retrospection. Over the past decade scholars such as Paul M. Sniderman, Richard Brody, and Philip E. Tetlock have argued that conditions exist wherein attentive citizens may engage not only in retrospective assessments of candidates and contexts but in prospective evaluations as well.[35] Such conditions, witnessed during normal times in intense issue campaigns but particularly likely amidst severe national crises, lead voters to look not only at the past but also at where the country is headed. In doing so, they may conclude that the economy is about to unravel or a regime is about to collapse and thus factor these concerns into their vote choice. But most important, they compare the prospective ability of candidates to address future problems. Citizens then vote, not only to punish or reward a performance, but also to select the candidate who appears most able to serve citizen interests in the future.

When conditions exist to engender prospective assessment, there is the possibility that voters will judge an incumbent as preferable over a challenger, even in the midst of growing crisis for which the incumbent has some considerable responsibility. They will do so because they have concluded that the incumbent, however problematic his performance in office, is still preferable to the inexperienced challenger in his ability to handle the presidency and address future problems. Yet citizens' capacity for prospection also opens another possibility. It allows citizens to judge a challenger by looking

35. Sniderman, Brody, and Tetlock (1991, chap. 9). See also Kahneman and Tversky (1979); Sniderman, Hagen, Tetlock, and Brady (1986); Marcus and MacKuen (1993); Lewis-Beck (1988); Marcus, Neuman, and MacKuen (2000); Popkin (1991); and B. D. Jones (2001, 78–81).

beyond her inexperience or weak party support to discover special attributes and capacities that may make her a viable presidential choice when more standard concerns like past governing experience would suggest otherwise. Seeing such special attributes, voters could embrace an inexperienced candidate over an experienced incumbent, even in the midst of crisis.

Observers of 1990 have found it surprising that citizens abandoned an experienced party and president who had worked so assiduously, in the face of considerable obstacles created by the United States, to reverse the vast poverty of the nation's citizens. The decision seems more incomprehensible when one considers the opponent. How mass citizens facing severe crisis could turn to an inexperienced candidate heading a fragile coalition dominated by parties historically linked to the old upper-class elite is difficult to understand. This decision is more puzzling given that Ortega entered the 1990 electoral campaign with a positive image, that Sandinista rallies attracted high attendance, and that the United States bore considerable responsibility for Nicaragua's crisis. Retrospective concerns about Ortega— and even prospective fears about the economy or regime—do not seem sufficient to explain such risky and momentous change.

The reason for such a choice ultimately lies, we argue, in prospective considerations whereby citizens assessed the promises Chamorro made and her capacity to deliver on those promises, and then voted on the basis of promise. In doing so, citizens gave strong consideration to her ability to end the war and embargo. But they also closely assessed her capacity to foster reconciliation and national reconstruction. From the outset of the campaign, citizens believed her election was more likely to generate rapprochement with the United States than was the reselection of Ortega. The increase in her support during the campaign paralleled a growing belief in her ameliorative skills, particularly a perception that she was concerned for the people and had the capacity to rebuild the nation. It seems clear, in other words, that citizens evaluated her as a prospective president who would be responsible for important policy initiatives, not just as a U.S. puppet whose election would lead to cessation of the war and embargo. They were considering not only whether her election was likely to end U.S. hostilities, but whether she could use the opportunity to generate national renewal. Her ability to unite a diverse range of parties and groups, combined with her personal and family history, her inclusive political style, and her aggressive early campaign in behalf of a freer and reconstructed Nicaragua, convinced citizens that she could do so.

The citizens' combined reliance on both retrospective and prospective assessments indicates the existence of an impressive process of voter decision making in the 1990 Nicaraguan election. This process, demonstrated by close statistical relationships between citizens' retrospective and prospective assessments and their vote intent, approximates and even surpasses that seen among experienced electorates in its complexity and sophistication. It demonstrates a greater willingness on the part of voters to reflect across prospective and retrospective concerns than has generally been seen in established democracies, a willingness we attribute to the special circumstances confronting voters in new third world democracies. These characteristics of the decision process help explain how it was that citizens could make such a momentous break with the past, doing so through reasoned choice rather than confusion, angry repudiation, cynical miscalculation, or resigned capitulation. They could make their momentous choice, despite poor education and inexperience with elections, because they followed the campaign closely, made discerning judgments about candidates and regime offers, matured in their attitudinal assessments during the campaign in response to information and growing awareness, looked forward as well as backward, and then trusted their judgment and made the leap into the future.

In doing so, Nicaraguans demonstrated that it is not just educated voters in established democracies who can engage in sophisticated reasoning and vote choice, but poorly educated citizens in third world settings as well.[36] They also demonstrated that citizens in such settings, deciding between the only elected government the nation has had and an inexperienced opponent, are not inherently trapped in affirming the status quo. Citizens in new democracies, even the less educated, can, with sufficient opportunity and incentive, make prospective judgments and move their nation into a new political path.

In the subsequent two elections, while the sense of severe national crisis decreased, the issues confronting the nation remained serious ones, so that voters remained concerned about politics and engaged in the presidential campaigns. The promise of free and fair elections, overseen by international observers, then drew them to the polls. In 1996, troubled by increasing poverty but enticed by a growing sense of national reconciliation and democratic liberties, citizens who were initially tempted to reembrace Ortega ultimately swung to the Liberal mayor of Managua, Arnoldo Alemán. With two presidential candidates who had highly visible experience in major public office, voters relied more on the retrospective assessment of both candidates than in 1990. Yet prospection still mattered, particularly because voters had

36. For a broad-ranging assessment of the role of citizens and public opinion in the more established democracies, see Dalton (2002).

not fully determined how strongly they embraced the new regime. Then, in 2001, repulsed by Alemán's corruption and authoritarian tendencies but drawn to improvements in the economy and social programs, citizens turned back Ortega's strongest effort since 1984 and elected Alemán's vice-president, Enrique Bolaños. They did so based largely on retrospection, including their sense that Bolaños had opposed Alemán's aggrandizing actions while Ortega himself had as president shown such tendencies.[37]

The move to a growing reliance on retrospective voting, present in 1996 and pronounced in 2001, points to the increased normalization of democratic politics in Nicaragua. With the major parties and candidates all having significant governing experience, citizens can base their electoral assessments more on the actual performance of candidates and parties in office and less on guesswork and estimated promise. This is a sign of a maturing democracy and a demonstration that Nicaraguan voters are continuing to behave in comprehensible ways consistent with voting theories. Observing the move from extensive prospective voting in 1990 to reliance on retrospective voting in 2001 also enriches our understanding of democratic transitions. It suggests that the capacity for prospection can be critical to democratization, particularly during the early period when most candidates and parties have had little or no governing opportunity. But once significant experience with democracy is under way so that all parties have seasoned candidates, then retrospective assessment of candidates and parties can ground democratic politics in the real-world experience of citizens. It gives citizens a relatively sound process to use in judging the competition, while making positive performance in office a major incentive for parties and politicians.

Across the three elections from 1990 to 2001, Nicaraguans engaged in a sustained process of reasoned, responsible voting and democratic adaptation that analysts need to understand, respect, and learn from even if it has not yielded the results many observers prefer. The more one immerses oneself in the public opinion data presented here, attempting to learn about and from Nicaragua, the more one sees an electorate grappling mightily with the decisions confronting it and doing so in a manner that fits the stereotypes of neither the left nor the right. Instead, one sees a heterogeneous yet pragmatic electorate composed of voters who approach their decisions from very different life experiences, assess their circumstances in distinctive ways, and yet together yield vote results that they collectively accept and honor. In the

---

37. Anderson and Dodd (2002b, 2004)

process they initiate and sustain a regime transition that ends the nation's immediate crisis and moves it toward some considerable reconciliation and national reconstruction. This transition allows for both the integration of the right-wing Contras into national life and the acceptance of the socialist Sandinista party as a viable contender for national power. It generates three conservative presidents who steer the nation toward neoliberal economics and yields a strong, continuing political presence for the socialist Sandinistas. This presence is seen in the Sandinistas' success in national legislative elections and in municipal elections nationwide, giving them political clout with which to continue the push for social reform.

The result is a contemporary Nicaragua that few observers would realistically have thought possible at the height of Somoza's authoritarian repression. Certainly it continues to face grave problems. These include social inequalities, ingrained poverty, and the potential for authoritarian resurgence on the right. Yet Nicaragua in the early twenty-first century is also characterized by competitive democratic elections, respect for civil liberties, pluralistic power sharing, increased egalitarianism, modest social programs providing education, health, and welfare, and a growing market economy. It is, moreover, a nation that reached this moment in time not through the actions of a farsighted, cohesive national elite guiding democratization, or through external occupation and imposition of democracy. Nicaragua reached this moment through the efforts of the citizens themselves.[38] They set the democratization process in motion first through a broadly supported social revolution that ended authoritarian dictatorship and initiated social and political reform, a revolution that they validated through national elections. They then pushed it forward, second, through an electoral revolution that used democratic processes to end the eleven-year revolutionary regime and institute a more conservative democracy. The new regime stabilized and routinized national governance, consolidating many of the gains of the revolutionary era and integrating the revolutionary party into a new pluralistic democratic politics that the citizens considered more respectful of civil liberties (Walker 1997d, 303–4; Selbin 1993, 143). That it did so through an eleven-year process of continuing contestation between right and left in nationwide elections, the national legislature, and mobilized protests only reinforces its democratic character.

In the face of these developments, it is vital to determine how voters made the decisions they did and why the nation's governing regime evolved

---

38. Our emphasis on the role of citizens in democratization is consistent with that of Dahl (1971); Putnam (1993); Thompson (1966, 1971); and Tilly (1995).

as it did. The bulk of this book explores these issues in detail, particularly chapters 3 through 8. Yet, seeing all that transpired in Nicaragua during these years, one is also left with an additional question: how could this quarter-century process of regime transformation and democratization have been possible at all in such a setting?

Why the Democratic Transition?

Our second question has even broader implications than the first, for it speaks to studies of democratic transition worldwide. That literature would deem Nicaragua an unlikely locale indeed for democratization. Here was an impoverished, poorly educated nation with a history of repression and international intervention, little experience with democratic procedure, vast social and economic inequalities, and a pattern of violence from above and below. Clearly, these are not the obvious "requisites for democracy" recommended by scholars to aspiring nations. The Nicaraguan experiment with democracy thus demands that we reassess such requisites and broaden our understanding of the democratization process.[39] We can do so by examining the Nicaraguan experience through the lenses of four general theoretical approaches to democratic study. These lenses have come to dominate scholarly analysis primarily as a result of their usefulness in explaining successful democratization among North Atlantic nations from the late eighteenth to the early twentieth century. They include a focus on affluence, on cohesive elite leadership, on a tradition of civic engagement derived from an extensive history of associational involvement, and on a conducive historical background devoid of socialist experience and preferably characterized by the gradualist evolution of democracy and a market economy. Here we present the core argument of each school and consider how it applies to Nicaragua in the late twentieth century.

Affluence

The first and most intuitively plausible theoretical approach suggests that affluence and its concomitant assets are essential to democracy. Accordingly, an affluent society should generate some significant degree of baseline equality enabling all citizens to participate meaningfully in political decisions. The

---

39. Remmer (1985a) reaches a similar conclusion in her study of "redemocratization" in Latin America, where she finds that democratization processes may not necessarily follow the paths previously foreseen by democratization experts.

literacy and widespread availability of information associated with an affluent society provide citizens with the skills and knowledge necessary for democratic decision making.[40] With the benefits of affluence spread throughout society, the severity of societal problems is reduced so that citizens have a mutual stake in cooperation and stability. Affluence also makes political engagement easier, as citizens have more time to participate in politics.

Proponents of this perspective, such as Seymour Martin Lipset, also stress the role that resource distribution plays in successful democratization.[41] A nation divided into a large impoverished mass and a small wealthy minority would be unlikely to embrace or sustain democracy because the latter would enjoy a disproportionate share of resources and use them to control the former. Moreover, should a nation facing such poverty experiment with democracy, elections would be dominated by unsophisticated voters and inadequate leadership, a combination antithetical to democracy, producing conflict and chaos instead.

Analyses exploring and expanding the link between affluence and democracy, such as Vanhanen's study (1992, 1997) of intellectual and economic resources and Robert Dahl's initial exploration in *Polyarchy*, demonstrate an empirical connection. But the real issue is not whether such an empirical association exists, testing data focused primarily on industrialized nations where democracy first took root, but whether affluence is so essential that its absence precludes democratization. The Nicaraguan case suggests that it is not, thereby raising the question of how citizens can embrace and participate in democracy without substantial material resources and in the face of the social difficulties endemic to poor societies.

Elite Leadership

A second theoretical explanation for democratization points toward elite guidance.[42] In this view the problems a nation faces can be managed through farsighted efforts by a cohesive elite committed to democracy, who guide the nation toward pluralism, carefully preparing citizens for democratic citizenship. Higley and Burton (1989) survey the experience

---

40. Participation, of course, is one of the primary bases of democracy, the other being contestation. See Dahl (1971).

41. Lipset (1959, 1960, 1963). More recently, see a similar argument by Janos (1991) to the effect that successful democratization in Russia would require massive infusion of resources designed to offset the nation's poverty. He maintains that these resources are unavailable in Russia or even from the international community, thereby limiting the prospects for Russian democracy.

42. See, for example, O'Donnell and Schmitter (1986).

of numerous established democracies and conclude that elite cohesion was the main factor accounting for democratic stability and suggest that without it breakdown can occur. Their data appear to indicate that, for advanced democracies, elite cohesion is the definitive explanatory variable, irrespective of differences in the nature of mass participation.

Looking beyond the developed world, Terry Karl underscores the value of elite pacting, as in Venezuela. In her view, successful democratization can occur in difficult conditions when elite actors agree to abide by democratic rules and to leave certain controversial questions out of the political agenda altogether. Karl does not suggest that elite pacting is essential to democratization, only that it is one path in the face of otherwise insurmountable divisions. She also recognizes that pacted democracy can be limited democracy, open to include only some issues and actors but "frozen" to exclude others.[43] Nevertheless, her argument has often been embraced to suggest the need for elite cohesion in support of democratization before successful movement in that direction becomes possible.[44]

We have no quarrel with the argument by these scholars that elite cohesion and pacting have proven critical in the historical development and contemporary performance of democracy. We also acknowledge that elites can play a broad range of critical roles in democratic transitions and will maintain that elites have done so in Nicaragua. In particular, elites of the right and left offered distinct alternative visions of Nicaragua's future in ways that facilitated citizen choice among them in 1990. They also honored citizen choice and respected basic civil liberties at key moments during the democratic transition. On the other hand, elite participation in democratic elections and respect for democratic outcomes in Nicaragua were in doubt throughout the late 1980s, on both the right and the left, and both sides repeatedly pushed for victory through military engagement. Selected elite members of both sides did work to engineer meaningful elections in 1990, but in a contentious rather than a cooperative manner that cast doubt on the motives and good faith of all sides.

43. The problem with such "frozen" democracy would seem clearly demonstrated in the years since Karl first introduced her argument by the experience of such Latin American nations as Chile and Colombia. See Karl (1987, 1986, 1997). For a discussion of the use of elite agreements to exclude some participants from the democratic game, see Hartlyn (1988); and for a more expansive perspective arguing that the strategic calculations and instrumental actions of elites are the primary factor shaping successful democratization, see Casper and Taylor (1996). For a more skeptical view of the democratic nature of pacts, see Shapiro (1996).

44. Another study of democratization that emphasized elite behavior in both Latin America and Eastern Europe is Przeworski (1991). Puryear (1994) sees democratic transition in Chile as fundamentally influenced by the behavior of intellectual elites.

Neither a "natural" cohesion nor a "pacted" agreement among elites would seem to explain events in Nicaragua, a nation where much of the elite was fighting among itself in a destructive civil war even in the months leading up to the 1990 election. Without sustained and cohesive elite guidance to prepare citizens for democracy, and in the face of severe intra-elite hostilities, how were citizens capable of engaging in electoral democracy and choosing among elite contestants? Moreover, why were fair elections held and honored? And what induced elites who lost at the ballot box to acquiesce rather than return to the battlefield, given their deep animosity toward one another and the lack of a pacted agreement among them? Perhaps elite cohesion and pacting, while helpful in many settings, are not essential ingredients of democratization, with the Nicaraguan case pointing us to other factors that may prove helpful when domestic elite cohesion and pacting are absent.[45]

Civic Engagement

A third perspective points to the importance of citizen activism and broadly shared civic values in fostering democracy. While the study of "civic culture" was originally used to gauge the depth of democratic commitment within established democracies,[46] Robert Putnam has recrafted the concept to consider how it can make democracy work.[47] He suggests that the historic experience of citizens with local forms of associational life engenders a capacity for movement toward and participation in regional and national democratization.[48] In his classic analysis of the dissimilar experience with democracy across Italian regions, Putnam makes a strong case that the reason for

---

45. Similar concerns about the necessity of elite cohesion or pacting are raised by Lindberg (2002), who notes that elite pacting does not appear to account well for democratic transitions in Africa, and by Dietz (1992, 252–55) in his assessment of Peru during the 1980s. Dietz notes that a democratic regime emerged in Peru in 1978 and had some considerable staying power throughout the 1980s despite weak "settlement" among contending elite groups. Left unclear is whether such settlement is essential to democratic consolidation. On this latter issue, see Burton, Gunther, and Higley (1992, 339–44). We note that the emergence of elite unity in support of democracy during consolidation is a separate issue from whether elite cohesion and pacting are essential to democratic transitions. Unified elite acceptance of democracy might not be necessary to an initial embrace of elections, but could be necessary (almost by definition) to long-term democratic consolidation.

46. Almond and Verba (1963). See also their later work, Almond and Verba (1989).

47. Putnam (1993).

48. In an important comparative study of democratization in Costa Rica and Guatemala, Yashar (1997, esp. 55) also argues that the rise of civic organization among elites as far back as the nineteenth and early twentieth centuries helps explain democratization in Costa Rica, whereas their absence in Guatemala helps account for its authoritarianism.

varying success levels lies in historic differences in associational patterns. He argues that democracy flourishes where it has been practiced in the community and private realms of citizens' lives through everything from labor unions to sports clubs to hobby and music associations. Cultural values and patterns from such private experiences become ingrained across generations and prepare citizens for the broader public exercise of democracy in cities and regions. By contrast, experiences that inhibit such cultural patterns include loyalty to the hierarchical decision-making process of Catholicism, excessive individualism, and regularized violence.

As the most recent of the theoretical arguments considered here, Putnam's work has generated extensive contemporary reaction. These include the feminist response, the challenge that some associational groups detract from social capital and democratic function,[49] and the accusation of insufficient attention to historic details that fall outside the broad general patterns Putnam describes.[50] Our critique is separate from these.

We find Putnam's focus on a citizen-centered understanding of democracy to be compelling and also believe it provides a suggestive way for understanding successful democratization experiences. Our argument is that his formulation of the processes whereby citizens develop their capacity for civic engagement is too limited when applied to developing nations. First, Putnam stresses extensive associational life of the sort likely to be seen in more affluent, industrialized, urban settings. Second, he appears to suggest that citizens socialized into hierarchical Catholic forms of obedience are unlikely to engage in the sort of personally assertive decision making essential to civic life, with the tradition of hierarchical obedience countermanding the benefits of associational life that the church might otherwise provide. Third, he seems to suggest that the positive aspects of associational life emerge only gradually across centuries of cultural evolution and citizen socialization.

None of Putnam's conditions points toward the likelihood of citizen-centered democratization in Nicaragua, a poor and largely Catholic nation whose mass citizenry enjoyed little opportunity for involvement in secular associations until recent decades. Yet democratization appears to be under way there, and its development seems reliant on a citizen-centered process of civic engagement. How are we to understand this? Are there other circumstances aside from long-term associational life that can induce civic engagement and foster citizen-centered democratization, circumstances so powerful that they can offset the influence of poverty and Catholicism?

49. Berman (1997); Kohn (1999).
50. Tarrow (1996).

Historical Background

A final perspective on democratization emphasizes the distinctive social and political experiences of a nation and the way these experiences aid or hinder democratic development. The notion that a nation's historical path and previous regime may shape its success with democracy is longstanding, reaching back at least to Tocqueville.[51] It was also seen in the early post–World War II years in Louis Hartz's *Liberal Tradition in America* (1955) and in Barrington Moore's *Social Origins of Dictatorship and Democracy* (1966). In such formulations, prior experiences with unrelenting social conflicts or inequities, and with regimes that sustain them, can poison the future. In contrast, experience with a new world, rugged self-reliance, and gradualist embrace of popular government or with the incremental crafting of liberal institutions in the disastrous aftermaths of old regimes can liberate, educate, and direct a people toward a freer future. Historical path matters for democracy. The issue is which historical pathway best engenders democracy.

Contemporary democratization theory, taken as a whole, tends to point to the gradualist co-evolution of democratic institutions and free market economies as the primary if not essential path to democracy and points strongly away from socialist revolution. Thus widespread affluence takes time to create, particularly affluence sustained through broad economic resources made available to citizens by free market enterprise. The emergence of a cohesive elite committed to democracy and its careful guidance of the masses toward democracy constitute an inherently gradualist process, particularly as they tend to involve skillful elite crafting of and experimentation with democratic constitutions and liberal institutions such as elections, slowly expanding suffrage, and legislative assemblies. And the emergence of civic society through long experience with private civic associations likewise requires a long evolutionary perspective.

In so far as all three of these foregoing "requisites" are deemed essential, then the gradual nature of democratization appears essential. This conclusion, most epitomized in the work of Samuel Huntington but implicit across much of the literature, holds out little hope for rapid democratization in contemporary third world nations. It is then reinforced by the concern among many analysts that revolution in the contemporary world, particularly socialist revolution, can so destabilize and poison the life of a nation as to foreclose hope for its subsequent democratization, should a nation embrace revolutionary action in an effort to redress its social liabilities.[52]

---

51. Tocqueville (1969). See also Tocqueville (1956).
52. See for example, Huntington (1991).

The concern with differential paths, and particularly with the detrimental aftereffects of socialist revolution, emerges most clearly in the work of Linz and Stepan (1996). Together they have undertaken the arduous task of categorizing democratizing nations into postauthoritarian and posttotalitarian groups and then subdividing the latter category by the degree of entrenchment or predemocratic thawing that has taken place under totalitarianism. Linz and Stepan's effort to differentiate the degree of totalitarian entrenchment or thawing that occurred in the previous regime and to relate that to democratic development is an important improvement upon arguments that treat the entire East European experience as one path toward democracy. Their sensitivity to historical path and to ways that different paths create different limits and possibilities is thus a major step toward understanding democratization in Nicaragua. Moreover, Linz and Stepan do not stress the necessity of gradualism in the emergence of democracy. But they do exhibit an unduly negative attitude toward socialist revolution. Since revolution is a primary way to move beyond gradualism, jump-starting a nation's efforts at societal restructuring and democratization, their dismissal of socialist revolution would seem to reinforce the gradualist perspective dominant in democratization theory. The Nicaragua experience challenges both this discounting of socialist revolution and the gradualist perspective on democratization that follows from it.[53]

Linz and Stepan see socialism as inherently totalitarian and, as such, antithetical to the citizen trust and belief in civic engagement that Putnam and others see as essential to democratic life. Moreover, the socialist experience offers no counterbalancing assets that aid democratization. Rather, the experience with the repressive and suppressive tendencies of revolutionary socialism cripples a people's capacity for democratic citizenship, perhaps permanently, while the "command economies" put in place through revolutionary socialism forestall the emergence of free market economics and the wide distribution of economic resources and affluence that a market economy is said to foster. Their indictment of socialism necessarily leaves us wondering how socialist Nicaragua moved so rapidly toward a broadly pluralistic and competitive democratic polity and a consumer-driven market economy, with the socialist party a consistent contender for national power and a strong legislative influence on social policy.

In sum, a theoretical literature focused on the necessity of specific substantive conditions—national affluence, elite cohesion, a historically

---

53. Similar concerns are raised by Rose, Mishler, and Haerpfer (1998, 140). They find that social structure is only weakly related to attitudes about democracy and its nondemocratic alternatives in postcommunist societies.

ingrained civic culture, or the avoidance of socialist revolution—leaves us unprepared to expect democratic transition in Nicaragua. It also makes difficult an explanation of the citizens' capacity to engage in meaningful electoral participation. Understanding how the citizens of Nicaragua were nevertheless able to engage in the transition to democracy, and able to exercise their right to vote in such a meaningful fashion, requires that we look beyond these dominant theoretical works stressing specific substantive conditions and consider another perspective on the requisites of democracy.

The Case for Democratic Learning

Our argument is that citizens and elites in developing nations like Nicaragua are far more capable of learning democracy, and of doing so relatively quickly, than analysts have realized.[54] They are intelligent, resourceful, and experienced in careful calculation and reasoning, attributes required to survive and flourish in the difficult circumstances of their daily lives. They are also concerned to find viable strategies for crisis resolution and civil social relations. While these attributes have not been fully appreciated by students of democracy, focused as they have been largely on the North Atlantic experience, scholars of peasant societies have long documented their existence in careful detail.[55] The savvy intelligence seen amidst the common citizens in such societies, combined with their aversion to perpetual crisis and violent conflict, prepares them to grasp the value of democracy and to adapt relatively quickly to the basic tasks of democratic citizenship, when confronted with facilitative circumstances.[56]

Given the inherent intelligence and crisis aversion of common citizens, the circumstances facilitative of democratization are much more common in the contemporary world than the experience of the North Atlantic nations during the previous two centuries would suggest. This is so partly because viable models of democracy are now widely prevalent, from which developing nations can learn, and partly because the commitment to democratization on the part of the international community is greater today and helps create

54. For an important exception, see Di Palma (1990).

55. Rokkan (1967); Thompson (1971); Scott (1976, 1985); Popkin (1979); Anderson (1994b); Tsing (1993).

56. Appreciation for the savvy awareness of common citizens in third world settings, particularly amidst economic crisis, also is seen in Dominguez and McCann's study (1996, 74–75) of presidential election in Mexico. As they write, "In conclusion, Mexicans were profoundly worried about the direction of their country in general, and of the nation's economy in particular. . . . But they were less gloomy in 1988 than in 1986. *In both years citizens showed a good grasp of reality*" (emphasis added).

incentives and oversight processes that facilitate local democratization efforts. But it is also true because democratization—even in seemingly unlikely contexts—may be facilitated by the existence of procedural foundations that enable elites to contest for power through elections and permit a broadly inclusive electorate to choose among elites in a meaningful manner. Such procedures can evolve amidst a history quite different from that of the North Atlantic nations, as seen in the experience of Nicaragua.

Building on the work of Robert Dahl and Anthony Downs, we suggest that three procedural foundations are particularly critical for rapid democratic learning and democratization. These are a political space in which information about contending ideas and policies can be presented and contested; a pluralistic and meaningful class structure that serves to simplify a nation's ideological conflicts in ways citizens can understand; and a well-defined party system composed of a modest number of autonomous electoral parties that articulate the major class or group interests of society and seek to govern accordingly. As with Nicaragua, such foundations may emerge not through the gradualist evolution of liberal democracy but during periods of violent contention among traditional elites, lower-class challenge to the domination of social elites, courageous dissent during authoritarian dictatorship, and most critically through social revolution.

A country with strong foundations of space, class, and party, whether derived through gradualist evolution or socialist revolution, has most of the domestic conditions necessary for rapid learning of electoral democracy—particularly in the contemporary period in which international support and viable models of democratization are present. The decline of Cold War animosities also facilitates the inclusion of a broad array of political parties, including right-wing and socialist ones, into the political life of developing societies. If citizens also believe in their own participatory power—a belief that may come not only through slow historical evolution but amidst rapid social revolution, egalitarian restructuring, and mass literacy—then an inclusive process of democratization may proceed rapidly once the nation embarks on the use of free and fair elections. This is true particularly if a society is characterized by certain other favorable circumstances, such as a small, relatively homogeneous population, cross-cutting social cleavages, and a stable, pluralist party system, factors that can somewhat diffuse the intensity of group conflict and help induce openness to political compromise and social reconciliation.[57] We argue in chapters 2, 7, and 9 that Nicaragua is precisely such a nation.

57. Dahl and Tufte (1973); Dahl (1956); Rae and Taylor (1970); Ross (1993); Dodd (1976, 1994); Anderson (2002).

Democratization has occurred in Nicaragua because procedural foundations, contemporary international developments, and revolution allowed citizens rapidly to grasp how to use electoral democracy to address the nation's most pressing problems and to craft an evolving regime structure of democratic processes. The Nicaraguan experience suggests that, while national affluence and broadly distributed material resources may facilitate such learning, they are not absolute necessities. Moreover, citizen choice and democratic initiative may take place in the absence of cohesive leadership from domestic elites or even when elites are actively opposing each other on the battlefield. Likewise, citizens may learn civic values and participatory skills in many different ways and in particular through a brief revolutionary experience that empowers citizens but ends before totalitarian socialism sets in. Such an experience with revolutionary socialism may even set in motion an egalitarianism and broad participatory experience that enable citizens to believe that they can have a sustained influence on their nation's politics and regime.

When social egalitarianism and mobilized politics combine with genuine electoral competition among candidates and parties offering meaningful alternatives, the poor and poorly educated citizens of one of the world's most impoverished nations can engage in extensive citizen participation and serious vote choice, thereby taking their fate and that of their nation into their own hands. We return to this argument in our final chapter. We outline there an alternative perspective on the requisites of democratization that emerges from the Nicaraguan experience.

This perspective argues that contemporary developing nations such as Nicaragua may be able to democratize through pathways to democracy different from those traveled by North Atlantic nations.[58] They can do so when "functionally equivalent" circumstances exist that play roughly the same role for them that the material circumstances of the North Atlantic nations played in their democratization processes. For example, universal primary education can help activate citizen capacity for democratic learning and political resourcefulness in settings where affluence is lacking. Authentic contestation among elites, combined with their willingness to abide by electoral outcomes they strenuously oppose, may allow democratization as well as or better than domestic elite pacting.

The flourishing of space, class, and party through revolutionary overthrow of an exploitive and authoritarian dictatorship may substitute for their

---

58. For an early effort to trace the differential patterns and paths by which nations democratize, see Flanigan and Fogelman (1971a and b).

gradualist emergence during the peaceful evolution of liberal democratic institutions, perhaps even inducing greater citizen appreciation for the right to participate freely in democratic elections. Political mobilization and mass participation through social revolution can foster a capacity for civic engagement by citizens in the absence of centuries-long experience with civic associations. And the egalitarian leveling that comes with social revolution may lead common citizens to believe that they can have a genuine influence on politics at least as effectively as can the legal-institutional protections of citizens' rights that emerge through the gradualist evolution of liberal constitutionalism. This would seem true particularly when such revolutions are followed by reasonably prompt restraints on the oppressive tendencies of revolutionary elites and a move to genuine competitive elections.

Such functionally equivalent circumstances had emerged in Nicaragua by the late 1980s, with the Sandinista revolution having played a decisive role in their development, together with international support of and pressure for elections. With their emergence the citizens then proved remarkably adept at participation in electoral democracy, despite their poverty. Their success in doing so highlights the democratic potential of citizens worldwide. If common citizens can learn democracy in Nicaragua, and act as responsible voters in the face of momentous decisions about regime direction and national reconstruction, then surely they should be able to do so in far less demanding situations elsewhere throughout the world, so long as it is clear that their votes will really matter and can have a meaningful impact on their lives and on the well-being of their nation.

Overview

We present our case for citizen choice and democratic learning in three parts. Part I sets the context of the 1990 election. Chapter 2 examines Nicaraguan history, considering how political space, class politics, and party legacy emerged from that history to provide important pillars upon which to rest competitive elections and democratization. Chapter 3 presents the story of the 1990 electoral campaign, detailing the immediate circumstances of the election and the move to democratic conservatism.

Part II examines the evidence for citizen choice in 1990. Chapter 4 presents a theory of reflective vote choice that we use to analyze public opinion and election results. Chapter 5 presents the evolution of citizen attitudes about the candidates, economic conditions, and regime options during the 1990 election campaign. Chapter 6 analyzes the relationship between citizen attitudes and vote decisions and examines the relationship between class, age, and gender and vote choice.

Part III turns to the aftermath of the 1990 election. Chapter 7 looks at the evolution of Nicaraguan democracy from 1990 to 2001, compares the election campaigns of 1996 and 2001 to the 1990 election, and examines citizens' comparative assessments of the performance of the revolutionary and postrevolutionary regimes. Chapter 8 examines the evolution of citizen attitudes toward candidates, the economy, and the regime across the 1996 and 2001 elections and examines the process of vote choice in those two elections. It also seeks to understand the implications that the voting patterns across 1990, 1996, and 2001 have for our understanding of democratization in Nicaragua. Chapter 9 concludes the book and considers its theoretical implications for the study of elections and democratization in contemporary third world nations.

PART I

Pathways toward Democracy:
The Case of Nicaragua

Chapter 2

Foundations of Nicaraguan Democracy:
Space, Class, and Party

Nicaragua's quarter-century move from severe human rights violations and extraordinary wealth accumulation by Somoza and his cronies to today's more egalitarian social structure and competitive democratic elections constitutes a substantial political and social transformation. This transformation is best characterized as a process of democratization, whereby citizens have sought greater influence over their daily lives, both through more equal distribution of resources and through political and governing arrangements responsive to their concerns. Democracy itself is a highly contested concept, so that there exists considerable disagreement on what constitutes evidence of a fully functioning democratic nation.[1] But there should be little disagreement that Nicaragua is a developing democracy, a nation seeking to replace a long tradition of authoritarian, elitist, extraconstitutional rule with constitutionally prescribed and regularized processes of popular participation and representative governance.[2] Nicaragua's effort at democratization would, in fact, seem virtually to define what that concept means in the real world of developing societies emerging from centuries of mass social and political exploitation.

Democracy in Nicaragua is real, if young. It is evident in substantial popular support for distinct parties and policies; electoral competition among

1. Diamond (1999); Diamond and Plattner (2001); Dahl (1971, 1998).
2. For similar assessments, see Walker (1997d) and P. J. Williams (1994). Robinson (1997) argues that Nicaragua falls well short of a purist democracy, more nearly approximating Dahl's (1971) conception of a polyarchical regime. Such a regime is, nevertheless, much preferable to authoritarianism and, from Dahl's perspective, constitutes clear movement toward a democratic polity.

those parties for all major government offices in elections deemed fair by external observers; distribution of power across executive, legislative, and local offices among parties of the left and right; and extensive popular participation both in elections and in social mobilization between elections. Such competition and popular participation have resulted in significant changes in government and in regime transition. Moreover, this process has gone forward within a constitutionally prescribed framework, amidst increased respect for civil liberties, human rights, and the rule of law. The power of process is evident both in the 1990 transition to democratic conservatism and in the 2000 municipal victories of the Sandinistas.

Our concern here is to understand why a process of democratization and significant electoral decision making could emerge in Nicaragua, a nation with few of the substantive or material "requisites of democracy." We argue that democratization has proven possible in Nicaragua because its history had generated procedural foundations of democracy that enabled citizens to embrace electoral politics and democratic development once domestic and international circumstances created the opportunity. Here we identify those procedural foundations, building on the work of Anthony Downs and Robert Dahl, and then we consider how the history of Nicaragua facilitated the emergence of these foundations.

The Procedural Foundations of Democracy

In *An Economic Theory of Democracy*, Anthony Downs argues that three foundations are essential for an electoral democracy that selects its governments through citizen choice: the presence of ideology for framing political understanding, a central role for parties in competing for votes, and the availability of information to citizens as they confront an uncertain political context in making their vote decision.[3] These three conditions ensure that citizens have the capacity to engage in the decision-making procedures at the heart of electoral democracy—making sense out of politics, enticing parties and candidates to address citizen policy concerns, and choosing the political options most in line with their priorities and interests. Downs suggests that ideology and political parties are essential to democracy because of the simplifying role they play in allowing citizens to comprehend politics and shape their

---

3. Downs (1957). For recent discussions of the ways in which "heuristics" such as party and ideology can aid citizens' ability to learn to comprehend politics and reason toward political choice, given sufficient information, see Sniderman, Brody, and Tetlock (1991); Lupia and McCubbins (1998); and Ferejohn and Kuklinski (1990).

vote choices. Ideology permits a simple, left/right categorization of political differences, allowing citizens to frame parties and other representative groups into basic opposing positions. Voters need not relate every position on every issue to their own views but can categorize parties ideologically and then compare party ideology with their own personal opinions. Ideological simplification is conducive to democracy because it increases understanding among all citizens and thus encourages political involvement. Downs's attention to parties likewise emphasizes simplicity, a limited number of divisions, and enhanced understanding. Downs thinks that parties, when linked to candidate or issue choice, enhance simplicity. The clarity of party division becomes still greater when nations enjoy a small number of parties with recognized meanings over time.[4]

Downs's third democratic foundation, information, stresses the need for alternative perspectives in the public arena. He emphasizes the exchange of information itself rather than any particular mode of exchange, such as a free press. The argument allows consideration of information exchanged even in predemocratic or authoritarian societies where a free press has not developed. There is room in the theory for popular memory, oral history, intellectual discussions within a university community, and fiction and poetry, all of which are ways of exchanging information, harboring alternative ideas, and expressing dissent before anything as visible and formal as a free press emerges.

Like Downs's, Dahl's theory of democracy also proposes foundational components. Dahl (1971, 1956) argues that two primary democratic institutions—contestation and inclusive participation—are prerequisites to genuine citizen decision making and thus to democratic development. With *contestation* Dahl is emphasizing that competition among political elites and parties must involve a meaningful contest among ideas and policies. Politics is not just a struggle for personal and factional power among contending elites who are in essential agreement over ideas and issues, but rather a conflict over alternative political visions that citizens care about. Moreover, for contestation to be real, it is important not just that different parties are on the ballot or in the legislature, but that constitutional, legal, and social arrangements ensure that alternative candidates and policies get a fair hearing and have some genuine chance to prevail. Major parties should have enough resources and popular support to have a viable chance to win power, and they should evidence enough ideological difference in policies that citizen choice among them matters. With *inclusive participation* Dahl is arguing not just that all citizens should have the right to

4. For discussion of the value of strong parties, see Mainwaring (1999, 12–13 and chap. 2); Mainwaring and Scully (1995); Hagopian (1996).

vote, but that there should be some substantial equality among citizens or groups of citizens so that all have some real chance to influence politics. It is thus vital that constitutional processes and social arrangements ensure equality among and respect for all citizens and facilitate their capacity to engage in participatory decision making. In sum, for genuine democracy to emerge, divergent opinions must present themselves, and citizens must take part in important political choices, with these capacities assured to some degree by constitutional, legal, and social arrangements.

This chapter shows how Downs's three foundations for democratic decision making and Dahl's two institutional requisites developed in Nicaragua in the years before 1990. It argues that they developed through the emergence of three specific historical conditions: political space, conscious class differences, and strong political parties, with these conditions emerging in a context that would seem antithetical to democracy, including extensive and violent conflict among the traditional elite, elite exploitation of the masses, brutal dictatorship, and socialist revolution. This was not a case of the gradualist evolution of liberal democratic institutions guided by a democratic elite. Yet together space, class, and party provided citizens with information, ideology, and party along the lines Downs requires. In addition, the way in which space, class, and party developed helped ensure the existence of inclusive contestation along the lines Dahl prescribes. We thus consider space, class, and party to be the vital foundations for Nicaraguan democracy.

Historically space, class, and party each served to enable the others, thereby driving the emergence of inclusive contestation in Nicaragua in ways that ultimately facilitated electoral democracy. Thus the growth of political space allowed the expression of dissent or contestation along simplified lines of class and party differences. Class differences simplified political contestation along the left/right ideological continuum Downs advocates, while also ensuring increased mass attention to politics. Political parties provided arrangements for organizing political contestation along class and ideological lines, further simplifying politics for citizens and providing them candidates and administrations to support. The growing contestation among classes and parties increased the inclusiveness of politics, bringing more citizens into the political fray. And as a broader array of citizens engaged in politics, they pushed for increased political space for dissent and contestation among competing classes and parties, ultimately demanding real political power and the right to choose their own leaders.

The slow and sometimes inadvertent development of these three foundations of democracy first over two centuries of history, then more rapidly in the revolutionary years, and finally in the preelectoral months prior to 1990 taught Nicaraguans how to use democracy to facilitate electoral choice. They learned to channel dissent into political parties, to define interests along a left/right political spectrum, and to place parties within that spectrum. They learned to absorb information from alternative perspectives, and they realized that their participation in the political process was permitted and necessary. Moreover, in the revolutionary experience they gained a degree of resource equality and an awareness of their participatory power along the lines that Dahl and Putnam see as critical to a vibrant civic life conducive to democratic participation.

Increased egalitarianism and political mobilization helped convince citizens that they could shape politics and society through mass participation in political life, given the right circumstances. Severe and unresolved conflict between the revolutionary regime and their U.S.-funded Contra opponents, combined with a deterioration in social and economic life, gave them the incentive to use their participatory power to resolve national stalemate. Pressure from the international community for free and fair elections in Nicaragua then gave citizens the option of going to the ballot box rather than to the battlefield to exercise their participatory power.

Our purpose here is to provide an overview of this history so as to understand the contemporary capacity for democratization in Nicaragua, taking the story up to the 1990 election campaign. Chapter 3 examines the exchange of information and the contestation and participation that emerged during that campaign, while chapter 7 looks at the evolution of space, class, and party in the eleven years following the 1990 decision.[5]

Our presentation of Nicaraguan history is thematic and chronological. We begin by demonstrating the development of space, class, and party under colonialism and in the Somoza years. The second section illustrates how the Sandinistas made their own unique contribution to democratization by providing citizens with specific requisites for democratic participation and choice. These included the social resources of collective action, popular empowerment through citizen initiative, and civic experiences in associations, organizations, collective action, and mutuality. Both the democratic foundations and the democratic requisites Downs and Dahl advocate were present in Nicaragua as the nation moved toward the 1990 choice. Their

5. For a discussion of democratic transitions in Central America that provides a broad assessment of the regional context within which Nicaraguan democratization was occurring, see Seligson and Booth (1995) and Dominguez and Lindenberg (1997).

presence enabled voters to make a reasoned choice even when observers and scholars were skeptical that they could.

The Inadvertent Legacy: Democratic Foundations in a Nondemocratic Era

The Colonial Years

Like most of Latin America, Nicaragua was colonized and controlled by Spain. The colonial centuries established a hierarchical political system, the Spanish language, and Catholicism. Colonial Nicaragua was a stratified society where fair-skinned descendants of the conquerors had political, social, and economic privileges and dominated the lives of a lower social strata of Indians and mestizos.[6] During these centuries the native experience was harsh. The population fell from approximately one million in the early 1520s to less than one hundred thousand several decades later. This decimation came from disease and from the exportation of four to five hundred thousand natives into slavery elsewhere in Latin America. Spanish conquerors and their descendants mined gold and raised corn, cacao, and cattle. Each enterprise pressed Nicaraguan labor into service for low wages under cruel conditions, while the Catholic Church perpetually pressured the indigenous population toward Christianity.

This harsh experience eventually produced disagreement, protest, and rebellion, and with them the beginnings of political space for contestation. Protest fell into two simple political divisions of either class or party. Contestation was either protest by the subordinate poor against the rich and thus followed lines of class, or it was disagreement that emerged among colonizers themselves and became reflected in two emerging parties. Let us examine each type of contestation.

Class, or subordinate, protest emerged first in response to the social divisions of colonialism itself. Nicaragua's relationship with Spain began as a class experience, with dark-skinned natives dominated by socially, economically, and militarily privileged Spaniards of fairer skin. Beginning then, class politics meant that a small upper class subjugated a large lower class. There was little upward mobility, and the native and later mestizo people remained beneath, while the Spaniards and their descendants were the upper class. The Spaniards became the large landowners; the mestizos became the workers or remained peasants.

6. Booth (1985, 13–14).

The first rebellions were rebellions of the poor against the rich so that contestation took the form of class protest and helped establish political space for dissent. The colonial centuries saw many incidents of popular protest and uprising, with several locales exhibiting protest so frequently and intensively that they gained reputations as centers of indigenous resentment. Two urban examples are the neighborhoods of Subtiava near the city of Leon, and Monimbó, near Masaya.[7] Additionally, rural areas, particularly the northeast jungle, always offered some degree of resistance, limiting Spanish control. These traditions of popular resistance and the space for contestation they created would resurface decades later with the Sandinista revolution. The colonial response to such protests was also a politics of class, in this case class oppression. Elites defined politics as a class exclusionary politics that omitted the poor. Efforts by the poor to enter the political dialogue met with oppression.

Contestation emerged second in disagreements between Spanish descendants and colonial authorities over trade. Unlike popular protest, divergent elite positions soon solidified into the Liberal and Conservative Parties. The formation of elite disagreement into political parties brought to Nicaragua a distinct advantage that would later favor democratization. From the colonial period forward, disagreement was articulated by a small number of parties that took relatively constant and distinct positions over time. The Liberals favored liberalization of trade and greater autonomy in international relations. The Conservatives were more cautious about the free market and more positively disposed toward Spain.[8] These alternative economic and political positions continued into the nineteenth century, providing names for different elite opinions.

The First One Hundred Years of Independence

Nicaragua received independence from Spain and established itself as an independent nation in the early nineteenth century. While independence came peacefully, political relations in the new nation were prone to strife. Conflict continued to follow class or party divisions. The politics of class exclusion remained, and the elite party divisions continued. Class oppression was such that political space in the nineteenth century was primarily preserved by elite disagreements along party lines.

In the nineteenth century the Conservatives and Liberals became parties of notables representing elite positions but without the mass support base of

7. Wheelock (1981).
8. Booth (1985, 11–13).

a modern party.[9] Far from being electoral parties, the Liberals and Conservatives instead competed for power by military means. Much of the nineteenth century witnessed repeated civil struggle and war between the armies of these two groups as each seized and held power until ousted militarily by the opposing group.[10] Although Liberal and Conservative conflict was violent rather than electoral, it nonetheless legitimized political competition along party lines. Nicaraguan parties thus continued to show a simple, bifurcated division and constant meanings. They also accustomed elites to different political and economic positions and to alternations in power. Although political space was officially closed to nonelites, its existence meant that it might be used by whoever was willing to try.

Party divisions among elites also shaped foreign affairs. The Liberals invited a U.S. citizen, William Walker, into a battle against the Conservatives. Afterward the discredited Liberals then saw thirty years of Conservative rule. As official relations developed with the United States, differences in attitudes toward the United States again followed party lines. In keeping with their precolonial preference for greater national independence, and as a result of the Walker affair, the Liberals were more cautious toward the United States, while the Conservatives were more amenable to U.S. involvement in domestic affairs and more deferential toward the northern neighbor.

In the late nineteenth and early twentieth century a Liberal, José Santos Zelaya, gained the presidency of Nicaragua with a nationalist agenda in mind. He soon disagreed with the United States over building a canal across Nicaragua. Zelaya opposed the canal unless it were controlled by Nicaraguans; the United States wanted canal control for itself.[11] Angered by Zelaya's opposition, the United States intervened militarily behind a Conservative effort to regain political control by military means. United States involvement with Zelaya's ouster initiated two years of armed conflict that ended when the United States installed the Marines to support the Conservative government.[12] Nevertheless, the Liberals had succeeded in posing a nationalist challenge to the United States. No canal was ever built across Nicaragua.

The canal incident and Zelaya's ouster established political precedents that would continue into the twentieth century. The United States was now domestically involved in a nondemocratic fashion. Moreover, it had been

9. For clarification of the difference between premodern and modern parties, see Mainwaring (1999, 64–65). For another Central American example of parties as an important democratic foundation, see Yashar (1997).

10. Booth (1985, 14–15).

11. Walker (1985, 12, 14–15).

12. Booth (1985, 23–24).

militaristic in pressing its own interests and supported a nondemocratic change of government. These patterns would reappear in the future. But the story also illustrates the continuation of contestation along party lines.

While remaining elitist and nonelectoral, the Liberal and Conservative Parties had demonstrated that competition between parties could highlight alternative political perspectives and shape national life in consequential ways. In doing so, they offered Nicaragua two opposing, constant sets of meanings. The first embraced the market and preferred national control over domestic decisions; the other was more cautious about market mechanisms, preferring some state restraint or regulation of the most extreme aspects of free market trade, and was more open to foreign involvement in political affairs. These divisions thus prepared citizens to think about politics and policy in partisan terms and to recognize the power that parties could exercise in national life. At the same time, they also symbolized the elitist nature of Nicaraguan politics. Lipset and Rokkan suggest that for parties to represent society fully, they must follow major lines of social cleavage, such as class, religion, region, or ethnicity.[13] The Liberal/Conservative division excluded most Nicaraguans. But this limitation on the party foundation of democracy would change with the arrival of Sandino.

The Sandino Affair

No event in Nicaraguan history exemplifies political dissent, class conflict, and contestation better than the rebellion of Augusto César Sandino and his Crazy Little Army of peasants during the 1920s. The son of a "smallholder from the mountainous region of Las Segovias . . . [Sandino did] agricultural labor under the commonplace debt bondage arrangements of the day."[14] This personal experience with class exploitation familiarized him with the plight of Nicaragua's poor, and he became politically active in their interest. As he did so, class politics stormed the stage, creating the mass consciousness of shared class interests that would help engender social revolution fifty years later, giving rise to the Sandinistas as Nicaragua's third major party and transforming the nation's social and political structure. Thus the Sandino affair is one of the pivotal moments in Nicaragua's history and a central factor in its ultimate move toward mass democracy.

Sandino's rebellion grew out of the nineteenth-century Liberal/Conservative conflicts that had continued into the twentieth century. The

13. Lipset and Rokkan (1967, 1–64); Rokkan (1970).
14. Booth (1985, 41–43).

United States supported the Conservatives in the early twenties and had placed Marines in Nicaragua to ensure Conservative power. In 1925, believing that the Conservative Party had firm control, the United States withdrew the Marines. But Liberal efforts to limit foreign influence continued, and soon thereafter an armed Liberal effort to oust the Conservatives ensued, drawing the Marines back to Nicaragua. In the struggle that followed, Sandino joined the Liberals. Sandino's entry into the battle can be understood in both party and class terms. As a nationalist who wanted the United States out of Nicaragua's domestic affairs, he joined the Liberal cause deliberately, his choice reflecting the enduring meanings the two parties enjoyed. These had, by now, permeated beyond the elite class, and Sandino shared the Liberal agenda of limiting U.S. influence. But his agenda also had a class aspect to it, and he also wanted social reforms that addressed poverty and redistributed land toward the poor.[15] Here he parted company from the Liberals.

When the Liberals agreed to halt conflict if the United States would supervise an election, Sandino refused to be a part of the truce. Since neither party represented the poor, elections would not have addressed his social concerns, and he was still determined to oust the Marines. Sandino fought on for six more years.[16] The space for political dissent in this instance proved quite literally to be the dense jungle of northeastern Nicaragua, into which Sandino's guerrillas could melt and escape, only to return and strike the Marines once again. Booth (1985) describes Sandino's army's tactics:

> The guerrillas often worked their fields by day, their weapons buried. Word of an approaching . . . marine patrol worked a terrible magic. . . . A chilling chorus of cries from the guerrillas' children . . . would sound disorientingly all around the patrol. Within seconds the ambush would begin with a withering crossfire from the steamy forest. . . . As unexpectedly as they appeared, Sandino's soldiers would then fade back into the jungle. (44)

Defeated and demoralized, the Marines withdrew, leaving Sandino's exercise in contestation to assume heroic proportions in popular history. Popular dissent had won the day.

Sandino's efforts broadened the representative capacity of Nicaragua's politics without factionalizing or confusing party meanings. With his presence, the two-way party division became a three-way division, although no official party emerged to give a name to this new voice. That the new voice

---

15. MacCaulay (1985).
16. Sandino (1980); Booth (1985, 44).

had a simple, easily recognized class meaning was immediately understood by Liberals and Conservatives alike. Sandino met unified elite opposition to his social reforms, and neither party objected when he was murdered. Sandino's arrival forced the issue of the party system's representative nature. His death temporarily permitted the exclusionary party system to return.

Sandino's military venture was the first point at which the politics of the lower class seriously challenged elite politics at a national level. It was also the first point at which class-based demands received a national hearing, however frightened and reluctant that hearing may have been. Fear of class politics prompted a temporary unity between the two elite parties, but that unity was too short-lived to undermine permanently the historical animosity between them.

Sandino's rebellion was thus a bold expression of political dissent. It also notified power holders what class interests were. But it affected the party system as well by underscoring the limits of agreement between the poor and either elite party, even when the former were nationalists. It accentuated the exclusive nature of the bifurcated party system. The long-term implications of these developments were postponed by the arrival of the Somoza dictatorship.

The Somoza Years

When the United States withdrew its Marines from the Sandino conflict, it left behind a new domestic military force, the National Guard, under the control of Anastasio Somoza Garcia. It also left the leader of the Liberal forces, Juan B. Sacasa, in the presidency and expecting to rule for several years. In response to U.S. withdrawal, Sandino ceased his rebellion and sent his army home. It seemed a peaceful moment, but no one anticipated the political ambitions and violent ruthlessness of Somoza. Somoza Garcia was the son of a "medium-scale coffee farmer [who] had worked his way into the top position in the Guard largely through his ability to ingratiate himself with the Americans."[17] A graduate of the Pierce School of Business Administration in Philadelphia who spoke fluent English, he was about to become the first of three Somoza dictators who would rule Nicaragua successively until 1979.

In 1934, after U.S. withdrawal, Somoza arranged for Sandino's assassination.[18] Then, in 1936, his troops surrounded Sacasa's presidential palace and ousted the president. Both the presidency of Sacasa (one element of elite

17. Booth (1985).
18. Walker (1985, 17); Booth (1985, 51, 53).

opinion) and the popular opinion represented by Sandino had fallen victim
to Somoza and the Guard. He then consolidated personal military and economic control of Nicaragua and remained president and commander of the
National Guard until his own assassination in 1956. He was succeeded by his
two sons, Luis Somoza Debayle and Anastasio Somoza Debayle.[19] Over the
course of their dictatorship, the Somozas gained financial control of much of
Nicaragua's economy, many of its factories, and 20 percent of its productive
land base. Financial elites who wished to do business in Nicaragua needed to
support the Somoza regime. Business elites who did not or who resisted the
Somocista accumulation of wealth and power found it very difficult to keep a
business afloat during the Somoza years. Although Somoza had overturned
the delicate political balance between Conservatives and Liberals that the
United States left behind, the latter accepted his political takeover because
Somoza Garcia and his sons were U.S. allies, first in World War II and later
in the Cold War.

After assuming power, Somoza Garcia began calling himself a Liberal,
and his sons also used that party label. However, some Liberals eventually
rejected the Somozas' self-professed representation of Liberalism and distanced themselves from the dictatorship by forming the Independent Liberal
Party, or PLI. In Nicaraguan society, members of both the Liberal and
Conservative parties who developed alliances with the regime came to be
called Somocistas. They comprised Nicaragua's wealthiest elite, and that
term, more than any party label, characterized their political allegiance.
With the defeat of Sandino and the rise of the Somoza dynasty, political
space for dissent reached an all-time low. Class politics were repressed more
heavily than before, and the vigorous Conservative/Liberal competition
became confined to the choice of whether or not to become a Somocista.[20]
In the course of such repression the Somoza-controlled National Guard
engaged in extensive human rights violations. Peasants, workers, students,
some clergy, and even members of the elite were jailed without trial, tor-
tured, and murdered while the legal system did not protect them. Such
repression provoked even greater popular resistance. At the height of its
repression, the Somoza regime, particularly under the last dictator, Anastasio

19. The Somoza family were as follows: Anastasio Somoza Garcia (Tacho), 1896–1956,
assassinated; Luis Somoza Debayle, 1922–67, died of heart attack before completing his second
term; Anastasio Somoza Debayle, 1925–79, overthrown July 1979 and assassinated in
September; Anastasio Somoza Portocarrero, 1951–, implicated in the assassination of Pedro
Joaquin Chamorro in January 1978. See Edmisten (1990, 1–3, 8, 10); Everingham (1996,
138–39); and Booth (1985, 159–60).

20. Booth (1985, 63).

Somoza Debayle, became the most brutal government Nicaragua has ever known.[21]

The Somozas' authoritarian system foreclosed both popular and elite policy input. But even authoritarians have limits, and the traditions of space, class, and party refused to be snuffed out, even under Somocismo. Some limited political space was preserved first among the Somozas themselves: Luis was more oriented toward limited social and political reform than the other two, while the harshest of the three was the last. Space for dissent also remained outside the dictatorship, and several fora of opposition developed. Of these one was popular, continuing the example of Sandino; the other was elitist, continuing the elite opposition tradition from the late colonial period. But a third forum of dissent and information also developed during the Somoza years, and this was a space created within the world of education, literature, and the intellect. Let us consider each of these spaces for contestation under Somocismo.

The Somozas forbade literature or discussion on Sandino. Such a prohibition restricted access to this aspect of history, but it also made Sandino's memory more important among nonelites.[22] Even remembering Sandino became the exchange of subversive information, an exercise in contestation and an act preserving political space under repression. Inhabitants of Nicaragua's northeastern jungle, in particular, preserved the hero's exploits in oral history, including his nationalism and his concern for the poor. Later, in the 1960s, the revolutionary movement of students, peasants, and workers would resurrect Sandino's name in that same region, becoming the Sandinista National Liberation Front (FSLN). Thus the Somozas could restrict but not eliminate the voices of popular dissent against the authoritarian dynasty. Nor could they eliminate the secret political spaces where dissent was nourished and spread. Popular contestation stood muted but not stifled.

Meanwhile, elite opposition to Somocismo developed as well. Since Somoza Garcia claimed to be a Liberal, Conservatives assumed the mantle of party opposition.[23] They plotted against the Somozas, attempted to remove the dictatorship by electoral means, and criticized the dynasty in the newspaper. Thus elite contestation also remained intact under Somocismo, contributing,

21. Anderson (1994b).
22. While interviewing peasants in rural Nicaragua in 1986 and 1987, Anderson discovered that rural dwellers, particularly the elderly, knew a great deal more about Sandino than could easily be found in written texts.
23. One example of a prominent Conservative family that opposed the Somozas was the Chamorros, including Pedro Joaquin. See Edmisten (1990).

along with popular dissent, to the preservation of political space for dissent. With Somoza's use of the Liberal party label and Conservative opposition to him, the long-standing meanings of these two elite parties solidified further. From then on the Liberals, by virtue of being the strongest advocates of the free market, were also the most rightist political force in Nicaragua, and this would come to have social and political significance as well as economic. The Conservatives, by contrast, seeking a softening and mitigation of most Liberal positions, became the less extreme and less rightist of the two elite political parties, and this softer position would become social and political as well. These differences continue into the twenty-first century.

Finally, during the Somoza years, the university and literary community became a stronghold of opposition, creating and using its political space for information and contestation. In response, in its last years, the dictatorship would single out students for repression.[24] University and intellectual opposition produced Rigoberto Lopez Perez, who assassinated the first Somoza in 1956, and eventually harbored the founders of the FSLN revolutionary movement. Student revolutionaries included Carlos Fonseca, Silvio Mayorga, and Tomas Borge.[25]

From this summary we see that Nicaragua's most authoritarian period inadvertently permitted the further development of democratic foundations. Eventually the political space for dissent that Somocismo was unable to close came to be filled with a powerful revolutionary movement capable of removing Somocismo. That movement would articulate itself along lines of class, picking up where Sandino left off. But the Sandinista revolutionary movement would also continue Nicaragua's tradition of a strong party system, first by finding allies among the Conservatives and Independent Liberals and second by adding to these two traditional elitist parties of the right a new nonelitist party of the left.

Democratic Foundations and Participatory Capacities under Sandinismo

Other scholars have argued that the Sandinista years contributed a grassroots, participatory democracy to Nicaragua's political history, a position that we likewise embrace.[26] The case rests on the level of mass involvement in the insurrection and the revolutionary regime's efforts to mobilize, organize, and

---

24. Anderson (1994b); Booth (1985, 70).
25. For a biography of Fonseca and extensive study of the early student revolutionaries, see Zimmerman (2000).
26. Ruchwarger (1987); Walker (1997b).

unionize the people. Yet Sandinismo did not initiate the democratic foundations of space, class, and party that already existed in Nicaragua prior to the revolution. Instead, the revolution provided specific popular experiences that enabled mass citizen participation, enhanced citizen capacity for reasoned choice, and, through these, fostered democratization.

These popular revolutionary era experiences differ from the democratic foundations we have found in the preinsurrectionary years. They include the ability of common citizens to organize, associate, and cooperate, the development of group participation skills, and the discovery of social resources in collective action. The revolution taught citizens that social resources might substitute for affluence as a source of power. It also provided opportunities for citizen initiative and for participation without elite guidance or leadership and sometimes even at odds with elite preferences. Sandinismo's contribution to democratization, then, lay first in strengthening the democratic foundations that preceded the revolution and second in fostering the participatory capacities of mass citizens. Let us see how these capacities developed with the revolution.

When the last of the three Somozas, Anastasio Somoza Debayle, assumed power in 1966, Nicaragua entered its darkest authoritarian period and its hour of greatest popular resistance. This second Somoza son eliminated the social reform efforts begun by his brother and allowed the economic system to concentrate income and increase poverty as never before.[27] Poverty soared, caloric intake dropped, illiteracy and illness were rampant, and deaths from preventable childhood disease were among the highest in Latin America. Carlos Vilas has called this a "deepening process of pauperization . . . of the popular classes which doubtless played a role in their integration into the revolutionary struggle."[28] In addition to total political control, Somoza concentrated land, industry, and financial control in his own hands. Somocista elites accumulated wealth while upper-class members not closely connected with the dictator found it increasingly difficult to be in business. Even among elites, the need for resistance grew. To maintain this financial and political control, Somoza resorted to repression beyond anything seen before in Nicaragua. Primarily the repression targeted peasants, workers, and students, but periodically it touched elites.[29]

27. Anderson (1994b).

28. Vilas (1986, 97–98). On poverty under Somoza, see also Booth (1985, 66).

29. The extreme repression that characterized the Somoza dictatorship in its final years can be seen as evidence that the state was cracking. Skocpol (1979) argues that revolutions become possible when the state "cracks" and subsequently becomes weaker and therefore vulnerable to revolution.

Throughout most of his reign, Somoza Debayle enjoyed staunch U.S. support. He was so reliable a Cold War ally that the United States turned a blind eye to the wealth concentration and political repression he established. U.S. endorsement, however, became more guarded after 1972, when a devastating Managua earthquake attracted international attention to the extraordinary poverty in Nicaragua, while disaster aid went to the Somozas rather than to the earthquake victims.

These extremes of poverty, wealth concentration, corruption, and repression evoked opposition that began secretly and became more overt. Using the protected spaces of the universities and the remote northeastern jungle, an underground revolutionary movement began in the 1960s, calling itself the Sandinista National Liberation Front. When the primarily rural efforts of the early 1960s failed, the FSLN "learned from their early mistakes and survived using a more diversified strategy."[30] Uniting students with the urban and rural poor, the movement grew steadily throughout the 1970s, eventually launching armed assault against the National Guard and other prominent symbols of Somocismo. With time, elite opposition to Somoza also grew, with Conservative Party leaders at the center of it. Most visible among these was Pedro Joaquín Chamorro, editor of the nation's main newspaper, *La Prensa*. Chamorro waged a war of the press against Somoza until the editor was assassinated in January 1978.

Despite repression, anti-Somoza opposition drew on the democratic foundations that had developed before this final dictator arrived. In that space for dissent, information was exchanged, contestation survived, and growing numbers of Nicaraguans participated in the struggle against the dictator. Opposition resumed the class basis Sandino's rebellion had assumed, even taking his name. But now class interests were framed in an explicitly ideological fashion by Marxist-influenced revolutionaries.[31] Since Sandinista Marxism was moderate and pragmatic, they accumulated many allies, giving the insurrection as much strength as possible.[32] Party divisions also entered the opposition, with the most visible anti-Somoza elites being members of the Conservative Party. These democratic foundations enabled anti-Somoza opposition to develop and flourish, bringing specific participatory resources and capacities to the population.

30. Prevost (1997, 150).
31. Prevost (1997, 1991). See also Vanden (1982) and Chavarria (1982).
32. Among those allies the revolution counted some elements of the Catholic Church leadership and followers. Such individuals were influenced by liberation theology. Dodson (1991). For an overview of liberation theology throughout Latin America, see Levine (1992, esp. chap 2).

The Insurrectionary Period

The Sandinista revolutionary movement began small and precarious but gained momentum and support over time. Participation came from across society, including the rural poor, the university community, urban areas, and even the elite, particularly Conservatives. After many years of guerrilla tactics, mass insurrection sparked in response to the assassination of Pedro Joaquin Chamorro, husband of Violeta Chamorro, in January 1978. About that murder Ricardo Chavarria writes, "The reaction of the Nicaraguan people was massive. Angry crowds attacked Somoza-owned business establishments and burned several buildings in Managua. And the business community conducted an 85% effective 'general strike' or business work stoppage which lasted for two weeks beginning January 22" (1982, 30). Subsequent to Chamorro's assassination, a major rebellion occurred in Monimbó, a neighborhood of Masaya, the city just south of Managua:

> the residents of the neighborhood closed off the main street entrance with a large FSLN banner. . . . With homemade weapons, machetes, clubs, and paving-block barricades, the Monimbóseños forced the [National] Guard out of their barrio, and from February 22 to February 27 held out against 600 [*sic*] soldiers with tanks, machine guns and helicopters under the command of the dictator's oldest son, Anastasio III. . . . Their rebellion illustrated one of the secrets of the Nicaraguan popular insurrection: neighborhood organizations are the backbone of revolutionary societies.[33]

The Monimbó riot would be followed by the flamboyant guerrilla capture of the legislature, led by Edén Pastora and Dora Maria Téllez, and a four-pronged military assault on Managua coming from the north, south, east, and west. Although many leaders were involved in this assault, three of the most visible were the young and courageous Ortega brothers, Camilo, Daniel, and Humberto. Camilo was killed in the Monimbó uprising, and a monument to him was eventually erected there. The other two brothers remained in the insurrectionary leadership and survived the revolutionary uprising.

In response to such mass participation and coordination, Somoza and his family fled to Miami on July 17, 1979, leaving the National Guard "an army of occupation operating in enemy territory." Finally "the Guard began to dissolve . . . [and] some 7000 Guards surrendered to the victorious FSLN forces."[34] On the night of July 17, the presidential jetliner of the government

---

33. Lopez, Nuñez, Chamorro, and Serres (1979, 179), *sic* in original.
34. Chavarria (1982, 31–37).

of Mexico flew the exiled FSLN leaders, including Daniel Ortega, from their
base in San Jose, where Costa Rica had allowed them to set up a government-
in-exile, to Managua, where "people danced for joy, cheered the victorious
Sandinistas and smashed symbols of the hated dynasty."[35] The FSLN leaders
and the Nicaraguan people gathered to commence rebuilding.

A governing junta formed, representing the most important social elements who had supported the insurrection. It included both Daniel Ortega
and Violeta Chamorro, representatives of the working poor and the Conservative Party, respectively. Humberto Ortega also played a central leadership role, and several of Chamorro's adult children stepped forward to
support the new government. Chamorro's daughter became the Nicaraguan
ambassador to Costa Rica.

With the insurrection we see contestation and participation articulated
along class and party lines within the space left open for dissent. In mass action
and in individual heroic acts, Nicaraguans gained the requisites of popular
engagement that are so fundamental to democracy. First, the insurrection
exploded its way into the restricted political space Somoza had unwillingly left
open and provided a forceful dissenting voice against the dynasty. Second, it
emphatically defended the interests of the poor but, as in Monimbó, found
itself also defended by the poor in turn. While enjoying elite support, the revolution, both ideologically and socially, was decidedly a movement of the
poor; its mass nature made that unavoidable in a society where most were
poor. And third, Sandinismo etched party politics more clearly onto national
debate, clarifying the limits of the more traditional parties and illustrating the
need for a party positioned to represent the poor majority. In this sense the
revolution placed party politics and the democratic contribution it made on
firmer and more inclusive footing than had been the case in the past. Thanks
to the establishment of the FSLN as a political party, the party system now
included representatives of *all* Nicaraguans, and not just elite Nicaraguans.
The new Sandinista party included a militia that had developed out of the
insurrection itself and whose members were deeply loyal to Ortega. The militia provided a radical power base for Ortega and the party, helping organize
and control grassroots support but also constituting a base to which the FSLN
leadership had to respond if they expected to retain their political dominance.

But fortification of the democratic foundations of space, class, and party was
only the beginning of the insurrectionary contribution to democracy. More
than any other event in Nicaraguan history up to that time, the insurrection

---

35. Seligson and Carroll (1982, esp. 336).

brought the *people* of Nicaragua into the politics of the nation. It involved many of the people; in some places it involved all of the people. It brought collective action and group participation to people's doorstep. Where citizens had been excluded before, in the insurrection their political participation was encouraged, needed, demanded. That included landless peasants, farm workers, urban workers, women, students, and neighborhood residents "[who] . . . played a decisive role in the victory over Somoza."[36] Citizens who had never before been given an opportunity for participation and choice now found that participatory chances were numerous. We know from studies of the Nicaraguan peasantry during the insurrectionary period that citizen participation changed during that time, becoming more frequent, widespread, skilled, and effective.[37] People moved from quiescence through growing political involvement to bold acts of revolutionary participation. Peasants say that they learned that participation was possible, desirable, and necessary.[38] The insurrection engulfed the nation in participation, empowerment, and self-help, in ousting a despised elite and seizing political initiative with popular hands. Deliberately and inadvertently, illegally and heroically the revolution brought politics to the people and delivered the people to political involvement. In this unexpected fashion the capacity for sophisticated choice began among the Nicaraguan people.

The insurrectionary experience itself gave citizens the beginning of the democratic requisites scholars have described as necessary for democratization. Where affluence theory calls for economic and intellectual resources, the insurrection substituted the social resource of mass collective action and mutually supportive popular participation. It used collective action to remove a dictator whom no other power had successfully ousted. While both nation and citizens were poor before the revolution and remained so afterward, the social resource of powerful mass action became a political resource citizens could draw upon if they ever needed it again. Through insurrection citizens learned that the social resource of mass action could promote citizen interests, remove unpopular leaders, and move the nation toward a more inclusive political configuration.

Moreover, many of the associational experiences Putnam describes began with the insurrection. It gave Nicaraguans new experiences in civic engagement and popular political initiative. Through secret organization and underground resistance, citizens learned to cooperate, to protect each other,

36. Ruchwarger (1987, 36).
37. Anderson (1997).
38. Anderson (1994b, 1990).

to trust one another, and to depend on each other and the community.[39] They found that by working together they could accomplish a political purpose that individual action could never bring about. Finally, in relying upon leaders who arose from among the popular masses, the insurrection showed Nicaraguans that political leadership and vision about the future need not always come from an elite class. Rather, it could come from among the people, and the people themselves could engage in effective political action.

The Early Revolutionary Years

The specific contributions of the insurrection to popular choice-making capacities increased after Sandinismo gained power in 1979. From the original governing junta, Daniel Ortega became the new president, while his brother, Humberto, became commander-in-chief of the armed forces. The new government drew together all the strands that had supported it in opposition to Somoza: the poor, intellectuals, Conservatives, and some Independent Liberals. Visible in this group were Violeta Chamorro, an active Conservative member of the ruling junta until resigning in the spring of 1980 over displeasure with its radical tendencies, and Virgilio Godoy from the Independent Liberals. As a result, dissent began within the new state itself. Conservatives and traditional elites within the new government wanted a free market, capitalist economy, absent the Somocista control. They wanted to produce, export freely, and maximize individual profits free of the corruption and control of a dictatorship.[40] Social reforms were not a part of that elite agenda. Many of their partners in government, however, were more influenced by revolutionary ideals than by market goals. Sandinista revolutionaries concerned about Nicaragua's poverty wanted a socialist system that would place first priority upon alleviating misery. This called for resource distribution, land reform, and extensive state investment in social programs of health, education, and income support.

Between these two positions, the government established a "mixed economy," incorporating elements of socialism and capitalism while also orienting policy toward alleviating poverty and encouraging popular participation.[41] It was an imperfect compromise between the demands of mass politics and the

---

39. On the development of coherent people's networks at the village level in the insurrectionary period, see Anderson (1994b), chaps. 6 and 7.

40. Spalding (1994).

41. In the late twentieth century, many socialist governments found it politically expedient and economically prudent to establish an economic program that combined socialist and capitalist policies. A similar case in Africa was Mozambique. See Pitcher (2002, esp. chap. 1).

desires of traditional elites who had joined the revolutionary coalition. Inescapably the compromise served to further the development of political space as all policies and government decisions were continually subject to discussion and disagreement within the government itself as well as in the society at large. It also solidified the implications of party and class divisions, making them a more salient part of everyday politics than ever before.

In economic and social policy the Sandinistas "democratized" the economy and the social priorities of the state. They brought land redistribution and economic control favoring the poor along with social welfare. Sandinista land reform aimed "to transform the rural social class structure by extending access of the landless and near-landless to land and work." By the mid-1980s 37 percent of the rural poor had received land, and by 1988 the percentage of land owned in large estates had dropped from 50 percent to 20 percent. More general economic policy included price controls, improving rural living standards, subsidies for rural products, and state spending on social welfare. The FSLN also established a National Social Security Institute (INSS), a Ministry of Social Welfare, and a Department of Family and Child Welfare, which focused on daycare, nutrition, elder care, and student scholarships. Sandinista social services included a literacy crusade, "[in which] . . . some 400,000 Nicaraguans mastered elementary reading and writing skills." Basic illiteracy was reduced from 50 percent to 13 percent. They also included a vaccination campaign against polio, measles, and other infectious diseases; it reached 85 percent of the population. The new Health Ministry distributed 4,200 latrines in the first six months after the revolution and set up 250 centers nationwide for oral rehydration and the treatment of diarrhea.[42]

Sandinismo in power drew upon the spontaneous popular organization that had emerged during the insurrection to encourage further and more formal organization of all previously excluded sectors of society.[43] The first revolutionary years witnessed the birth of unions of peasants, workers, rural proletarians, women, students at all levels, teachers and other professionals, widows and families of soldiers, and members of urban and rural cooperatives.[44] To encourage involvement in group organizations, regular revolutionary celebrations continually reminded citizens of the power and results

42. Quotations in this paragraph are in the following works: Jonakin (1997, 82, 97–114, esp. 98); Ricciardi (1991, esp. 251–52); Baumeister (1991); V. Miller (1982, esp. 255–56); and Bossert (1985, esp. 265–66).

43. Ruchwarger (1987, chaps. 2 and 10).

44. McClintock (1981) has also found that the formation of cooperatives, in this case in Peru, contributed to citizen empowerment.

of mass action.[45] Once established, these groups promoted their own interests both vis-à-vis Nicaragua's traditional elite class and vis-à-vis the government itself.

A number of scholars have described the grassroots, participatory system
Sandinismo established. Luis Serra writes that "the grassroots organizations
served as important channels for the democratic expression of popular
interests and for the resolution of the most pressing problems and adverse
conditions brought on by the war, the economic crisis, and the inheritances
of the past" (1991, 73). Gary Ruchwarger describes the Sandinista mass
organizations as "schools of democracy" in which, for the first time, citizens
learned to "1) democratically select their leaders, 2) participate in decision-
making, 3) ensure the accountability of their leaders and 4) guarantee the
political equality of all members." Although there were limits, imperfections,
and slippages in these organizations, "there is no doubt that, during the little
over a decade of Sandinista rule, enormous advances in political participation
at the grass roots [took] place."[46]

There were even instances when popular organizations pushed for more
and faster redistribution than the Sandinista government wanted.[47] Through
the popular organizations "many people . . . had learned to state their opinions, criticize, be informed about the policies of the government, and organize
in collective attempts to attain satisfaction of their common needs."[48] Worker
organizations demanded raises more often and for greater amounts than the
Sandinista government desired. This placed the FSLN government in a position of trying to get workers to moderate their demands. As each group promoted its own interests, Nicaraguan citizens discovered that popular unity was

45. One such example was the annual Repliegue, a citizen march from Managua to
Masaya, commemorating the revolutionary retreat from Somoza's bombing of a working-class
Managua neighborhood to Masaya, where the revolutionaries were in military control. In the
insurrection the retreat had been a strategic move that allowed the revolutionary forces to
collect and launch a final assault on Somoza-controlled Managua. In the retreat, women, men,
children, and old people crept out of Managua at night, moving with the revolutionaries, and
making the long walk with them into the next city, Masaya. Under the Sandinista government
the date was commemorated by a reenacted citizen and soldier march overnight from Managua
into Masaya. Foreign visitors were invited to join the annual march. As the nocturnal hours
rolled on and marchers grew silent with exhaustion, they would reach for each other's hands,
silent, wasting no energy on words. Holding hands, they would move onward toward Masaya.
Some citizens learn civic engagement through bowling leagues (Putnam, 2000); Nicaraguans
learned it in part through revolutionary action and reenactments such as the Repliegue.

46. Ruchwarger (1987, 116 and chap. 5). See Serra (1991, esp. 74).

47. Probably the best example of this occurred in the area of agrarian reform in which the
peasant union, UNAG, often pushed for more land redistribution than the state envisioned
(Luciak, 1995).

48. Serra (1991, esp. 74); Perez-Stable (1982, esp. 138–40).

a powerful political tool that could be directed toward actors who, as individuals, had more resources (affluence, education) than the poor, but who, when targeted by collective action, might be defeated. Moreover, when the popular organizations opposed the state, citizens found that they could not always depend on elites to defend popular interests, as when Sandinista leaders opposed salary increases. Sometimes citizen initiative was necessary to promote collective demands. The social resources of collective action and citizen initiative became commonplace tools average people used against the elite resources of wealth and class advantage and against the state resources of power.

While collective action offered new experiences in the use of social resources, interactions inside the popular organizations provided opportunities for civic engagement and the growth of skills derived therefrom. Members of popular organizations found themselves drawn out of their individual lives and into interaction with others in the promotion of common interests. Citizens who had previously been isolated when dealing with power now operated in alliance with others. Association, civic engagement, cooperation, and mutual support became normal experiences within the activities of popular organizations.

Yet the poor were not the only groups to mobilize and voice their concerns. One group that mobilized almost immediately was the paramilitary Contras. Originating with members of Somoza's former National Guard, the Contras mobilized in Honduras to avoid being arrested, tried, and jailed by the new FSLN government, whose overthrow they sought. At first they had little domestic support in Nicaragua and might have disappeared entirely had they not received U.S. political, economic, and military backing. Later, as Sandinista policies alienated some Atlantic region residents and other rural dwellers, the Contra ranks grew. Eventually the Contras became a military concern for the Sandinista government and a reason for the draft. Never militarily strong enough to fight the Sandinista army, the Contras hid in the forests and attacked civilian communities instead. They aimed to undermine Sandinista development projects and skilled project workers. They blew up agricultural silos, destroyed wells and irrigation pumps, and killed nurses, teachers, and agricultural technicians, including a number of non-Nicaraguans. They sought to destabilize the regime and destroy it, rather than working to shape and influence it.

While the Contras have received extensive journalistic and scholarly attention, less well-known outside of Nicaragua is the organization of rightist groups within the confines of the Sandinista regime and their decision to participate through more normal processes. In reaction to popular mobilization, many citizens within the wealthy and propertied classes organized into business associations, professional associations, landowners' unions, and associations of ranchers, coffee growers, and sugar producers. While many of the wealthiest Nicaraguans left for Miami, other land and business owners stayed in Nicaragua and voiced their interests through these new organizations. One example is Enrique Bolaños, who rose to leadership in COSEP (Consejo Supremo de Entreprises Privadas), the business owners' organization, and from that position repeatedly challenged Sandinista policies and decisions. Similarly, Arnoldo Alemán opposed Sandinista land reform policies and made his opposition visible. Likewise, after leaving the Sandinista government in 1980, Violeta Chamorro joined with her eldest son, Pedro, who had become the editor of *La Prensa*, in voicing opposition to government policies through the newspaper. The Chamorros were split, however, with another group departing *La Prensa* to open a pro-Sandinista newspaper, *El Nuevo Diario*, and yet a third group of Chamorros running the official Sandinista newspaper, *Barricada*.

Through such extensive participation by citizens from across all socioeconomic levels, the democratic foundations of contestation, participation, and the exchange of information became a regular part of politics. Citizens experienced the power of unity, the possibilities of independent political action, and the advantages of increasing their skills of associational interaction. Certainly the organizations of private entrepreneurs met with less state enthusiasm and had less state influence than the popular associations. But the democratic requisites of collective action, citizen initiative, and civic association were present nonetheless. Through state-sponsored and state-opposed organizations, the experiences in dialogue, disagreement, social power, and civic engagement that began with the insurrection continued through the revolutionary years.

Apart from civic organization, the Sandinista government institutionalized formal pluralism beyond anything Nicaragua had seen previously. This effort began with the national legislature, which initially directly reflected the popular organizations. Early Sandinismo began with a sectoral legislature, the Council of State. Unions of peasants, rural workers, factory workers, women, and students, in proportion to their numbers, elected members who would become council deputies, again using skills of cooperation and association in the selection process itself and in the legislative discussion.[49] Organizations of private interests, also in proportion to their numbers, sent

---

49. Interviews with Leticia Herrera, Reinaldo Téfel, Sergio Ramirez, Alfredo Cesar and other members of the Legislative Assembly by Anderson, Managua, 1995, 1996; Anderson (1995).

deputies to the legislature, being forced in the process to present their interests through formal state channels rather than through the invisible connections of kinship and corruption that had traditionally characterized economic relations among the privileged. In the first years after the revolution, the sectoral legislature functioned as a second branch of state power. Representatives from peasant and worker organizations outnumbered the representatives of private producers, bringing class politics inside the legislature.[50] The legislature became a place where political space was institutionalized but also where the implications of class and party politics clarified with each debate and each vote. Legislative dialogue also developed skills in group unity, civic association, and nonelite initiative.

There were, of course, limits on the pluralism that flourished under early Sandinismo. These limitations are discussed at length elsewhere,[51] but briefly the principal shortcomings of Sandinista pluralism were inadequate formal mechanisms within which to channel opposition to the government, the underrepresentation of certain groups, and the limitation of pluralism primarily to fora below the level of the national state. The informal nature of Sandinista pluralism limited its effectiveness and placed disproportionate power in the hands of the revolutionary party and the executive. If popular organizations enhanced citizen representation, they were often overly deferential to Sandinista preferences. The sectoral legislature overrepresented Managua at the expense of the interior and remained institutionally subordinate to the executive. Because it drew deputies from popular groups organized by the FSLN, the legislature exhibited a strong majority of pro-Sandinista deputies, making it unlikely that the legislature would vote to check the executive. Additionally, pluralism in elections for presidents of cooperatives or unions was not the equivalent of national pluralism that accompanies presidential elections. Yet popular realization of the limits of Sandinista pluralism only increased awareness of the constraints of elite guidance in democratization and encouraged citizens to have confidence in themselves rather than relying upon elites to lead them to some democratic promised land.

Pluralism in Sandinista Nicaragua was both present and imperfect. Political space was broader, more inclusive, and more formal than it had ever been under any previous government, but it was less formal than the United States wanted.[52] Participation and contestation were greater than ever before. They had grown with the revolution, and alternative presentations of

---

50. Anderson (1995).
51. Luciak (1995).
52. Linfield (1991). According to Walker (1997b), this was Linfield's conclusion as well.

information abounded. Moreover, limits on and imperfections in pluralism did not keep the population from gaining the participatory experiences and democratic requisites described here. Indeed, the informality of pluralism may well have provided more associational experiences to a broader spectrum of the population than formal, institutionalized pluralism would have done. Informal organizations saw citizen participation depart from elite guidance at times, exhibiting self-confidence and political efficacy that can only have come from the learned experience of the popular organizations themselves. Both in the insurrection and during the early Sandinista years, citizens honed skills they would need as democracy became more formal and electoral choice arrived.

Just as earlier Nicaraguan history included significant foreign involvement, so the Sandinista years also saw international attention. Neighboring Latin American governments opposed Somoza and facilitated the FSLN leaders in the final moments of insurrection. With the revolution in power, foreign influence continued.[53] Even hostile U.S. efforts, including funding for the Contras beginning after 1981 and the economic embargo, eventually contributed to citizen capacities for choice.[54] By pressuring for elections, the United States helped create an opportunity in which citizen choice would assume center stage, the people's party would be institutionally legitimate, and the people's decisions would be honored by the international community, if not by the United States.

The 1984 Election

While the Sandinistas encouraged grassroots pluralism, they were considerably less enthusiastic about national elections. They argued that popular support for the insurrection was a stronger expression of opinion than voting could ever be and that further appeals to popular support were an unnecessary use of scarce national resources. International opinion and domestic opposition disagreed, however, and pressed the government for national

---

53. LeoGrande (1985, 1998); Schwab and Sims (1985); Morales and Vanden (1985); Malley (1985); and Axicri (1985).

54. The Contras were not funded by the United States while Jimmy Carter was president. Reagan took office in January 1981. Although funding was clandestine and we do not know exactly when it started or how much funding was passed, we do know that U.S. support for the Contras began early in the Reagan presidency. By 1983 the Contra military operations were in full swing with U.S. support. The economic embargo became official policy in 1983. The United States stopped all exports to and imports from Nicaragua. It also denied all but one flight per day from Miami to Managua. Most travelers had to fly first to another Central American nation and from there to Nicaragua.

elections. Eventually the Sandinistas scheduled an election for November 1984 to select a president and change the legislature to a National Assembly.

As with politics before it, the 1984 election drew upon the democratic foundations of political space, class politics, and parties. It enhanced democratic qualities of ideology as formulated by Downs; provided a forum for all parties; and encouraged contestation and participation as formulated by Dahl. It was itself an exercise in dissent within the growing political space offered under the new regime. It offered a chance to exchange information and express alternative opinions about the state of the nation.

Both class and party interests shaped the electoral competition. The FSLN's electoral strategy formalized and institutionalized its class representation of the poor. The party put forward Daniel Ortega as its presidential candidate, stressing his class origins, his involvement in the insurrection, his revolutionary credentials, and his efforts in office to aid the poor. In his 1984 campaign Ortega promised continued reforms and appealed to revolutionary loyalties. For the first time in Nicaraguan party politics, the poor now had a party of their own. While the opposition campaign also defended class interests, its electoral strategy was primarily shaped by historic party divisions. True to their traditional position, the opposition parties did not woo lower-class voters but restricted their attention to the interests of the upper class. As parties of notables competing in a national election that would depend upon mass participation, the Conservatives and Liberals were at a distinct disadvantage. But their greatest disadvantage was party division itself. More focused upon each other than upon defining their class interests vis-à-vis the poor, the Conservatives and Liberals ran against each other as much as against the FSLN. Their candidates were figures with historical ties to factions of the two major parties: Miriam Arguello for the Conservatives and Virgilio Godoy for the Independent Liberal Party.

Such an approach had worked when most Nicaraguans did not vote; it was a recipe for disaster when most did. Now, as the nation took its first step toward electoral democracy, the irrelevance of the elite agenda to Nicaragua's poor majority was clear. United, with the support of the poor behind them, and speaking as the representatives of the third and historically neglected voice, the Sandinistas won a resounding victory, 63 percent of the vote, becoming the first socialist regime to attain electoral legitimacy as well as insurrectionary victory. The largest opposition contender, the Conservative Party, won only 13 percent.[55] The Liberal faction represented by the Independent Liberal Party was third. The election was the first formal

---

55. Latin American Studies Association (1984).

indication that popular participation and association had helped capacitate the citizens for electoral choice. Voters knew who represented their interests and who did not. When given the chance, they delivered a resounding defeat to the traditional parties and their rightist political agenda. The electoral results offered strong support for Ortega's contention that his party already had popular support; they were stunning confirmation that the historical pattern of elite politics no longer worked in the new Nicaragua.

While the Conservative and Liberal (PLI) showings indicate that these two traditional groups were the least weak opposition parties, the 1984 outcome also illustrates that a small number of clear party divisions favors democracy. Conversely, a large number of splintered, factionalized parties does not. In 1984 the elite party behavior did not facilitate true electoral competition and distracted anti-FSLN forces into infighting instead of concentrating their efforts on competing with the FSLN. The FSLN victory that year resulted in part from the Sandinistas' continued revolutionary popularity but also from the factionalization of the opposition that produced no viable opposition to the FSLN ticket.

The 1984 election reveals the contribution and the limits of elite guidance in Nicaragua's democratization. On the one hand, FSLN leaders offered a program that appealed to voters and appeared to address critical problems. On the other hand, Liberal and Conservative leaders focused upon their mutual animosities rather than upon the electorate. In doing so, they rendered themselves, their parties, and their electoral offer irrelevant. Nicaraguan democracy unfolded one step further with the guidance of some elites and entirely without the guidance of others.

The 1984 Aftermath

With the 1984 victory the FSLN government began a new era of legitimacy. Ironically, the elected government also faced greater hostility than ever from the United States. Jimmy Carter had somewhat reversed the long-standing U.S. support for the Somozas in view of growing information on human rights violations and had accepted the Sandinista victory in 1979. But Ronald Reagan's presidency inaugurated a renewed period of support or expanded tolerance of conservative and authoritarian regimes in Latin America and, with this policy, strong opposition to the Sandinista experiment in Nicaragua. The efforts in Nicaragua against the FSLN included support for the Contras beginning in 1981 and an economic embargo beginning in 1983. The ill effects of these policies began to mount in the mid to late 1980s, undercutting the social policies of the Sandinistas and helping to reverse the improvements in health care, education, and agriculture that had come early in the FSLN era. Despite growing international concern about the consequences of U.S. policies for Nicaragua's poor, Reagan continued the embargo and war. He did so, moreover, in the face of the Iran-Contra scandal, which engulfed his administration at home when it was discovered that it had been selling arms to Iran and illegally diverting some proceeds from those sales to help the Contras.[56]

This hostility of the U.S. government, when combined with the sense within Nicaragua that the 1984 election had instituted a legitimately elected Sandinista regime, would have surprising and disconcerting effects on political space for pluralism in Nicaragua. On the one hand, political space became more formal and constitutional. Walker (1997a, 12–13) has called this the "Constitutional Period" of Sandinismo. On the other hand, combined revolutionary and electoral victory raised Sandinista self-confidence so high that they became inflexible and heavy-handed, particularly with respect to war policy, drafting underage and infirm youth. They also briefly closed *La Prensa* for irresponsible publications and jailed some political dissidents, including Alemán. Eventually popular patience wore thin. Yet throughout these changes in formal and informal space, citizens continued to develop the democratic requisites of civic engagement, participation, collective action, and popular initiative. Nicaraguan democracy devoted considerable energy to institutional and constitutional development, including writing a new constitution, approved in 1987, a Statute of the Republic, and a Statute of Rights and Guarantees. Democratic development also included writing and approving rules for regional autonomy and local democracy. Four branches of state were established: the executive, the legislature, the Supreme Court, and "an electoral branch headed by a Supreme Electoral Council." Each of these was approved by the newly elected legislature.[57]

Institutional and formal democracy also improved among the opposition parties. The 1984 defeat caused them to wonder if the traditional Conservative/Liberal animosity was the best way to promote their class and party interests in a new electoral era. The anti-FSLN groups searched for common ground on some issues to improve their electoral challenge. Both Costa Rica and Venezuela urged the opposition parties to work together. Kenneth M. Coleman and Douglas H. Stuart have used the term "families of parties" to see beyond the factionalization that characterized the parties,

---

56. Malbin (1989).
57. Vanden (1991); Reding (1991); and Serra (1991). See Walker (1997a, introduction) and McConnell (1997).

particularly those right of center in the period around 1984. Factionalization is only the natural and temporary response of a party system that has received the shock of great expansion in a short time period. The search for electoral cooperation was an important step toward democratization among Nicaragua's opposition parties after 1984. Eventually common ground was found on the issues of ending the Contra War, stopping the draft, making the army less partisan, and pointing toward a new election in 1990. In that search, Liberals and Conservatives again emerged as the strongest families of parties looking toward 1990.[58]

On the other hand, while formal political space broadened after 1984, informal pluralism deteriorated.[59] The FSLN responded to U.S. hostility with growing forcefulness, decreasing internal discussion, insensitivity to popular concerns, arrogant behavior, and abuse of power. While some mass organizations, such as UNAG (Unión Nacional de Agricultores y Ganaderos), retained relatively high levels of autonomy, others had more problems with vertical control. Additionally, it was increasingly evident that the revolutionary reforms had bypassed some groups, particularly women and non-Hispanics. Among ethnic peoples, inadequate reforms led first to Contra support and then to demands for autonomy.[60]

Perhaps the best indication of growing FSLN rigidity and distance from the public was the solidification of a new class of revolutionary elites, above the population and apart from the traditional upper class. Originally intended to serve the poor, by the mid-1980s they resembled a second, revolutionary elite, less wealthy than the old elite but more financially secure than the average citizen. They were government employees and soldiers, safe in their positions even as social benefits declined and the war lost popular support. One of the only benefits unaffected by the economic decline was free university education, and students came to be a third privileged group.

Nicaragua now had three classes instead of two: an old, traditional wealthy elite; a new, relatively financially secure revolutionary elite; and the masses. The demographic characteristics of these groups in 1990 are presented in

58. Weaver and Barnes (1991) and Coleman (1997).

59. Personal interviews with members of La Concepcion village in Carazo, Nicaragua, by Anderson, September–November 1987 and October 1989.

60. Prevost (1997) and J. Butler (1997); Chuchryk (1991); J. Butler (1997); Luciak (1995); Polakoff and La Ramee (1997, esp. 185).

Habermas (1979, 178–206) writes that the state must increase its efforts to attain legitimacy if it increases its demands on citizens. Otherwise, it will come to be seen as illegitimate. After the 1984 election the Sandinista-run state increased its demands on citizens but did not try to increase its own legitimacy, becoming less legitimate in the process.

table 2.1, with these data drawn from a pooled set of national surveys taken during the 1990 election campaign. The survey results also allow us to estimate the approximate size of each class within the adult population. In the categorization of citizens according to class, the *new elites* were civil servants, students, and soldiers; *old elites* were private business people and pensioners; the *employed masses* were day laborers, peasants, and domestic workers; the *unemployed* identified themselves as such. The working-class masses constituted 60 percent of the country and tended to be less educated, older, and living in impoverished dwellings. Among the masses, men tended to be unemployed and the women employed. Overall, there were far fewer men than women in the mass population, owing to deaths in the revolution, to early deaths in manual labor, and to involvement in the civil war either as Contras who had withdrawn into the mountains or as members of the nation's military. The new elite, roughly 30 percent of the country, were younger, better educated, and living in somewhat better but not luxurious conditions. They included more men, reflecting the extent to which the militant insurrectionary activists were now at the heart of the new elite, and anticipating as well the extent to which Sandinista reforms addressed men's concerns more than those of women. The traditional elite, never large to begin with, had shrunk still further with the exodus to Miami and now constituted around 7–8 percent of the nation. Those who stayed in Nicaragua lived in more luxury than any other class and had a broad distribution of education but included many with advanced technical, professional, or university education.

This new class division posed a special irony for Nicaragua. The revolution had been fought in behalf of freedom from elite oppression and the betterment of the masses. Progress had been made on both fronts during the Sandinista reforms of the 1980s. But in the process the greatest benefits had gone to the new Sandinista elite, whose close ties to the revolutionary state through military service, public sector employment, and educational support provided them a stable income and decent lifestyle. They were thus somewhat cushioned from the social and economic difficulties of the late 1980s that came with the U.S. embargo, Contra War, and economic deterioration. In addition, directly dependent on the FSLN regime for their income and personal opportunity, the members of the new elite had considerable incentive to remain loyal to the regime.

In contrast to the new elite, the remnants of the old traditional elite, while also better off than the masses, had suffered serious reversals with the revolution and had reason to oppose the regime. Yet such opposition varied considerably in its nature. The far right sought removal of the FSLN from national life, preferably with their imprisonment or exile, and a return to rule

Table 2.1 Nicaraguan Class Structure and Selected Demographic Characteristics, 1989–1990 (%)

Class	New elite	Employed masses	Unemployed masses	Old elite
Gender				
Men	53.6	36.1	62.4	58.7
Women	46.4	63.9	37.9	41.3
Total	100	100	100.1	100
Age				
≤ 24	64.0	28.0	39.0	25.9
25–44	32.8	51.2	51.7	47.7
> 44	3.2	20.8	9.4	26.4
Total	100	100	100.1	100
Lifestyle				
Luxury	4.6	2.3	0.5	8.3
Modest	59.3	42.3	44.8	54.4
Poor	36.1	55.4	54.6	37.3
Total	100	100	99.9	100
Education				
Illiterate	2.0	13.8	10.7	6.2
Primary school	18.6	48.6	31.7	34.4
Junior high	40.9	21.1	25.4	20.3
High school	20.2	9.0	14.1	12.2
Advanced	18.2	7.5	18.1	27.0
Total	100	100	100	100.1

Source: Pooled DOXA surveys for November and December 1989 and January and February 1990, with a combined *N* of 5480. For details about these surveys, see the appendix.

Notes: New elites were civil servants, students, and soldiers and constituted 31.2% of the interviewees; old elites were private business people and retirees and constituted 7.7% of the sample; employed masses were workers, peasants, and domestic workers and were 53% of the sample; the unemployed identified themselves as such and were 7.1% of the sample; 1% of the sample could not be given a class designation. Lifestyle was based on a visual assessment of the respondent's home by the interviewer. Under education, the illiterate identified themselves as such, while the advanced category refers to university students or those with technical/professional or some university education. In the table there were no missing cases for gender attribution, 89 missing cases on age, 53 missing cases on lifestyle attribution, and no missing cases on education. Totals do not all equal 100 due to rounding error.

by old-guard devotees of Somoza. This position was seen amidst the Contras. In contrast, moderate voices within the traditional elite sought the installation of a conservative democratic regime, committed to civil liberties, electoral democracy, and some version of free market economics. This group, epitomized by Violeta Chamorro, was more prepared to accept the Sandinistas' participation in national life and electoral politics so long as their leaders demonstrated authentic commitment to civil liberties and democratic process. Thus while challenging the Sandinista regime, owing partly to its casual regard for civil liberties and partly to its socialist programs, these more moderate forces acknowledged the Sandinistas as representatives of a portion of Nicaragua's electorate. At issue was whether the FSLN represented primarily the military, public sector employees, and students, as well as former militant Sandinista activists still deeply involved in party activities, or whether it also continued to enjoy the broad support of the masses who had rallied to the Sandinistas in the revolution and the 1984 elections.

While the masses appeared better off in absolute terms than at the end of the Somoza era in terms of social benefits, personal opportunity, and political freedom, they were also the greatest victims of the conflict between the U.S. government and Contras, on the one hand, and the Sandinista regime on the other. Less cushioned than the two elite groups by public sector income or private sector resources, they experienced the social and economic effects of the conflict on a daily basis and in a direct, negative, and personal manner. And it was their husbands, fathers, and sons who were drafted—often involuntarily and even illegally—to man the government's military effort against the Contras. The masses confronted such difficulties knowing that the new elite governing in their name tended to enjoy a better life—perhaps quite modest compared with that of the Somoza era elite but superior to their own.

The new elite was committed to alleviating the long-term plight of the masses. But it believed that doing so required staying the course in its conflict with the United States, subjecting the masses to short-term difficulties that the Sandinista elite more easily avoided. The conservative opposition, in contrast, was prepared to reconcile with the United States, ending the short-term instability associated with war and embargo, but in doing so could move the nation back toward a Somoza-style government should a change in regime come through military victory by the Contras. Even to the war-weary masses, a Contra victory was worse than continuation of the war.

By the late 1980s the masses faced the prospect that revolutionary struggle and domestic deterioration could persist indefinitely, with the FSLN dragging them deeper into a morass in behalf of policies that it justified in their name. The most evident alternative, the Contras, offered an even more unsavory future. Buffeted mercilessly by the immediate difficulties induced by war, embargo, and societal disintegration, the masses faced a quandary. At issue was what to do about the crisis enveloping them and threatening to pull them under, and how best to do it.

Nicaragua at the Crossroads

The crisis confronting the citizens of Nicaragua in the late 1980s was a severe one. Between 1984 and 1990 overt and covert U.S. Contra funding increased. The war mounted, drawing manpower and resources away from economic productivity and further decimating the male population already depleted by revolution and its aftereffects. Simultaneously, the U.S. embargo continued and tightened, leading to a decline in exports for Nicaragua, since the United States was its primary trading partner, and producing additional economic contraction. The United States also continued to challenge the legitimacy of the FSLN regime, claiming that the 1984 election had been unfair and refusing to deal with the government that resulted from that election.[61]

Clearly the United States wanted regime change and a rightist government in Nicaragua, whether through overthrow of the FSLN by the Contras or through defeat at the polls. Just as clearly, the Sandinistas intended to maintain their hold on power, seeking to defeat the Contras on the battlefield and expecting to prevail over any right-wing challengers at the polls. They expected the mass citizens to stand with them in the upcoming election, given the social improvements the regime had delivered. A second and massive FSLN victory would then shame the Bush administration into acceptance of the regime, or so the Sandinista leaders were prepared to argue.

In the face of the stalemate between the United States and the Sandinistas, the masses had the option of taking voluntarily to the battlefield, throwing their sizable numbers in decisive support of either the Contras or the government. No such movement occurred. Worn down by revolution and domestic turmoil, the citizens withheld enthusiastic military support from either side. In fact, not only was there scant movement of volunteers to the mountains in support of the Contras; there was growing hostility and resistance to conscription. Instead, citizens waited warily for the upcoming presidential election, seeking to clarify whether the Sandinistas would in fact hold a fair election and whether a viable opposition candidate would emerge.

Most regimes, facing external pressure and internal civil war, would have yielded to repression, and the Sandinistas did become oppressive, as we have seen. Yet as Nicaragua approached the 1990 election, "the [FSLN] regime still granted substantial political space . . . inviting opposition participation in . . . the institutionalization of a new political order."[62] Class and party politics remained strong. The FSLN framed its agenda in ideological and class terms

---

61. Gibson (1991).
62. Weaver and Barnes (1991, 139).

and continued to prioritize the poor. The traditional elites still focused upon their own class economic advantage and opposed policies for the poor. And party politics had strengthened after 1984 to include greater cooperation among rightist parties inside a political system that by the late 1980s represented the population more inclusively and formally than ever before.

The Sandinista party was now an electoral party that had won the presidency with a huge margin of victory in the nation's first true national election. In doing so, it had learned how to construct a well-organized electoral machine and mount a popular campaign. It was preparing to put that capacity into action again in 1990. This time it appeared it could face a more united opposition than in 1984, with efforts afoot to present a cross-party coalition that included the Conservatives and the Liberals in support of a common presidential candidate. Rather than dissolving after their defeat in 1984, the traditional rightist parties, having survived the Somoza dictatorship, were evolving in new ways, preparing to cooperate and challenge the socialist regime in order to flourish once more. Efforts were also under way to find a candidate with the stature and skills to cement such a unified opposition on the right and also appeal to mass citizens. Hoping against hope, key opposition leaders worked to persuade Violeta Chamorro to take up the challenge. A more united opposition might seriously test the Sandinistas' hold on the masses, particularly if led by such a broadly admired figure who also symbolized opposition to the Somoza regime.

With these developments, a genuine and competitive election increasingly seemed possible as 1990 approached, offering the citizens some chance to choose between the Sandinista regime and a viable alternative. Perhaps more than anyone suspected at the time, the citizens were poised to make such a choice.

Preparing for Citizen Choice

Nicaragua and its citizens had come an immense distance in the decade since the 1979 revolution. Gone was the system of concentrated economic power that had allowed a small and wealthy elite to dominate national life during the repressive Somoza years. Had that elite survived into a period of competitive electoral politics, it could undoubtedly have used its wealth and social position to dominate campaigns and tilt elections its way or to foster fear among mass citizens that it would do so. Without massive wealth and property, the remnants of the old elite were, to some extent, just an affluent political faction instead of an overwhelming social force. They were even a group with whom the masses might safely ally.

With the significant social leveling that the FSLN had engineered, the mass citizens enjoyed some considerable political equality and could truly believe that their voice would matter in election outcomes, given a free and fair election. Moreover, the FSLN had not only generated a more egalitarian Nicaragua but also a better-educated one, with the substantial improvement in literacy aiding the informed participation of the masses. It was also a somewhat more propertied population, so that citizens would see that much was at stake in ensuring a legitimate regime that could stabilize the nation. Additionally, they had learned through mass mobilization and revolutionary engagement a sense of efficacy that would enable participatory engagement.

In describing citizen life in Sandinista Nicaragua, Ruchwarger (1987) writes:

> through their involvement in the day-to-day life of the popular associations, hundreds of thousands of Nicaraguan citizens [received] training in democratic participation. Theorists such as Rousseau and Mill argue that such participation in all aspects of public affairs is the only way to create and maintain a democratic society. Individuals who participate in public affairs learn to gain other people's cooperation through the careful consideration of matters beyond their own private interests. Moreover, this participatory form of democracy is self-sustaining because the more individuals participate, the better they are able to do so. It is precisely through participation that cultural change and individual development—necessary ingredients for democracy—can happen. Thus, if democracy is to flourish in Nicaragua, the mass organizations must continue to serve as training grounds for democratic participation. (135–36)

By 1990 the decade-long immersion of the masses in revolutionary life and political reorganization of their society had served as a vital training ground for the citizens. It had created among them a capacity for self-sustaining participation in politics, enabling citizens to move beyond revolutionary fervor and engage in democratic elections with self-confident reliance on their own judgment.

Voters already versed in participation, collective action, and associational interaction had found in 1984 that mass unity could translate into an electoral outcome with a formal and institutional impact in determining who held national power. And they had had the trial run at democratic elections in 1984 by which to understand better the nature of electoral participation. By the late 1980s the revolutionary era had helped generate among citizens considerable resources for democratic citizenship and experience in exercising such resources. Ironically, the emerging crisis in the revolutionary regime also gave them considerable incentive to use such resources and experience, taking the future of the nation in their own hands through the ballot box. Externally the nation faced the hostility of the world's leading political hegemon, the United States, hostility manifest in economic embargo against the tiny nation and in support for the Contras trying to overthrow its government. Internally, citizens faced civil war and an increasingly oppressive government. Daily, they faced growing impoverishment and the death of loved ones in seemingly endless conflict. Yet in contrast to the decades and centuries of difficulty earlier in the history of Nicaragua, now they had the experience with political mobilization and participatory involvement gained during the revolutionary years to draw on as they considered how best to break the political stalemate. And they had an upcoming election at which they conceivably might do so.

The question at this vital crossroad in Nicaraguan history was whether mass engagement in a momentous and competitive election could yield a winning candidate who had the skills and vision to lead the nation forward and could bestow sufficient legitimacy on the victor to enable him or her to succeed.

Conclusion

As Nicaraguans approached the 1990 election their entire future was at play. Free and fair elections could give them the chance to legitimize a clear direction to national life that might lead the United States to cease its aggression. Such a victory might also rally the international community to provide expanded aid to Nicaragua for rebuilding the country. With peace, international assistance, and skillful domestic leadership might come domestic healing, social progress, and economic improvement, possibly through continued social reconstruction should the left triumph or through some as yet undefined and more conservative path should the right or center win.

This moment of democratic decision seemed from afar to confront a backward citizenry lacking long-term electoral experience with an almost impossible task. In truth their history and contemporary experience had prepared them better than observers realized, laying democratic foundations on which citizens could now rely as they faced their moment of truth.

While the nation's movement toward democracy had never been unidirectional, by 1990 that movement had yielded a citizenry experienced in political contestation among conflicting ideologies and interests, attentive to political mobilization in behalf of personal and group interests, and aware of the role parties could play in articulating and fostering those interests. There had been periods throughout history when regimes and leaders tried brutally to curtail political space, exclude class interests, and override party divisions. But eventually space reopened, class interests reemerged to shape contestation, and strong party loyalties resurfaced. Similarly, the development of democratic requisites during the revolutionary years was not linear. After doing much to enhance collective unity, citizen initiative, and civic experience during the insurrection and early revolutionary years, Sandinismo moved after 1984 to restrict space and assert greater control over society. In the process it rejected some collective demands, periodically quashed citizen initiative, and tried to control civic associations, thus limiting contestation and participation. Yet these efforts were no more successful than were previous attempts to weaken Nicaragua's democratic foundations. By 1990 the requisites of space, class, and party were well established in Nicaragua, and it was too late for citizens to forget the lessons in democracy they had already learned.

In the 1990 election the citizens would have the opportunity to put these lessons in democratic participation to use, if only there were truly viable alternatives among which to choose, a clear delineation of the differences between candidates and their proposed regimes, and a free and fair election in which to exercise such choice. In such an election, they could reaffirm the Sandinistas in power, cementing in place a party system tilted to the left. They might even give the FSLN such strong legitimation as to lessen U.S. opposition to it and further empower the Sandinista regime in its efforts on behalf of national reconstruction and social justice. Alternatively, they could move rightward, choosing a more conservative democratic regime and inducing a potential realignment in the partisan and electoral structure of Nicaragua. With such a development would surely come rapprochement with the United States, an end to the embargo and Contra War, and more conservative and even austere social and economic policies. With it might also come expanded commitment to civil liberties and electoral democracy, depending on whether it was a candidate of the far right or of the more moderate right-center who emerged victorious. We turn now to the story of the 1990 election, detailing the candidates, campaign strategies, pivotal developments, and political discourse that emerged during it and providing initial assessments of its outcome that will help guide us as we turn in part II to explain citizen choice.

Chapter 3

Embracing Electoral Choice: Political Discourse and the 1990 Campaign

The 1990 election pitted one hero of the revolutionary struggle against the widow of another hero. Daniel Ortega and Violeta Chamorro each represented a set of aspirations and ideals beyond Somocista repression and greed, although theirs were very different sets of ideals. Moreover, each had played a visible role in the post-1979 political moment, thereby representing the confluence of opinions and visions that had united to oust Somoza and that sought in 1979 to shape Nicaragua's future. Ortega, hailing from Nicaragua's working class, symbolized the mass desire to overturn social and economic inequality as well as political repression. His priorities rested with the poor and with social and economic reforms that would directly address poverty. Chamorro, by contrast, a member of the nation's elite classes, albeit a somewhat more progressive group among them, symbolized the concern of some elites to install political democracy, elections, civil liberties, and a free market economy. In the post-1979 struggle between these two alternative and somewhat incompatible visions, it was Ortega's ideals that had won the initial phase and prevailed for the first eleven years.

The question facing citizens in 1990 was a reconsideration of that initial victory. Should they stay with Ortega and his Sandinista regime or embark on Chamorro's experiment with democratic conservatism? Nicaraguan history had prepared the electorate for this moment of choice better than observers surmised. Yet if the historical emergence of space, class, and party had prepared citizens for this decision, these factors were even more critical in the election campaign itself. The campaign epitomized the exchange of information and diverse political opinions Downs describes as necessary to help citizens understand political options. The space for peaceful electoral contestation helped encourage mass participation and induced at least some elite partisans to leave the Contra battlefield, if only momentarily, and seek citizen support at the ballot box.

This chapter scrutinizes the campaign discourse between these alternative visions that citizens heard as they approached this important vote decision. It describes the election contest itself.[1] It assesses domestic news coverage of the election and how voters responded to the campaign and news coverage in terms of interest and involvement. Finally, it looks at the electoral outcome, at pollsters' accuracy in predicting that outcome, and at survey results that help us better understand the campaign and its outcome.

The 1990 Presidential Campaign

Setting the Electoral Stage: Spring and Summer 1989

As the 1990 campaign approached, Daniel Ortega faced extraordinary problems as president. After ten years of a socialist economy and in the midst of the U.S. embargo and Contra War, the nation was struggling with negative economic growth, hyperinflation, and a severe import/export imbalance. In 1988 inflation had hit 36,000 percent, war damage had reached $12 billion, and the weather had caused another $800 million in damage. Despite Sandinista efforts to improve the lives of the poor majority, recent years had instead seen growing poverty, increases in deaths from preventable childhood disease, and reduced caloric intake. Ortega and his government had sought to address the problems through policy reforms that included (1) realigning prices, (2) decreasing inflation by cutting the deficit, (3) relaxing price controls to raise productivity, and (4) dismantling wage constraints to raise labor productivity.[2] Yet these steps undermined still further the revolution's benefits for the poor, reducing Sandinista resolve to implement them.

---

1. Our description of the campaign and related events in Nicaragua from March 1989 to March 1990 relies extensively on international news coverage, as well as on academic sources and domestic coverage. For space reasons we do not give specific citations to the numerous non-Nicaraguan news sources, unless a specific fact is involved. The list of international news sources consulted include: Associated Press, BBC World News, *Boston Globe, Christian Science Monitor, Current Digest of the Soviet Press, Daily Telegraph,* Gannett News Service, *Le Monde* (France), *Los Angeles Times, Manchester Guardian* (United Kingdom), *New York Times, Revista Nexos* (Mexico), *San Diego Union-Tribune, San Francisco Chronicle, St. Louis Post-Dispatch, St. Petersburg Times,* Tass (Soviet Union), *Times* (London), *Toronto Star,* United Press International, *Washington Post,* and *USA Today.*

2. Ricciardi (1991, 263).

The FSLN leadership believed that the nation's economic problems were primarily the fault of the United States and could be reversed if the United States would end the embargo and Contra support. They saw new elections as a way of demonstrating the regime's legitimacy and convincing the Republican administration to end its antagonism.[3] Accordingly, Ortega entered negotiations in late spring and summer 1989 with opposition parties, refining procedures for holding the national elections that were already scheduled for November 1990. He entered an agreement with other Central American presidents to move the election forward by nine months, to February 1990.[4] He did so to send a clear signal to the United States and the international community that he was serious. He also did so at a point in time when most polls, including CID-Gallup of Costa Rica, showed strong citizen support for Ortega's reelection.

To underscore his desire for rapprochement with the United States, Ortega was also prepared to suspend the draft for six months, decrease his military efforts, and consider an extended cease-fire with the Contras. These decisions were popular abroad as well as at home with citizens opposed to the war and draft-age young men. Yet during the summer, always concerned to maintain his militant image with the FSLN militia, Ortega sent other signals as well. He expelled several U.S. diplomats for inciting civil disturbance, asked the United States to limit its embassy personnel, and began requiring visas for U.S. visitors. These actions diffused the short-term benefit he might have gained in the United States by moving the electoral calendar forward, so that little movement came in easing the embargo or decreasing support for the Contras. But domestically Ortega did gain momentum for elections while maintaining his hold on his party.

In early August the five Central American presidents met to agree on several important international issues affecting the region and to help set the stage for the Nicaraguan elections. The result of that meeting, the Tela Accord, provided that Ortega would recognize the outcome of El Salvador's recent election while, in return, Honduras and the other Central American nations agreed to support Ortega's demand that the Contras be demobilized. President Bush objected to the Tela Accord, preferring to keep the Contras mobilized until after the election. The Central American presidents stood

3. Reding (1991, esp. 39–44).

4. The 1987 constitution called for elections every six years. The 1984 election had been in November. However, the FSLN moved the election forward to February 1990, a date that deferred to opposition pressure and that fit better with the agricultural crop cycle and the monsoon rains. Armony (1997, 204).

firm, however, and Bush ultimately accepted their position, unwilling to undermine an accord supported by all the leaders of the isthmus. Ortega later made good on his agreement by releasing fifteen hundred Contra and former National Guard prisoners.

Organizing for the Election

The Tela Accord and the support Ortega received in Central America turned attention to organizing the election. The FSLN and the opposition parties agreed to guarantee the holding of the election, and all parties began urging citizens to register to vote. Additionally, pressured by the United States and some Latin American nations to set aside differences in favor of electoral unity, Nicaragua's traditional parties coalesced behind a ticket combining Conservative and Liberal leadership.[5] In late August the fledgling UNO (Union Nacional Opositora) coalition unveiled specifics of an electoral platform[6] and named Violeta Chamorro as their candidate. UNO included the following parties: Conservatives, Independent Liberals, Social Christians, Social Democrats, Socialists, and the Communists. With Chamorro, the coalition put forth perhaps the only candidate from the traditional parties who could claim enough visibility and respect among the voting public to pose a real challenge to Ortega. Despite Chamorro's acceptance of the nomination, the rightist parties continued to be influenced by old habits of elite infighting and found it hard to present a united opposition. Unifying UNO presented an enormous challenge to Chamorro as she began her campaign. Simultaneously, various minor parties on the right and left chose to mount campaigns for their own presidential candidates, thereby threatening to divide the opposition vote even if Chamorro unified the Conservative and Liberal Parties behind her.

As autumn approached, skepticism about Ortega's intentions[7] and the opposition's capacity to compete gradually yielded to a belief that the election would occur, which in turn led to a focus on the issues. Chamorro began to act and sound like a real candidate, criticizing government policy, stressing the nation's troubles since 1979, and calling for expanded civil liberties. Bush

---

5. Robinson (1992).

6. *Los Angeles Times*, 8/23/89, 5.

7. *Revista Nexos*, 2/1/90. For discussions of the Soviet position in support of elections, see, for example, *Los Angeles Times*, 10/27/89, A8; *St Louis Post-Dispatch*, 10/29/90, 3B; *Manchester Guardian Weekly*, 3/11/90, 10; *San Diego Union-Tribune*, 9/27/89, A11; *Toronto Star*, 7/17/89, A14; Morley (1994).

searched for ways to fund her campaign through the National Endowment for Democracy. And Ortega emphasized his party's revolutionary legitimacy and his own experience as president. Both campaigns seemed to gather steam, freed of concerns about whether the election would be held. Then disaster struck, with Ortega suffering a setback from which his personal image would never fully recover. Ironically, it was the voter registration process that opened the door for this setback.

The Cease-Fire Fiasco

On the morning of Sunday, October 22, 1989, a group of soldiers on their way to register to vote were ambushed by Contras. Between eighteen and twenty-one were killed. Ortega waited four days before responding and then chose an internationally visible forum for doing so. He had previously been invited to a dinner in San Jose, Costa Rica, to celebrate the Tela Accord. Ortega arrived in military dress, denounced the Contra attack, and declared that he would now refuse to extend the cease-fire, due to expire in a few days. His announcement was greeted with disbelief. The governments of Costa Rica, Venezuela, and Argentina as well as the U.N. Secretary General all urged him to reconsider.[8] President Bush reacted with anger, calling Ortega a "little man in his military uniform," "an unwanted animal at a garden party." Bush and UNO predicted that this was Ortega's first step toward canceling the election.

Ortega initially responded to international pressure with defiance. He said the Sandinista government could not continue to honor a one-sided cease-fire. He noted that Nicaraguan soldiers were being killed by U.S.-sponsored attackers even while he himself was honoring his electoral promises. Yet however justified Ortega might have been, it was not just Bush or the international community that responded with suspicion about his motives, but citizens at home. His response seemed an overreaction, using the incident to political advantage or even as an excuse to cancel the election. His willingness to end the cease-fire made him look weak and deceitful.

---

8. Orozco (1999) argues that the international community played a key role in Nicaragua's democratization. He highlights positive contributions made by the United States, Costa Rica, the OAS, the UN, the European Union, and the Carter Center. For a general discussion of the contribution of the international context to democratic development, see Di Palma (1990, esp. chaps. 2 and 4).

After several days, as the magnitude of his mistake became clear, he moderated his position, saying that the cease-fire would continue if the Contras could be demobilized and refraining from intense military action when the cease-fire did, in fact, end. Within a week, Ortega issued reassurances that the elections would proceed on schedule, while Bush's aides said they would cease all funding to that particular Contra unit if, in fact, the unit had carried out the ambush. Bush asked the Contras to refrain from armed action, and the U.S. media concluded that while Ortega's timing had been poor, his position had some merit. Yet Ortega's overwrought and theatrical response to the ambush had raised deep concerns among Nicaraguan citizens about his desire to end the Contra War and reconcile with the United States. He also appeared erratic, fueling an underlying concern about his suitability for the presidency.

November 1989

With the cease-fire fiasco highlighting the tenuousness of the electoral process and amidst the highly charged international events of November 1989, Nicaragua's 1990 contest became one of the most watched and overseen elections in history.[9] International involvement included official and private funding from the United States for UNO, election oversight from the Carter Center, nonpartisan financial contributions from several Western European powers,[10] and encouragement for the election from the Soviet Union and Central America. Observers from around the world were already on the ground, including a team of 240 observers sent by the United Nations. The international community again began to anticipate a free and fair electoral process.

November also saw domestic attention return to the campaign. Ortega appeared eager to repair his damaged image by dialogue with Contra leaders, offering amnesty, demobilization, and resettlement. He also restrained military activity and moderated his language. Following these moves, a national poll by DOXA of Venezuela showed that 70 percent of Nicaraguans wanted blanket amnesty and 77 percent opposed renewed combat with the Contras. And Ortega's image had sustained damage. Thus 60 percent questioned the success of the FSLN in fostering peace, with only 19 percent seeing progress. The country was sick of war and was concerned about Ortega's ability or desire to end it.

9. Reding (1991, 42).

10. *Report of the Latin American Studies Association to Observe the Nicaraguan Election*, 1990.

Chamorro took immediate advantage of the situation, portraying herself as the "peace candidate."[11] She and her campaign also challenged the Sandinistas' record, criticizing violations of press freedom and civil liberties, disregard for private property, and the nation's economic difficulties. At a time when DOXA's polls showed 69 percent wanting the draft abolished, she highlighted the Sandinistas' continued refusal to end conscription. She sought U.S. publicity with a fund-raising trip to Miami and an editorial and interview for the *Washington Post*.

Yet Chamorro also faced problems. While promising campaign funds, Bush had yet to deliver. Her rallies were often disrupted by violence, with 47 percent of the public blaming the FSLN, but 20 percent attributing the violence to conflicts within UNO. She was mired in controversy over her choice of Alfredo César, a former Contra, as UNO director. Most polls predicted an FSLN win, although CID-Gallup gave her the lead. But the real surprise was UNO's progress in unifying and in mounting an aggressive campaign. Precisely when Ortega was lowering his profile and moderating his image, Chamorro was attacking.

December 1989

Ortega continued his conciliatory approach into December, extending the Contra demobilization deadline and participating in the Central American peace process. On the campaign trail he presented himself as the vigorous, idealistic, youthful revolutionary he had once been, seeking to create a better world, rather than the hardened, calculating leader many believed he had become. He reminded citizens of the revolution's successes in redistributing property and meeting social needs, all in the face of U.S. opposition and sabotage. Yet he continued to send mixed signals. While he attempted to appear more moderate, his foreign minister, Miguel D'Escoto, denied entry visas to several U.S. congressmen coming to observe the campaign. D'Escoto argued that the U.S. Congress had approved funding for the UNO campaign and that the congressmen could not now pretend to be "impartial election observers."[12]

---

11. Chamorro's effective portrayal of herself as the "peace candidate" when Ortega could also have made an argument to that effect is a good example of using the media to seize ownership of an issue. By emphasizing UNO's international legitimacy while *El Nuevo Diario* failed to do the same for the FSLN, *La Prensa* appeared to seize for Chamorro the mantle of international legitimacy. On issue ownership, see Ansolabehere and Iyengar (1994).

12. *Washington Post*, 12/1/89, A51; UPI, 12/1/89.

Despite the contradictions between Ortega's efforts to appear more moderate and his government's defiant actions, he continued to bask in the polls. A December Greenberg-Lake survey gave him a substantial lead and appeared to confirm the findings of a Nicaraguan poll earlier that month. Such polls suggested that Ortega was weathering the autumn storm. Citizens might be disappointed with his recent behavior, but the deep reservoir of support for his revolutionary mission remained.

For her part, Chamorro continued to stress the need for national reconciliation, her strong sense of family, and her success in unifying UNO. To underscore her diplomatic capacities, her campaign emphasized her success in bringing together her own contentious adult children and their families for holiday celebrations, despite their division into Sandinista, Conservative, and Contra factions. She also promised that if she won an electoral victory, the United States would end the embargo and its Contra support and initiate aid to Nicaragua, allowing reconstruction. But with the long delay in U.S. campaign funds, such promises looked less convincing, while UNO, if more united, was still factionalized and ideologically diverse. It was hard to imagine the coalition sufficiently unified to outvote the FSLN in the National Assembly. In the polls, Chamorro's campaign appeared to sputter. But then came another bombshell.

On December 20, the United States invaded Panama. It captured the Panamanian dictator, Manuel Noriega, flew him to the States for trial on drug-smuggling charges, and invaded the home of a Nicaraguan diplomat based in Panama City. The unilateral, heavy-handed actions seemed disturbing to the international community, even if Noriega was a dictator and drug lord. They were particularly troubling in Central America, demonstrating scant U.S. regard for the sovereignty of small nations and disdain for the ongoing regional process of peacemaking. The timing, two months before the Nicaraguan election, looked particularly suspect. If anything was likely to throw the electoral process into upheaval, intimidating citizens into supporting Chamorro or giving Ortega an excuse to end the election, this invasion was it.

January 1990

Ortega began January condemning the U.S. invasion of the Nicaraguan diplomat's home in Panama, suggesting it foretold a U.S. invasion of Nicaragua itself. Clearly he and his government were angry over the U.S. actions and disturbed about their timing. His government continued to deny entry visas, and a Contra attack on four unarmed nuns and clergy, including one U.S. citizen, illustrated that domestic hostilities continued and helped explain some of Ortega's intransigence. Yet he also maintained a sense of balance, immediately reassuring everyone that the election would occur on schedule and continuing to campaign. Unlike the cease-fire, this crisis left Ortega stronger, with the invasion reigniting some of the spark and old revolutionary style without leading him to go too far in statements or actions.

International coverage in January contrasted Ortega's strength and skill with the weakness, whining, and unsportsmanlike behavior of Chamorro's campaign. Correspondents reported that Ortega's campaign was well run, well financed, and effective, drawing huge crowds. By contrast, Chamorro broke a leg, left for surgery in the United States, and returned in a wheelchair. Her campaign organizers grumbled to the press about alleged Sandinista violence at UNO rallies or about the lack of U.S. funds. UNO appeared factionalized and juvenile, with leaders engaging in a fistfight at a key UNO rally. UNO campaign managers even admitted they were inexperienced and that the FSLN campaign was better.

Some reporters stressed positive aspects of Chamorro's campaign, including her emphasis on peace, reconciliation, and national reconstruction and the challenge that UNO unity now posed for Ortega. They underscored her skill in blaming the FSLN for economic decline and calling for market reforms, while admitting that U.S. sanctions had damaged the economy as well. They also noted that her offer of a market economy and expanded civil liberties constituted a clear message of an alternative regime. But despite these achievements, it was difficult to ignore the appearance of an organized, efficient political leader running a hard-hitting, effective campaign against an aging, infirm, disorganized political novice whose beleaguered campaign diverted attention from its failings by stressing the unfair behavior of domestic adversaries and its weak foreign support. No one was surprised when Greenberg-Lake and other late January polls predicted an Ortega victory.[13]

Yet if the contest looked like an emerging Ortega landslide, preparations for the elections indicated that a free and fair vote was under way. Jimmy Carter praised the preparations for election day and worked to remove blemishes on the incumbent government by gaining visas for the congressmen. The UN and OAS were visible, and the Soviet press reported fifteen hundred observers in Nicaragua. The whole world would be watching as Nicaraguans went to the polls.

---

13. *LASA Report*, 1990; *San Diego Union-Tribune*, 1/31/90, A5; *Boston Globe*, 1/27/90, 14; *New York Times*, 1/27/90.

February 1990

February found observers from all major international newspapers descending on Nicaragua, generating a plethora of perspectives on the campaign. With this onslaught, the collective sense that Ortega would win lessened, and alternative perspectives gained credence. Coverage of Chamorro became more serious and detailed, with her distinctive personal history becoming clearer. An interview stressed her reconciliation skills, developed within her own highly visible but fractious family, and reported the respect she received from Nicaraguans. Even Ortega was unwilling to criticize her directly. Journalists described growing crowds at UNO rallies, and some polls predicted an UNO victory.

Still, most observers continued to expect Ortega to win. His political machine continued to generate massive rallies.[14] Emboldened by his January success in striking an aggressive stance while maintaining a moderate image, he increased his attacks against the United States and UNO. He also tried to attract the female vote. Primarily, however, he stressed his party's governing experience and its revolutionary commitment to the poor. The party had proven that commitment both in insurrection and in governance. His strategy seemed to work; again in February major pollsters reported an Ortega lead, and some purportedly saw a decline in UNO support.[15]

The last two weeks of the campaign saw international attention to Nicaragua crescendo. Like the candidates themselves, international reporters stressed regime differences. Chamorro was the proponent of a conservative, market-based Nicaragua committed to electoral democracy, personal freedom, and close relations with the United States. Ortega was the champion of social justice, mass political mobilization, and a powerful but popularly constrained socialist state capable of completing the revolution even in the face of U.S. opposition. Observers noted the nation's severe economic problems and said that candidates in an established democracy would focus on them. Yet the Nicaraguan struggle was a deeper one, focused on the nature of the state itself and the power it needed, and could be safely accorded, to ensure economic and social progress.

In the final preelectoral days, correspondents reported that both candidates looked good but that an UNO win would be difficult. The massive attendance at FSLN rallies combined with polling predictions reinforced the

14. Barnes (1992, 1990).

15. U.S. scholars also argued Ortega had run the better campaign. See Robinson (1992, esp. the afterword by Robert Pastor, 181–83). See also Oquist (1992, 22, 30–32). *Revista Nexos* (Mexico) wrote (2/1/90) that Sandinista supporters included urban workers, peasant members of cooperatives, students, soldiers, and bureaucrats, while UNO supporters were ranchers, merchants, and artisans. Those whose vote was most uncertain were peasant smallholders.

perception of an Ortega victory. American newscaster Peter Jennings and *ABC News* were so confident of their February poll that his analysis in the days prior to the election treated Ortega's win as a virtual certainty. Yet some seasoned international journalists were still cautious, admiring Chamorro's pluck and refusing to dismiss scattered polls suggesting she might win. Finding unease about the election as he interviewed FSLN rally participants, one distinguished journalist wondered whether such gatherings were reflections of electoral support for Ortega or nostalgic celebrations of a revolution that had run its course. The campaign ended with observers awaiting the citizens' verdict, concerned to discover who they supported and what the vote would mean for Nicaragua's future.

Nicaraguan Newspaper Coverage of the Campaign

As Nicaraguans considered their decisions, they relied on their own media for information and perspective. High-intensity, opinionated political coverage was a long-standing characteristic of Nicaragua's media and one that had continued throughout the Sandinista years.[16] Nicaragua boasted multiple media outlets.[17] It had more than fifty radio stations, three television channels, three daily newspapers (*La Prensa*, *El Nuevo Diario*, and *Barricada*), and a weekly, *La Cronica*.[18] Citizens used the information available: 43 percent relied primarily on radio for information; 31.1 percent relied on the newspapers as their first source; and 25.7 percent used the television as their main news source.[19] Yet citizens respected and trusted the newspapers most, according to a 1989–90 poll by CID-Gallup of Costa Rica that ranked them as the most trusted news source.[20]

---

16. Norsworthy (1997, esp. 281).

17. Students of the linkage between journalism and opinion formation argue that the media exert a powerful influence over the political agenda discussed by the public. In particular such influence is exerted through elites, who may read newspapers more than average citizens, and who then transfer the agenda on to the general public. See Cook (1998, 10). Candidate usage of the media, moreover, powerfully influences the message voters receive and how they vote. The media can cause voters to distinguish among more important versus less important issues. See Edwards, Mitchell, and Welch (1995). Additionally, by the way they frame their media presentation candidates can gain "issue ownership" and also influence voters that way. See Ansolabehere and Iyengar (1994). On the more general linkage of news and the construction of political meaning among citizens, see Neuman, Just, and Crigler (1992)

18. Banks and Muller (1998, 675).

19. Norsworthy (1997, 287); Cook (1998, 186).

20. The CID-Gallup poll, conducted by a survey team from Costa Rica, is available from the Roper Institute. CID-Gallup found that 35.8 percent of respondents trusted the newspapers most as a source of news, while 28.7 percent trusted the radio most, and only 22.7 percent trusted the television most (N = 1,226).

Among newspapers, a majority of citizens (51.6 percent) selected either *La Prensa* or *El Nuevo Diario* as one of their top two preferences. This selection reflected the effort of these two major dailies, Nicaragua's most independent newspapers, to achieve some degree of journalistic integrity. Their approach contrasts with that of *Barricada*, the third daily newspaper, which was "the official organ of the FSLN."[21] Yet in keeping with Nicaraguan tradition, each of these dailies was partisan, with *La Prensa* being "an anti-Sandinista voice-piece for the Nicaraguan capitalists,"[22] and *El Nuevo Diario* "supporting the government."[23] In fact, the *St. Petersburg Times* noted that the two were campaigning equally hard on each side of the election.[24]

To get further perspective on the campaign and a sense of what citizens were hearing, we turn now to an examination of campaign coverage by *La Prensa* and *El Nuevo Diario*.[25] Our concern here is to clarify the portrait of the campaign that these two respected and preferred yet partisan newspapers presented to the citizens. We use content analysis of their campaign coverage, utilizing the procedures presented in the appendix to the book. In coding the topical content of articles in these two newspapers, we determined whether articles on the campaign addressed five broad categories: the candidates and their parties, domestic concerns, regime choice issues, international topics, and the Contra War.

Table 3.1 presents the coverage in each category by *La Prensa* and *El Nuevo Diario* by month during the campaign, together with the total coverage for the four months combined. As the last column shows, both newspapers emphasized regime concerns. Such articles gave attention both to general support for or opposition to the regimes offered by Ortega or Chamorro and to specific problems associated with them. Attention to regime predominated in 29 percent of all articles across the two newspapers, roughly 23 percent of *El Nuevo Diario*'s coverage and 33 percent of *La Prensa*'s. *La Prensa*, supporting the candidate wanting regime change, gave regime issues more coverage than *El Nuevo Diario*, supporting the status quo.

In discussing regime more than traditional domestic concerns such as the economy, the news coverage by Nicaragua's two leading papers paralleled

21. Norsworthy (1997, 287). See also Conroy (1985, 220); and Enriquez (1985, 276).
22. Spalding (1994, 141); see also Booth (1985, 198–99).
23. Dore (1985, 420–21).
24. For a discussion of the value of bias in newspaper coverage for citizen evaluations, see Calvert (1985b).
25. The use of newspapers to uncover underlying political dynamics and patterns in the study of developing democracy finds precedent in the study of developing democracy in Britain. See Tilly (1995).

Table 3.1   The Primary Campaign Topics Covered by *La Prensa* and *El Nuevo Diario*
Month by Month during the 1990 Presidential Campaign (%)

	November	December	January	February	Total
	I. La Prensa				
Candidates/parties	13.2	37.3	23.8	5.2	18.8
Domestic issues					
Economy	8.2	4.0	10.4	12.2	8.9
Social issues	4.9	6.3	3.0	4.5	4.6
Religion	1.6	2.4	4.3	0.6	2.2
Regime concerns					
General	11.0	9.5	3.7	16.0	10.0
Specific behavior	24.2	19.0	26.8	22.4	23.4
Int'l concerns	26.4	13.5	20.7	34.0	24.2
Contra War	10.4	7.9	7.3	5.1	7.8
Total	99.9	99.9	100	100	99.9
N	182	126	164	156	628
	II. El Nuevo Diario				
Candidates/parties	28.4	34.5	34.0	20.8	28.3
Domestic issues					
Economy	6.2	4.8	3.5	1.7	3.5
Social issues	8.6	3.6	14.9	14.6	11.8
Religion	6.2	5.9	2.1	6.2	5.0
Regime concerns					
General	24.7	15.5	12.1	19.7	17.6
Specific behavior	2.5	6.0	5.0	7.9	5.8
Int'l concerns	11.1	17.9	19.1	21.9	18.6
Contra War	12.3	11.9	9.2	7.3	9.5
Total	100	100.1	99.9	100.1	100.1
N	81	84	141	178	484

Source: Content analysis of *La Prensa* and *El Nuevo Diario*, as detailed in the appendix.
Note: This table reports the primary topic of all campaign-related articles within each newspaper and the percentage of articles devoted to each topic, by month and in total, during the 1990 presidential campaign. Percentage estimates were derived through content analysis of the newspapers' campaign coverage. These procedures yielded 628 articles for analysis within *La Prensa*, distributed across the months as specified in the table, and 484 articles within *El Nuevo Diario*.

that of the foreign newspapers. Yet both papers also provided extensive coverage of the candidates and parties (22.9 percent of total coverage), international concerns (21.8 percent), and domestic issues (17.7 percent). In addition, the Contra War as a separate category received 7.8 percent of *La Prensa*'s coverage and 9.5 percent of *El Nuevo Diario*'s, demonstrating its salience in the campaign.

When the newspapers' coverage is contrasted by month, a variety of patterns emerge. First, *El Nuevo Diario* early on focused more on candidate and party concerns than did *La Prensa*, paralleling international media reports that Ortega and his supporters were stressing his personality, past experience, and the historic role the Sandinistas had played in contemporary Nicaragua. That focus increased even more in the middle two months, then decreased substantially in February. For comparison, *La Prensa*'s party and candidate focus was modest in November, became stronger in December with the effort to highlight Chamorro's personal and family background, moderated in January when she went to the United States for surgery, and virtually disappeared in February. This pattern paralleled media reports that Chamorro and her supporters were spending more time on the attack against the Sandinista regime and its policies than on discussing candidates and parties, deliberately underplaying the importance of party because of UNO's coalitional weakness.

In contrast to *El Nuevo Diario*'s early focus on candidates and parties, *La Prensa* began the campaign stressing regime issues, maintained this emphasis strongly in the middle months, and then gave predominant attention to regime in February. Such articles raised concerns about Sandinista performance in office and highlighted Chamorro's call for a more democratic Nicaragua. These articles exceeded *El Nuevo Diario*'s regime focus month by month as well as in total coverage. Yet the latter did pay considerable attention to regime as well, giving strong attention to it early on and predominant attention in the final month.

With respect to domestic issues, *La Prensa* focused more on the economy, while *El Nuevo Diario* stressed social concerns. This pattern fits with *La Prensa*'s position as "the voice of the capitalists" and *El Nuevo Diario*'s prorevolutionary position. *La Prensa*'s stress on the economy was particularly pronounced in January and February, while *El Nuevo Diario*'s attention to social issues was also strongest then, indicating that the second half of the campaign was the period when the candidates and their supporters gave greatest attention to domestic policy problems. With respect to the Contra War, which raised domestic as well as international concerns, both newspapers gave at least 10 percent of their coverage to it early on, following the cease-fire controversy. But thereafter attention to it declined, with the papers focusing more on international issues.

The articles on international concerns reached their highest point in February when they constituted 34 percent of the coverage in *La Prensa* and 22 percent in *El Nuevo Diario*. These articles focused on a range of international topics, such as the need for foreign acceptance of the nation's governing regime, the importance of future donor aid, and the necessity of maintaining Nicaragua's autonomy within the international community. Such international concerns were necessarily connected to issues of regime, reinforcing the importance of regime choice in the election. Combining the results for international topics and for articles directly on regime, we see that in the final month *La Prensa* devoted over 70 percent of its articles to these two topics, while *El Nuevo Diario* gave them roughly 50 percent of its coverage. Meanwhile, concern with candidates and parties faded.

The image that emerges from the pattern of the newspapers' topical coverage is of a vibrant, spirited campaign focused on issues of great consequence for Nicaragua's future. The February convergence by both newspapers toward articles on regime choice and international issues also suggests that Chamorro and her supporters had succeeded by the end of the campaign in having their central concerns dominate the closing days of campaign dialogue. Perhaps more than international observers realized, Chamorro's early and continuous attack on the Sandinista regime and her growing focus on international concerns ultimately drew Ortega and the Sandinistas to wage the campaign battle on her turf. His hesitancy to attack her directly may have contributed to this development, since it would be difficult to sustain a strategy focused on differences between candidates without taking on the opposing candidate in some direct and critical manner.

An indication of the partisan intensity of newspaper coverage can be gleaned by comparing the number and percentage of election articles in each newspaper that were partisan or neutral. In doing so, we find that *El Nuevo Diario* published 484 articles across the four months of the campaign (on the selected days specified in the procedures outlined in the appendix) and that 88 percent favored Ortega while 12 percent were neutral. *La Prensa* was even more strongly partisan, publishing 628 articles of which 94 percent favored Chamorro and 6 percent were neutral. The vast majority of articles in each newspaper thus favored the candidate supported by the newspaper, with the conservative *La Prensa* outstripping the Sandinista *El Nuevo Diario* in the quantity and partisan character of its election articles across the campaign.

The broad story conveyed by these patterns—an aggressive and partisan coverage by the conservative press, a somewhat less intense partisan coverage by the Sandinista press—is qualified by examining the newspapers' month by month coverage. *El Nuevo Diario* started the campaign in a relatively less partisan manner than *La Prensa*. November and December were the months when Ortega was most on the defensive over his ending of the cease-fire and over his electoral intentions generally. His own restraint and moderation were reflected in *El Nuevo Diario*'s restrained partisan coverage during these two months, so that 144 of its 165 election articles were partisan in nature. Simultaneously, Chamorro was reported in the international press to have begun the campaign in a surprisingly aggressive manner, a tack echoed in *La Prensa's* more partisan and intense coverage. Thus *La Prensa* published more articles on the campaign than did *El Nuevo Diario* across these early months—310 in contrast to 165—and more of them were partisan in nature—95.8 percent (297) in contrast to 91.4 percent (144).

In the final two months of the campaign, a reenergized Ortega took a more aggressive approach while Chamorro, preoccupied by illness and surgery, was less visible. Reflecting these developments, *El Nuevo Diario* greatly expanded its coverage of the campaign in January, with its 141 articles that month approximating the 165 articles across the two previous months combined. Although only 83 percent (or 117) of these articles were partisan, the overall number of partisan articles published on behalf of Ortega had increased substantially. Simultaneously, *La Prensa* published 166 articles on the election in January, only a slight increase over the 155 articles it had averaged in the two previous months. Moreover, the percentage of partisan articles in *La Prensa* dropped to 89.8 percent (or 149 articles). These shifts in partisan coverage by the two newspapers parallel developments in the campaign, mirroring Ortega's growing intensity and assertiveness and Chamorro's momentary preoccupation with surgery in the United States. Nevertheless, even in January the pro-Sandinista newspaper printed fewer articles on the campaign than *La Prensa*, and fewer of them were partisan.

In February *El Nuevo Diario* began to outdistance *La Prensa* in the number of articles on the campaign and nearly matched it in terms of partisan intensity. Thus in February it published 178 election articles, in contrast to 157 published by *La Prensa*, and 165 (or 92.7 percent) were partisan, in contrast to 149 (or 94.9 percent) that were partisan in *La Prensa*. The conservative *La Prensa* was still more partisan in percentage terms than *El Nuevo Diario*, but the pro-Sandinista newspaper was closing the gap at campaign's end and actually publishing more partisan articles in total. Yet ironically, as detailed in table 3.1, the topics of *El Nuevo Diario's* coverage had also shifted, focusing less on the concerns with candidates and parties that had been central to Ortega's early campaign strategy, and more on concerns about regime choice and international legitimacy that Chamorro's campaign had highlighted. As *El Nuevo Diario* became more partisan, it also became more preoccupied with the issues that Chamorro had made the early focus of her campaign.

The difference in partisan intensity between these two most trusted newspapers portrays an early aggressiveness in the media presentation of

Chamorro's message that was missing with Ortega and his supporters. The pattern also reinforces the sense that, by the end of the campaign, Chamorro and her supporters had drawn Ortega and his camp into a real and contentious electoral battle. As such, the election came to be focused less on a ritualistic and pro forma legitimation of Ortega and his regime, and more on a choice between contending candidates and the regime offers they were making. As a result, the voters following the campaign through these two key newspapers or indirectly influenced by their coverage received a strong message making clear that a real election contest was under way.[26] At issue was whether voters would take that contest seriously and closely consider the alternatives at hand.

Citizens Respond: From Apathy to Engaged Choice

Citizen engagement in an electoral contest despite civil war, economic crisis, and growing poverty is no small achievement. It is all too easy for citizens to become absorbed in personal lives and problems to which an election appears irrelevant, particularly if they have little experience in the use of elections and face doubts about whether one will be held or honored. And yet, in order to influence their future through elections, citizens must be willing to risk disappointment, focus on the contest, listen to alternative positions, and absorb enough information to make a reasoned choice.[27] And they must also be matched in their democratic aspirations by an elite that makes clear its commitment to fair, meaningful elections.

As we have seen, by November the governing Sandinistas had signaled that a genuine election was under way, and a coalition of opposition parties was presenting a visible candidate offering a clear alternative. Thereafter a contentious campaign unfolded, even if it was attended by moments of uncertainty about Ortega's true intentions and about Chamorro's viability. The well-oiled Sandinista machine mounted impressively organized rallies on behalf of Ortega's revolutionary leadership and the party's historic mission. The opposition delivered an aggressive message attacking the Sandinistas' performance in office, calling for national renewal, and offering Chamorro's well-honed familial skills at reconciling disparate political factions. The

---

26. Shaw (1999) writes that some campaigns are simply better at getting their message across. Although the newspapers were not officially part of either campaign, these findings indicate that the newspaper that favored Chamorro was better at conveying its message than was the pro-FSLN *El Nuevo Diario*.

27. Tichenor, Donohue, and Olien (1970); Markus (1982, 1986); Miller and Shanks (1982, 299–356); Marcus and MacKuen (1993).

nation's partisan press covered these developments closely, capturing the growing partisan intensity and giving readers a strong sense of shifting campaign messages. The pressing question was how citizens were interpreting these developments and whether they were connecting to the campaign.

To probe citizen response, we examine nationwide surveys that the Venezuelan firm DOXA conducted between November 1989 and February 1990. November's survey covered 800 respondents. The December data draw upon two waves of surveys that together included 2,280 respondents, 1,200 in the first and 1,080 in the second. The January and February surveys were 1,200 each. Surveys were illegal in Nicaragua in the last two weeks before the election, so our last data are from mid-February; the election was February 25.

In November citizen disengagement and apathy were pronounced. It was unclear whether Ortega would hold or honor the election, and Chamorro was still trying to unify UNO and mount a campaign. Disengagement was evident in two ways: (1) in low levels of response to important questions about political choice and (2) in the citizens' own perception of apathy around them. A question about presidential vote intent got a 32 percent nonresponse rate, while a question asking whether or not they were confident they would vote drew a 34 percent nonresponse rate, with only 64 percent answering affirmatively in a nation where voting is mandatory but enforcement lax. Similarly, when citizens were asked whether they perceived apathy toward the campaign, 55 percent of interviewees reported modest levels of apathy, defined as seeing apathy in 10 percent or more of citizens. Twenty-three percent saw high levels of apathy, defined as seeing it among 26 percent or more of the citizens.

As the campaign proceeded, nonresponse to questions about the campaign as well as perceptions of voter apathy steadily declined.[28] Nonresponse to DOXA's question on vote intent dropped to 20 percent in January and 15 percent in February, with the later figure roughly paralleling the percentage of citizens who failed to vote. Nonresponse on whether respondents intended to vote at all declined to 20 percent by late December, with 72 percent saying they expected to vote. This question was not asked after December 1989. Likewise, in January the proportion reporting that they perceived moderate apathy had dropped from 55 percent to 28 percent, while only 18 percent saw high apathy.

To gauge whether citizens' growing connection with the campaign reflected an increased sense that a genuine election was under way, we look

28. This process is similar to the one Gelman and King (1993) describe for electorates in established democracies, with voters gathering enough information during a campaign to make an "enlightened" choice.

now at how voters assessed the election. By December, 63 percent were expecting the election to be fair, with 16 percent predicting it would be unfair. By February, 70 percent predicted a fair election, 15 percent an unfair one. Similarly, when asked in late December whether the electorate was fearful about voting, 10 percent perceived "much fear," and only 44 percent perceived "no fear." But by February, those perceiving "much fear" had dropped to 5 percent, and those seeing "no fear" had risen to 59 percent. Additionally, citizens were focusing on whether or not the FSLN would concede defeat, so that in mid-February a majority of respondents had concluded that the Sandinistas would leave office if defeated. Such results suggest that most respondents concluded that a true election was under way and that Ortega would respect the outcome.

As citizen expectations of a fair election grew, so too did their sense that UNO was a viable political coalition. This conclusion is based on a question that asked citizens whether they saw UNO as fragmented. Those seeing fragmentation had exceeded those seeing a more unified UNO by 25 percent in November. By February that difference had shrunk to 5 percent.

The success of Chamorro and UNO in generating a viable opposition, as well as Ortega's ability to maintain his own viability, is captured in DOXA's probes of citizens' openness to supporting one or both major contenders. In both November and early December, DOXA asked citizens which candidate they would never support. In both polls, a quarter of the interviewees responded by saying that they could never support Ortega, whereas roughly 15 percent reported an unwillingness ever to support Chamorro. A substantial proportion of the population appeared willing to consider both Chamorro and Ortega.

Finally, as citizens watched the struggle to ensure a fair election, and as they saw Chamorro's effort to unify her coalition, did they suspect that any of this really mattered? Did they foresee a real contest?[29] One way to estimate this is to look at which candidate they thought would win. The results are startling, as presented in figure 3.1. In November, when most major polls except CID-Gallup of Costa Rica were predicting an easy Ortega win, almost as many respondents expected a Chamorro victory as did an Ortega one. Then December saw citizen predictions give a slight edge to Chamorro, while in January she moved decisively ahead. As citizens prepared to go to the polls in February, they were almost equally divided in their expectations of a Chamorro or Ortega victory, clearly perceiving a real contest at hand.

---

29. Studies of U.S. elections also show that campaigns matter even when the issues seem etched clearly beforehand. Moreover, within the campaign, effective use of the media matters. See Shaw (1999).

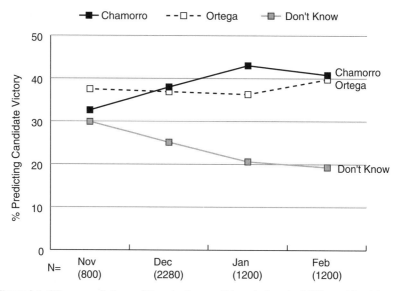

Figure 3.1 Citizen predictions of the winning candidate during the 1990 presidential campaign, by month

Source: DOXA nationwide monthly surveys asking, "Which candidate will get the most votes?"

The Electoral Outcome and Its Aftermath

When the citizens voted on February 25, 1990, Chamorro won by a land-slide, leading Ortega 54 percent to 41 percent among certified ballots.[30] The outcome was anticipated by neither the FSLN nor most major visible poll-sters, although the citizens themselves may have been less surprised. Ortega visited Chamorro's home to concede, and they embraced. She received him graciously, remarking, "There are neither victors nor vanquished." Shaken, tearful, but dignified, he announced that he would "respect and obey the mandate of the people."[31] He urged Nicaraguans "to ensure a peaceful tran-sition and begin a process of national reconciliation and economic recov-ery."[32] The French press noted that the immediate postelectoral mood was somber as the victors preferred to celebrate at home in a low-profile fashion, and FSLN party militants waited for signals from Sandinista leaders about

30. The Consejo Supremo Electoral reported 1,752,088 registered voters, 1,510,838 of whom voted, and 1,420,584 of whose votes were valid. CSE, Managua, 1990. For a non-Nicaraguan report on final electoral percentages see *LASA Report*, 1990, 34–35.

31. *San Francisco Chronicle*, 2/27/90, A1; Associated Press, 2/26/90; UPI, 2/26/90.

32. *Boston Globe*, 2/27/90, 1.

how to handle an event none had anticipated. Peter Jennings apologized on his nightly *ABC News* for the dramatic miscall of the election. The Sandinista Party began the process of relinquishing control of the state and turning the reins of government over to a new president and regime.

With the outcome Nicaragua was turned into a frenzy of anticipation on the right and concern on the left. Anxious to protect Sandinista supporters, the lame-duck government legalized Sandinista holdings of property confiscated during the revolution, doing so in a hurried and opportunistic fashion that many citizens perceived as wrong.[33] This perception was aggravated by efforts of visible Sandinistas to claim upscale property in Managua, a move that came to be called the "piñata." The transition was also marred by a struggle over the size and control of the military, by continued U.S. interference, and by the unemployment that resulted from demobilization of both the Contras and the military. In addition, the transition period and the months thereafter found the Sandinistas assessing what the election meant for them as a future political force. This assessment led the party to conclude that it had engaged in power abuses in office that it had to acknowledge and renounce if it were to play a leading political role in the new era.

The 1990 outcome also produced reassessment of the public opinion polls reported during the campaign. Fourteen of the preelectoral polls had predicted a Sandinista win, particularly some highly visible ones, while thirteen gave UNO the lead.[34] One of the most widely cited polls, by Greenberg-Lake out of the United States, had consistently predicted an FSLN victory, with the widely reported Washington Post/ABC poll and a Univision poll doing so as well. Why had such polls been wrong, and why did those predicting an UNO victory receive so little attention?

A variety of answers emerged. Mark Penn, a New York-based pollster, concluded that "people [felt] intimidated and I think they [were] reluctant to reveal their true intentions . . . particularly when their true intentions [were] anti-government." Sergio Bendixen of the Washington-based firm of Bendixen-Schroth, which had conducted the Univision poll, suggested that the Sandinistas might have skewed his interviews by infiltrating his pool of interviewees. Carlos Denton of CID-Gallup, Costa Rica, which had correctly predicted Chamorro's win, attributed error to respondents' reluctance to share their true views, the practical difficulties of polling in Nicaragua, and government regulations surrounding surveys. Accurate polling had

33. Prevost (1997, 162).
34. *Washington Post*, 2/27/90, A17. The *Post* also reported that five of the last nine polls showed the Sandinistas leading.

required attentiveness to the unique Nicaraguan circumstances, particularly the creation of an image of absolute impartiality on the part of interview teams. Janice Ballou of the Commission on Nicaraguan Preelection Polls reinforced Denton's sense that accurate polling had been possible, saying that the mispredictions were due to sampling errors by pollsters who failed to survey all groups representatively.[35]

Others noted that the inaccurate polls came largely from Nicaraguan sources, which generally predicted outcomes that fit with the partisan biases of the organizations involved, or from large U.S. firms unfamiliar with Nicaragua. The accurate surveys tended to come from Latin American pollsters from outside Nicaragua. Such firms were experienced with similar electorates elsewhere, attentive to the coverage of remote areas and less accessible barrios, and familiar with the Nicaraguan context but less partisan than domestic pollsters. They were also less visible than either the Nicaraguan firms or the high-profile U.S. pollsters.[36]

As pollsters and observers looked back over the campaign, a few signals of the impending UNO victory were now apparent. While Sandinista rallies were huge, some included government employees who may have had little choice about being there. Some observers suspected that UNO supporters had avoided undue attention and pressure, while UNO itself stressed the secrecy of the vote. Mark Uhlig of the *New York Times*, one of the closest journalistic observers during the campaign's last two months, had warned that the election was "hard to predict," noting an unease surrounding Sandinista rallies and a growth in UNO turnout.[37] In retrospect it seemed that many observers, inattentive to Uhlig's warnings, had allowed the glitzy and well-organized Sandinista campaign to warp their own perceptions. They had thus readily accepted the affirmation of an FSLN victory by established international firms with limited experience in Nicaragua, or had embraced polls conducted by local firms loyal to the Sandinistas, while overlooking or dismissing the other half of the polls that predicted an UNO win.[38]

---

35. The quotes from pollsters are presented in the *Washington Post*, 2/27/90, A17.

36. Barnes (1992). See also the *Washington Times*, 2/27/90, A8, and the Associated Press report by Mike Feinsilber, "The Landslide That Slid the Other Way," 2/28/90, both of which stressed the accuracy of Latin American pollsters from outside of Nicaragua, in contrast to the predictive failures of United States and Nicaraguan pollsters. On the need for greater attention by pollsters to working-class urban areas and rural voters, see the *New York Times*, 2/27/90, A1, and the Associated Press report by Feinsilber, 2/28/90.

37. *New York Times*, 2/18/90, sec. 1, p. 1.

38. For Uhlig's follow-up article immediately after the election, see the *New York Times*, 2/27/90, 1A. In it, Uhlig takes political analysts to task for failing to heed reporters' warnings that polls predicting an Ortega victory were misleading.

Some polls pointing to Chamorro clearly came from sources within Nicaragua favorable to UNO, but others came from respected Latin public opinion firms like CID-Gallup of Costa Rica and DOXA of Venezuela. These firms enjoyed reputations for objectivity, accuracy, and polling expertise in Latin American settings. A look back after the election at their polls presents a more complete and reliable picture of the campaign than that captured by observers at the time. This picture puts the subsequent debate over the causes of the "election upset"—whether it was an accident, a repudiation, a choice, a miscalculation, or a capitulation—in a substantially different light. Among these surveys, those taken by DOXA provide the broadest available array of questions.

Reassessing the 1990 Campaign

Figure 3.2 presents DOXA's survey results month by month from November through February. As with CID-Gallup of Costa Rica, DOXA found Chamorro already leading Ortega in November, by 34 percent to 28.9 percent, though this result was accompanied by a high level of nonresponse. More than 30 percent of interviewees (31.4 percent) failed to give a vote preference, and another 5.8 percent or so chose minor party candidates. Although Ortega was in trouble, 37 percent of the public had not yet chosen between the two major candidates, so the race was by no means already determined.

Following Chamorro's five-point advantage in November, DOXA's month-by-month results show her jumping to an 8.5 percent lead among interviewees in December, rising to a 10.6 percent margin in January, and then settling at an 8.3 percent advantage in mid-February. Among respondents to DOXA's vote intent question in its final, mid-February poll, omitting interviewees who failed to give a vote intent, 49.6 percent reported an intention to vote for Chamorro, whereas she drew 53.7 percent of the vote two weeks later; 39.8 percent reported a vote intent in favor of Ortega, whereas he drew 40.8 percent two weeks later. And 10.6 percent said they would vote for minor parties, while these drew 5.5 percent on election day.[39] These survey forecasts, completed two weeks prior to the election, lend support to the assessment of Denton and Ballou that the fundamental problems with inaccurate surveys lay not with interviewees but with interview teams

39. Among DOXA interviewees as a whole, including nonrespondents in the base, the February totals were 33.8 percent for Ortega, 42.1 percent for Chamorro, 9.0 percent for the minor parties, and 15.1 percent giving no response. N = 1,200 voting age adults.

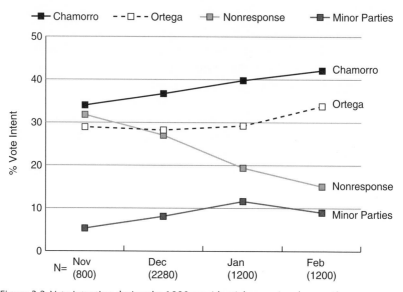

Figure 3.2 Vote intention during the 1990 presidential campaign, by month

Source: DOXA nationwide monthly surveys asking, "Which candidate will you vote for?"

and survey samples. DOXA's February survey combined with its polls of the previous months thus portrays an election that unfolded in surprising ways and differs substantially from the reading of various observers at the time or analysts since the election.

The Panama Effect

A first surprise in the DOXA data is that the turn away from Ortega and toward Chamorro had occurred by November, preceding the Panama invasion rather than resulting from it. In fact, Ortega's support increased after the invasion. This finding is supported by subdividing DOXA's December results. The first wave of December interviews occurred before the invasion, and the second immediately after it. In the first, Ortega's support had declined 4 points from November, to 24.8 percent. At this point, Chamorro had the support of 36.3 percent of interviewees, up roughly 2 points from November. Yet 32.3 percent were now undecided, and minor parties drew the rest (6.7 percent). But after the invasion, Ortega's support jumped to 32 percent. Chamorro's support held at 37.2 percent and nonresponse dropped suddenly by 11 points, to 21 percent, with the remaining interviewees (9.7 percent) supporting the minor parties.

Viewed sequentially, the two December surveys suggest that the Panama invasion crystallized movement toward the FSLN and stopped a virtual collapse in Ortega's support, rather than inducing his defeat. From the point of the invasion onward, Ortega stayed at or above his November support level of 29 percent, drawing 34 percent from DOXA interviewees by the final poll. His February numbers increased by 5 percent over his November ratings, and by 9 percent over his early December support. This movement toward Ortega apparently came to some extent from those who were undecided in November or early December, judging from the decrease in nonresponse. The Panama invasion thus appears to have had the opposite effect from that stressed by analysts who believe that it produced a capitulation among Nicaraguan citizens.

Possibly it was Ortega's awareness of the invasion's value in solidifying his support that led him to highlight it in his campaign appeals—though assumedly he did not realize how badly he needed the support. He also may not have realized the limited play he could get from stressing it. While 66 percent of DOXA interviewees opposed the invasion in late December, only 17 percent thought an invasion of Nicaragua was a realistic concern. This does not signal the sort of massive apprehension that would lead to public capitulation to the United States or allow Ortega to whip the nation into a nationalistic frenzy. It does point to a level of concern that could help a faltering leader appeal to his base, particularly to voters with military experience and nationalist concerns.

A Forthright, Sensible, Attentive Public

The DOXA surveys indicate, second, that voters behaved during the campaign in a more straightforward and discerning manner than many may have believed.[40] In fact, they seemed more cognizant of a close election than did many observers. This is evident not only in their collective prediction of a close outcome. Starting in November, DOXA also asked citizens whether or not they saw support for the FSLN changing. In November, in the aftermath of the cease-fire controversy and following Chamorro's strong entry into the campaign, 48 percent of interviewees saw FSLN support as decreasing, and only 12.5 percent saw it increasing. It was not until January, after the Panama invasion, that the percentage seeing FSLN support as falling began to decline, and the percentage reporting an increase in FSLN support rose.

---

40. Geddes and Zaller (1989) also find that an attentive electorate is more able to make discerning judgments in the context of campaign propaganda. See also Key (1961, 1966)

This would seem a clear indication of citizens' close, accurate attentiveness to the nation's political pulse. Such attentiveness is also seen in the dramatic decrease in nonresponse on vote intent that occurred during the campaign and, as we see in chapter 5, in growing response to questions about candidates, the economy, and the regime.

The citizens also increasingly expected a fair election, as we saw earlier, and seemed to anticipate Ortega's acceptance of electoral defeat. In addition, citizens shared with DOXA a set of vote intentions that corresponded closely to the final election result. DOXA forecast a 9.8 percent Chamorro victory in early to mid February, based on respondents who gave a vote intent; two weeks later she won by 13 percent. And DOXA forecast a combined lead of 20.4 percent by the opposition over Ortega, including UNO and the minor parties in the opposition category. In the end the lead was 18.4 percent. The accuracy of the DOXA results, not just in predicting Ortega's defeat but in approximating the election margin two weeks out, suggests that citizens were not responding to pollsters in a secretive, deceitful manner, but were quite forthright.

This is not to paint an overly refined or placid portrait of the electorate. While fear had declined and most citizens expected Ortega to concede, a minority harbored doubts about his good intentions, just as some feared a U.S. invasion if he won. But these were not predominant perceptions. Similarly, while citizens performed their duty to vote in an impressive manner, there was a substantial proportion of the voters, 6 percent, who mismarked their ballots, leading them to be discarded. These discarded ballots indicate the presence of confusion and inexperience. Yet there were not enough of these to affect the election outcome, nor widespread accusations of fraud. And of course the mismarking of ballots is not the sole province of inexperienced citizens in new democracies.

It is difficult to conclude from these surveys that the election was an accident resulting from citizen incomprehension and blundering, or a result of their strategic miscalculation in expecting a massive Ortega win or his refusal to concede. By and large, citizens appeared not only attentive to the campaign but sensible, forthright, and prescient in their perspectives on the election. This shifts the effort to explain the outcome more to repudiation, capitulation, or choice, highlighting a third surprise in the DOXA data.

The Blame Game

The debate over repudiation versus capitulation revolves around alternative perceptions about whom citizens blamed for Nicaragua's crisis. Those stressing repudiation believe Nicaraguans held the Sandinistas primarily responsible for the nation's problems, thus explaining the Chamorro vote. Those emphasizing capitulation believe that citizens blamed the United States, voting against Ortega to appease Bush. This debate has been inflamed by the results of a December 1989 Greenberg-Lake poll reporting that most citizens held the United States rather than the FSLN responsible for the nation's crisis (with 57 percent blaming the former, 29 percent blaming the latter).[41] This poll appeared to lend credence to the argument that the Chamorro vote was capitulation to the United States. Those holding the repudiation view argue that the unexpected nature of the 1990 outcome indicates that citizens were secretly opposed to Ortega, afraid to admit it to the pollsters, and only biding their time. Ironically, such analysts point to the failure of surveys by Greenberg-Lake and others to predict Chamorro's victory as proof of how frightened citizens were and how willing to hide their opinions. In fact, such firms may simply have used sampling procedures that inadvertently over-polled Sandinista supporters, such as university students and civil servants who tend to live in accessible urban areas rather than rural communities or poor barrios. The results of such polls would have overwhelmingly blamed the United States for the nation's crisis and predicted a sizable Sandinista victory.

To ascertain more accurately how citizens ascribed responsibility for the nation's difficulties, consider the results from DOXA's November survey, presented in figure 3.3. This early survey, which already showed a slight Chamorro lead, indicates that as the campaign began citizens distributed blame more widely than either the repudiation or the capitulation thesis suggests. Substantially more citizens held the Sandinistas responsible for the economy than the United States. Simultaneously, slightly more held the United States responsible for the war than the Sandinistas. Overall, the Sandinistas bore more responsibility for the general state of crisis than the United States, just the opposite of the Greenberg-Lake findings, with UNO, the Contras, and Cuba also sharing some of the blame. If we distinguish between two groups—a *right wing* composed of UNO, the Contras, and the United States and a *left wing* composed of the FSLN and Cuba—citizens split almost evenly in attributing culpability. The left bore slightly more responsibility for the economy than the right (42 percent to 38 percent), the right substantially more for the war (46.5 percent to 36 percent), and the right slightly more for the overall crisis (40.4 percent to 36.1 percent).

41. See Reding (1991, 47 n. 38).

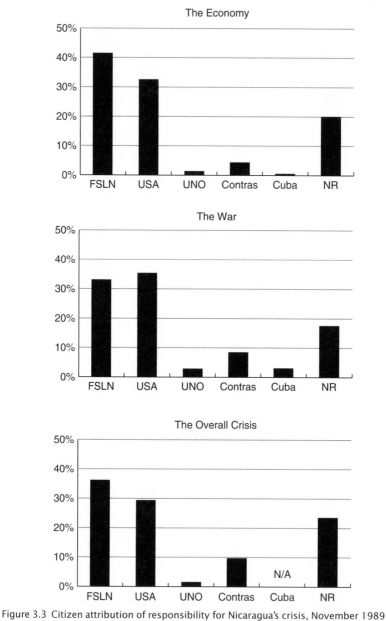

Figure 3.3 Citizen attribution of responsibility for Nicaragua's crisis, November 1989

Source: DOXA nationwide November 1989 survey asking, "Who is responsible for . . . the economy / the war / the overall crisis?" (N = 800).

While many citizens attributed major responsibility to the United States for Nicaragua's problems, that number was not so large as to indicate a nation on the verge of capitulation. From the perspective of observers living in the United States or influenced by its media, the role of the Reagan-Bush administration in Nicaragua may have loomed large, with this perception magnified by the indefensible nature of U.S. aggression. But Nicaraguans themselves concluded that there was enough blame to go around, with much or most of it focused on domestic actors, including the FSLN, Contras, and UNO. The domestic blame game, however, likewise fails to yield an easy explanation of the election.

Citizens who blamed domestic actors focused primarily on the Sandinistas, but they were not so numerous as to suggest the imminent, massive repudiation of a secretly despised regime. The public was quite prepared to criticize the FSLN, so that more than 40 percent held it responsible for the economy, with only 18 percent unresponsive. Yet this seems less a sign of repudiation than evidence that citizens felt free to express frustrations with the regime, even in November, when holding the election was still somewhat in doubt. But citizens did not appear convinced that the Sandinistas were the essence of their problem. Only 36 percent held the FSLN responsible for the overall crisis, a sizable but not overwhelming number. The DOXA data portray an electorate with a nuanced and complex view of its contemporary circumstances, but undecided about how best to address them. Citizens were more than prepared to criticize the elite actors. But when asked in November whom they would support, almost 40 percent were undecided or selected a minor party, rather than choosing between Ortega and Chamorro. Why?

The Responsible Electorate

The reason for early indecision lay in voter preoccupation with the national crisis, including difficulties that demanded thoughtful judgment, not just blame and emotional reaction. Some observers may have seen the election as a moment of truth between Ortega and Reagan-Bush, determining who had been right all along. Other observers concentrated on the question of whether a contest was occurring at all between the experienced president and an ailing housewife. But the citizens saw the election as an opportunity to address national crisis. The extent to which citizens perceived a looming crisis, and their desire to address it in the election, are DOXA's fourth surprise.

Asked in early December whether the nation faced a crisis, 95.3 percent of interviewees said yes. Asked what its most severe problem was, 56.5 percent said poverty, hunger, and the economy, and 25.7 percent said the war. Only 4.5 percent said the United States, and only 6 percent said the FSLN. Their central concern appeared to be neither the Sandinistas nor the United States, but rather how best to respond to immediate and severe problems. Asked in a separate question what the determining factor would be in the election—the need to change the government or the need to address the war and domestic problems—only 28 percent said it would be changing the government, a number close to the 25 percent who said they would never support the FSLN. Fifty-two percent indicated that the decisive factor would be the need to bring peace and solve economic and social problems.

Faced with severe crisis, citizens were struggling to determine which alternative would free the nation to move forward. Most of them ruled out neither Ortega nor Chamorro. There were, of course, partisans and ideologues who embraced one or the other early, and most citizens had a good idea of what they believed had led to this difficult moment. But at the crossroads between two dramatically different paths, many citizens withheld judgment, while others showed a willingness to reassess first preferences in response to new information and events. When citizens decided, they did so not primarily out of anger, bitterness, fear, vindictiveness, or inadvertence, but thoughtfully, responsibly, soberly, seeking to shape the nation's future through reasoned and conscious choice.

Conclusion

The core of this book will demonstrate that Nicaraguans engaged in a process of reasoned choice as they selected Chamorro over Ortega in 1990 and reaffirmed their chosen direction thereafter. This choice took place among citizens with divided historic loyalties and contemporary experiences. It also took place despite severe crisis and substantial U.S. aggression, doing so through the use of the traditions of space, class, and party that helped citizens make sense out of those drawbacks. And it took place in an intense campaign that, in its earliest weeks, even raised questions about whether the election would be held.

Voters could have responded to such circumstances in a disconnected and unreflective manner, with the campaign having little impact and with scant evidence of attitudinal maturation or reasoned decision making. Instead, as it became clear that a genuine election was under way, citizens became attentive and involved. The campaign took on additional life and momentum. Rallies for both candidates grew. The major newspapers reported intense, partisan interpretations of events. The candidates took their case to the people. In response, the people listened, reflected, and assessed what they heard.

As citizens connected with the campaign, they engaged in a decision process closely corresponding to that expected of educated voters in established, affluent democracies. In doing so, as analysis of DOXA's surveys will indicate, they demonstrated a maturation in attitudinal assessments and reasoning beyond that normally documented for poorer, less-educated electorates. This was particularly true in 1990, but also evident in 1996 and 2001. Perhaps the 1990 outcome ultimately proved unexpected because the citizens were engaged in a sophisticated process of decision making that analysts did not conceive as possible and did not examine. Survey data will provide unexpected but powerful evidence of citizen choice.

To understand that process and the survey evidence of it, let us turn to a discussion of voting theory in established democracies and the ways it can be adapted and applied to the study of new democracies such as Nicaragua. In doing so, we will argue that the theories and methods of contemporary voting analysis, properly adapted to the special contexts of new third world democracies, provide powerful strategies for gauging the existence of thoughtful voter assessment and reasoning in such settings. In so far as such reflective reasoning and vote choice occurred in Nicaragua, we then have a good sense of how possible such reasoning is amidst poor and poorly educated citizens elsewhere, including both in new democracies and in established democracies, so long as circumstances—such as free and fair elections and a meaningful opportunity for citizens to influence their nation's future—facilitate serious mass engagement in electoral choice.

PART II

Choice amidst Crisis:
Public Opinion in 1990

Chapter 4

An Empirical Theory of Electoral Choice

Students of elections have struggled to understand why citizens vote as they do and what the answer tells us about democracy.[1] Early in the advent of mass elections, proponents of expanded democracy thought that universal male suffrage would hand power to the working classes who predominated in industrializing societies. Later, some observers anticipated that women's suffrage would change electoral outcomes little since women would follow the lead of husbands. Neither expectation proved true: working-class parties seldom sustained majority dominance, and women often voted quite distinctly from men.[2] In time, group-based conceptions of voting yielded to the study of individual vote choice, and again early theoretical expectations proved incorrect.

Belief in the informed citizen of democratic philosophers fell in the face of survey evidence that citizens knew little about the intricacies of politics. Upon close inspection, analysts found a proliferation of unsophisticated voters who often knew almost nothing about the candidate they supported. With such findings emerged the possibility that citizens approached voting in a random, unreasoning, or impressionistic manner. Elections were thus a game of chance. Results were important to winners and losers but signified nothing. In such circumstances, the failure of the working class to establish electoral dominance or the disassociation between the voting patterns of men and women could simply reflect accident, confusion, intimidation, or misinformation.

---

1. For a review discussion see B. D. Jones (2001, 78–81).
2. Przeworski and Sprague (1986); Conway, Steuernagel, and Ahern (1997); and Burns (2002, especially 477-483).

In response, a reassessment of voters and voting emerged.[3] Perhaps citizens need not have a detailed understanding of politics in order to know whether the government is doing a good or bad job. Perhaps some citizens are more attentive and thoughtful, giving direction to politics amidst the randomness or simplistic choices of the majority. Or perhaps there are critical moments when citizens do attend to politics, making decisive choices about their nation's future. These theoretical possibilities have led analysts to develop empirical strategies for determining when and how reasoned vote choice occurs among citizens by scrutinizing their attitudes and vote intentions.

The debate over citizens and voting took on special meaning for democratizing nations with the 1990 Nicaraguan election. Once again, voters behaved in unexpected ways, raising doubts about their adequacy as democratic citizens. The surprising nature of the results also raised issues about the legitimacy of the outcome. Even if no vote fraud had occurred, how could a result so inexplicable to many observers be considered a reasonable outcome of citizen choice? The results also raise concerns about whether poorly educated citizens in new democracies can be entrusted with momentous decisions about regime direction, particularly since they so often face constrained, complicated circumstances characterized by intimidation, ignorance, inadvertence, and fear.

Our concern here is to address these issues by assessing how theories of vote choice apply to the Nicaraguan electorate. We seek to determine whether strategies of empirical analysis drawn from established democracies can help clarify whether citizen choice was present in 1990 and thereafter. We build our analysis around the two dominant theories of vote choice: the retrospective theory associated with V. O. Key and Morris Fiorina and the prospective theory associated with Paul M. Sniderman, Richard Brody, and Philip E. Tetlock. To these we add a theory of reflective and evolving choice that combines and modifies the retrospective/prospective perspectives to reflect the realities of new and developing democracies. The latter is more useful in understanding the Nicaraguan elections than either existing theory separately. To help in contrasting these theories, we begin by considering an additional reason the 1990 outcome seemed unexpected, quite apart from the mispredictions of pollsters. This clarification, centering on the role of social class in the election, helps underscore the full significance of what the citizens of Nicaragua did in 1990.

3. For a review of the literature challenging the democratic capacities of voters and the justifications analysts give for reassessment of this challenge, see Key (1966, 1-8) and Fiorina (1981, 3–17). Much of the broader framework within which this reassessment occurred is developed in Key (1961).

Social Class and Nicaraguan Vote Patterns

Given the historic importance of class in Nicaragua, observers expected it to predominate in 1990 as it had throughout the revolution. The expectation was that the Sandinistas would again be swept to victory, as they had in 1984, by the poor majority in whose name they governed. The vote of the poor would be led by that of a committed revolutionary elite who now administered the revolutionary reforms.

Table 4.1 links class structure and vote intent in DOXA's final campaign poll, in mid-February 1990. It demonstrates that the expectations about the behavior of the poor were wrong. The poor majority supported Chamorro and UNO in 1990, as did the traditional old elite. Moreover, among the poor, the unemployed poor were even less inclined to support Ortega than were the employed. In fact, the vote margin of the unemployed in behalf of Chamorro over Ortega approximated that of the old traditional elite. Only the new elite, composed of the military, state bureaucrats, and students, tilted decisively toward Ortega and the Sandinistas. Within the new elite, the military provided Ortega overwhelming support, the bureaucrats were roughly twice as likely to support him as Chamorro, and students provided him a modest plurality over her.

These voting patterns shed additional light on the problems that pollsters faced in 1990 and on why many polls had difficulty predicting the election. The pivotal voters turned out to be the poor, especially the poorest of the poor, living in Nicaragua's most impoverished and least accessible places. Whether rural or urban, such areas lack the most basic amenities,

Table 4.1   Class and Vote Intent Two Weeks Prior to the 1990 Presidential Election (%)

	UNO	FSLN	Minor parties	Nonresponse	Total
The New Elite					
Military	0.0	95.2	4.8	0.0	100
Bureaucrats	28.6	56.5	7.7	7.1	100
Students	37.3	48.1	5.2	9.0	100
The Masses					
Employed w/training	41.5	31.4	11.9	19.3	100
Employed w/o training	48.5	20.6	9.1	21.8	100
Unemployed	50.0	15.3	12.5	22.2	100
The Old Elite	58.5	21.3	15.0	5.0	100

Source: DOXA nationwide monthly survey in February 1990, which ended two weeks prior to the election in accord with the national law prohibiting surveys within two weeks of elections.
Note: N for this table is 1,187, with 13 of the original 1,200 interviewees omitted owing to the lack of class designation.

making polling access difficult and the interview process unpleasant. Analysts expecting the least fortunate to support Ortega, and thus concentrating on the more accessible and affluent citizens who were assumedly less certain about their vote, would have totally misread the election.

The 1990 outcome, and the deviation of the poor majority from predominant expectations, open the question of why the poor voted as they did. Did the 1990 election constitute a change in partisan loyalties among Nicaragua's voters, or had earlier assumptions about class support for the Sandinistas been wrong? This question is fueled by the lack of extensive survey data on citizen attitudes and partisan loyalties in earlier decades in Nicaragua. To provide empirical perspective and help determine how best to study electoral politics in Nicaragua, we can look at special data collected by DOXA in 1996, as it surveyed voters in early October, immediately before that election.

DOXA's 1996 preelection survey not only asked about the upcoming election but also collected recall data for 1984 and 1990. The answers to these questions from older interviewees who had voted in 1984 give us a window back into that earlier time and allow us to look at reported patterns of vote stability and change for the same individuals across three elections. The resulting information provides the only data of which we are aware that allow examination both of class voting patterns in 1984 and of changes in those patterns thereafter.

Figure 4.1 compares vote recall and intent across 1984, 1990, and 1996. The comparison is limited to respondents who had voted in both 1984 and 1990 and intended to vote in 1996. Additionally, it draws on voters' income level in 1996 to estimate class. While limited by the use of recall data, and by reliance on 1996 class determination, the data provide useful insight into class voting patterns in Nicaragua across these years. Interestingly, the 63.1 percent who reported having voted for Ortega in 1984 corresponds closely to the estimated vote totals for 1984, which range from 63 percent to 67 percent.[4]

The data reveal a two-step shift in class loyalties between the mid 1980s and the mid 1990s, pointing to what the voting studies literature has called a "partisan realignment."[5] The most extraordinary pattern in the data is for the mass citizens in the three lowest income groups. In 1984 the destitute voted for Ortega by more than 70 percent, and the other two low-income

---

4. Many nations and organizations sent delegations to observe the 1984 election. A delegation of scholars from the Latin American Studies Association concluded that, on top of the 63 percent who had voted for Ortega, an additional 4 percent may not have understood how to mark the ballot, marking out, for example, all parties but the FSLN. Such incorrectly marked ballots were excluded from the final vote tally but may have been votes for Ortega. See *LASA Report* (1984).

5. Key (1955).

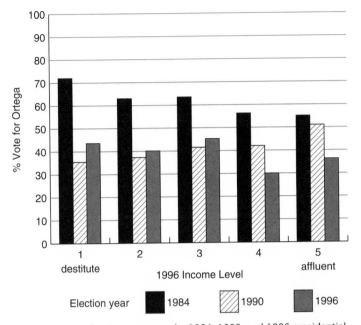

Figure 4.1 Vote support for Ortega across the 1984, 1990, and 1996 presidential elections among interviewees voting in all three elections, grouped by 1996 income level

Source: DOXA nationwide survey in early October 1996 asking, "Who did you vote for in 1984/1990 and who will you vote for in 1996?" The figure reports responses for those 352 interviewees who said that they voted in 1984 and 1990 and intended to vote in 1996. An additional 17 interviewees reported voting in 1984 but not doing so (or intending to do so) in one or both of the subsequent elections.

Notes: Interviewees are grouped according to their monthly income in cordobas in 1996. The income range and numerical distribution of interviewees by group is as follows. Group 1 ($N = 55$) had a monthly income of 500 cordobas or below and were destitute by Nicaraguan standards in 1996; group 2 (75) had an income of 501 to 1,000 cordobas; group 3 (142) received 1,001 to 2,000 cordobas; group 4 (33) received 2,001 to 2,500 cordobas; group 5 (47) had either a monthly income over 2,500 cordobas or help from abroad, making them affluent by Nicaraguan standards.

groups voted for him by more than 60 percent. Yet six years later, in 1990, their support for him had essentially collapsed, declining to 36 percent among the destitute and only slightly above that for the other two groups. These are dramatic shifts by any standard. The importance of this shift is reinforced by the finding that only 5.1 percent of lower-class respondents who supported Ortega in 1984, looking back on the 1984 election, said that it had been unfair. Moreover, only 8.7 percent of those supporting Ortega in 1984 but switching to Chamorro or a minor party in 1990 perceived the 1984 election as unfair. These figures reveal that low-income citizens felt that their vote in 1984 had been freely given to Ortega. The assumption made by observers in 1990 that Ortega had previously enjoyed wide support among the poor was correct. These data also provide support for the legitimacy of the 1984 election, indicating broad citizen belief in its free and fair conduct, despite allegations by the Reagan administration to the contrary and the use of those allegations to justify hostility and aggression toward Sandinista Nicaragua.

After the massive shift of low-income citizens away from Ortega in 1990, he enjoyed small increases in support among them in 1996. This included a 7.5 percent increase among the destitute. Yet these increases did not reverse the substantial loss of support he experienced between 1984 and 1990. In the 1984 election he received 65 percent of the vote from citizens across these three low-income levels. In 1990 he drew 39 percent. In 1996 his support among them rose only 4 percent, to 43 percent.

In contrast, the elite shift away from Ortega came more slowly. In 1984 our top two income groups—Nicaragua's income elite—had provided Ortega with majority support, though less than that provided by the low-income groups. In 1990, when the lower classes were shifting massively away from Ortega, the elite showed a greater tendency to stay with him. As a result it was the elite who provided Ortega his strongest support in 1990, including a majority among those who were the most affluent. This tendency of many upper-income citizens to stand with him in 1990 is owing to the fact that while some in the higher-income group came from the traditional elite that had always opposed the FSLN, others came from among the Sandinista elite of the 1980s who were serving in the military, working in the bureaucracy, or studying at the universities. They had been directly involved with the Sandinista regime and benefited from it. Therefore, the upper-income groups divided in 1990 between Ortega and Chamorro, giving considerable support to Ortega.

The decisive shift away from Ortega among the income elite came in 1996, when vote support for him in the two top income groups fell to the mid to low thirties. No longer dependent on the FSLN regime and increasingly drawn into professional jobs within the new market economy, a portion of the previous Sandinista elite broke with Ortega and voted more conservatively. As they did so and as the lower classes simultaneously moved slightly toward Ortega, the wealthier groups became the most conservative voting bloc, and the 1984 ordering of class and vote reappeared. The poorest voters again gave Ortega his highest level of support, and the most affluent again voted more conservatively. Yet by 1996 all groups were supporting Ortega at levels 20 percent to 30 percent below 1984, having reached these substantially lower levels through two phases of partisan reorientation.

The recall and vote intent data across these three elections, based as it is on the voting patterns of an identical group of citizens, points to a genuine realignment in class voting among citizens who had come of age by Nicaragua's first election in 1984. The electorate's shift from the FSLN to democratic conservatism is not simply or primarily a result of such factors as differential turnout, or the entrance of new voters, but is a change in the voting behavior of individual Nicaraguans across time. This realignment in individual loyalties is supplemented in various ways by voting patterns among the newer voters that we will address later. Our concern at this point is to understand why such a realignment occurred. How do citizens—particularly poor, modestly educated, inexperienced voters in a new democracy—decide to abandon a party and regime that they have supported both in revolution and at the polls in order to embrace a new president and regime?

Citizen Choice in Established versus Developing Democracies: The Logic and Relevance of Vote Choice Theories

To understand how voters decided to break with past partisan patterns, we turn for guidance to theories about how individuals reach their vote choice. In particular we look at the argument for retrospective voting which says that citizens reason based on assessments of candidates' past performance, and the argument for prospective voting, which says they reason by looking at candidates' future governing potential.[6] Yet we do so with caution.

Existing theories of vote choice have been created to explain voting in established democracies, particularly the United States. As a result, the arguments of such theories are based not only on the specific types of reasoning processes that the theorists attribute to citizens. The arguments also assume the existence of stable and well-established democratic politics. Such politics allows citizens to employ retrospective and prospective reasoning in a relatively straightforward manner. By contrast, citizens in emerging democracies that lack a stable democratic history may face more complex considerations when they attempt to reason through retrospection or prospection. Only by understanding these more complex considerations can we explain how Nicaraguans were able to move beyond Ortega and embrace Chamorro through reasoned choice.

Our purpose here is to present the traditional arguments for retrospec-

---

6. For previous work on retrospective and prospective voting in Latin America, see Dominguez and McCann (1996, 106–7); Anderson and Dodd (2002a); Magaloni and Poiré (2004); Anderson and Dodd (2004); and Dominguez (2004).

tive and prospective voting and indicate how they can be restructured to apply to new democracies. We then turn to the theory of voter decision making in new democracies that emerges from this reformulation. It stresses voter reflection across retrospection and prospection, providing our explanation of the 1990 Nicaraguan election. In addition, it argues that patterns of voter reasoning evolve as a new democracy matures, thereby explaining the logic of vote choice for the 1996 and 2001 elections.

The Theory of Retrospective Voting

V. O. Key (1966) and Morris Fiorina (1981), pioneers in the study of vote choice, argue that reasoned choice is present when voters use retrospective assessments of an incumbent's governing performance to determine their vote. While Key was the first to note the possibility of citizen retrospection, Fiorina developed the idea of retrospective thinking into a theory of individual vote choice. Building on Downs's argument that individuals reason to vote decisions through reliance on parties' past performance as a guide to their probable future behavior, Fiorina argued that voter reasoning could be understood by the systematic examination of citizen attitudes about the past performance of parties, candidates, and governments. While there are a series of debates among retrospective voting theorists about precisely how and why citizens engage in such reasoning,[7] the bottom line is that individual citizens determine their vote intent by looking at past performance rather than relying on new and unfettered assessments of future potential.

Retrospective voting, within this perspective, is demonstrated by a close correlation between citizens' attitudes about candidates' past behavior and their vote intentions in an upcoming election. Relevant attitudes could include their images of candidates, particularly incumbents, which would gauge citizen response to candidates' past political and governing behavior. In addition, analysts look at citizen assessments of the past performance of the

---

7. We refer here to Key's argument on behalf of a strict punishment-reward logic to retrospective voting, focused on the immediate performance of an incumbent party, and Downs's argument that retrospection occurs as a voter assesses parties' consistent past performance as a guide to their future behavior. Fiorina (1981, 6–16) makes a strong case for close attention to Downs's perspective, particularly under specialized election circumstances and when rich opinion data are available. Yet he suggests (197–98) analysts draw on elements of both perspectives, and warrants that Key's perspective will yield the same empirical outcome as Downs's in most circumstances. We use Key's punishment-reward characterization of retrospection because it seems more appropriate for the study of elections in new democracies wherein most parties will lack the long-term governing experience necessary for the application of Downsian-style retrospection by voters.

economy under the incumbent. Close association between such attitudes and presidential vote choice could address concerns about vote randomness and pinpoint the factors citizens considered as they reasoned to a vote decision. This strategy of electoral analysis, introduced by Fiorina, has provided extensive verification of retrospective voting in the United States and Western Europe, a conclusion reinforced by research on aggregate voting patterns of electorates. Citizens appear to vote in response to the retrospective assessments of candidates and governments.[8]

The evidence on behalf of retrospection has led analysts to conclude that voters in established democracies regularly engage in serious electoral choice. In Key's pithy phrase, "voters are not fools" stumbling through an electoral maze, generating random or manipulated, deceitful or cynical electoral results (1966, 7). Rather, particularly in settings characterized by competitive parties and a free press, voters act in intelligent and intelligible ways. They may cast ballots with only modest information about candidates and governing performance. But the votes they cast, in good times or bad, are based on real-world observations that correlate closely with reported vote decisions. These individual choices then generate aggregate vote patterns that make sense and look systematic. Across time, citizens do appear to respond in their voting to actual government performance, once the distinctive group interests and experiences of voters are considered.

Retrospection is a particularly sensible way to determine vote choice because it is grounded in actual experience. Citizens have lived with the government's performance and can judge it, particularly when their personal experience combines with media information. The result is a simple formula for citizen choice: if the government has succeeded in the immediate past in serving a citizen's interests, he or she rewards the government (or its incumbent or dominant party) by voting for it. If the government has failed, the voter punishes it by voting for the opposition.

From the perspective of democratic theory, retrospective voting has a constructive result. It provides a logic whereby citizens hold government accountable for its performance. This logic provides government with a strong incentive to listen and respond to the public. In fact, as Key was the first to argue, governments may fail so dramatically and groups may shift so decisively away from the incumbent that a "critical election" takes place and partisan realignment occurs. This creates a long-term disinclination by citi-

8. See, for example, Abramson, Aldrich, and Rohde (2002, 150–67); Miller and Wattenberg, (1985); Kramer (1971); Tufte (1978); Kiewiet and Rivers (1984); Kiewiet (1983); Lewis-Beck (1988).

zens to support a particular incumbent or party.[9] The possibility of realignment reinforces the incentive for a governing party to listen to citizens and govern responsively. It also encourages a party to disassociate itself from an incumbent who leads it to disaster and seek new party leadership that can convince voters to give it another chance.

In established democracies all citizens should be able to engage in retrospective voting.[10] Everyone has some sense of how the incumbent performed, based on personal experiences during the preceding administration, even if new campaign information is lacking or minimal. In addition, established democracies have well-developed party systems and a loyal opposition with past experience in government. In such conditions, a citizen frustrated with the incumbent can consider voting for the opposition without wondering if it knows how to govern or will keep the democratic system. Thus in an established democracy, where candidates and parties abound with experience, retrospective comparisons and vote decisions can be relatively straightforward and almost automatic, seemingly with no need for citizens to engage in extensive assessments and elaborate reasoning.

The theory of retrospective voting and its utility in enabling citizens to hold governments accountable has helped scholars understand the dynamic resilience of established democracies. Building on Key, Burnham (1970, 1976) suggests that citizens' capacity to hold governing regimes accountable for profound governing failure, shifting their dominant partisan loyalties to a new governing party or regime through critical realignment of voter attachments, is the key to the continuing and peaceful revitalization of such nations. Such electoral revolutions accomplish dramatic change in government within the confines of civil society and without resorting to the violent revolutions that are often used to change authoritarian or totalitarian governments. The question is whether retrospection and critical elections can be of similar use in developing democracies.

Retrospective Voting in Developing Democracies

Reasoned, retrospective evaluations of incumbents and government performance should also be possible in developing democracies, since citizens there can likewise judge their personal experience under incumbent govern-

9. See Key (1955). For extensions and qualifications of this argument, see Burnham (1970); Chubb, Flanigan, and Zingale (1980); Sundquist (1983); Burnham (1994); Nardulli (1995); and Mayhew (2002).

10. Kiewiet and Rivers (1984); Markus (1988); Miller and Wattenberg (1985); and Dalton (1996).

ments. Fiorina's strategy of correlating retrospective attitudes and vote should allow us to gauge choice in new electorates. Yet there are constraints on citizens' reliance on retrospection in newly democratic settings that are absent in developed democracies.[11]

Key and Fiorina assume the existence of parties and candidates, both incumbents and oppositions, who are experienced in governing and loyal to democracy. Only with such viable alternatives can voters feel free to punish the incumbent and elect the opposition. Additionally, in an established democracy, a newly elected government should have a strong, experienced legislative bench that can help constrain and correct mistakes the government might make. Moreover, other major parties, including those recently defeated, will also have a strong legislative presence that can help counterbalance the new government. Given such experience, stability, and safeguards, voters can reward or punish incumbents without worrying about endangering the polity itself.

The assumption of a loyal opposition that believes in democracy works in older democracies, for which retrospective theory was created. But it is a more questionable assumption in new democracies where at least some interests have historically gotten what they wanted by avoiding democracy and may be tempted to try that path again.[12] Moreover, in new democracies the governing incumbent and his party may be the only experienced leadership the nation has. Or the incumbent party may be the only cohesive party the nation has. Additionally, the incumbent leader and party may have come to power in an extra-electoral fashion and then subsequently used elections only as confirmation and legitimation. These various scenarios are quite likely in contexts where democracy is new and the number of democratic governments is quite limited.

A particular problem in new democracies occurs, as in Nicaragua, when the incumbent party led the nation out of authoritarianism, through revolution, and into electoral politics, while the major opposition party or parties include elements linked to the ousted authoritarian regime. Even if the opposition is willing to forgo the direct leadership of former authoritarians,

11. On the difficulties that new, unstable, and poorly established mass party systems can create for democratic transition, see LaPalombara and Weiner (1966); Huntington (1968); and Sartori (1976). For a specific case in which the absence of parties has a negative effect on democratic development, see Mainwaring (1999).

12. The notion of democratic loyalty draws upon Valenzuela (1978) and his discussion of parties in Latin America more generally. In developing democracies parties may be fully loyal to democratic governance, disloyal to democracy and desirous of its ouster, or semiloyal and containing both members who support and those who do not support democracy. Linz and Stepan (1996) also use these distinctions.

it may have few other leadership alternatives. Moreover, public caution about returning to power former authoritarians could be greatest at times of turmoil, since the risks of their return to authoritarian behavior in order to manage such turmoil could be greater then. Yet those are precisely the circumstances under which citizens engaged in retrospection may most desire new leadership.

In such new democracies, lacking an experienced, safe set of alternatives, voters may find it extremely difficult to rely on retrospective voting in an authentic evaluative manner that could lead to the defeat of an incumbent. Instead, citizens may hold the incumbent to low standards of performance, concluding that poor incumbent performance is preferable to risking renewed authoritarianism or governing incompetence. Absent a loyal, experienced, well-known opposition whom voters can trust, citizens in new democracies facing severe crisis would seem to have little alternative other than staying with the incumbent, if retrospection is their only way of making a choice. Such a choice would appear cruel and would deny citizens any way to move forward beyond an unsatisfactory incumbent and toward greater democratic accountability. There is, however, another form of voter reasoning: prospective candidate assessment.

The Theory of Prospective Voting

During the 1990s, new work on political psychology pioneered by Sniderman, Brody, and Tetlock offered electoral studies a prospective theory of voting.[13] It argues that an informed, engaged electorate is capable of a sophisticated form of reasoning wherein citizens make an intelligent guess about what candidates can offer in the future.[14] Such reasoning draws upon more than past political performance. It requires voters to assess personal characteristics, policy orientations, and context in determining which candidate may perform best in the future. Citizens resort to prospective evaluation when retrospection fails to produce a satisfying vote choice or when new information convinces them that an alternative candidate is preferable for addressing future problems, even if the incumbent has been satisfactory. As they do so, they develop an increasingly complex reasoning process in determining their vote. This process is evident in the growing range of

13. Sniderman, Brody, and Tetlock (1991). They build on and yet move beyond Stimson's (1976) pathbreaking work on how consistency in voter reasoning and choice varies with "cognitive ability."

14. Lewis-Beck (1988, chap. 8). See also Kuklinski and West (1981); Miller and Wattenberg (1985); and Abramson, Aldrich, and Rohde (2002, 128–48).

retrospective and prospective concerns that correlate with vote intent.

According to Sniderman et al., voters initially focus on the incumbent candidate or party and do normally make a retrospective "first cut" decision, determining whether to stay with the incumbent or look to the opposition. This first cut may be sufficient for many voters to determine their vote choice: they may be sufficiently satisfied with the incumbent that they choose him/her, or so dissatisfied that they opt for his opponent. But sometimes the choice is not so easy based solely on retrospection. In addition, even when inclined toward an incumbent, some citizens may remain open to additional information. Seeking to resolve a hard choice, or just to double-check their initial inclinations, they will turn to considering which candidate would be most competent in addressing the nation's future problems. The willingness to assess and compare the prospective competence of candidates is particularly likely among educated citizens who may follow politics more closely and can process information more easily and rapidly than the less educated. While some prospection may happen among the educated in any election, it is particularly likely in close and issue-oriented campaigns concerned with serious problems of governance.

When the more educated look beyond retrospection and seek to compare the prospective governing competence of candidates, they become more attentive to the campaign and focus on a broader array of factors. They may consider what the future problems of the country will be, perhaps focused on the direction the economy will take. But they will also consider the candidates' proposals about how they will address problems, and whether they have the skills and temperament to do so successfully. Thinking in this manner, a voter may conclude that the incumbent has a better perspective on the future. After some prospective consideration of the challenger, the voter will solidify her support for the incumbent. Alternatively, she may conclude that, while an incumbent did well in addressing past problems, for which his skills were well suited, he now lacks the capacity to address future dilemmas, a capacity the opponent may possess. She would then support the challenger. Either decision will rest on more than simple retrospective analysis, showing some complexity. But an inclination to throw the incumbent out requires close, extensive, and prospective attention to how the new government will govern, particularly if the nation faces severe problems.

As voters engage in close prospective evaluation of candidates, they seek to increase their knowledge about them and to resolve inconsistencies in perception. In the process, retrospective and prospective perceptions become more crystallized, and voters gain more information about contenders. Then voters begin to see differences between candidates more clearly and to develop more coherent and distinctive interpretations of them. In these assessments, voters consider how the candidates affect their own personal interests, and these considerations reflect a wider array of personal and collective interests as the campaign progresses. Because of their attentiveness to personal interests and values, citizens' candidate assessments are likely to resemble those of others with like class, gender, age, and social interests. Simultaneously, interpretations of the candidates across groups with different interests will become increasingly different.

Citizens' tendency to differentiate between candidates according to the voters' social and political characteristics produces a pattern of group polarization within the electorate as a whole. Some groups favor one candidate strongly and see him as more competent to address future problems; other groups prefer the opposition and see her as more competent. As voters move to see the candidates more fully, they begin to reason toward a vote choice by considering several dimensions of identity, self-interest, and experience instead of only one dimension, like social class, which may have primarily determined vote choice in the past. For example, women within a social class may find that they have had different or more pronounced experiences than men in the same class so that they become as deeply engaged in the campaign as men but with different preferences. And among women, one generation may have had experiences different from those of another generation so that one age group departs from the predominant voting patterns of women as a whole.[15]

Such rich, complex, and polarized individual reasoning introduces its own distinctive form of pluralism into democratic politics, so that one dimension of life does not predominate in politics. Instead many differentiated groups emerge. Moreover, as such engaged and differentiated voters think in new ways and listen to the opposition message, they may also see the importance of new principles that they had not recognized in the past. Such discoveries can lead voters to change partisan voting patterns based on expectations that they share with the new party's elite.[16]

---

15. On the role that social identities of citizens play in fostering partisan attachments and vote choice, see Green, Palmquist, and Schickler (2002).

16. Green, Palmquist, and Schickler (2002) suggest that such shifts are particularly likely when a party's principles are couched in terms of new social imagery that connects strongly with the social identities of citizens who had previously supported another party. Violeta Chamorro was engaged in the skillful use of such imagery when she emphasized her efforts as a mother to bring peace and reconciliation among her politically divided children, comparing this effort to the task of bringing national peace and reconciliation. In so doing, she was connecting core principles of her proposed regime with the social identity of mothers throughout Nicaragua in a way that affirmed that identity and made the political affirmation of it a route by which former Sandinista supporters could embrace the conservative regime. On the critical value of metaphorical reasoning to political learning and change, see Dodd (1994, 348–54).

By generating shared governing principles among leaders and supporters of a new government, intense elections characterized by prospective reasoning can provide an additional and perhaps more sustainable basis for partisan realignments, aside from retrospective frustrations. Such elections can generate common understanding about the goals a new governing party seeks to achieve and to which its core voters will hold it accountable. This understanding can also provide the government a basis on which to evoke support from its base, even in difficult times. Prospection can thus generate both "electoral revolutions" and stable new regimes. Seen in this way, prospective voting can be a vital resource for citizens in new democracies, particularly under conditions that encourage the poor and uneducated to use it.

Prospective Voting in Developing Societies

The theory of prospective voting has been developed and utilized primarily to account for voting patterns among the educated in affluent, established democracies like the United States, with retrospective voting seen as more appropriate for explaining the behavior of the less educated. Utilizing Fiorina's strategy of correlating attitudes and vote intent, Sniderman et al. demonstrate that the less educated do vote more nearly based on retrospective image assessments of candidates, whereas the more-educated voters are more likely to consider the prospective policies and governing capacities of candidates. Yet they acknowledge that education is not the only basis for prospective voting.[17] An intense campaign with extensive coverage might attract so much attention and pose such vital concerns that even the less educated look beyond retrospection to consider the future competence of candidates.

The relationship between intense campaigns and prospective reasoning makes prospective reasoning particularly important for new democracies in third world nations. Such new democracies tend to face crises that induce intense elections, and they generally have a large low-income, poorly educated component to their electorates. Such underclass citizens are more likely to be mobilized by an intense campaign because they are searching for electoral solutions to personal crises. In such moments, while retrospective reasoning may yield little basis for rejecting an incumbent and selecting the inexperienced opposition, prospection provides a way out.

Even if only one candidate or party has the governing experience necessary for the reliable use of retrospection, poorly educated citizens in new democracies can still make a genuine choice using prospection. They can do

17. Sniderman, Brody, and Tetlock (1991, 20).

so by considering the prospective problems their nation faces and by determining which candidate seems more able to address those problems in an effective and democratic manner. Of course, engaging in prospection requires that less-educated voters have considerable incentive for doing so, since they must overcome the limits of low education and their lack of experience with complex reasoning.

Ironically it is the crisis-prone nature of new democracies in less-developed societies that provides the poorly educated with the incentive to engage in prospection. It is crisis that makes retrospection risky and less satisfactory while simultaneously making prospection more viable. As the work of George E. Marcus and Michael B. MacKuen demonstrates, crisis not only generates intense campaigns and high domestic and international media coverage and attention; it also induces citizen anxiety and increases voter attention to the election.[18] As citizens become more anxious, they become more open to the possibility of breaking with old patterns and considering new ones. Anxiety and focused attention then lead citizens to think prospectively, maybe even embracing a critical change in government or a new regime. In so doing, they can move their nation forward beyond crisis.

Seen in this way, prospective voting can be quite relevant to a developing democracy, and may even be essential to democratization. It can allow voters to determine whether a real choice is possible and to estimate the retrospective standards that can be used to assess the incumbent. In addition, should they find the incumbent wanting, prospection then provides a strategy for elevating the opposition in a reasoned manner, moving the nation forward and out of crisis. Prospection provides a rationale for such a choice even if it means discarding the very government that instituted elections and democracy and even in the absence of experienced opposition candidates. Yet precisely how prospection combines with retrospection in new democracies is somewhat different from the ways Sniderman et al. suggest for established democracies, so a distinct voting theory is necessary for new democracies, built around a different logic and process.

As we move to present this theory, we do so with one caveat: while prospection offers exciting possibilities for new democracies, it is not an inherently superior way of reasoning toward a vote choice. Rather, both retrospection and prospection have unique advantages that enable choice and reflection. Retrospection, as a way of thinking, is more grounded in real life experience than is prospection. When using retrospection, voters are using

18. Marcus and MacKuen (1993); see also Dodd (1994); Kinder and Kiewiet (1979).

concrete knowledge about past realities. In this sense, retrospection is a very data-oriented way of making vote choice. On the other hand, prospection requires the use of imagination, a kind of future-oriented estimate about the capabilities of the challenger. Thoughtful estimation, when buttressed by extensive information from the campaign itself or from the media, can enable reflective comparison about the future even in the absence of concrete life experience with the challenger or her party. While prospection is less based in life experiences, it opens up possibilities that would be foreclosed if voters only looked backward in making their evaluations. Taken together and considered as equally important, retrospection and prospection can allow thoughtful electoral choice in new democracies as they do in old. At issue is how voters in new democracies combine these two forms of reasoning in order to make responsible vote choices.

A Reflective Theory of Evolving Vote Choice: Voter Decision Making in New Democracies

We propose that citizens in new democracies reach their vote decisions through a process of reflective and evolving vote choice. This theory gives more weight to explicit election context than do retrospective and prospective theories. It also allows for more reflection across retrospective and prospective concerns by educated and uneducated voters than these theories suppose. We present it as a perspective on how voters in new and developing democracies reason, given the circumstances generally present in such societies. It also could be relevant to older democracies when democratic loyalty or governing competence of parties and candidates is in doubt.

The Logic of Reflective Vote Choice

We suggest that in new democracies, if elections are fair and competitive, voters approach their decisions more attentive to prospective concerns than in established democracies. This is because the relative inexperience of most candidates and parties is such that retrospective assessment alone is meaningless. In order to choose among parties with little or no governing experience, citizens must estimate whether the parties challenging have some reasonable likelihood of honoring democracy and performing satisfactorily once in office. Prospection will matter even when an experienced governing party is running for reelection, since citizens cannot freely choose to stay with the incumbent party without comparing it with an alternative. Such a comparison within a new democracy requires prospective thinking, since the alternative parties will have no prior governing experience to assess. Thus some prospection is needed even when evaluating the incumbent.

The first-cut decision for citizens in a new electorate will be composed of both retrospective assessment of the incumbent and a broadly reflective assessment of the opposition—across retrospective and prospective concerns—to determine whether he/she is sufficiently viable that serious retrospective standards can be applied to the incumbent. Once voters make such a combined retrospective and prospective assessment, they may find the opposition so deficient that no real choice exists. Apathy and disengagement are then likely to envelop the electorate, while the election becomes a runaway for the incumbent. Alternatively, citizens could determine that the opposition is so much superior to the incumbent, on grounds of democratic loyalty or policy or both, that the incumbent is summarily rejected and the opposition soars to victory. But if voters decide that viable competing candidates and parties exist, meaningful choice becomes possible. Given the importance of elections in new democracies, citizens then engage in the campaign.

As engaged citizens in new democracies move beyond their first-cut determination, they may look more closely at the incumbent, hold him to reasonable standards, and conclude that he deserves another term. Citizens could make this decision in ways that closely resemble the choices of voters in older democracies, determining that the incumbent is good enough that they need not engage in the more difficult decision process of further retrospection and prospection. In such a decision-making process, voters will move from an early stage of considering both candidates retrospectively and prospectively to a final stage where they are primarily concerned about incumbent retrospection.

Alternatively, once citizens conclude that viable choice exists, they may be sufficiently attracted to both candidates and sufficiently concerned about the nation that a more sustained comparison of the two emerges. Voters in such a scenario will become increasingly attentive to politics, seeking a broad range of information that will allow them to differentiate more fully among the candidates and also to gauge prospectively what issues they are likely to confront in office. This process of attitudinal crystallization and differentiation would necessarily include close comparison of the candidates' prospective capacities to address pressing policy problems and to do so democratically. Prospection is the primary dimension across which such candidates can be compared, given the challenger's inexperience. Such movement toward closer prospective comparison may prove particularly likely among citizens who are suffering the most amidst national crisis and seeking to use the election to solve the crisis. Such citizens, united by common characteristics and experiences, could become sufficiently attentive as to challenge preexisting group alignments that undermine current interests. That challenge would then produce a new polarization in the electorate and new patterns of group voting behavior.

In the end, many or even most voters still may conclude that the incumbent is preferable, but they would hold him to higher standards that included both retrospective and prospective considerations. In the process, they may have clarified for themselves governing principles or ideals that they share with the incumbent government. Others, sometimes even the majority of voters, could conclude that a challenger is preferable, even an inexperienced challenger, if she has the skills, temperament, and strategy to solve the crisis. Such citizens would reach this decision through prospective reasoning about the candidates and context facing them, as well as retrospection about the incumbent's performance.

In embracing an opposition candidate and party, citizens may become so attentive to and attracted by its arguments that they consciously embrace new political principles and governing possibilities espoused by it, principles and possibilities they find more compelling than those witnessed in the performance and promise of the existing government. Such conscious embrace of new principles through prospective reasoning can be seen as a decision by voters to invest in a new governing party. This decision would carry with it a willingness to give the party time to deliver on its promises before subjecting it to critical reassessment, particularly if its early performance in office shows a good-faith effort to honor its espoused principles and promises. This combination of prospective and retrospective reasoning creates a kind of "investment/reassessment" logic to citizen vote choice in new democracies wherein the process of punishment or reward is constrained by some modest willingness to give new parties, candidates, and governments reasonable time to succeed.

Given the stakes involved in crisis-prone new democracies, and the need to assess candidates and parties with little or no past governing record, it is highly unlikely that meaningful campaigns in new democracies can start and end in a retrospective mode for either the educated or the uneducated. In fact, the uneducated, who also have low incomes and tend to be those most affected by crisis, would seem to have greater incentive for prospection in a new democracy, particularly with respect to challengers. At the same time, voters would seem unlikely to rely solely on prospection, since they would need some sense of what is realistically possible in a new democracy and would need to look back toward recent reality to gain some sense of the experience of challenger and incumbent alike.

In sum, the theory of reflective voting differs from the theories of retro-spective and of prospective voting in two critical ways. First, it does not assume the existence of experienced, competent, and democratically commit-ted opposition parties who can step into the void should voters wish to reject a governing incumbent. Rather, it assumes that voters will have to examine parties and candidates closely to determine whether they are competent and democratic, and that such determination will have to include attention to fac-tors other than their prior political performance or experience in office. These factors will include special attributes that candidates, parties, or coalitions may have, and also their programmatic promises and visions of the future. Second, attention to such factors, including assessments about the prospective govern-ing capacities of the opposition, will have to come at the very outset of a cam-paign. Retrospective assessment of an incumbent can occur only against some sense of the standards to which he/she is to be held, which in new democracies requires an assessment of the prospective capacities of the opposition based on factors other than prior governing performance.

Reflection across retrospective and prospective concerns is thus inherent to responsible vote choice in new democracies, particularly at the outset of a campaign. How vote choice evolves during the campaign, whether toward voter reliance by the end on retrospection, prospection, or both, is then the result of special voter concerns and distinctive election context.

The Evolution of Vote Choice during Campaigns

Precisely how the process of vote choice proceeds during a campaign would seem very much dependent on a nation's distinctive social and political con-text, and would be likely to produce patterns of vote choice by groups in new democracies that differ from the patterns of choice among counterpart groups in older democracies. Thus the poor and less educated in new democ-racies may be prone to vote in prospective ways, even though they have the same educational limits that lead the uneducated in older democracies to be more retrospective. Their openness to prospection would come from the greater life difficulties they face, giving them greater incentive to focus on politics and causing them to look for solutions in politics more readily than the poor in established democracies do. This greater incentive would be par-ticularly strong if they constitute a relatively large segment of the population and live in a relatively egalitarian society in which they could believe that their votes could truly change public policy to some significant degree.

The incentive for the poor and uneducated to vote prospectively could be reinforced by the presence early in the democratization process of momentous choice about regime direction or economic system that would dramatically influence their lives. In addition, their tendency to reason and vote prospectively could arise from occasional success in using their mass power to address crisis, such as in social movements or social revolution.

In contrast, the more educated in new democracies may be more prone to retrospective assessment than their counterparts in older democracies. They share with the more educated in established democracies the cognitive skills that lead the latter to reason prospectively. But because of their smaller numbers in developing societies, and because government may have been their primary employer, they will often be more integral to the regime than they are in older democracies. Experience in assisting the government (in civil service, the military, public education) can lead them to understand the government's governing difficulties and be more willing to stay the course with the incumbent. Their economic dependence on the government can also lead them to prioritize regime stability out of personal interest. Finally, they may have helped bring the current government to power and have special loyalty to it.

Because of their special relationship with the incumbent government, the better educated in developing societies can see elections as opportunities to legitimate the incumbent, focusing on its positive attributes and voting retrospectively. Of course, if the educated who are part of an incumbent government face regime change induced by the less educated, their vote patterns might change to incorporate more prospection as they struggle to determine where their interests lie after the old regime collapses.

Overall, as with the less educated, the process by which educated citizens in new democracies reason their way to a vote choice may be more tied to their group circumstances and interests, and less a direct result of educational level, than in established, stable, more affluent democracies. Both groups should begin an election campaign by weighing retrospective and prospective assessments in order to establish standards by which to make their vote decision. Some focus on deriving such standards will be necessary, given their nation's meager experience with democracy. Then as the campaign progresses it is quite possible that less-educated mass citizens will sustain or expand their attention to prospective concerns, as they look for a viable way out of crisis. In contrast, the better-educated elite may attend more to retrospective concerns as they highlight the progress in crisis resolution made by the government to which many and perhaps most are attached. Less-educated citizens in new democracies thus may evidence more of a focus on prospection as they reach their final vote choice, and better-educated citizens more of a focus on retrospection, than is the case for established democracies. However, such vote choice patterns also should change as a new democracy ages.

The Evolution of Vote Choice across Elections

Across elections in a new democracy, some evolution should occur in the vote choice patterns of all citizens. During early phases of democratization, when most parties and candidates have little or no governing experience, we would expect all groups to use reflective choice, giving substantial attention early in a campaign to both retrospection and prospection. But as the democracy ages and matures into a fully competitive electoral system, more parties and candidates will become experienced with governance. This experience can come not only at the national level but at the regional level and through legislative service as well.

As democratization generates more experienced candidates and parties, the electorate will move toward more retrospection, though citizens will tend to remain more attentive to prospection than in older democracies. Some continuing prospection will increase the chances of electing candidates and parties loyal to democracy and will be necessary as these new democracies continue to struggle with societal instability. Nevertheless, an electorate will move toward more retrospection as the range of experienced viable candidates and parties widens. How swiftly a nation moves to a greater reliance on retrospection depends on how successful it is in staging elections that are fair and competitive, how fully governing power is shared, and how successful government is.

With the normalization of electoral processes and a reduction in crisis, the vote choice patterns of new democracies will more closely resemble those of older democracies.[19] The less educated may rely increasingly on retrospection, and the more educated may move to greater prospection. Early signs of such patterns may serve as indicators of the emerging maturation of democracy, indicating the presence of a larger number of experienced candidates, greater mass satisfaction with democratic policies and accountability, and a growing body of educated voters who are not closely tied to the government.

Yet all such signs must be treated with caution. New democracies necessarily face adverse social, political, and economic realities that can destabilize electoral politics. Assessments of voter reasoning in such contexts must address the interplay between context and vote choice. Even with the arrival of social and political stability, voters confronting mass poverty may be open

---

19. For a similar argument concerning economic voting alone, see Anderson, Lewis-Beck, and Stegmaier (2003).

to new policy leadership so that such nations can be prone to complex vote decisions and dramatic partisan swings. This is particularly true if voters have become aware that politics can change their lives. Similarly, the spread of education can produce elite groups independent of the regime and prepared to challenge it. Masses seeking renewed hope, combined with educated activists anxious to lead, could introduce such transient election outcomes that new regimes would be unable to govern. The ability of new democracies to overcome this problem depends on the kind of vote choice that elections offer, particularly on whether voter reasoning and choice have been sufficient to yield stable partisan commitment among voters.

Vote Choice, Partisan Alignments, and Regime Stability

As with established democracies, the ability of developing democracies to stabilize politics and govern may depend on critical moments at which voters, especially the masses, become so attentive and engaged that they make conscious decisions to reorient or validate the direction of their government and become committed to that direction. For committed choices to occur, citizens would need to be attentive both to past performance and to future governing potential. This would include assessments of whether candidates were up to the job and had the personal skills to address critical problems. But citizens would also need to be attentive to the distinctive principles guiding the future performance of the incumbents as well. Such ideals would include policy concerns like the tradeoff between liberal democracy and democratic socialism. And they could involve voter assessment of whether candidates, parties, and regimes would govern in a democratic manner.

Committed vote choice in favor of viable democratic parties provides a solid foundation for stable and constructive democratic regimes. The subsequent stability of such a regime depends on its ability to deliver on its most basic promises, addressing the problems that led citizens to elect it, and doing so in ways that create acceptable social and political conditions. Voter willingness to sustain the regime would also depend on the presence of highly respected opinion leaders within society prepared to highlight the regime's accomplishments. And such willingness would depend on the regime's ability to respond effectively to severely disruptive issues that could arise and destabilize it if left unaddressed.

Of course, a regime may survive momentarily even without citizen commitment or without being responsive, particularly if it uses coercion. But such survival is precarious. A vibrant and constructive regime is most likely to emerge and survive when citizens are committed to its core governing principles and when it delivers on its promises in ways that earn citizen reaffirmation. Stability and institutionalization develop as those core principles become part of the nation's constitutional and legal doctrine and as opposition parties integrate those principles into their own governance perspectives.

The institutionalization of a democratic regime thus can depend on the nature of vote choice and citizen commitment associated with its initial election and subsequent electoral affirmations, as well as on its performance in office and on a supportive international climate. If voters initially engage in serious reasoning about alternative candidates and governing principles, and then make an informed, reflective choice of one path, the conditions exist for them to hold government accountable to those principles. The conditions also exist for government to appeal to voters to stay the course with the regime, even in the face of difficulties. Such an appeal can rally supporters, stabilize the government, and sustain it through a new election. The study of vote choice is thus critical to understanding both how regimes transition and how they can stabilize and govern.

Conclusion

This, then, is our assessment of vote choice theories as they apply to new democracies. The perspective we offer, reflective and evolving vote choice, emphasizes that citizens in such settings face severe societal problems and may need to look across both retrospection and prospection from the outset in order to judge their governing alternatives adequately, particularly if the democratic loyalty of one or more contenders is in doubt. In developing societies with severe problems to solve, continued prospective reasoning may be necessary in electoral choice. In emphasizing the use of prospection and insisting that citizens can have the necessary cognitive skills for such reasoning, we agree with Sniderman et al. Yet we see prospection as more integral to vote choice among the poor and uneducated than they do. In explaining the use of prospection by the uneducated and poor, we emphasize the centrality of self-interest among these voters and thus reaffirm Fiorina's use of rational calculations of self-interest in understanding vote choice.[20] In the end, how voters reason and decide will be shaped by the interaction of both

---

20. Aside from Fiorina's (1981) focus on voters' retrospective assessment of the performance of candidates and parties in their calculation of their presidential vote, see also his argument (1977) that voters consider legislators' performance as in casework and constituent service in their vote for Congress. The relevance of this latter argument outside the United States is explored in Cain, Ferejohn, and Fiorina (1987).

cognitive skills and self-interest, requiring that analysts integrate both when explaining vote choice.

Self-interest can be so strong and clear amidst severe crisis in new democracies that the poor have an incentive to overcome cognitive limits created by low education. They can do so by paying close attention to the campaign and engaging in careful, reflective reasoning. In doing so, like the more educated, they will draw on personal retrospective experience and prospective best judgment. They may be slower to reach a stable vote choice than the better educated, who rely more on extensive media coverage and can easily digest and process larger amounts of information. And they may depend less on refined political knowledge and more on simplified, commonsense concerns, thereby responding to simple analogies such as Chamorro's campaign comparison of national reconciliation with reconciliation within her family. Yet in the end they can make their own independent judgments about who should govern and will seek to do so, especially if it is clear that real choice exists and the outcome will be honored. And they may do this more widely and on a more sustained basis, even amidst poverty and low education, than voting analysts have realized.

Our immediate concern now is with whether compelling evidence exists, along the lines suggested by voting theory, to demonstrate that reflective reasoning and serious citizen choice shaped Nicaragua's 1990 electoral outcome. We know already that as the campaign got under way, apathy was decreasing and citizens were becoming more engaged and attentive. We also know that in November 1990 they wanted to address their nation's momentous problems through responsible vote choice. But what happened then? Does the available evidence indicate that citizens, including the poor and uneducated, reasoned reflectively and shaped their vote according to their subsequent judgments? Does the evidence account for unexpected voting patterns, such as those associated with lower-class support for Chamorro?

To determine whether public opinion and vote intent patterns accord with theory, we will follow Fiorina and Sniderman et al., looking at the relationship between citizen attitudes and vote intent. In this endeavor, we utilize the five surveys conducted by DOXA during the 1990 campaign. These surveys allow us to determine whether Ortega and Chamorro appeared viable early in the campaign on retrospective image and prospective governing assessments. Such results will help us gauge whether voters approached the election as a genuine choice. The data also allow us to look at changes during the campaign in citizens' attitudes about the candidates, the economy, and the regime and at how these changes shaped the patterns of vote choice. As we explore these patterns, we will look closely at differences by class, gender, age, and education in an effort to clarify and explain class and group voting patterns.

Chapters 5 and 6 present our findings in detail. We believe that the evidence strongly supports the conclusion that citizens chose Violeta Chamorro consciously, though they were constrained in this choice by the conditions, candidates, and context. Moreover, Chamorro won the 1990 election not solely because her victory would lead to an end of the U.S. embargo and Contra War, but because citizens embraced her regime vision and long-term neoconstructionist agenda.

Thereafter, our concern is to determine why citizens continued to support a regime of democratic conservatism in 1996 and 2001. In making this determination, we will draw on four surveys taken by DOXA in the 1996 election and on three conducted by the Nicaraguan firm CINASE in 2001. The 1996 and 2001 surveys, designed and conducted under the guidance of the authors, provide a unique window into the evolution of democratic politics within a new democracy.

Our argument is that a critically momentous election such as Nicaragua's in 1990 can lead elites to offer such explicit and contrasting governing visions and citizens to make such engaged, committed vote choices between these visions that a special agreement emerges between victorious leaders and their supporters. This agreement generates "governing capital" that both leaders and followers can draw upon to ensure that their interests and values are respected in the future.[21]

Governing capital is defined by the extent to which explicit and shared agreement exists among leaders and supporters about the policies, principles, and prospective expectations of the new regime. With strong agreement, followers who have invested in the new government can hold it accountable to such principles and prospective expectations, reminding it of campaign promises through lobbying, protests, and voting. Government is accountable

---

21. This argument is related to but distinct from that of Rahn, Brehm, and Carlson (1999). They focus on the ways that elections can generate social capital, particularly in fostering in citizens a diffuse sense of political efficacy, trust in government, and collective solidarity. Much of this happens through engagement in the rite of elections, as well as through attitudinal change or reinforcement generated by that engagement.

In arguing that elections can also generate "governing capital," we are suggesting that elite presentation of distinctive governing visions and citizen reasoning to vote choice through assessment of those alternative visions, *in their interaction*, can generate shared elite/mass commitment to an agenda and governing regime that enhances the regime's governing effectiveness and persistence. We take the concept of "governing capital" to be an extended implication of Downs's logic of party competition and vote choice.

to the electorate. But by the same token leaders can point to the mutual agreement made with the public, asking that voters stay the course in the face of hard choices and tough times. In electing a new regime and charting a new direction, voters thus have a responsibility to the new government, owing it some time to deliver before they engage in far-reaching critical reassessment and electoral punishment, so long as the government makes good faith efforts early on to fulfill key expectations.

Seen in this manner, a mutual agreement on policy and governing vision, reached through authentic contestation and choice, can generate considerable shared capital for both elites and the public. Such capital can be replenished in subsequent elections that center on the same shared principles. Alternatively, with time, poor government performance, or shifting circumstances, voters can engage in a critical reassessment of the party and invest in a new government, thereby reinforcing the principle of government accountability, while the new government can call on voters to give it some sustained opportunity to prove itself, reinforcing the responsibilities of citizens.[22]

The intriguing issue is whether the 1990 election generated shared governing capital among voters and elected leaders, and whether citizens and leaders then drew on that capital in crafting and stabilizing the new regime. Did the campaign produce such a clear sense of the policy direction promised by the new regime that mass supporters could hold Chamorro and her government accountable to the policy promise voters embraced in installing the regime? And did the voters in fact do so, demanding such accountability through citizen protest, by lobbying the legislature, at the polls in subsequent elections, and otherwise? Similarly, did the 1990 election generate such committed vote choice by citizens, and such a genuine effort by victorious leaders to fulfill their policy promise, that Chamorro and subsequent

22. This process of investment/reassessment early in the life of a new democracy can gradually generate sustained voter experience with different parties in government, thereby making possible the purer retrospective logic that Downs and Fiorina attribute to voters in established democracies.

It is also possible that such an "investment/reassessment" logic comes to the fore in established democracies in periods of severe system crisis, partisan realignment, and regime change, as in the 1930s in the United States. During such periods, citizens' vote choice may involve not only rejecting a failed governing party but also investing in a new one, based on prospective assessments of its governing potential. Citizens' calculated investment in a new party government or regime, and their willingness to give the investment some time to pay off, may be one of the aspects of a critical election that can create a propensity toward moderate-term stability of "partisan attachments" and thereby foster immediate stability of the new regime. In such a logic, citizens give their "party investment" time to mature before subjecting it to tough-minded reassessment, particularly if there are early signs that the new government or regime is acting in good faith to fulfill its promises.

leaders then drew on their governing capital to help sustain the new regime in power? Did Chamorro and her government truly seek to deliver on the promises made in 1990? As the 1996 and 2001 elections approached, did she and other conservatives make a case for supporters to stay the course and for previous opponents to join in? As the electorate continued to vote conservatively, did it do so out of continuing affirmation of the new regime through reflective choice? Did the regime's stability continue to be rooted in citizen support for its core principles? Or did conservative victory come in response to intimidation of voters by the conservative regime? We address these concerns in part III.

Chapter 5

Citizen Attitudes in 1990: Candidates, the Economy, and the Regime

As we examine the evolution of citizen attitudes during the 1990 campaign, we introduce a new dimension into our analysis. Thus far we have focused on the story of the election as seen against the backdrop of history, through the eyes of observers, and through the lenses of voting theory. Now we clarify how it looked to citizens. The campaign confronted them with two contrasting candidates and with a political context that rivaled that of any election in modern history in the severity of the circumstances.[1] Moreover, in the middle of the campaign the United States invaded one of Nicaragua's Central American neighbors, seeming to some observers to warn voters about their prospective fate should they elect the "wrong" candidate. Faced with such circumstances, how were citizens evaluating the choices and context confronting them, and when did they make their determinant assessments? In the campaign's first month? After the Panama invasion? In the final weeks? At different times for different citizens? To address these issues, we look closely at the development of attitudes across four dimensions: candidate image, candidate competence, the economy, and the regime.

Candidate Image

Voting studies from advanced democracies argue that candidates' personal attributes are as important as or more important than any other factor in

---

1. The most comparable cases can be found in the 1930s, prior to the advent of modern survey analysis, as democracies worldwide struggled to respond to the Great Depression and rising militarism. For an insightful analysis of elections and regime stability during that era, see Hill (1988). For an instructive study of voting in the Weimar case, see Shively (1972)

influencing vote choice.[2] In particular, positive retrospective assessments of an incumbent create a strong predisposition toward reelection largely irrespective of equally strong or stronger assessments of a challenger.[3] A key dimension of such assessments is candidate image, as introduced by Fiorina in his study of American presidential elections. Sniderman, Brody, and Tetlock rely on image as their gauge of retrospective views of a candidate's political performance. They find image valuable because it taps general perceptions of candidates' past performance apart from recent or specific controversies or prospective governing concerns.

Image is a particularly useful indicator of candidates' retrospective performance in a study of the 1990 Nicaraguan election. Both major candidates were important national symbols, with their visibility tied to distinctive roles during and after the revolution. This provided citizens considerable information with which to evaluate image. Additionally, image assessments are simple cognitive evaluations that all citizens can undertake, regardless of educational level. We draw on eight image questions about each major candidate, asked by DOXA across all 1990 surveys, to determine citizens' retrospective image assessments. These questions are detailed in figure 5.1, which pools all the image data on each candidate across the four months of the campaign. The pooled data create an aggregate portrait of the candidates based on the percentage of interviewees who gave them a positive rating on each question. The figure is arranged so that those image items on which citizens preferred Ortega more than Chamorro (as on experience) are on the left and those where they preferred her (as on honesty) are on the right.

The Pooled Image Data

We see immediately that citizen images of both candidates were positive. There can be little doubt that both candidates enjoyed positive reputations for their past activities. A majority of citizens saw each as a leader, patriotic, close to the people, respected, and brave. Neither was being repudiated for past performance. Yet there were distinctions. Ortega was seen as more experienced, but Chamorro was seen as more honest and respected. Moreover, citizens had qualms about whether either was up to the job of president, with

2. Dalton and Wattenberg (1993); Abramson, Aldrich, and Rohde (1999); Markus and Converse (1979). For a study of candidate image and impression in determining voter choice in the United States, see Lodge, McGraw, and Stroh (1989). Dominguez and McCann (1996, 102–5) also find that candidate image or "personality traits" were relevant in Mexico's 1988 presidential election and that candidate likability was relevant in the 1994 presidential election (206–7).

3. Rabinowitz, Prothrow, and Jacoby (1982); Calvert (1985a); Rosenberg (1986).

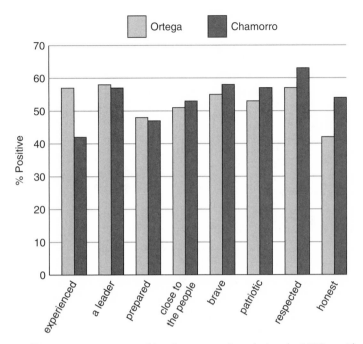

Figure 5.1 Citizen responses on candidate image questions during the 1990 presidential campaign

Source: Pooled results from DOXA nationwide monthly surveys during the 1990 presidential campaign ($N = 5,480$). The results report the percentage of interviewees giving a positive response on eight candidate image questions, with nonresponse included in the base. The questions asked, "Is Chamorro/Ortega . . . experienced / a leader / prepared / close to the people / brave / patriotic / respected / honest?"

the question about their preparation or readiness for office being the one on which neither received majority support.

Chamorro received slightly more support on average than Ortega, with 54 percent of her assessments being positive across the eight items, in contrast to 52.6 percent for him, but his image rating was still strong for a long-term incumbent governing amidst crisis. While she led him on five of the eight items, both seemed in good shape in retrospective terms. This should give an advantage to an experienced incumbent with a strong organization. However, averages can be deceiving and mask variations in opinion within the respondent pool. These averages might have occurred because most citizens gave each candidate positive scores on most questions. But they might also have occurred because one group of citizens gave very high marks to one candidate, while another group scored the other candidate highly. The two patterns would have very different meanings.

A clearer portrait of how individuals assessed the two candidates' images comes by combining individual responses into an Overall Candidate Image Index for each candidate. In this index, interviewees who answered at least one question for either candidate are treated as *respondents* on both indices, since they indicated that they understood the image questions and had an image preference. When these *respondents* gave a nonresponse to any specific image question, it was treated as a neutral evaluation. Interviewees who failed to answer any image question across both candidates are *nonrespondents*. This group was 8.9 percent of DOXA's total pool of 5,480 across all four months. The low nonresponse rate on image indicates that virtually all citizens had some awareness of the candidates and were willing to react when probed, at least minimally.

In creating our Overall Candidate Image Index, we have summed the number of positive image assessments respondents gave to a candidate. Those giving a candidate at least five positive scores out of a possible eight were treated as having a *positive image* of that candidate. Those who gave a candidate no positive scores, giving only negative assessments or nonresponses, were listed as having a *negative image* of that candidate. And respondents who gave a candidate one to four positive scores are listed as having an *ambivalent image* of that candidate.

Table 5.1 presents the combined results of the interviewees' overall image assessments of the two candidates. Ortega's ratings sum down the columns; Chamorro's sum across the rows. Looking at the cell for column A and row H, we see that 48.3 percent gave him a positive image rating, while 52.3 percent (column D, row E) gave her a positive rating. Her four-percentage-point advantage on these scores indicates that she led Ortega not only on average scores but also in the percentage of citizens giving the candidates positive overall ratings. But what do these percentages mean? Was Nicaragua a cleaved society, half of which rated Ortega's past performance highly and the other half of which gave her high marks? Or did a substantial number of citizens see both in positive terms? We can determine this by looking at the cells within the table.

When we look at the overlap in citizens' assessments, we can see that Nicaraguans were not polarized into two camps, each liking one candidate and hating the other. Rather, only 36.2 percent preferred one candidate, giving him/her a positive rating and the other a negative rating on overall image. This percentage combines the 19.9 percent of the citizenry that liked Chamorro and disliked Ortega (column C, row E) and the 16.3 percent that liked him but disliked her (column A, row G).

The most surprising pattern in Table 5.1 is the extent to which individual Nicaraguans gave favorable responses to *both* Chamorro and Ortega. Seventeen percent of all interviewees during the 1990 election campaign gave

Table 5.1   Citizens' Combined Image Assessments of Chamorro and Ortega during the 1990 Presidential Campaign (%)

Citizen Assessment of Chamorro	Citizen Assessment of Ortega			
	A. Positive (5 to 8 "yes" responses)	B. Ambivalent (1 to 4 "yes" responses)	C. Negative (0 "yes" responses)	D. Total
E. Positive (5 to 8 "yes" responses)	17.0	15.4	19.9	52.3
F. Ambivalent (1 to 4 "yes" responses)	15.0	4.0	1.2	20.2
G. Negative (0 "yes" responses)	16.3	0.9	1.4	18.6
H. Total	48.3	20.3	22.5	91.1%

Source: DOXA nationwide monthly surveys during the 1990 presidential campaign.
Notes: This table pools the results for November, December, January, and February so as to create a combined data base for the entire campaign. N is 5,480, with a nonresponse of 8.9%. The percentages include nonresponse in the base.

strongly positive assessments to both (column A, row E). And an additional 34.4 percent gave at least one positive assessment to each candidate (column A, row F, and column B, rows E and F). A majority of Nicaraguans (51.4 percent) thus had something positive to say about both Ortega and Chamorro.

Far from being highly polarized between the two, across the campaign most citizens attributed some positive traits to each candidate. This result suggests that the two candidates enjoyed greater acceptability to the public than observers had surmised. Yet this result does not necessarily mean that citizens were well disposed to both candidates on image terms as they cast their votes on election day. These image assessments come from surveys across all four months of the campaign, with the data from these surveys pooled together to create an overview snapshot of citizen attitudes for the four months taken as a whole. Voting theory suggests that an intense campaign such as the one that occurred in Nicaragua in 1990 will generate growing differentiation and polarization in citizens' assessments of candidates' images. To explore whether this occurred during the 1990 campaign, so that by election day citizens held polarized image preferences for Ortega or Chamorro, let us subdivide our pooled data and compare the results by month.

Citizens' Image Preferences by Month

Figure 5.2 presents citizens' image preferences for the two candidates month by month, considering overlap in candidate ratings. To determine image preferences, we divide individuals' ratings of the candidates into five mutually exclusive categories: "Prefer Chamorro" and "Prefer Ortega" refer to individuals who gave a positive rating, five or over, to the preferred candidate and a zero or negative rating to the other. "Prefer both" refers to individuals who gave positive ratings to both candidates. "Prefer neither" applies to respondents who did not give either candidate a positive rating; fewer than 2.5 percent of the interviewees fell in this category in any survey and thus these scores are omitted from the figure.[4] "Ambivalent" refers to those who gave a positive rating of one or more to each candidate, so long as they did not prefer both. We rate such individuals as ambivalent, even if they gave five or more positive ratings to one of the candidates, because they recognized positive features of each and could have felt cross-pressured in relying on image assessments alone to shape vote intent.

The image preference scores for November indicate that neither candidate had emerged as dominant based on image as the campaign began. Thus 12.8 percent of respondents preferred Chamorro and opposed Ortega, while 9 percent preferred him and opposed her. Combining the two percentages, only 21.8 percent of respondents held polarized image assessments that favored one candidate to the complete detriment of the other. By contrast, 18.9 percent gave both candidates favorable image ratings. And most interviewees (52.4 percent) indicated ambivalent image assessments, with some positive inclination toward each candidate but not enough to prefer both. Only 3 out of 800 interviewees had negative views of both. Finally, virtually all interviewees showed some attentiveness to the campaign, with more than 93 percent in November answering at least one image question.

The pattern of image assessments for November indicates that early in the campaign, virtually all citizens had an opinion about the candidates, and relatively few had ruled out either on image terms. The challenger had a slight edge on retrospective image. Yet despite the period of crisis over which he had presided, the incumbent enjoyed broad, diffuse appreciation. He certainly did not appear subject to the repudiation that conservative campaign commentators expected. Most critically, when one combines those holding ambivalent views and those rating both candidates highly, more than 70 percent of interviewees appeared open to considering both candidates as a potential president, ruling neither of them totally out of contention based on retrospective image. As the campaign intensified, these assessments shifted.

---

4. For November the "Neither" category was 0.4 percent; December, 1.4 percent; January, 2.3 percent; and February, 1.3 percent.

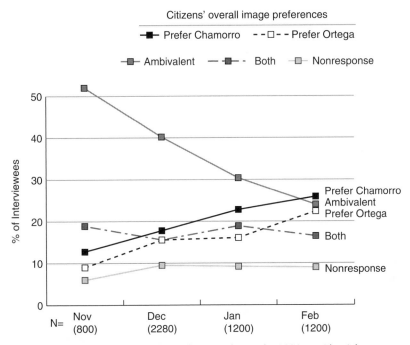

Figure 5.2 Citizens' candidate image preferences during the 1990 presidential campaign, by month

Source: DOXA nationwide monthly surveys.
Notes: "Prefer Chamorro" indicates interviewees who gave her five or more positive image ratings and Ortega none. "Prefer Ortega" indicates interviewees with the reverse scoring pattern. "Both" refers to interviewees who gave both Chamorro and Ortega positive ratings on five or more items. "Ambivalent" refers to interviewees who gave both candidates at least one positive rating but who did not give both five or more positive ratings. "Nonresponse" refers to interviewees who failed to answer all eight questions across both candidates. Interviewees were coded as preferring "neither" who gave no positive rating to either candidate, giving only negative assessments when they responded; fewer than 2.5% did so in any survey and thus these scores are omitted from the figure.

Month by month, the percentage of interviewees preferring a specific candidate on image rose while the percentage who were ambivalent fell. By February, the percentage preferring either Ortega or Chamorro on image terms had more than doubled from the November level while the percentage of citizens who were ambivalent between the two candidates had been cut in half. Thus in February 48.6 percent of interviewees preferred one or the other candidate on image, with 25.9 percent tilting strongly toward Chamorro and 22.7 percent toward Ortega. Another 16 percent still gave positive image ratings to both. Approximately 25 percent were ambivalent, while 1.3 percent gave negative ratings to both. These developments point toward citizens who were steadily clarifying their attitudes toward the candidates. In the process their image assessments were becoming increasingly differentiated.

Image Differentiation

Increased attitudinal differentiation exists when a growing number of interviewees like one candidate and dislike the other. We can determine the extent to which such differentiation on image was occurring month by month by creating an Image Differentiation Index. It sums together the percentage of interviewees within a group who prefer Chamorro on image and the percentage who prefer Ortega on image. This sum gives us the overall percentage of group members who held differentiated attitudes on candidate image, giving five or more positive ratings to one candidate (either one) and no positive ratings to the other. Figure 5.3 presents the results when we apply this index month by month to the entire sample as a whole and to social classes within it. In this figure, a low percentage indicates that few citizens held differentiated assessments of Ortega and Chamorro, so that their positive assessments were diffused across both candidates. A high score denotes high differentiation, with individuals liking one candidate a lot and the other not at all.

The month-by-month patterns for image differentiation indicate that substantial change occurred during the campaign in the image assessments of the two major candidates. Early in the campaign, a candidate's positive image assessments were diffused throughout the interviewee pool. Less than a quarter of all interviewees were clearly preferring one candidate over another in image terms in November. Low differentiation was likewise evident among the social classes, with only the new elite edging up to a 27 percent differentiation score. In contrast, by the end of the campaign roughly half of all individuals in the survey had strong opinions favoring one or the other contender on image. Moreover, this process of increasing differentiation occurred across all classes, led by the new Sandinista elite but with the masses and the old elite not far behind

The move from diffuse to differentiated attitudes can be a critically important development in a campaign. When positive image responses are diffused and either candidate appears acceptable to citizens, glitzy campaigns and well-organized turnout efforts can make the difference in convincing citizens to support one candidate and go to the polls in his or her behalf. Under such conditions, a well-run campaign and a strong party organization can be decisive in determining the eventual winner. But when image responses become differentiated, with voters intensely attracted to specific candidates, the outcome of the campaign can depend on whether citizens of similar class,

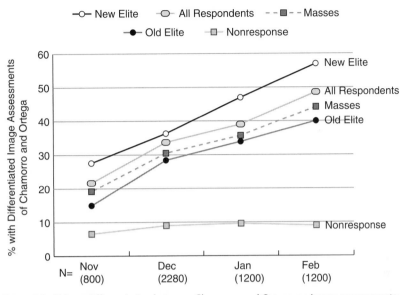

Figure 5.3 Citizen differentiation between Chamorro and Ortega on image assessments during the 1990 presidential campaign: class percentages by month

Source: DOXA nationwide monthly surveys.
Notes: Differentiation between candidates exists when an interviewee rates one candidate positively on a majority of the image questions while giving the other candidate no positive image assessments.
Percentage differentiation for a group indicates the proportion of its members that scored either candidate positively on a majority of questions while giving the other candidate no positive assessments.

age, or gender are polarizing toward the same candidate. When citizens of similar backgrounds and general orientations polarize toward a specific candidate on image terms, they reinforce one another's candidate assessments and encourage group turnout in the candidate's behalf, somewhat irrespective of factors such as party organization. In such situations, group polarization on candidate image can greatly shape an election outcome. In addition, the rapid emergence of extensive group polarization on candidate image may allow candidate retrospection to dominate vote choice. Alternatively, if campaign intensity increases but groups fail to develop strong image preferences for one candidate or the other, or do so slowly, then other attitudinal concerns may come to influence the decision, including prospective assessments.

Image Polarization

We utilize a Class Polarization Index to determine the extent to which the growing image differentiation among citizens translated into polarized group response to Ortega and Chamorro. This index subtracts the percentage of class members who gave a polarized image response preferring Ortega (giving him five or more positive ratings and Chamorro none) from the percentage who gave a polarized response preferring Chamorro. If all members of a class gave her five or more positive image scores and him none, the polarization score for that class would be 100 (100 minus 0), indicating a class totally polarized toward her. If 25 percent preferred her and 75 percent preferred him, the class polarization score would be –50 (25 minus 75) and would indicate a class tilting strongly toward him. Figure 5.4 presents the resulting polarization scores across the campaign by class. It subdivides the polarization result for December into the first and second wave of interviews in order to clarify the effect of the Panama invasion.

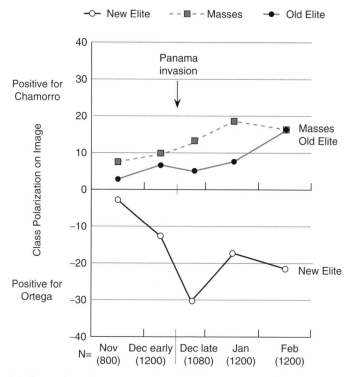

Figure 5.4 Class polarization on candidate image assessments during the 1990 presidential campaign, by month

Source: DOXA nationwide monthly surveys.
Notes: Class polarization is determined by subtracting the percentage of class members who prefer Ortega on image from the percentage who prefer Chamorro. A positive score indicates the % tilt toward Chamorro. A negative score indicates the % tilt toward Ortega.

As the campaign began, the masses were slightly tilted toward Chamorro, while the two elite groups showed little clear preference on image assessments. The modest orientation of the masses toward her in November makes clear that she enjoyed high visibility within the nation, even at the outset, and had a sufficiently positive personal identity that she could challenge Ortega among his mass supporters. Yet she was less clearly embraced among her own traditional elite class, perhaps owing not only to her inexperience but also probably to gender prejudice and possibly to her own strong support for political democracy.

Finally, the polarization score for the new elite is particularly striking. The division within the new elite in November over the image of the two candidates indicates that Ortega's base was considerably more hesitant about his retrospective performance, and more attracted to her, than observers understood. This division owed in large part to problems with the university students. His regime had given them free education and based much of its hope for the future on their growing national role. Yet students also included a large number of young men threatened by the draft should peace efforts fail. In November it was the students, nearly half of the new elite, who had the greatest doubts about his retrospective image, tilting slightly toward Chamorro. In contrast, those in the military overwhelmingly preferred Ortega on retrospective image, while the government bureaucrats fell roughly midway between the military and the students.

As the campaign progressed, the classes polarized in candidate image. The new elite came to see Ortega positively and dismiss Chamorro. The old elite and masses moved in the opposite direction. Yet these developments came slowly and at different points in the campaign. The new elite tilted first, shifting toward Ortega in late December, following the Panama invasion, when students and bureaucrats joined the military in preferring him on retrospective image. Thereafter, their polarization toward him moderated, but still remained well above the level seen prior to the invasion. The masses shifted more gradually, reaching their most polarized positive position favoring Chamorro in January. And the old elites moved more slowly still. They reached their most polarized position in February, following the masses rather than leading them.

In the end, significant image polarization occurred during the 1990 campaign, but not in such a way as to ensure that image retrospection would dominate citizen reasoning and vote choice. Weak class polarization early in the campaign meant that citizens accustomed to looking to class unity to guide and reinforce their political assessments could not easily do so on the issue of retrospective image, thereby providing an early opportunity for other concerns to rise to the fore. In addition, insofar as class polarization did exist in November, it went against historic class alignments, with the masses tilting away from the Sandinista candidate and toward the more conservative contender. This may well have created cross-pressures on mass citizens that gave them additional incentive to look at other concerns when they considered their vote decision during the early phase of the campaign.

Perhaps most important, once the classes polarized on candidate image, starting in late December, they did not do so in a decisive manner that would create powerful momentum toward the preferred candidate. The masses and old elite reached only a 16 percent tilt toward Chamorro. In standardized terms, where we use percentage tilt to estimate the natural underlying division of an entire class, this polarization score points to a 58–42 percent split toward her on image. This would not appear to be a strong tilt, putting pressure on wavering class members to move toward Chamorro. The new elite did reach a 21.5 percent tilt toward Ortega, indicating a 61–39 percent split on his behalf. Yet this is hardly a rousing affirmation of a revolutionary leader and long-term president pointing to a solid base prepared to sweep him back into power. Neither the masses nor the elites tended to show a decisive preference for Ortega or for Chamorro in image terms. For this reason, as well as citizens' need in a new democracy to be especially careful in choosing a president, their prospective assessments of the candidates' governing competence took on special importance.

Candidate Governing Competence

Candidate governing competence is a more substantive assessment than image and comprises a future-oriented estimate of candidates' abilities to solve major problems.[5] As with image, voting studies have found competence to be a key determinant of the vote. Sniderman et al. use it as their primary indicator of prospection. In their study and in ours, competence questions ask citizens to assess candidates' ability to address major policy problems or issues.

Measuring Candidate Competence

Our measure of candidate competence is based on respondents' answers to eight simple questions about Nicaragua's major problems in 1990. These

---

5. Funk (1996) has found that competence matters more than personality or image. Additional studies of candidate competence and vote choice include Mann and Wolfinger (1980); Miller and Wattenberg (1985); and Shanks and Miller (1991).

asked respondents to indicate which of the two major candidates "has the greater likelihood to" address each of the following: (1) end the war; (2) end/solve the overall state of crisis; (3) address the economy; (4) get foreign aid; (5) bring peace; (6) bring reconciliation; (7) rebuild the country; (8) help the people. We organize these concerns into four categories: (I) End the Wartime Crisis; (II) Improve the Economy; (III) Bring Peace and Reconciliation; (IV) Build a Better Nicaragua.

These four categories capture the broad prospective concerns that pre-occupied Nicaragua during the 1990 election. They also point to different expectations surrounding the election of Chamorro or Ortega. The first category, addressing the wartime crisis, speaks to the perception that her election would lead the United States to forgo support for the Contras, in effect ending the war, while his election could sustain it. Alternatively, a respondent could support Ortega by concluding that a decisive win by him would bring international pressure on the United States to end hostilities, while electing Chamorro to appease the United States could risk rebellion on the left. The second category, improving the economy, certainly might require the United States to end its embargo and join other countries in aiding Nicaragua, an outcome Chamorro's election was said to ensure. Yet citizens could support Ortega on this issue, believing that his defeat would lead to reductions in state spending and public employment, thereby increasing economic problems, while his victory might lead to expanded international aid for a regime that had repeatedly earned and proven its legitimacy.

The third and fourth categories are more subtle than the first two. Their accomplishment required much more than the cessation of U.S. hostilities or the presence of international support. Instead, they tap whether a candidate's leadership skills and goals are appropriate to long-term governing tasks within Nicaragua. The third category, bringing peace and reconciliation, focuses on whether a candidate and governing approach can generate harmony and healing among Nicaraguans themselves, bridging the nation's deep divisions. And the fourth, building a better Nicaragua, points to the need to rebuild a country devastated by decades of right-wing repression, natural disasters, revolution, and political turmoil. This task was the most serious long-term challenge facing the next president, and its difficulty centered in particular on how best to approach rebuilding while being sensitive to the needs of the people. Answering the questions about "building a better Nicaragua" and "bringing peace and reconciliation" required citizens to make judgments about the candidates' leadership skills and their alternative visions for the future.

Competence Assessments Month by Month

Unlike the image questions, the competence questions asked respondents to choose between the two candidates on each separate question. They also were given the option to choose "neither candidate" but no option to choose both. The monthly results for each question are presented in table 5.2. The percentages include nonresponse in the base. Summing the percentages for Ortega, Chamorro, or neither indicates that roughly 80 percent of interviewees were prepared to respond on *each* competence question in November.

The high November response rate for the individual questions indicates that citizens were attentive to competence issues early, as the theory of reflective voting predicts. Nicaraguans faced a momentous decision about regime direction, in a context where they could not assume the existence of an experienced and loyal opposition. Moreover, they faced questions about the democratic credentials and honesty of the incumbent president. While both candidates were highly regarded for their historic roles, neither was clearly preferable on image terms. To determine if a real choice were possible between them, citizens focused on the prospective competence of the candidates. In doing so, they reached a conclusion at odds with the expectations of many observers.

While observers may have worried that the opposition was so inexperienced or questionable that real choice was impossible, the citizens disagreed. A substantial proportion of interviewees saw each candidate as competent. Moreover, Chamorro consistently received higher competence scores than Ortega on each question for each month. Across all questions for all four months, citizens chose Chamorro roughly 43 percent of the time and Ortega roughly 30 percent. Yet there are differences in choice patterns by question, and critical shifts in competence assessments across time.

From the outset, far more people believed that Chamorro could end the war and improve the economy. These were concerns in which her close ties with the United States played a substantial role. She received the support of 40 percent of interviewees during November on each question and led Ortega by about 12–15 percentage points. Citizens also saw her as more likely to have the skills to bring peace and reconciliation. This was an area in which her reputation for playing a conciliatory role within her divided and politicized family created a positive perception of her, while the growth of hostilities during Ortega's incumbency damaged him. Again, she topped 40 percent on the two questions about peace and reconciliation and led Ortega in November by 13–15 percentage points.

As the campaign progressed, she improved somewhat in citizen assess-

Table 5.2   Citizens' Competence Assessments of Chamorro and Ortega by Month during the 1990 Presidential Campaign (%)

Dimension, Question, and Candidate	November	December	January	February	Change[a]
I. Ending the wartime crisis					
End war					
Ortega	27.3	28.2	28.2	32.3	+5.0
Chamorro	42.0	41.3	42.8	44.3	+2.3
Neither	11.4	14.2	15.4	13.1	+1.7
End crisis					
Ortega	27.9	28.4	29.0	33.4	+5.5
Chamorro	40.4	42.1	44.3	45.9	+5.5
Neither	10.3	12.7	13.9	10.6	+0.3
II. Improving the economy					
Address the economy					
Ortega	28.8	29.4	29.1	33.2	+4.4
Chamorro	40.4	43.1	45.7	46.5	+6.1
Neither	10.3	11.8	11.9	10.6	+0.3
Get foreign aid					
Ortega	29.4	29.0	28.5	33.8	+4.4
Chamorro	44.6	46.3	47.7	46.9	+2.3
Neither	5.5	8.3	11.2	9.4	+3.9
III. Bringing peace and reconciliation					
Bring peace					
Ortega	28.9	28.8	28.7	32.6	+3.7
Chamorro	41.9	42.1	42.5	44.0	+2.1
Neither	10.3	13.5	15.3	13.1	+2.8
Bring reconciliation					
Ortega	26.9	26.1	27.8	33.8	+6.9
Chamorro	42.3	41.3	44.3	44.6	+2.3
Neither	11.6	13.0	14.8	11.5	−0.1
IV. Building a better Nicaragua					
Rebuild the country					
Ortega	31.1	31.2	29.0	33.6	+2.5
Chamorro	36.1	41.0	44.6	45.0	+8.9
Neither	9.6	11.1	12.4	11.6	+2.0
Help the people					
Ortega	32.1	31.0	29.9	34.8	+2.5
Chamorro	38.5	41.0	43.8	45.2	+6.7
Neither	8.1	10.2	13.0	10.7	+2.6

Source: DOXA nationwide monthly surveys during the 1990 presidential campaign.

Note: Percentages indicate interviewees choosing Ortega, Chamorro, or neither as more competent on the specific item, with nonrespondents included in the base. There were 800 interviewees in November, 2,280 in December, 1,200 in January, and 1,200 in February.

[a] Change refers to the percent difference when the first survey is subtracted from the last survey. A plus sign indicates an increase in the percentage of positive assessments across the campaign.

ments on these first three categories of questions, so that by the end she was seen as more competent on them by 44–47 percent of interviewees. However, it was Ortega who improved more during the campaign on most of these items. His efforts to moderate during the campaign clearly paid off. Still, in the end, only about a third of the interviewees embraced him as the candidate most likely to end the wartime crisis, improve the economy, or bring peace and reconciliation. In February she led him on all of these items by 11–14 percentage points.

The most striking change evident in table 5.2 is the growing proportion of citizens who believed that Chamorro could build a better Nicaragua. In November she faced more doubts on this issue than on any other, being seen as competent by only 36–38 percent on these items, well below her other scores. In contrast, Ortega was seen in a more favorable light than on the other categories, being rated as more competent by 31 percent to 32 percent, which was well above his other scores. Ortega's relatively high early ratings reflected the FSLN's historic commitment to reconstructing Nicaragua into a more equitable and just society and his devotion to this enterprise during his presidency. Chamorro's problems in this area may have been caused by her inexperience in governing and by early doubts about whether her stress on U.S.-style democracy and a market economy served the interests of Nicaragua's citizens. Her percentages then increased steadily month by month, whereas his wavered during the campaign, shooting up somewhat only at the end.

By February, roughly 45 percent of the public saw Chamorro as the more competent to build a better Nicaragua, whereas only a third chose Ortega. Her early, aggressive attacks on him and her emphasis on the price the people had paid during his presidency, combined with her stress on expanded liberties, helped fuel her improvement. His passivity early in the campaign and hesitancy to attack Chamorro gave her the opening to make her case. As a result, between November and February, she doubled the distance between herself and Ortega on this issue.

Overall, the changes evident in the competence evaluations across all four categories leave little doubt that Chamorro did better in citizens' competence estimates, including those requiring considerable vision and leadership skills, than her inexperience in governing led observers to anticipate. Yet these are citizen responses to individual questions, so that the impression they create of strong citizen preference for her on competence evaluations could be deceptive. Possibly Chamorro's positive assessments were dispersed throughout society, with almost all citizens giving her some positive assessments, but only a small cadre giving her positive assessments across all items. In contrast, Ortega could have enjoyed positive, well-differentiated assessments from a sizable and cohesive group, such as the new Sandinista elite.

Competence Differentiation

To determine how differentiated the competence evaluations were, we combine citizens' separate, discrete evaluations into an Overall Candidate Competence Index. It gauges how strongly individuals preferred one candidate or the other on competence issues. In constructing it, we gave a +1 to those who chose Ortega as more competent on each separate question, a −1 to those who chose Chamorro, and a 0 to those saying neither. We then summed the responses that each individual gave across the eight questions. Those having a score of +5 or more were treated as seeing Ortega as more competent, and those with a score of −5 or more were treated as seeing Chamorro as more competent. If the absolute sum was less than five for both candidates, we considered the individual to be ambivalent between the two. If an interviewee declined to rate the candidates on one or more of the eight questions, we treated him/her as a nonrespondent in our calculation of the competence index score. We used this stringent standard in order to set a high bar in determining how attentive citizens were to prospective candidate competence.

Figure 5.5 presents the patterns for the citizens' Overall Candidate Competence responses by month during the 1990 campaign. As the month-by-month drop in nonresponse indicates, competence evaluations crystallized steadily over the campaign. Roughly 60 percent of interviewees were prepared to answer *all* of the competence questions in November. By February, two weeks before the election, roughly 85 percent answered all eight competence questions.

As attitude crystallization increased month by month, so too did differentiation on candidate competence. In November, slightly more than 50 percent of the interviewees were clearly differentiating between Ortega and Chamorro, and those who tilted strongly toward Chamorro exceeded those tilting toward Ortega, by 30 percent to 21 percent. By February, Chamorro was leading Ortega on overall competence assessments, 43 percent to 31 percent. At this point, a remarkable 74 percent of interviewees gave responses on the candidates that differentiated between them on candidate competence. This means that these citizens answered all eight questions and that the bulk of their answers substantially favored one candidate over the other. Prospective candidate assessments clearly mattered to the citizens. But it is

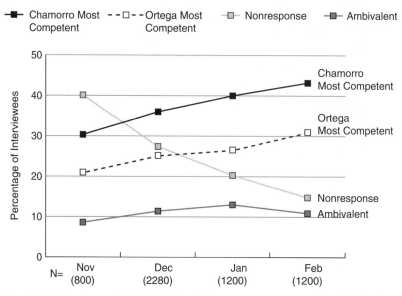

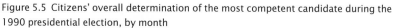

Figure 5.5 Citizens' overall determination of the most competent candidate during the 1990 presidential election, by month

Source: DOXA nationwide monthly surveys.

Notes: An interviewee's overall competence assessment of the two candidates is determined by summing the number of positive ratings given to Ortega on the eight competence questions (scored as +1 for each item) and the number of positive ratings given to Chamorro (scored as –1). When an interviewee indicates that "neither" is competent on an item, that response is scored as a zero. Interviewees whose sum is +5 or more see Ortega as most competent, and those whose sum is –5 or more see Chamorro as most competent. Interviewees who give neither candidate an absolute score of 5 or more are ambivalent. Interviewees who decline to rate the candidates on one or more of the eight competence questions are treated as nonrespondents in the calculation of citizens' overall competence assessment of the candidates.

unclear whether groups of citizens were developing differentiated attitudes that tilted decisively toward one candidate or the other. Did social groups polarize in their competence assessments, as they did with image assessments?

Group Polarization on Candidate Competence

In measuring group polarization on candidate competence, we subtracted the percentage of citizens in each group who gave Ortega a positive overall candidate competence evaluation from the percentage who gave the same to Chamorro. Class polarization scores can range from –1.00 to +1.00. The former indicates a class in which all members gave Ortega an overall positive competence assessment; the latter represents a class that favored Chamorro as more competent. Intermediate scores indicate the degree of tilt toward one or the other. Figure 5.6 gives the results.

More than with candidate image, classes polarized on candidate competence at the campaign outset. In November, the masses and old elite tilted strongly toward Chamorro, the new elite more hesitantly toward Ortega. The early December interviews show the former swinging even more strongly toward Chamorro on governing competence, while the new elite increased their tilt toward Ortega. A steady growth in class polarization appeared under way. But then came the U.S. invasion of Panama.

With the invasion, the swing of the masses and old elite toward Chamorro on candidate competence stopped momentarily, while the movement of the new elite toward Ortega magnified. In the late December interviews, the

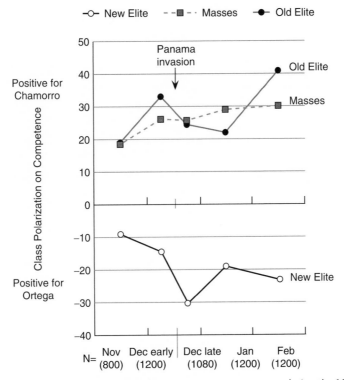

Figure 5.6 Class polarization on candidate competence assessments during the 1990 presidential campaign, by month

Source: DOXA nationwide monthly surveys.
Notes: Class polarization is determined by subtracting the percentage of class members who consider Ortega to be the more competent candidate from the percentage rating Chamorro as more competent. A positive score indicates the % tilt toward Chamorro. A negative score indicates the % tilt toward Ortega.

masses held steady at their early December level of polarization, and the old elite decreased markedly in their tilt toward Chamorro. In contrast, the tilt of the new elite toward Ortega on competence issues doubled from 14.5 percent to 30.3 percent. The immediate effect of the invasion appears to have been to stall the polarization of the masses toward Chamorro on competence issues, to reverse the movement toward her among the old elite, and to fuel the polarization of the new elite toward Ortega.

The final two months of the campaign saw Chamorro rebound on competence issues among the masses and old elite, while Ortega held his own among the new elite, down from late December but above his preinvasion scores. If we combine the masses and old elite, we find that their polarized tilt toward Chamorro in February was 30.2 percent, while the tilt for the new elite toward Ortega was –23.1 percent, so that the polarized gap between the classes at this point was 53.3 percentage points. This gap had doubled since November, with the major increase coming in late December.

The campaign also saw substantial growth in polarization along age and gender lines. With respect to gender, men were tilted slightly toward Chamorro early on in their competence assessments (with a 4.1 percent polarization score in November), and women were moderately polarized toward her (with a 13.5 percent score). By February men were slightly less supportive of her (with a 2.2 percent score), while women had moved decisively toward her (with a 19.9 percent score). Over the four months the polarization gap between men and women on the competence of the two candidates had virtually doubled, moving from 9.4 percent early on to 17.7 percent two weeks prior to the election.

The growth in polarization over candidate competence by age was even greater than that by gender. Early on those twenty-four years of age or under were almost evenly divided between the two candidates in competence assessments (with a 1.9 percent polarization score in November) while those forty-five years or older clearly preferred her (with a 19.3 percent polarization score). By the end of the campaign, the young were still divided (with a – 0.8 score in February) while the older citizens had moved dramatically toward Chamorro (with a 39.5 percent polarization score).[6] The polarization gap between the young and old had more than doubled from November to

6. The middle age groups fell between the young and older voters in their competence assessments throughout the campaign, increasing moderately in their polarization toward Chamorro as the election neared. In November those citizens 25 to 34 years of age had a 13 percent polarization score, tilted toward Chamorro; by February this tilt had increased slightly to 15.5 percent . Those citizens falling between 35 and 44 started with a 9.5 percent tilt toward her and ended with a 13 percent tilt in her behalf.

February, from 17.4 percent to 40.3 percent. Clearly, women and older voters increasingly saw Chamorro as the more competent, while men and the young each continued to divide in assessments of the candidates.

At the end of the 1990 campaign, it was citizens closest to the margin of existence—the poor, women, older voters—who had the greatest qualms about Ortega's governing competence and were most inclined to support Chamorro. Those with more security—the new elite, men, and the young—were less inclined to see her positively and more open to him. Unfortunately for Ortega, the former composed the bulk of the electorate. Thus, as citizens prepared to go to the polls, assessments of candidate competence were so polarized by class, gender, and age, and so benefited Chamorro, that only a powerful countervailing factor would probably have propelled them to reelect Ortega. One such factor could have been satisfaction with the economy or belief that his policy was generating its imminent improvement. Another could have been a belief that, whatever Ortega's limits and Chamorro's assets, the Sandinista regime deserved continuing support based on past accomplishments and future promise. Such concerns required citizens to look beyond the candidates and to assess context. Of course, such assessments can be a double-edged sword.

While positive assessments of context can lead citizens to override doubts about an incumbent and vote to reelect him, negative assessments can reinforce their opposition. When strongly negative, such assessments may not only lead citizens to alter historic voting patterns but encourage them to rethink partisan and regime loyalties. We turn now to clarify how citizens evaluated economic and regime context.

Assessing Context: The Economy and Regime

The Economy

Like candidate assessments, citizens' economic evaluations receive considerable attention in voting studies of established democracies.[7] Such studies find that citizens' economic assessments have a strong effect on vote choice that is separate from the effect of candidate evaluations.[8] As we would expect,

---

7. Tufte (1978); Lewis-Beck (1988); MacKuen, Erikson, and Stimson (1992). For the role of economic assessments in a Latin American context, see the analysis of the Mexican presidential election of 1988 by Dominguez and McCann (1996, esp. chaps. 3 and 4).

8. Williams (1990); Lewis-Beck (1988); Hibbs and Vasilatos (1982, 259–79); Hibbs, Rivers, and Vasilatos (1982); and Hibbs (1981).

negative assessments hurt incumbent candidates, while positive economic evaluations help them.[9] Following the lead of existing literature, we analyze opinion through two sociotropic questions that probed views of the overall state of the economy rather than personal economic circumstances.[10] The first, retrospective in nature, asked, "In your opinion, is Nicaragua's economy getting better, worse, or staying the same?" The second, prospective in nature, asked, "Over the next twelve months, do you think the economy will be better, worse, or the same as it is now?" Figure 5.7 presents the percentage of *respondents* who saw the economy in positive terms, retrospectively and prospectively, across the campaign. We focus on respondents rather than interviewees because of high nonresponse on prospective assessments. The percentage who failed to respond to each question is listed beneath the figure, with *N* indicating the total number of interviewees.[11]

Clearly the economy was in trouble according to the citizens. As one would expect in the midst of severe inflation and economic collapse, both the retrospective and prospective ratings were dismal. In November, at

9. On the relationship between economic performance and electoral outcomes, see Lewis-Beck (1988); Remmer (1993); Hibbs (1987); and Hibbs and Fassbinder with the assistance of Rivers (1981). Scholars have come to note that the connection between economics and elections is so close and regular that there is even a political business cycle in which politicians attempt to manipulate the economy for electoral advantage. Landmark contributions in this genre include Nordhaus (1975); MacRae (1977); Lowery (1985); Powell and Whitten (1993).

10. Most students of U.S. elections agree that sociotropic perspectives are more powerful determinants of the vote than are pocketbook perceptions. For a pioneering early study, see Kinder and Kiewiet (1981). As survey research on elections has proceeded, scholars have increasingly differentiated between different kinds of economic assessments and vote choice, looking at pocketbook, group, and sociotropic perspectives (Markus 1988, 1992; Kinder, Adams, and Gronke 1989), while still stressing a sociotropic perspective.

Despite the efforts at disentangling different types of economic reasoning, there remains disagreement as to whether sociotropic questions are eliciting concern solely about collective experience and interests, or reflect attention to individual and group self-interest. Like Marcus, Neuman, and MacKuen (2000, 135), we see voters as exercising "a rather sophisticated calculus engaging their sense of both individual and collective benefit" when responding to sociotropic questions (see also Mutz 1998).

We see intense personal experience and related self-interest as helping shape citizens' perceptions of collective experience, so that variation in survey responses on sociotropic questions reflects some degree of personal and group interest. Yet such responses in the aggregate will also reflect concern for general systemic performance beyond individual experience and self-interest. Thus we seek in our discussion both to make clear the broad context within which a citizenry is operating when responding to surveys and to clarify the distinctive experience that can lead to differential sociotropic assessments across groups of citizens.

11. For early attention by survey analysts to voter evaluations of the economic past as compared with the economic future, see MacKuen, Erikson, and Stimson (1992); Alesina, Londregan, and Rosenthal (1993); and Muller and Seligson (1994).

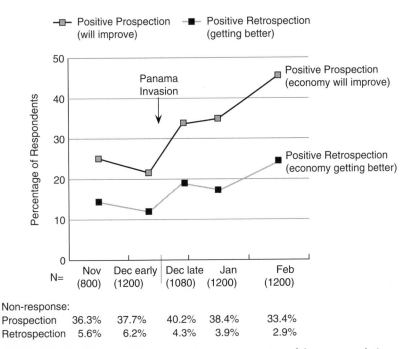

Figure 5.7 Citizens' retrospective and prospective assessments of the economy during the 1990 presidential election, by month

Source: DOXA nationwide monthly surveys asking, "In your opinion, is Nicaragua's economy getting better, worse, or staying the same?" (retrospection) and "Over the next twelve months, do you think the economy here will be better, worse, or the same as it is now?" (prospection). Percentages omit nonresponses.

campaign outset, only 14.4 percent of respondents gave the economy a positive retrospective evaluation, and only 25 percent gave it a positive prospective assessment. Moreover, as the candidates began to campaign, public disillusionment with the economy appeared to grow. In early December only 12 percent gave a positive retrospective assessment of the economy, and only 22 percent gave a positive prospective assessment. But then positive assessments increased. A first jump came immediately after the Panama invasion. This surge in positive assessments was driven by a sudden rallying of the new elite behind the economy. Their positive ratings jumped roughly 11 to 12 percent on both retrospective and prospective assessments, while that of the masses and old elite increased by less than 2 percent. In January, assessments leveled off, and then in February another jump occurred. This jump was most pronounced among the new elite, whose positive assessments across both dimensions increased between January and February by roughly 14 percent. Yet it was also evident among the masses and old elite, particularly on prospective assessment, where their positive assessments increased by around 7 to 8 percent.

The surge at the end had no relationship to any real economic improvement in Nicaragua and more nearly reflects citizens' views that a genuine election was about to occur that could break the stalemate with the United States and end the embargo. Similarly, the higher prospective scores throughout the campaign may reflect respondents' views that, while the past had been abysmal, the election could put the nation on a stronger economic path. Still, the consistent high nonresponse on "future economy" suggests great voter anxiety and underscores the difficult choices confronting them.

The poor state of the economy naturally would convince citizens to think hard about who best to lead them. Moreover, those most concerned about the economy were the poorer, more vulnerable respondents. It was the masses who generally gave the economy its lowest ratings, ranging from 9.4 percent and 16.5 percent positive assessments on past and future economy in November to 15 percent and 36 percent in February. The new elite gave it the highest, ranging from 24 percent and 38.8 percent early on to 42.4 percent and 61.4 percent across the two dimensions at the end, with the old elite generally falling closer to the masses than the new elite. Yet all classes experienced the counterfactual jump in prospective scores in February. This reinforces the sense that citizens across the board were anticipating that the election outcome—perhaps particularly the anticipated election of their candidate—could solve the economic crisis. The fact that the approaching election elicited such an anticipatory response indicates how concerned citizens were about the economy and how vital they saw the election as being to economic recovery.

The Regime

In contrast to economic evaluations, regime assessments are difficult to explore in a manner informed by the survey literature on established democracies.[12] Such nations have little experience with the regime concerns that confronted Nicaragua in 1990, and thus there are no widely accepted questions to use in studying regime evaluations. In the absence of established questions, the 1990 surveys used two questions on regime worded to fit the

---

12. For a study of postcommunist societies that advances the measurement and interpretation of citizens' attitudes toward regimes, see Rose, Mishler, and Haerpfer (1998). For a study contrasting regime concerns in a first postsocialist election across the cases of Nicaragua and Hungary, see Anderson, Lewis-Beck, and Stegmaier (2003).

specific conditions of Nicaragua. The retrospective question asked citizens to consider comparative regime performance over the past decades and implicitly contained a reference to the Somoza years. This question read: "Was the country better off before or after the revolution?" The prospective question asked respondents to evaluate the future direction that the regime was taking the country. It read: "Is Nicaragua going in a good or bad direction?"

At the heart of the regime questions lies a basic concern: did voters still believe in the viability of the revolutionary regime, based on either its past accomplishments or its prospective promise?[13] Underlying this concern is the issue of whether citizens believed that the current political order could address problems of governance in ways they considered legitimate and desirable. Citizens who supported the existing regime, including its determination to face down the embargo, overcome the Contras, and return to socialist reforms, would assumedly tilt toward Ortega, perhaps irrespective of candidate or economic assessments. But voters disillusioned with the regime could be open to an electoral realignment and the reconstruction of the political order. In their disillusionment, they might even embrace a politically inexperienced candidate. Much thus depended on regime evaluations.

Table 5.3 presents the pattern for citizens' retrospective and prospective regime assessments. As on the economy, these results present an electorate deeply troubled by the context confronting them. In November, when contrasting the revolutionary period with the preceding era, a slight majority of interviewees found life better in the earlier period, while only 26.6 percent preferred life after the revolution. Approximately a fifth failed to respond to this question early in the campaign. As citizens responded more fully, they divided, so that percentages preferring life before and after the revolution rise survey by survey. With respect to regime prospection, a clear majority consistently saw the country heading in a bad direction, while roughly 25–35 percent saw it heading in a good direction. A slight upturn in prospective assessments at the end, much as with economic assessments, could reflect anticipation that the election would bring beneficial clarity to the nation's future.

These patterns indicate strongly that citizens were unhappy with the existing political order during the 1990 campaign, though the results do need some qualification. We do not see the results as suggesting that citizens preferred

13. On the critical role of regime legitimacy in modern societies, see Schaar, (1981); Useem and Useem (1979); and Easton (1976).

Assessments of regime performance are proving critical among citizens in post-Soviet societies as well. See Miller, Reisinger, and Hesli (1993); and Anderson, Lewis-Beck, and Stegmaier (2003). For an early discussion of the importance of looking at regime issues, see Rose and Urwin (1969).

Table 5.3   Retrospective and Prospective Regime Assessments by Month during the
1990 Presidential Campaign (%)

	November	December (early)	December (late)	January	February
Retrospective: Was life better before or after the revolution?					
Before	51.4	55.7	58.7	61.0	60.8
After	26.6	28.0	30.6	30.2	32.8
NR	22.0	16.4	10.6	8.8	6.4
Total	100.0	100.1	99.9	100	100
Prospective: Is Nicaragua headed in a good or bad direction?					
Good	29.6	23.4	30.1	31.4	38.3
Bad	56.0	62.2	61.5	60.1	56.0
NR	14.4	14.4	8.4	8.5	5.8
Total	100.0	100	100	100	100.1
N	800	1200	1080	1200	1200

Source: DOXA nationwide monthly surveys during the 1990 presidential campaign.
Note: There were 800 interviewees in November, 1,200 in early December, 1,080 in late December, 1,200
in January, and 1,200 in February. The late December survey was taken immediately following the Panama
invasion.

Somoza over Ortega, or preferred the Somoza dictatorship as a government
instead of the Sandinista regime. In fact, other data in the 1990 survey reveal
that Nicaraguans did not prefer Somoza over Ortega. When asked directly in
December 1990 whether they liked Somoza (a lot, some, a little, not at all),
84.8 percent said "not at all," and only 1.1 percent said "a lot" or "some." In
contrast, as we have seen, Ortega received decent retrospective evaluations
from many respondents, with no evidence of a near-universal repudiation
along the lines seen with Somoza. Our sense is that these questions tap regime
performance and current direction, not regime preference. In making these
assessments, citizens necessarily recognized that daily life was easier for many
and perhaps most citizens without civil war, embargo, and revolutionary
reconstruction, even in a repressive dictatorship.

Despite this qualification, it is nevertheless clear that voters did have
deep concerns with the Sandinista regime. Not only did they believe that
life had been better in the previous era, they were not sure that the current
order was leading in a fruitful direction, at least under existing conditions.
As with the economy, it was the most vulnerable citizens who again had the
greatest regime concerns. Looking at respondents only, from the outset of
the campaign roughly 70 percent or more of the masses saw the period
before the revolution as preferable in each poll. A similar percentage also
saw the country heading in a bad direction. In addition, even the new elite

respondents acknowledged severe problems with the performance of the existing political order, splitting roughly 50–50 on both regime questions.[14]

The regime patterns reinforce the sense that citizens had strong reasons for engaging in the campaign and subjecting the candidates to close scrutiny. While voters had complex perspectives on who was to blame for Nicaragua's state of crisis, as we saw in chapter 3, they were also clear that life amidst perpetual revolutionary struggle was difficult. Moreover, the current direction of the country appeared to hold out little hope for future respite from their trials and tribulations.

Given these perceptions, the pressing question is whether the electorate, or pivotal groups within it, actually changed their minds about politics in some fundamental way during the election campaign. As they assessed the context around them and reflected across the images and prospective competence of the contenders, did they focus solely on ending the immediate crisis? Or did they see new and compelling possibilities, even learning to think in terms of a new set of governing principles? Did they begin to embrace a new vision and regime path for Nicaragua?

Reassessing Candidate Competence: The Case for Reflective Learning

As the 1990 election approached, Nicaraguan history suggested that most citizens, particularly the poorer and more vulnerable, would stay with Ortega and the FSLN out of their deep belief in the Sandinistas' long-term revolutionary vision. If nothing else, they should see Ortega as more devoted to constructing a better Nicaragua and, given his experience as president, as more competent to do so. They might also imagine that his long-term commitment to social justice would enable him to bring genuine peace and reconciliation to the citizens by addressing historic grievances through reconstruction. Meaningful acceptance of Chamorro, the kind that would signal commitment to a new governing regime, required that citizens not only acknowledge the respite from civil war and embargo that her election could bring. It required that they accept her longer-term governing vision as the better path for reconciliation and national reconstruction, doing so in the face of her governing inexperience.

14. On the critical role that a sense of deep dissatisfaction, injustice, and grievance can play in undermining citizen support for candidates, institutions, and regimes, see Tyler, Rasinski, and McGraw (1985). For evidence that the difficulties of regime transition can induce nostalgia for a previous regime, even one deemed totalitarian in nature, see Finifter and Mickiewicz (1992); Finifter (1996); and Miller, Reisinger, and Hesli (1996).

Our most direct evidence of citizens' attitudes toward the candidates' governing visions during the 1990 election is contained in the survey questions on candidate competence. The competence questions probe voter perceptions about which candidate could best end the war or address the economy. But they also include four questions probing citizens' perspectives on the candidates' abilities to bring peace and reconciliation and to build a better Nicaragua. Our concern is whether change occurred during the campaign on any of these questions that would point to a fundamental alteration or relearning of citizens' regime loyalties during the 1990 campaign. To address this concern and to gain a more precise understanding of the challenges facing the candidates as they sought to rally supporters, we reexamine the individual competence questions and subject them to more systematic and detailed scrutiny. In doing so, we will closely assess the changing patterns of class polarization on the questions, as presented in table 5.4.

Looking down the competence polarization scores for November, we see a striking difference in class response between the first three categories and the fourth. The new elite was divided at the outset over whether Ortega was more competent than Chamorro to end the wartime crisis, address the economy, or bring peace and reconciliation. Ortega's difficulty on these issues is seen in polarization scores for the new elite that fall below −.10 on all six of the relevant questions. In other words, the new elite could not even reach a 55–45 percent split in his behalf on these items. In contrast, the masses and the old elite appeared relatively sure that she would do better than he on these issues. They polarized strongly toward her across all three categories, with polarization scores that exceeded .20 on each of the six questions. In standardized terms, the masses and old elite exceeded a 60–40 percent split in support of Chamorro on each question.

On the fourth category, who would build a better Nicaragua, the confidence of the new elite in Ortega was substantially higher. Their polarization scores in his behalf were three to four times larger than on the first three categories, approximating .18 to .20 on the two relevant questions. Simultaneously, the confidence of the masses and the old elite in Chamorro decreased on this issue, as seen in the drop in their polarization scores below .20 on the two questions. The contrasts in class response between the first three categories and the fourth, we believe, is a critical key to understanding the 1990 election and its implication for citizen learning.

The polarization patterns for November point to the central dilemma each campaign faced as the election period began. Ortega's strength among many citizens, particularly the new elite, lay in his historic commitment to the Sandinista vision of a new Nicaragua. The question was whether he

Table 5.4 Class Polarization on Individual Candidate Competence Questions by Month during the 1990 Presidential Campaign

Dimension, Question, and Candidate	November	February	% Change (Nov. minus Feb.)
I. Ending the wartime crisis			
End war			
New elite	−.038	−.221	.183
Others	.245	.303	.058
% difference	.283	.524	.241
End crisis			
New elite	−.050	−.228	.178
Others	.218	.315	.097
% difference	.268	.543	.275
II. Improving the economy			
Address economy			
New elite	−.095	−.228	.133
Others	.228	.328	.100
% difference	.323	.556	.233
Get foreign aid			
New elite	−.08	−.216	.136
Others	.28	.317	.037
% difference	.36	.533	.173
III. Bringing peace and reconciliation			
Bring peace			
New elite	−.079	−.24	.161
Others	.239	.30	.061
% difference	.318	.54	.222
Reconcile Nicaraguans			
New elite	−.080	−.24	.16
Others	.277	.30	.023
% difference	.357	.54	.183
IV. Building a better Nicaragua			
Rebuild the country			
New elite	−.203	−.242	.039
Others	.175	.306	.131
% difference	.378	.548	.170
Help people			
New elite	−.178	−.253	.075
Others	.189	.296	.107
% difference	.367	.549	.182

Source: DOXA nationwide monthly surveys in November 1989 and February 1990.
Notes: The scores in the first and second columns indicate the polarization on a candidate competence question within the specified group. "Others" combines the responses of the masses and the old elite into one category. Polarization is determined by subtracting the percentage of group members preferring Ortega on the item from the percentage of group members preferring Chamorro. A positive score indicates a preference for Chamorro, and a negative score indicates a preference for Ortega. The "% difference" score indicates the absolute difference in polarization tilt between the elite and other classes. The scores in the third column indicate the change in polarization from November to February. A positive number indicates an increase in polarization.

could overcome immediate obstacles such as war and embargo in order to realize that vision. Unfortunately, he faced such concerns not only among the masses, but among his own elite. The new elite tilted strongly toward the belief that Ortega could build a better Nicaragua, should he have a real opportunity to do so. But early on they doubted whether he could solve the short-term problems inhibiting his pursuit of the long-term vision.

With respect to Chamorro, her strength lay in a widespread belief that her election would lead the United States to end its hostilities toward Nicaragua. She gained additional support for her warm personality and family history, both of which suggested that she could foster peace and reconciliation within the nation once the war and embargo ended. Of greater concern was her ability to provide long-term leadership and a vision for national reconstruction. Even the masses and old elite who tilted toward her on the first three categories were considerably more divided on the fourth, as seen in her lower polarization scores for them on these questions.

As the election progressed, each campaign generated considerable attitudinal movement on its behalf, thereby addressing its core dilemma. However, the movement Ortega generated among the new elite meant something quite different from the movement Chamorro produced among the masses and old elite.

As evidenced by the February polarization scores, Ortega successfully redressed doubts among his elite supporters about his immediate problem-solving capacities, convincing them he could end the war, improve the economy, and bring reconciliation. He did not generate as much support on those items as Chamorro generated within her base. Yet his ability to generate substantial opinion shifts across these six core questions was impressive, particularly in view of continuing U.S. hostility and his October missteps. He moved the new elite from a standardized divide of 53.5 percent to 46.5 percent in November, averaged across these six questions, to a 61.5 percent to 38.5 percent divide in February. Yet he was not seeking to change core beliefs of the new elite, only to convince them to remain true to those beliefs. He was asking them to continue to prioritize the Sandinista long-term vision of social reconstruction and, in doing so, to give him the benefit of the doubt about his short-term problem-solving capacities. In the process, he was generating attitudinal reinforcement, bringing short-term transitory and strategic assessments in line with long-term political principles.

By contrast, Chamorro convinced a large proportion of the masses and old elite to embrace her vision for Nicaragua and to trust that she could pursue it effectively. Between November and February the polarization toward her among the masses and old elite increased more in the category of building a better Nicaragua than on any other topic. She moved the masses and old elite, as a group, from a 59/41 percent split in her behalf on these questions in November to a 65/35 percent preference for her on these questions in February. In doing so, she was generating a substantial shift within the voting population, given that the masses and old elite constituted roughly two-thirds of the electorate. Moreover, she appeared to be generating this shift amidst a lower-class population that had embraced Ortega in the 1984 election, had been the primary intended beneficiary of the social restructuring his government had pursued, and had long been thought by observers to be "true believers" in the Sandinista cause.

Simultaneously, Ortega's campaign solidified the belief among the new elite in his vision and capacities for reconstruction. In November the new elite had tilted toward him across these two questions, on average, by a 59/41 percent split. In February, they tilted toward him by a 62/38 percent division. As a result, at the end of the campaign the polarized division between the new elite and the other two classes was greater for this category of competence concerns than for any other. On the issue of which candidate could build a better Nicaragua, a larger percentage of the new elite was polarized against a larger percentage of the masses and old elite than on any other concern.

The growing polarization of the masses and old elite toward Chamorro on the issue of building a better Nicaragua would seem to point toward a substantial change in the political beliefs of Nicaragua's poor majority. However, the polarization scores in table 5.4 combine results for the old elite and masses, so that the results there could be misleading when used to make inferences about polarization among the masses as a separate group. In addition, we are making our inferences about class views of the candidate best able to build a better Nicaragua based on averaging the polarization scores for two separate questions—which candidate could rebuild the country and which candidate would help the people. It is possible that different citizens within each class group were preferring a candidate on each question, so that there was far less class support for that candidate on the two questions in combination than seems to be the case based on such averages.

To clarify the extent of polarization among the separate classes on this issue, we have constructed a new set of class polarization scores. In doing so we have created a new measure—competence to build a better Nicaragua— by assessing how an interviewee answered both questions listed under this heading in table 5.4. Citizens are counted as signaling a preference for Chamorro or Ortega only if they give one candidate or the other a positive assessment on both questions. In other words, an interviewee is treated as seeing a candidate as "competent to build a better Nicaragua" only if the

respondent agrees that the candidate will be better at "rebuilding the country" *and* at "helping the people." We then construct our class polarization
scores by subtracting the percentage of citizens within a class whose combined scores on the two questions favored Ortega from the percentage of citizens within the class whose combined scores favored Chamorro. A negative
score indicates a tilt toward Ortega on the overall issue of building a better
Nicaragua; a positive score indicates a tilt to Chamorro. The results are
striking, especially for the masses.

Across the 1990 campaign, the polarization of the masses toward
Chamorro on the issue of building a better Nicaragua increased by 15.1 percent—more than doubling from 14.3 percent in November to 29.4 percent
in February. Since the masses constituted a majority of the electorate, this
percentage change among them translated into shifts among tens of thou-
sands of citizens. In standardized terms, they moved from a 57 percent to 43
percent tilt for Chamorro over Ortega on this issue early on to an approximately 65 percent to 35 percent tilt toward her two weeks prior to the election. Simultaneously, polarization toward Ortega among the new elite grew
by 5.8 percent, increasing from – 18.6 percent in November to –24.4 percent
in February. And the polarization of the old elite toward Chamorro
increased by 16.1 percent, from 18.8 percent in November to 34.9 percent in
February.

Given the support that mass citizens had given the FSLN in 1984, and
through insurrection in 1979, their movement toward Chamorro and away
from Ortega on the issue of building a better Nicaragua must be considered a
remarkable development in the contemporary history of Nicaragua. While
we lack individual-level panel data for verification, it seems relatively certain
from the size of the shift involved that she was persuading a substantial segment of the mass citizenry to engage in transformative attitudinal change,
going against their historic loyalties and principles and embracing new ones.
This decision could not have been made lightly. Yet by the end of the 1990
campaign these lower-class citizens were tilting strongly toward Chamorro
on the issue of building a better Nicaragua, preparing to take the nation's
future into their own hands.

Simultaneously, similar shifts toward Chamorro occurred among women
(whose polarization tilt toward her on this issue more than doubled across
the campaign) and among older citizens (whose tilt toward her increased by
an astounding 31.6 percent). With these shifts, more happened in 1990 than
a decision to elect a candidate who would end the war and embargo. The
most vulnerable of Nicaragua's citizens—the poor, women, and older voters—considered the longer-term direction of the nation and determined that

Chamorro's offer of democratic conservatism appeared the more promising long-term path. At this critical moment of choice in Nicaragua's history, much of the support base whose loyalty had been essential to the Sandinistas' rise and governing legitimacy now saw Chamorro's proposed neoconservative regime as the preferable strategy for building a better Nicaragua, thereby justifying a move beyond the revolutionary government that had come to power in their name. They reasoned to this position, moreover, by concluding that she would be better at rebuilding the country and would help the people more than would Ortega.

Conclusion

Clearly, Nicaraguans took their electoral responsibility seriously during the 1990 campaign, closely assessing the candidates and the context confronting them. At campaign outset, uncertainty existed as to how they would ultimately evaluate the situation, with that uncertainty reflected in high nonresponse on overall candidate competence, the economic future, and regime performance. By campaign end, however, voters had well-developed differentiated attitudes toward both candidates, the economy, and the regime. Such firm attitudes demonstrated extensive retrospective and prospective reflection. For the new elite, these attitudes tended to crystallize in response to the Panama invasion, which polarized them toward Ortega. The attitudes of the masses, pointing them toward Chamorro, developed more steadily, month by month, like a snowball rolling slowly forward and gaining size with each roll. And for the old elite, the campaign evoked a struggle between their attraction to Chamorro's conservative economic policies and their doubts about her capacity to govern. That competence struggle resolved itself only in February, when they tilted strongly in her direction.

In citizen responses to the candidates, economy, and regime, we see an earnest yet conflicted electorate, struggling to act responsibly and make the right choice. There can be little doubt that many voters appreciated Ortega and the Sandinista regime. The retrospective image scores testify to that, revealing respect and affection for him even in the midst of national crisis. In light of the severe situation, his selection by a third or more of the February interviewees on questions about future direction shows support for him and for the revolution that observers must recognize and respect. Even under assault from the United States and confronted by Ortega's own mistakes, a sizable bloc of citizens wanted to stay the course.

Yet ultimately the election was neither about appreciation of Ortega nor about the ideals his regime represented and the material improvements it had produced. It was not about gratitude for ending Somocista dictatorship or respect for courage in holding the United States at bay. It was about where the nation should go now, in 1990. To be responsible, this judgment had to be made both in light of such accomplishments and failures and in recognition of Nicaragua's realities in the hemisphere and the world at large. It also had to reflect a clearheaded assessment of the character, governing competence, and promise of the candidates and their regime offers. As the citizens who had to live with the consequences of these assessments made their judgments, they increasingly tilted toward Chamorro and democratic conservatism. This was especially true of the people living closest to the edge and who had the most to lose by making a mistake.

As citizens entered the last campaign weeks, armed with attitudes and preferences rather than guns and bullets, the critical issue was which attitudes would most shape their vote choice, thereby determining not only a president and regime but the meaning of the election itself. At issue was not just whether citizens would vote for Ortega and the FSLN or for Chamorro and democratic conservatism. Equally if not more important was *why* they would vote as they did. Would they make a responsible choice, grounded in a serious process of reflective reasoning? And would the reasons that guided them generate a sense of commitment and loyalty to the eventual winner and regime? Or would those reasons serve only momentarily to end electoral stalemate and governing crisis without pointing toward a future path? We can address such questions by looking at the process of vote choice.

Chapter 6

The Voters Are Not Fools: Modeling
the 1990 Presidential Election

Responsible decision making and citizen choice exist when the attitudes and beliefs of attentive citizens shape their vote decision. This perspective on voting, foreshadowed in V. O. Key's classic study *The Responsible Electorate*, was developed into a systematic strategy of empirical inquiry by Morris Fiorina. According to Fiorina, analysis of public opinion surveys taken during or immediately following an election provides a way to determine whether citizens' attitudes have shaped vote decision making. Weak and illogical statistical associations between citizens' attitudes and their reported vote intent suggest limited reasoning as voters make their decision; strong and internally consistent statistical associations point toward reasoned choice.

This strategy provides a more systematic, empirically grounded, and detached way of evaluating voting behavior than relying on whether the vote outcome accords with political preferences or interpretive biases of observers. The question is not whether citizens voted for the "right" candidate from the analyst's perspective. It is whether citizens voted in ways that appear reasoned and sensible *within their own* context and perspective. Evidence of a close, logical association between attitudes and vote intent makes a strong case for the presence of a cognitive process of reasoning through which citizens reached a vote decision. Moreover, examination of statistical associations between attitudes and vote intent can then help clarify the nature of the reasoning process, enabling analysts to ascertain whether citizens were primarily thinking retrospectively or prospectively and whether they were focusing on candidates, the economy, the regime, or some combination of these. It also helps illuminate how voter reasoning evolved across a campaign, whether the process varied among citizens along dimensions such as education or class, and the precise concerns that mattered most to citizens in their final vote intent.

This chapter examines the relationship between citizen attitudes and vote intent in order to assess the extent to which reasoned, responsible vote choice occurred during the 1990 election and to clarify the nature of such decision making. In doing so, it seeks to give clear voice to the reasoning the citizens employed as they approached their difficult, momentous decision about regime direction. We then seek to understand how that reasoning process helped generate the historic shifts in group voting that occurred during the election.

The Vote Choice Model: 1990

In examining the relationship between attitudes and vote intent, we seek to identify the statistical models that best represent the reasoning of the electorate in 1990. Our *dependent variable*, vote intent, is categorical in nature, meaning that voters chose between two different vote options rather than among a range of options on an ordered scale. Thus the models use logistic regression to test for statistical associations. The models seek to determine which attitudes best predict vote intent rather than to explain variance around a mean, the traditional goal of regression analysis of ordinal or interval data. In constructing our dependent variable, we score Ortega as the outcome to be predicted and thus as zero. Votes for Chamorro or the minor parties are combined into an opposition category and coded as 1. The *independent variables* are the seven attitudinal foci presented in chapter 5. These gauge the retrospective and prospective concerns citizens considered as they made a vote choice.

The focus on predicting a vote for Ortega comes from the factual reality that most observers expected him to win. Understanding why citizens voted for or against Ortega is the central issue in the 1990 election. Additionally, Ortega is the one constant candidate we have across all three elections of 1990, 1996, and 2001, as well as in 1984. Using an Ortega vote as the predicted outcome creates continuity and comparability across elections. This is similar to the routine use of the Democratic presidential vote as the predicted outcome in the study of U.S. elections.

Table 6.1 presents the expected relationship between each attitudinal variable and vote intent. The one surprise may be the alternative prediction listed for future economic assessments. Analysts generally believe that voters who see an economy about to improve will reward the incumbent. This is our first-listed expectation. But in the unique circumstances of Nicaragua in 1990, an alternative expectation is possible. Many citizens anticipated a Chamorro win *and* that her election would improve the economy. They may have been more likely to support her precisely because they anticipated that

Table 6.1   Dependent and Independent Variables

I. Dependent Variables: Vote Intent: O = Ortega; I = Chamorro/Opposition

II. Independent Variables: All significant in bivariate model (.0000 level): November survey

A. Chamorro's image
Coded: from 0=no positive image assessments to 6 = six + positive assessments
Expected Relationship: Positive—Low Chamorro image (0) likely to yield Ortega vote (0)
83.3% Prediction Success in November Survey
Coefficient = .7494

B. Ortega's image
Coded same as for Chamorro
Expected Relationship: Negative—Low Ortega image (0) likely to yield Chamorro
vote (1)
85.95% Prediction Success
Coefficient = −1.2331

C. Candidate competence
Coded: −1 = Chamorro; 0 = Ambivalent; 1 = Ortega
Expected Relationship: Negative—Seeing Chamorro as competent (−1) likely to yield
Chamorro vote (1)
86.84% Prediction Success
Coefficient = −3.6012

D. Current economy: *previous 12 months*
Coded: 1 = Better; 2 = Same; 3 = Worse
Expected Relationship: Positive—Seeing Better (1) likely to yield a vote for Ortega (0)
80.37% Prediction Success
Coefficient = 1.9023

E. Future economy: *next twelve months*
Coded: 1 = Better; 2 = Same; 3 = Worse
Expected Relationship: Positive—Seeing economy as likely to get better (1) should
yield vote for incumbent Ortega (0)
Alternative Relationship: "anticipatory/reinforcement effect": Negative—Expecting
Chamorro to win and improve economy, thus voting for her
72.5% Prediction Success
Coefficient = .5999

F. Regime performance
Coded: Country better off before (=1) or after (=2) revolution
Expected Relationship: Negative—Seeing the country as better before the revolution
(1) should lead to a vote for Chamorro (1)
85.02% Prediction Success
Coefficient = −3.4868

G. Regime direction
Coded: Country on a good path = 1 or on a bad path = 2
Expected Relationship: Positive—Seeing the country on a good path (1) should be an
affirmation of the nation's regime direction and lead to a vote for Ortega (0)
82.16% Prediction Success
Coefficient = 1.5083

her imminent election would improve the economy. Such anticipatory reinforcement may well have existed among some who expected Ortega to win
and improve the economy. But there were far more citizens holding such
expectations of Chamorro, so their countervailing anticipation may have
proved stronger. Under such conditions, a negative relationship would exist
between a future economic improvement and the vote for Ortega.

Aside from future economic direction, the expected relationship between
each variable and vote intent is straightforward, once the coding of each variable is accounted for. Logistic regression requires that the predicted outcome
be scored zero, with the alternative as 1. As a result, certain natural modes of
coding, such as having Ortega's score increase from one to six as citizens give
him a higher image rating, produce a negative sign in the relationship between
his image and a vote for him. In this case, as in certain others, the negative sign
indicates that an increase in the variable produces an expected increase in the
predicted outcome. We provide this table to make clear the theoretical meaning associated with each sign.

Table 6.1 indicates that the expected relationship between each variable and
vote intent does exist in the November survey. The likelihood that a citizen will
vote for Ortega increases with a low image of Chamorro, a high image of
Ortega, an assessment of Ortega as the more competent candidate, positive
assessments of the current economy and its future direction, and positive evaluations of the current regime's performance and its future direction. Moreover,
the predictive success of each separate variable is notable, with all except "future
economy" ranging above the 80 percent level. The critical question in modeling vote choice, however, is not the relationship between separate variables and
vote intent, but how they perform in a multivariate model to predict vote outcome. Once all are taken into account, some variables will prove statistically significant and important in shaping vote; others will appear less so or not at all.

The combination of influential variables that emerge within a statistical
model will indicate the attitudes that most shaped voters' decision making at
a specific point in time and thereby clarify the retrospective, prospective, or
reflective character of their reasoning. The predictive success enjoyed by
a combination of variables likewise serves as a useful indicator of how well
citizen attitudes are shaping the overall process of vote choice. Across surveys during an election campaign the variables that best model vote choice
may shift, indicating changes in the nature of voter reasoning, and the predictive success of models may increase or decrease in ways that alert us to the
changing power of voter reasoning in shaping overall vote intent. Analyzing
surveys across time thus allows us to see whether voters become more retrospective, prospective, or broadly reflective, to determine whether assess-

ments of candidates, the economy, or the regime become more or less central, and to ascertain how well a particular model of reasoning accounts for the vote intent across all citizens. To explore these and related issues, we model the relationship between citizen attitudes and vote intent for each of DOXA's five surveys from November through February.

Modeling Vote Choice across Time

Table 6.2 presents the multivariate model for each survey. It separates out the first and second wave of December interviews in order to examine the effect of the Panama invasion on voter reasoning. The models demonstrate that Nicaraguans drew extensively on their attitudinal assessments as they reasoned to a vote choice. As the predictive success of each model indicates, the independent variables account for more than 94 percent of the vote decisions in every survey taken by DOXA during the 1990 campaign. This is a high level of predictive accuracy. In addition, accuracy generally improves month by month. The high and improving rate of accuracy points strongly to citizen choice as the explanation of the vote and away from arguments stressing randomness, emotional reaction, or intimidation. Moreover, the patterning of the multivariate relationship between attitudes and vote reinforces the case for citizen choice.

The five statistical models demonstrate that voters reflected across retrospective and prospective considerations throughout the campaign as they shaped their vote intent. They also took into account all three dimensions—candidate assessments, economic evaluations, and regime choice. We see this by looking at the variables that proved statistically significant for each model. The significant variables were the ones that best "modeled" citizen decision processes for a particular survey. Each attitudinal variable played a role in citizens' reasoning at some point during the campaign. In addition, in every situation where a variable is significant, the relationship is in the predicted direction, except for future economic assessments. "Anticipatory reinforcement" accounts for the latter pattern.[1]

1. The role of anticipatory reinforcement in Nicaragua in 1990 is similar to the finding of Dominguez and McCann (1996, 107) for the 1988 presidential election in Mexico: "We conclude, therefore, that Mexicans did not plan to vote in terms of general retrospective or general prospective assessments of the economy or their finances, or in terms of specific economic policy issues. Instead, they focused on a particular kind of prospective judgment: the connection between the future of the 'party of the state' and the impact of its fate on the future of the economy." This focus led to support of the incumbent party.

The difference between the 1988 Mexican election and the 1990 election in Nicaragua was that in the former voters were considering the incumbent to be the party of the state, whereas in Nicaragua mass voters were considering the challenger to be the 'prospective' party of the state. In both cases the expectation that the economy would improve with the party's anticipated election reinforced a vote for the party.

Table 6.2 Modeling Vote Choice in the 1990 Presidential Campaign, by Month: Retrospective and Prospective Evaluations of Candidates, the Economy, and the Regime

Survey	November 1989	December 1989 (early)	December 1989 (late)	January 1990	February 1990
Chamorro's image	.0955	.091	.4094***	.4149	.1265
	(.1243)	(.077)	(.1398)	(.1748)	(.1561)
Ortega's image	-.5735****	-.279***	-.4234***	-1.0180****	-1.0273**
	(.1507)	(.092)	(.1634)	(.3100)	(.4061)
Candidate competence	-2.6832****	-1.8078****	-2.4364****	-2.0200****	-3.1816****
	(.4740)	(.323)	(.5383)	(.4043)	(.5931)
Current economy	.6101	-.118	.0021	.2809	.9254**
	(.4210)	(.153)	(.3375)	(.5546)	(.4377)
Future economy	-.1432	-.256*	-.1226	-.6514**	-.6530**
	(.2122)	(.155)	(.2273)	(.3084)	(.2892)
Regime performance	-.8233	-.336	-2.3602****	-2.5039	-1.9191***
	(.5557)	(.445)	(.5938)	(.8770)	(.7134)
Regime direction	.5189**	.863****	.9388***	1.3676***	.9642***
	(.2709)	(.199)	(.3088)	(.4212)	(.3168)
Constant	1.2674	.007	2.6189*	5.1927**	5.8178**
	(1.9116)	(1.166)	(1.5633)	(2.5620)	(2.5640)
N	404	619	690	792	859
Chi square	413.485****	588.834****	830.502****	959.400****	1057.282****
Predictive strength	94.55%	94.5%	97.39%	98.11%	97.79%

Source: DOXA nationwide monthly surveys during the 1990 presidential campaign.
Note: The table utilizes logistic regression analysis. Entries are maximum likelihood coefficients. Standard errors are in parenthesis.
****p < .001 ***p < .01 **p < .05 *p < .1

Our concern, however, is not just to determine that retrospective and prospective attitudes mattered in shaping voter intent in 1990, but to determine when and how such variables mattered. This determination allows us to clarify the precise nature and evolving character of the reasoning processes that underlay citizens' shifting vote preferences during the campaign. Did citizens start in a broadly reflective manner, using both retrospective and prospective concerns to shape vote intent? Did they become increasingly retrospective or prospective as the campaign proceeded? Was their attention to candidates, the economy, and regime constant across the campaign, or did the mix of these concerns shift as citizens contemplated their vote intent month by month? Were there dramatic changes in reasoning during the campaign, such as notable alterations between the second and third surveys in response to the U.S. invasion of Panama in mid-December?

Most critically, we are particularly concerned to specify the pattern of reasoning that shaped citizens' final vote intent at campaign's end. As they prepared to go to the polls in the weeks prior to the February election, were citizens thinking primarily or exclusively in a retrospective, a prospective, or a broadly reflective manner? And at this critical juncture in Nicaraguan history, did they seem truly attentive to the daunting issues of regime assessment and choice that confronted them, or were they focused on candidate attributes and the economy?

We can address these issues by looking at the pattern of voter reasoning that occurred survey by survey across the four months. In doing so, we gain greater depth in our understanding of the 1990 campaign, augmenting the analysis presented in chapter 3. In particular, we can account in a more systematic manner for the month-by-month swings in candidate support and specify with some considerable precision the factors voters were weighing most heavily as they prepared to vote in February.

Voter Reasoning across Time

Voters began the campaign in November by shaping candidate preferences according to their retrospective image of Ortega and their prospective comparison of the governing competence of Ortega and Chamorro. They also gave weight to their perception of the regime's future direction. These patterns indicate that much of the citizenry was already engaged in close and thoughtful assessment of the choices at hand. Moreover, these early patterns point to the kind of reflective reasoning that we expect among citizens in a developing context like Nicaragua's in 1990. In such situations, retrospection about the incumbent clearly matters, but cannot be probed too extensively until voters determine whether a real choice exists. Determining whether a real choice exists requires prospective evaluation of candidate competence. It is also aided by assessing whether the regime direction looks good or bad, since that assessment helps the voters determine how closely to assess the challenger's governing competence.

In November 1989 voters clearly believed that the future would be difficult under the current regime, as we saw in chapter 5. Reflecting on this awareness, they began to look seriously at Chamorro. As they did so, they discovered positive dimensions to her prospective governing competence that helped offset her political inexperience. This discovery made for a competitive race, with citizens concluding that Chamorro was a viable alternative to Ortega. Taking into consideration retrospective assessment of the incumbent, the future direction of the current regime, and the comparative competence of the two candidates, citizens reasoned to a 5 percent vote margin in behalf of Chamorro over Ortega in November.

Once it was clear to voters that the challenger was sufficiently viable to generate a meaningful contest and that the prospective context under the incumbent regime was problematic, the voters broadened the factors they considered. In December, prior to the Panama invasion, they continued to look at Ortega's image, candidate competence, and regime direction, and also considered the direction of the economy. Thus three prospective factors emerged as significant influences on vote intent, together with incumbent image. Citizens' focus on them in early December generated a 4-point drop in Ortega's vote support and a 2-point increase in Chamorro's support, so that her 5-point November lead increased to 11 points. It appeared that the election was rolling toward a Chamorro landslide.

Following the U.S. invasion of Panama, Nicaraguans remembered Ortega's leadership and courage in standing up to Somoza and the United States. An expanded version of retrospection suddenly dominated voter decision. Three retrospective and two prospective considerations loomed large at this point. Voters looked not only at Ortega's image, governing competence, and regime direction but also at Chamorro's image and regime performance. Economic direction receded into the background. This shift toward retrospection reversed the emerging collapse of Ortega's support and generated a substantial increase in response levels on vote intent. Instead of being routed, Ortega experienced an increase of 7 percentage points, while Chamorro's support remained virtually unchanged, and the minor parties increased by 3 percentage points. December ended with a 5-point margin of Chamorro over Ortega, signaling the return of a close and competitive race.

The late December surge toward Ortega proved short-lived, as did the focus on retrospection. Perhaps in response to the momentum toward Ortega created by the Panama invasion, which raised the prospect that he might win, voters again emphasized prospective considerations in January. Three prospective variables and one retrospective variable appear decisive in shaping vote intent. These considerations mirrored the early December model and produced a decline in Ortega's vote and a jump in support for the opposition, with Chamorro's margin increasing to 9.7 percent.

The campaign ended with voters balancing three retrospective and three prospective concerns. They looked backward at Ortega's performance, the economy's performance, and regime performance and forward at the candidates' future governing competence, the economic future, and regime direction. These concerns generated an additional increase of 4.6 percentage points in Ortega's support and 5 percentage points for the opposition. The final results point toward a substantial Chamorro victory, with her leading by more than 8 percent. This forecast is based on a model that predicts more than 97 percent of all vote decisions, indicating a well-developed reasoning process amidst the electorate.

An Overview Assessment

Across the campaign, citizen reasoning processes moved from a simple consideration of three concerns to a complex reflection across six. This move from simplicity to complexity is precisely the pattern we expect among a highly engaged citizenry facing an intense campaign and the prospect of regime change. With this growing complexity came increased predictive accuracy over the simple three-variable model of November. Additionally, in contrasting the maximum likelihood coefficients for February with those from November, we see that the effect of the independent variables on vote intent increased across the four months. A change in one unit of measurement in each independent variable produced a greater change in the dependent variable in February than in November.

Three concerns were continuously present in the vote models: the incumbent's image, the comparison of the candidates' governing competence, and regime direction. The continuing presence of these three variables highlights the major decision at the center of citizen choice: whether to stay with the experienced incumbent and his regime, with all the problems that implied for the future, or to bet on the governing competence of an inexperienced challenger. These variables also underscore the extent to which this was an election about the future more than the past. However much citizens may have despised Somoza, however patriotic and brave they may have considered Ortega, and however much they may have supported the revolution and subsequent reforms, the issue at the heart of the election was not whether to affirm the revolution of 1979 or the revolutionaries. Assumedly that had been done in 1984. Now the pressing issue was where the country was going in 1990.

To underscore the extent to which the election was future oriented, let us note that two of the three attitudinal variables continuously present in each vote model are prospective in nature. One of these, notably, was regime direction. Far more than economic direction, this concern encompassed the broad future of the nation and made clear that citizens were concerned not just with a particular program or one dimension of governance but with the political order itself. The other prospective variable, governing competence, also focused on where the country was likely to go in the future. In fact, it is the variable that reached the highest level of statistical significance in each vote model.

These results indicate that Nicaraguans were reflecting broadly across the vital issues confronting them and in doing so were incorporating prospection into their decision. This was not just an unhappy electorate throwing the rascals out based on poor past performance. These were voters who were thinking about the shape of the future, considering who best could lead the country and voting accordingly. Or were they?

Refining the Vote Choice Models

The close association between attitudes and vote creates a presumption of responsible choice by Nicaragua's electorate in 1990. It suggests that at this critical moment, Nicaraguans considered not only retrospective performance but also whether the alternative candidates were competent to govern, given the conditions of the country. Such prospective assessment is critical in a nation where opposition politicians and parties have so little prior governing experience: voters must be especially attentive to such challengers' competence before throwing the incumbent out. And it is critical for voters to be attentive in this way when their choice entails not simply a change in politicians, parties, and programs but also a change in regime.

However, demonstration of a statistical association between competence and vote intent does not demonstrate that citizens voting for change were attentive to long-term governing competence. Strong statistical association can exist between competence and vote intent even if long-term capacity to reconstruct Nicaragua did not generate that association. Instead, voters may have focused on immediate crisis resolution, with that concern driving the statistical relationship between competence and vote. Similarly, the citizens most responsible for regime change may not have been the ones most concerned with competence and most engaged in thoughtful, reflective, complex reasoning. Citizens in general may have looked sober and sensible in the reasoning through which they decided their vote, while regime change was generated by the least thoughtful and responsible among them. To get a more precise sense of what the voters were stressing in candidate competence, and to clarify the reasoning of different groups of citizens, let us turn to some refinements in the vote models.

Reasoning about the Future: Crisis Resolution or National Reconstruction?

Our first concern relates to how deeply citizens were thinking about the future as they made their vote choice. Two alternative scenarios exist. It is possible, as one scenario, that citizens were focused primarily on the immediate benefit that Chamorro's election might bring in convincing the United States to cease military and economic hostilities. In this case, citizens would be taking responsibility for deposing Ortega and the Sandinista regime through conscious vote choice, installing Chamorro as a strategic way to end the crisis. But they would be taking responsibility for little else, simply giving Chamorro's regime a chance to rise or fall based on whether or not the good times rolled, once American hostilities ceased.

Alternatively, it is possible that citizens were looking to the longer-term challenges of the nation and concluding that Chamorro and her proposed regime genuinely offered a more promising governing approach than did Ortega and the FSLN. In this scenario, voters would be making judgments—perhaps rightly, perhaps wrongly, depending on the observer's perspective—about which candidate and regime offered the most viable, attractive long-term future path. In voting based on this consideration, citizens would be taking responsibility for the nation's future direction, responsibility that could carry with it some degree of psychological commitment to the new president and regime. This deeper form of "future thinking" would point to responsible voting of a more sophisticated nature, capable of laying the foundation for a stable and legitimate new regime.

The most direct way of probing the future thinking of voters is to determine whether it was immediate crisis resolution or longer-term reconstruction that played the more decisive role in shaping the relationship between competence assessments and vote choice. To do so, we can divide our questions about candidate competence according to which of these two dimensions they tap into or best reflect, using them to create two new competence variables along the lines discussed in our construction of the Overall Candidate Competence Index in chapter 5. Citizens' assessments of candidate competence at *crisis resolution* can be estimated by combining their answers to the four questions focused on ending the wartime crisis and improving the economy. Their assessments of candidate competence at *national reconstruction* can be estimated by combining their answers to the four questions focused on bringing peace and reconciliation and building a better Nicaragua.

When we develop a simple two-variable model of vote choice for each of our 1990 surveys utilizing these two competence dimensions, we find that voter assessments of candidate competence at national reconstruction performs substantially better than does competence at crisis resolution. The national reconstruction dimension is statistically significant (at the >.001 level) in each of the five models, with crisis resolution significant—at a lower level—only in the two December models. Moreover, the maximum likelihood coefficients for the national reconstruction dimension are quite strong in each model (reaching −1.409 in the final model, with a .222 standard error). The predictive strength of these two-variable models is also impressive, ranging above 91 percent in each survey.

Citizens gave more consideration month by month to the long-term reconstruction of Nicaragua than to the immediate issues of the war and economy. Solving the immediate crisis was important. But from start to finish, the decisive concern appears to have been competence at reconstruction.

This conclusion is reinforced when we incorporate the two competence dimensions into our overall analysis of vote choice in table 6.3. This table provides several alternative ways to examine the effect of competence within our multivariate analysis for February. In model 1, we use nine variables, adding the reconstruction and crisis resolution variables to our earlier seven-variable model presented in table 6.2. These nine variables predict 98.1 percent of the cases, with national reconstruction being the one competence variable that is significant, along with the other five variables that were also significant for February in table 6.2. Models 2 and 3 give the multivariate results when we drop Chamorro's image, which repeatedly failed to reach statistical significance, and utilize our measures of the two separate dimensions of competence, searching for the "best fit" model. As the results indicate, national reconstruction (model 3) continues to produce the strongest overall results in terms of predicting cases, accounting for 97.9 percent. In addition, the maximum likelihood coefficient for national reconstruction (− .959) indicates that it had a greater effect on vote intent than did competence at crisis resolution (with a coefficient of −.724, as seen in model 2). This is a powerful finding since both of these variables are scaled in precisely the same manner. In contrast, when we utilize the overall candidate competence variable in a similar six-variable model, excluding Chamorro's image, it does more poorly than either of these two dimensions, predicting 97.5 percent of the cases. Our "best fit" model is thus the one utilizing candidate competence at national reconstruction (model 3).

The electorate as a whole gave primary concern to a candidate's competence at national reconstruction as it shaped its final vote choice, rather than to overall competence or competence at crisis resolution. This finding strengthens the case for responsible vote choice, indicating that the electorate as a whole was genuinely attentive to the long-term implications of the vote decision. But was this concern evident among those most responsible

Table 6.3   Modeling Vote Choice for President in February 1990 Using Different Measures of Candidate Competence

	Model 1	Model 2	Model 3
Chamorro's image	.084		
	(.159)		
Ortega's image	−.898**	−.968***	−.882**
	(.414)	(.337)	(.346)
Current economy	1.039**	.854**)	.901**
	(.470)	(.411)	(.442)
Future economy	−.741**	−.407*	−.558**
	(.343)	(.236)	(.276)
Regime performance	−1.631**	−2.170****	−1.947***
	(.727)	(.598)	(.652)
Regime direction	1.312****	1.172****	1.319****
	(.374)	(.288)	(.328)
Competence overall	1.401		
	(1.990)		
Competence at crisis	.131	−.724****	
	(.424)	(.111)	
Competence at reconstruction	−1.499***		−.959****
	(.467)		(.148)
Constant	4.711*	5.297**	4.894**
	(2.683)		(2.385)
N	859	904	904
Chi square	1071.723****	1108.472****	1125.748****
Predictive strength	98.1%	97.8%	97.9%

Source: DOXA nationwide survey in February 1990.
Note: The table utilizes logistic regression analysis. Entries are maximum likelihood coefficients. Standard errors are in parenthesis.
****$p < .001$ ***$p < .01$ **$p < .05$ *$p < .1$

for generating regime change, who—as we know from the opening discussion of chapter 4—came predominately from the masses? Because the masses tended to be composed of less-educated citizens who should find it difficult to make complex, reflective vote decisions, this is a serious issue. The state of crisis in Nicaragua certainly gave these less-advantaged citizens an incentive to push themselves and engage in reflective decision making. But were they able to do so? Did limited education inhibit their capacity for reflective reasoning and long-term regime assessment?

In light of the importance of this concern, both in understanding vote choice in Nicaragua and in assessing the potential for complex and prospective reasoning among less-educated citizens worldwide, let us compare vote choice models for the educated and less-educated citizens of Nicaragua to see how detrimental limited education was to voter reasoning. Were the less educated able to engage in complex reasoning and also embrace long-term prospective voting, thereby positioning the common citizens of Nicaragua to grapple in a responsible manner with the momentous choice facing them?

Vote Choice among the Educated versus Less Educated

To examine whether educational level influenced citizens in reaching their vote choice, we divide our survey data for November and February according to whether respondents were more or less educated. In doing so, we combine formal education and professional occupation to estimate education level. The result is one pool of respondents who appear, by Nicaraguan standards, to be better educated and another pool composed of individuals with less education. The *more educated* are those who have gone beyond high school. This includes citizens with technical, secretarial, and similar training, those with some college training, or those who have a professional occupation that would provide on-the-job training. The *less educated* are those with a high school education or less who do not have a professional occupation. Of these, about 72 percent had a sixth-grade education or less. This distinction between the more and less educated divides the interviewees roughly in half.

Our concern in contrasting citizens of differing educational levels is to clarify whether their reasoning processes during the 1990 election differed and, if so, what the implications of those differences are for interpreting vote choice. Responsible vote choice would seem to require that the less educated engaged in prospective as well as retrospective voting, since they constituted the demographic groups most responsible for Chamorro's election. By contrast, the better educated were more supportive of Ortega, in significant degree because they composed much of the new Sandinista elite, so that they could have given more consideration to retrospection. However, these expectations fly in the face of theoretical expectations derived from voting studies in established democracies. Those expectations, presented most compellingly by Sniderman, Brody, and Tetlock, suggest that the limited cognitive capacities of the less educated make it difficult for them to engage in prospective reasoning, though in highly intense campaigns they may do so. Yet, even when they do, their reasoning process should be less complex and prospective than that of the more educated.

We agree with the general arguments about the role of cognition put forward by Sniderman, Brody, and Tetlock and acknowledge that better-educated voters may reflect more naturally and rapidly across retrospective and prospective concerns than the less educated. But, as with Fiorina and Key, we see citizens as having self-conscious concerns with self-interest that also impact their reasoning. Strong concern with the effect of an election on personal interests can lead the less educated to put special energy into vote choice. In doing so, if they have sufficient time and information, they can overcome cognitive limits and make complex assessments even in difficult conditions. Moreover, the less educated may have self-interested concerns that make a vote decision critical to them—concerns related to the difficulties that attend the impoverished life that often characterizes limited education. Such concerns can even lead them to be more attentive to prospection than better-educated and more affluent citizens, should the self-interest considerations of the latter lead them to rely on retrospective satisfaction with an incumbent.

This is not to understate the impact that cognitive capacity has on citizens' reasoning capacities. It is quite likely that the less educated will move more slowly in their reasoning processes, particularly in circumstances requiring complex reflection. Some among them, particularly the least educated, may be so overwhelmed by difficult choices that they withdraw from electoral engagement.[2] As a result, a dual process of vote decision making may characterize electorates: a faster and more inclusive process for the better educated; a slower and somewhat less inclusive process for the less educated. In addition, the character of the reasoning seen in these dual processes may differ among more- and less-educated citizens, as Sniderman and his colleagues argue. We suggest, however, that such differences can result not only from the contrasting cognitive capacities of educated and less-educated

---

2. This expectation is supported by Wolfinger and Rosenstone's (1980, 13-36) demonstration that formal education is the most important variable shaping turnout. See also Abramson, Aldrich, and Rohde (2002, 77–91).

citizens, which would lead the latter to be less prospective, but also from different patterns of self-interest linked to life circumstances.

Because the less educated respond not only to their own cognitive limits but to self-interest, the potential exists for them to rise to the occasion in severe circumstances and employ a complex and reflective process of reasoning. Moreover, such processes can involve the sort of prospective assessments that would seem necessary for third world citizens to change governments and regimes through responsible vote choice. By contrast, better-educated citizens, particularly if heavily benefiting from the existing government, might find it in their self-interest to affirm the government and its performance in office, relying more fully than the less educated on retrospection. A dual process of reasoning and choice thus could exist across the better-and less-educated citizens, with the latter slower in their reasoning processes but also, when self-interest demands, more prone to prospection than the former.

Initial evidence of a dual process of vote choice in the 1990 Nicaraguan election is seen in the fact that the less educated moved more slowly than the better educated in making their vote choice. In November nonresponse on vote intent was 56 percent among illiterates, 30.6 percent among citizens with a high school education or less, and 24.5 percent among those with training beyond high school. By February, nonresponse had fallen among all groups but still varied in direct relation to education: 41.1 percent among illiterates; 16.8 percent among those with some primary education; 10.9 percent for those with some junior or high school education;10.8 percent for those with some university education; and 9.5 percent among those with technical or professional training. Looking at our measure of education based on formal training and professional occupation, we see that in November nonresponse was 38.2 percent among the less educated and 24.9 percent among the better educated. In February it had declined to 21.1 percent and 9.4 percent, respectively. The less educated thus do appear to move more slowly toward vote choice. Nevertheless, as election day approached, 80 percent had reached a decision, except among illiterates. The critical issue is whether and how their reasoning differed from that of the educated.

Table 6.4 presents our "best fit" models of the multivariate relationship between the attitudinal variables and vote intent for the separate educational groups in November and February. In these models we utilize the reconstruction dimension to estimate candidate competence because it (again) consistently performed better for both the educated and less-educated voters than did the overall candidate competence variable or the crisis resolution variable. We also drop from the models those variables that were statistically insignificant. The resulting patterns indicate that, early in the campaign, both the less educated and more educated were engaged in reflecting across retrospective and prospective concerns. Yet as one might expect early in a campaign, the less educated did have a simpler reasoning process that looked solely at Ortega's image and the candidates' competence at reconstructing the nation, whereas the more educated had a slightly more complex process that also included assessment of regime direction. However, by the end the less educated were employing a reasoning process that was at least as complex as that of the more educated and more focused on prospection. In February the less educated drew significantly on all three prospective concerns: the future direction of the economy, regime direction, and candidate competence at national reconstruction. They also drew on one retrospective concern: assessment of regime performance. The better educated drew on two prospective concerns: candidate competence at reconstruction and regime direction. To these they added two retrospective concerns: their image of Ortega and retrospective assessment of the economy.

Table 6.4   Modeling Vote Choice for President in November 1989 and February 1990: Contrasts between the Better Educated and Less Educated Voters

	The Better Educated		The Less Educated	
	November	February	November	February
Chamorro's image				
Ortega's image	−.639****	−.916**	−.977****	
	(.158)	(.440)	(.272)	
Current economy		1.639**		
		(.639)		
Future economy				−.959**
				(.421)
Regime performance				−2.752***
				(.940)
Regime direction	.669**	1.562****		1.673****
	(.294)	(.380)		(.474)
Competence at	−.832****	−.972****	−.840****	−1.456****
reconstruction	(.125)	(.190)	(.142)	(.334)
Constant	1.771*	−1.097	5.243****	4.522**
	(1.058)	(3.023)	(1.499)	(1.995)
N	273	510	231	434
Chi square	290.676****	650.565****	227.650****	473.941****
Predictive strength	95.6%	97.8%	95.2%	97.5%

Source: DOXA nationwide surveys in November 1989 and February 1990.
Note: The table utilizes logistic regression analysis. Entries are maximum likelihood coefficients. Standard errors are in parenthesis.
****$p < .001$ ***$p < .01$ **$p < .05$ *$p < .1$

These results indicate that the less educated were reasoning prospectively as they shaped their vote choice during the 1990 election, and that, in doing so, they were considering which candidate could best reconstruct Nicaragua. Poor education did not deter citizens from engaging in complex, reflective, future-oriented thinking during the campaign. It is thus reasonable to expect that the mass citizens most responsible for Chamorro's election and Nicaragua's regime change were engaged in reflective reasoning and responsible vote choice as they set the nation on a new path, despite the poor education most had received. But is this expectation actually borne out by close assessment of vote choice patterns? After all, while education is a reasonable surrogate for class, it is not an exact one. Given the importance of class voting to our interpretation of the 1990 election, it is important that we look at the reasoning processes of the classes in a more precise and concentrated manner. In addition, to assess the dominance of class voting in 1990, and to gauge the complexity of the vote decision that year, it is important to compare the influence of class on vote choice with the influence of other demographic characteristics, particularly gender and age.

To clarify group voting patterns, we turn now to the evolution of vote choice among social groups, focused primarily but not exclusively on social class. Our first concern will be to compare the voting patterns of class, age, and gender groups in the 1990 election and assess the changing influence that these demographic characteristics had on vote intent during the campaign. This discussion will highlight the importance of class in shaping the 1990 vote, in contrast to age and gender. Our second concern will be to examine the processes of reasoning that the social classes employed as they reached their vote decisions in 1990. We will do so by comparing the reasoning processes employed by elites, as a group, with the reasoning processes employed by the masses. In this comparison, we will give special attention to how and why the mass citizens who constituted the bulk of the nation's voters, and who provided Chamorro with her landslide victory, chose her as president, thereby setting regime change in motion.

Demographic Modeling and Vote Choice: Class, Gender, and Age in the 1990 Election

Central to demographic analysis of elections is the effect of social class on voting behavior.[3] This is particularly true in nations, like Nicaragua, with

---

3. For research demonstrating the critical influence of class on voting behavior in established democracies, see Weatherford (1978) and Lijphart (1971).

histories of class conflict. In such societies, with deeply embedded and politicized class structures, individual interests tend to be shaped by the expectations, opportunities, and hurdles associated with class. Self-interest is thus linked to class interest, with changes in class opportunities and resources directly affecting individuals. As a result, a nation's class structure often determines the broad outlines of its partisan arrangements, and class association tends to shape individual partisan loyalties. Socialist parties capture the loyalty of the masses, whereas parties of the right draw the loyalty of the middle classes and elite.

However, as Adam Przeworski and John Sprague remind us, class is not the only dimension of social and political life.[4] A range of other social associations can shape self-interest and personal perspective on politics, cutting across class alignments and reducing the influence of class on politics. It is for this reason that working-class and socialist parties, which, as representatives of the majority of citizens, would seem destined to dominate politics in many societies, are in actuality seldom able to emerge as majority parties or to sustain majority status. This failure of working-class and socialist parties owes also to circumstances that convince the lower classes that their historic party has lost sight of their interests, as many appeared to believe in Nicaragua in 1990.

Depending on a nation's social composition, history, and momentary circumstance, factors aside from class that can shape citizens' political perspectives include age, gender, race, ethnicity, religion, and urban or rural location. In chapter 5 two such variables were salient in shaping attitudes in 1990, as seen in the discussion of group polarization on candidate competence. Respondent age proved critical because it captured differences in generational experiences. Older citizens had direct experience with the Somoza regime, with those 45 or older living much of their lives during the dictatorship. Those in midlife, age 25-44 by Nicaraguan standards, had experienced the Revolution of 1979 as a major formative event during their teenage or early adult years. And those aged 16-24 had come of age during the revolutionary era itself, an era of great promise and popular empowerment, and had often benefited from its strong support for education. Older citizens, coming of age before the FSLN had initiated its support for education, were

---

4. Przeworski and Sprague (1986). The literature on the numerous social forces that shape citizens' approach to politics is voluminous. See, for example, Alford (1963); Lipset (1960, 1981); Michelat and Simon (1975, 1977); Sarlvik (1969); and Dalton (2002). For evidence about the continuing power of such demographic factors in American presidential politics and relevant discussion of the burgeoning literature across the United States and other democracies, see Abramson, Aldrich, and Rohde (2002, esp. chap. 5).

less likely to have received the kinds of educational opportunities enjoyed by the young and also were less likely to have received the political socialization that went with it.

Similarly, gender emerged as an important factor in 1990. Women were more likely to have been responsible for the family household because men were involved in military service or political action and because a large number of men were killed during the revolution and Contra War. As a result, women faced the daily household hardship that came with scarcity during the insurrection and the Sandinista era. In contrast, the men who survived the revolution and its aftermath tended to be less involved with families and more oriented outward toward political activism, military service, and revolutionary reform. Additionally, given the traditional character of Nicaraguan society, women were less likely to have received advanced education or to obtain professional jobs than men. Finally, despite their rhetoric and best intentions, the Sandinistas were less successful in addressing the gender inequalities that existed in Nicaragua than they were in addressing general social and economic inequalities.[5] Like socialists everywhere, the Sandinistas saw class exploitation but were often blind to the gender exploitation within the household or workplace perpetrated by men who, within the class system, were themselves victims.[6] This failure to address gender exploitation was felt most keenly by older women who had families and jobs, while younger women, still of university age, were as yet less affected by such dynamics. As a result, men and women even of the same class background could have experienced the Sandinista years quite differently, particularly among the older age groups, and therefore could vote differently in the choice between Ortega and Chamorro. Let us turn now to determine how the social groups voted.

1990 Demographics and Vote Intent

Table 6.5 presents vote intention by our three salient demographic groups in February 1990. As they prepared to go to the polls, women greatly preferred Chamorro, doing so by a 16 percent margin, while men slightly preferred Ortega by about 1.5 points (well within the survey's 3 percent margin of error). Women thus voted more conservatively than men. This finding

---

5. Isbester (2001). Despite gender inequities under Sandinismo, there were women who became committed revolutionaries. For an examination of these women and their subsequent involvement in the democratic transition, see Luciak (2001).

6. Przeworski and Sprague (1986, esp. 440).

reverses what we know about electorates in older democracies, where the gender gap finds women voting for the left and men for the right.[7] Moreover, women's conservative tilt had a dramatic impact on the election. Chamorro might well have lost the election narrowly had suffrage been male only, while Ortega would have suffered a massive defeat had the suffrage been only female.

In contrast to gender, the finding for age follows patterns evident in established democracies, with the oldest citizens voting more conservatively—giving Chamorro a 33 percent vote margin over Ortega—and the youngest being more leftist in orientation.[8] The strong rightward tilt of the older voters reflected their desire for the normalization of Nicaragua after more than a decade of revolution, social restructuring, and domestic turmoil. The slight leftward tilt of the young undoubtedly reflected a mix of normal youthful idealism and personal self-interest, with the latter owing to the free education provided them by the Sandinistas. In fact, close examination of the data indicates that the move of the young leftward was pronounced not only

Table 6.5   Vote Intention by Age, Gender, and Class Groups in February 1990 Survey (%)

	UNO	FSLN	Minor parties	Nonresponse	Total
Age					
16–24	37.6	42.2	5.0	15.2	100
25–34	44.4	32.7	10.1	12.8	100
35–44	41.7	29.8	12.0	16.5	100
> 44	51.4	18.6	13.6	16.4	100
Gender					
Men	37.7	39.3	9.7	13.3	100
Women	45.7	29.3	8.5	16.5	100
Class					
New elites	30.3	56.2	6.2	7.3	100
Masses	47.4	21.9	9.9	20.8	100
Old elites	58.8	21.3	15.0	4.9	100

Source: DOXA nationwide survey in February 1990.
Note: $N = 1,198$ for age, with 2 of the 1,200 original interviewees refusing to give age. $N = 1,200$ for gender. $N = 1,187$ for class, with class designations missing for 13 of the original 1,200 interviewees.

7. For more extensive discussion of women and participation, and some caveats, see Conway, Steuernagel, and Ahern (1997); Klein (1984); Gilens (1988); Glenn (1974); Inglehart (1977, 1994); and Burns, Schlozman, and Verba (2001).

8. Glenn (1974); Inglehart (1977, 1994). In contrast to earlier studies, some more recent work on age and the vote in the United States finds that the youngest voters may be the most conservative. See Abramson, Aldrich, and Rohde (1994, 1998, 1999).

for men but also particularly among women.[9] This tendency almost certainly was reinforced if not propelled by the fact that student benefits, especially government university benefits, went to both men and women, providing a special incentive for young woman as well as young men to vote Sandinista. The youngest voters thus would have reelected Ortega by a 5 percent margin, whereas all other age groups preferred Chamorro.

Finally, class vote intention patterns reversed historic expectations, with the masses voting conservatively, while only the new elite supported Ortega. Thus the masses gave Chamorro a 25 percent vote margin over Ortega while the old elite gave her a 37 percent margin. In contrast, the new elite voted for Ortega over Chamorro by a 26 percent margin. This polarization of the classes in their voting patterns parallels results reported in chapter 5, where the masses and old elite polarized in support of Chamorro on image and competence grounds and questioned the past performance and future direction of the existing regime, while the new elite moved in the opposite direction. Clearly, Chamorro's support lay with the masses and old elite, while Ortega's lay with the new elite.

These patterns demonstrate that social factors helped shape citizens' final vote intent. But did these patterns emerge during the campaign, possibly provoked by the Panama invasion, or were they there from the outset? To clarify this issue we can examine class voting across time.

Class Vote Intent Patterns across Time

Figure 6.1 explores the evolution of class vote intention during the 1990 campaign by looking at shifts in the polarized vote support across our five surveys. The figure presents the polarized vote margin for each class when we subtract its aggregate support for Chamorro from its support for Ortega. A positive score indicates Ortega's margin over Chamorro, while a negative score indicates the reverse. The scores indicate the vote margin between the incumbent and his primary competitor, ignoring the minor parties.

---

9. Thus when we break down the vote intent data by age and gender for DOXA's February 1990 survey, both the young men and the young women provided Ortega his strongest support within the two gender categories. Among men, the vote for Ortega versus Chamorro was 45.6 percent to 33.2 percent among those under 25; 38.5 percent to 38.2 percent among those from age 25 to age 44; and 17 percent versus 54 percent among men 45 or older. Among women the vote for Ortega versus Chamorro was 38.6 percent to 41.9 percent among those under 25; 21.2 percent to 41.2 percent among those 25 to 44; and 19.5 percent to 50 percent among those 45 or over. These percentages are based on totals that include nonrespondents and those supporting minor parties.

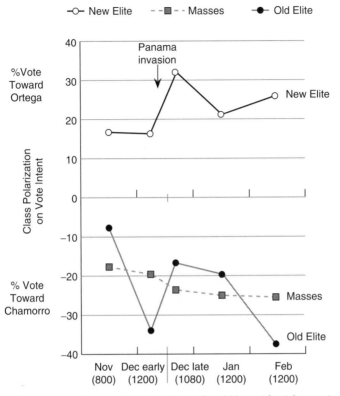

Figure 6.1 Class polarization on vote intent during the 1990 presidential campaign, by month

Source: DOXA nationwide monthly surveys.

Notes: Class polarization is determined by subtracting the percentage of class members intending to vote for Chamorro from the percentage intending to vote for Ortega. A positive percentage indicates the % tilt toward Ortega. A negative percentage indicates the % tilt toward Chamorro.

As the survey results in figure 6.1 indicate, Ortega enjoyed plurality support only from the new elite as the campaign began in November. Chamorro already had substantial plurality support from the masses and old elite. The opposition to Ortega from the masses was not a move that came late in the campaign but was present early on. In fact, Ortega at this early point actually had more support from the old elite than from the masses, a reflection of the qualms about Chamorro that the old elite brought to the campaign. As the masses' preferred candidate, Chamorro already looked poised for a surprising upset. Yet neither Ortega nor the opposition had majority support from any class, as demonstrated in chapter 3, and nearly a third of interviewees were undecided.

With the high level of indecision about vote intent in November, Ortega had an opportunity to rebound, rally the masses, and surge past Chamorro. Instead, as citizens approached election day in February, the masses and old elite still supported Chamorro, while the new elite preferred Ortega. The primary difference in class voting between November and February is that each class supported its preferred candidate at a much higher level at the end of the campaign than at the outset. Clearly, the primary effect of the campaign was to reinforce the initial candidate preferences of the three classes. The critical question is how this reinforcement occurred, whether it seemed to come through a gradual decision process or in response to a critical event such as the Panama invasion. The answer to this question differs for the two campaigns.

With respect to Ortega, the increase in his polarized class support during the campaign followed the U.S. invasion of Panama. During the first two months of the campaign, prior to the invasion, his support was stagnant or declining across all classes. He suffered a slight decrease of 1 percent or so among the new elite between the November and early December surveys, a 26 percent decrease among the old elite, and a 2 percent decrease among the masses.

After the invasion, the masses continued their move away from Ortega and toward Chamorro. In contrast, both the new elite and the old elite reversed course and shifted dramatically toward him. The sudden increase in Ortega's elite support following the invasion, a jump of 15.3 percent among the new elite and 17.3 percent among the old, served to reverse the stagnation and decline in their support for him early on. He consolidated most of this increased support among the former, but in the end lost the latter. Nevertheless, the invasion was a pivotal moment for Ortega, jump-starting his campaign among the new elite and giving him an opportunity among the old.

In contrast to Ortega, the evolution of Chamorro's support among the masses, her primary base, appeared relatively unaffected by the Panama invasion. After increasing by 2 percentage points in early December, her margin among the masses increased by 4 percentage points following the invasion, by 2 more percentage points in January, and then held constant. Chamorro's increase in mass support appeared gradual and continuous across the campaign, stalling only in the last month. The masses were already clearly polarized toward her in November, and were continuing to move in her direction in early December. More rapid movement occurred toward her in late December following the invasion and continued into January. Overall this movement was consistent with a process of growing polarization in her behalf evident in the campaign's first month, a polarization seen not only in vote intent but in assessments of her image and competence presented in chapter 5.

The reinforcement of Chamorro's mass support during the campaign appeared to result from a process of steady movement toward her, the sort of movement consistent with the effort of a poor and less-educated citizenry to grapple with difficult choices and reach a painful, final decision. Already well in motion prior to the invasion, the polarized tilt of the masses toward her was not induced by the Panama invasion but continued despite the furor it caused. The reinforcement of Ortega's support among the new elite did appear to result, at least in part, from a dramatic event-driven moment of recognition and reassessment, with the invasion reminding Ortega's elite base of the regime's historic purpose. His growing assertiveness in January undoubtedly aided his consolidation of this support. Finally, the reaffirmation in February of the old elite's initial polarization toward Chamorro came despite their early doubts about her governing competence, doubts momentarily fueled by the invasion.

In the end, the classes tilted in February in the same partisan direction evident in November, only more so. Yet class association did not totally determine citizens' vote choice, as each class included a substantial bloc that voted against its preferred candidate. To determine how strongly class shaped the evolution of vote intent, and the role that age and gender played in dividing the classes, we model the relationship between these three variables and vote intent across the campaign.

Modeling the Vote Demographics

Table 6.6 presents demographic models of vote intent for age, gender, and class across the five 1990 surveys. We expect a positive relationship between each variable and vote intent, such that being young, male, and a member of the new elite should yield support for Ortega. We do not expect the high predictive success in the demographic models that were found in the attitudinal models, since the latter examine the relationship between distinctly personal and salient perceptions and individual vote intent, whereas these models examine the extent to which vote intent was shaped by citizens' group characteristics, which may or may not be personally salient. Nevertheless, demographic modeling can help us gauge whether a group association did tend to shape vote intent, pointing to the shared experience and concerns that may have led groups of citizens to tilt one way or another in attitudes and vote.

As table 6.6 indicates, class had the most continuous and dominant

Table 6.6 Modeling Vote Choice in the 1990 Presidential Campaign by Month Using Demographic Variables

	November	Early December	Late December	January	February
Age	.226*	-.023	.046	.110	.228***
	(.089)	(.076)	(.072)	(.069)	(.068)
Gender	.098	-.029	.053	-.251*	.361***
	(.181)	(.153)	(.150)	(.141)	(.135)
Class	.590****	1.003****	1.239****	.919****	.805*****
	(.156)	(.147)	(.148)	(.136)	(.127)
Constant	-1.297***	-1.091***	-1.864*****	-1.599****	-1.938*****
	(.381)	(.331)	(.318)	(.302)	(.288)
N	533	798	849	952	1017
Chi square	29.896****	55.590****	94.326****	71.755****	99.292*****
% predicted	61.5%	66.9%	70.1%	67.7%	67.6%

Source: DOXA nationwide monthly surveys during the 1990 presidential campaign.

Notes: For this analysis Age is scored according to the four levels presented in table 6.5, where the category 16–24 is 1 and >44 is 4. Gender is scored with 1 for male and 2 for female. Class is scored with the new elite as 1, masses as 2, and old elite as 3. The table utilizes logistic regression analysis. Entries are maximum likelihood coefficients. Standard errors are in parenthesis.

****p < .001 *** p < .01 **p < .05 *p < .1

influence on vote intent. It was statistically significant in each survey and was the sole variable shaping vote intent in the two December surveys. The size of the maximum likelihood coefficients indicates that class had its greatest effect in late December, immediately after the Panama invasion, when the new elite surged toward Ortega while the masses continued to move toward Chamorro and the opposition. Prior to the invasion, the only other variable that was significant was age, which did shape vote intent in November. This was before Chamorro's attacks on Ortega for failing to end the war momentarily weakened his support among the young.

After the invasion, age and gender as well as class reached statistical significance, doing so in ways that clarify final vote decisions. Following class polarization in late December, men tilted toward Ortega in January and women toward Chamorro. The men affirmed a past as revolutionary militants, while women reflected desire for a stable social structure wherein families could reconcile and prosper. Gender thus enters our model as statistically significant in the last two surveys. In February, within the class and gender groupings, generational experience produced additional refinement in vote decision. The young, imbued with hopefulness and self-interest, moved toward Ortega. Older citizens, reflecting on life in a more stable era, moved to Chamorro. Age is thus statistically significant for the last survey prior to the election, along with class and gender.

While class remained central throughout the campaign, age and gender influenced how citizens reasoned as election day approached and helped determine which members of each class tilted left or right. This points to an increasingly refined process of individual reasoning as the campaign progressed, with voters taking into account an increased range of group-based concerns. This process accords with the expectations presented in chapter 4, according to which an intense campaign, particularly one that engages citizens in prospective voting, will lead them to look at the myriad of ways that a vote choice can affect their personal interests. In doing so, they assess the implications of a vote not just along general class lines, but according to specialized implications for a citizen's gender concerns, age-based concerns, and so forth. Such assessments will then generate complex patterns of group-specific voting, as clearly happened in the intense and future-oriented election of 1990 in Nicaragua.

Nevertheless, the results in table 6.6 make clear that class was the most persistent and significant demographic characteristic that shaped vote choice. This finding thus underscores our emphasis on class in our interpretation of the 1990 election and the need to look closely at the reasoning processes whereby the classes reached their vote choice in behalf of Ortega or Chamorro.

We have detailed already the reasoning process of the more educated and less educated, with those results pointing to the prospect that the masses as well as the elite engaged in a thoughtful and future-oriented decision process as they reached their vote intent, but we hesitate to rely solely on that analysis as our indicator of class reasoning. There is considerable overlap between the masses and less educated, and between the elites and better educated, but the overlay is not perfect. The better educated constituted approximately 90 percent of the elite and the less educated roughly 75–80 percent of the masses. With the slippage between education level and class, it is possible that class reasoning varied in distinct ways from those associated with education.

To determine precisely how the masses reasoned to their vote intent across the campaign, in contrast to the elite, we can compare the vote choice models for the masses in November and February with the analogous models for the elite. In making these comparisons, we combine the new and old elite into one group, since they were the mirror images of each other: the new elite voting as expected for Ortega and the old as expected for Chamorro. In contrast, the bulk of the masses were voting for Chamorro and regime change, against historic expectations. It is the contrast between elite groups voting as historical loyalties would predict and the vast majority of the masses voting against their historic alignment that has so puzzled observers, leading many to question the authenticity of the vote outcome. What were the considerations that led the masses to abandon historic ties, whereas the elite voted true to form. Did the masses actually engage in a reasoned process of vote choice, and if so, what was that process?

Modeling Vote Choice for the Elites and Masses

Table 6.7 presents the best-fit models of vote choice for elites and masses in November and February. In these models, we determined which of the competence variables performed best when the other six attitudinal variables were also present. Then we removed the insignificant variables for that model and prepared the final best-fit models. The results are quite telling.

Despite significant overlap between the class groups and educational levels, the regression results for the classes are distinct from those presented earlier for education levels. The elite had a simpler reasoning process by which they reached a vote choice than did the more educated as a whole. The masses had a more complex reasoning process than did the less educated as a whole. There were also more pronounced differences in nature between the reasoning of the elite and that of mass citizens than there were between the reasoning of the better educated and that of the less educated.

Table 6.7 Modeling Vote Choice for President in November 1989 and February 1990: Contrasts between Elite and Mass Voters

	Elites		Masses	
	November	February	November	February
Chamorro's image				
Ortega's image	−.581****		−1.679***	−.889**
	(.166)		(.630)	(.889)
Current economy				
Future economy				−.973**
				(.402)
Regime performance		−3.796****		−2.206**
		(.865)		(.922)
Regime direction	.512*		.888***	1.689***
	(.302)		(.318)	(.504)
Competence overall		−3.832****	−2.836****	
		(.537)	(.613)	
Competence at crisis resolution				
Competence at reconstruction	−.868****			−1.165****
	(.139)			(.262)
Constant	1.671	5.378****	7.741**	7.373***
	(1.109)	(1.112)	(3.579)	(2.390)
N	238	429	256	491
Chi square	247.138****	524.701****	247.017****	526.475****
Predictive strength	95.0%	97.7%	94.9%	97.8%

Source: DOXA nationwide surveys in November 1989 and February 1990.
Notes: The "elites" category combines the Sandinista "new elites" with the traditional "old elites." The table utilizes logistic regression analysis. Entries are maximum likelihood coefficients. Standard errors are in parenthesis.
****$p < .001$ *** $p < .01$ **$p < .05$ *$p < .1$

The elite began by reflecting across one retrospective and two prospective concerns and ended by concentrating on one retrospective and one prospective concern. Early on, as a group composed largely of new elite members committed to the Sandinista vision, they focused on which candidate could best reconstruct the country and on Ortega's record. They also focused on the future direction of the country. A significant plurality chose Ortega based on this reasoning.

By the end of the campaign, following Ortega's efforts to reassure the elite that he could solve the immediate crisis as well as reconstruct the nation, the one prospective concern that guided this group was overall candidate competence. In addition, perhaps because of the invasion, the elites' one retrospective concern was with whether or not the revolution was worth it, leaving Nicaragua better off than it had been under Somoza. Utilizing this concern as well as overall competence, 56 percent of the elite favored Ortega in February. The old elite naturally provided a bloc of dissidents within the elite. Nevertheless, the overall reasoning process looks like one we would expect of privileged citizens benefiting from the regime and prepared to stay with it.

The masses began the campaign focused on one retrospective concern and two prospective concerns. They ended attentive to two retrospective and three prospective concerns. Whereas the elite moved to a very simple reasoning process balancing one retrospective and one prospective concern, the masses moved by the end to a complex reasoning process with a future-oriented tilt.

Early on, the masses closely assessed the candidates' overall governing competence. In doing so, they had little doubt that Chamorro's election would resolve the immediate crisis. But they were less sure of her long-term capacities to reconstruct the nation. Thus they weighed the issue of crisis resolution versus national reconstruction. In addition, as with the elite, the masses looked closely at where the country was headed and at Ortega's past governing record. Mass citizens, utilizing this reasoning process, tilted by a significant plurality to Chamorro.

By campaign end, following Chamorro's aggressive efforts to challenge the adequacy of the Sandinista regime and present her own governing vision, the masses had come to concentrate on which candidate could best reconstruct the nation, more than on which could best resolve the nation's crisis. Prospectively, the masses also considered where the country was headed and its future economic prospects, with their anticipation of a Chamorro victory and better economic times reinforcing their support for her. Retrospectively, they considered Ortega's past record and whether the revolutionary government had really performed as it should have, against the backdrop of the pre-revolutionary era. Accounting for all of these factors, the bulk of the masses voted against Ortega and for Chamorro's regime change.

The choice of Chamorro over Ortega by the masses was based on a highly sophisticated and complex reasoning process that reflected across prospective as well as retrospective concerns, had a future-oriented tilt to it, and exceeded the complexity of the reasoning process whereby the elite chose to support Ortega. The reasoning process demonstrated by the masses as they reached their vote choice in 1990 must be considered impressive by any realistic standard of voter decision making and a considerable testament to the potential for poor and poorly educated citizens to participate in electoral politics in engaged, thoughtful, and responsible ways, particularly under conditions where they believe that their vote can make a true difference in their lives. Whether or not one agrees with the decision they made, respect is due for the process by which they made it.

Conclusion

With Chamorro's victory, Nicaragua moved into a new political era and began anew the process of constructing a viable governing regime. Within the context of the times, this transition looked less like a reactive counterrevolution designed to move Nicaragua back to Somoza-style authoritarianism and more like something new and proactive in its own right. Chamorro had promised not only to end the war and embargo, using her association with the United States to do so, but to move toward expanded civil liberties, national reconciliation, and a more formally democratic polity. And she had promised free market policies that would strengthen the economy while also showing concern for the people. Her vision was both conservative and democratic.

Her agenda was a challenging one whose success could not be guaranteed by the United States or any external force. Moreover, it was an agenda vague in details, with much of the substance yet to be specified. And it was an agenda that would be pursued within a relatively pluralistic and mobilized political setting by a government whose core justificatory principles of civil liberties and democratic process required respect for pluralism and power sharing. The nature of the new regime would be a constructed and contested one, not one preordained or imposed from above or outside. At issue was whether she and her supporters but also her Sandinista opponents could cooperate and realize the potential for healing that her regime offered.[10]

10. The difficulties the Chamorro regime confronted and limits on the ability of any actor to guarantee its success is evident in the essays in Walker (1997b) focused on the economy, agrarian reforms, and social policies. Chamorro also faced an additional irony: "In all, the democratic legacy of . . . Sandinista rule . . . was also reflected in the existence of a highly mobilized population with experience in grass-roots participation and little reticence about making demands. Accordingly and ironically, civilian rule in Nicaragua in the 1990s would be much more difficult than in other countries. Elsewhere, outgoing dictatorships and incoming opposition elites could negotiate transitions without being overly concerned with the interests of disadvantaged classes, the latter having been politically demobilized through years of government sponsored terror. In Nicaragua, however, the poor majority could not be ignored" (Walker 1997a, 15). This insured that neither Chamorro nor the United States could dictate the character of the new regime but that it would emerge from domestic political contestation, thereby making institutional politics and electoral processes critical aspects of regime crafting.

The election itself suggests that Nicaraguans were ready to face the test of a regime change. Chamorro had acted responsibly in offering both an end to crisis and a vision for the future. She and her regime had a blueprint for the future, vague in details but clear in its neoliberal and democratic parameters. Her offer of a new Nicaragua created a kind of contract with the citizens to which they could hold her accountable and on the basis of which she could call for their continuing support. Similarly, Ortega and the Sandinistas had acted responsibly in seeking to govern in a manner consistent with the broad socialist vision they had espoused in coming to power, by holding a fair and free election in which citizens could assess their performance and vision, and by honoring its outcome. In time, the Sandinistas' vital role in moving Nicaragua toward democracy would become clearer.[11] It was a role that had begun with the overthrow of a murderous dictatorship. It had continued through egalitarian social and economic reforms, institutionalized constitutional restructuring, a legitimizing election in 1984, and an electoral calendar. It now continued with a relinquishment of power in deference to popular will.

The responsible behavior of Chamorro and Ortega, while in no sense providing evidence of a cohesive, pacted elite guiding Nicaragua to democracy, underscores vital ways elite actors can contribute to democratization despite substantial elite conflict. They can do so, in particular, by offering distinctive, meaningful, and alternative visions to a nation's citizenry, by seeking to engage citizens in political participation in pursuit of one or the other vision, and by respecting voters' choice between the visions when that choice is clearly, freely, and responsibly expressed.

Finally, the people had acted responsibly in their role as democratic citizens. Resisting the entreaties of the left and right to join with them in civil war, the vast bulk of Nicaragua's citizens held out for a peaceful and democratic resolution of civil strife. At least as much as the international community, the citizens of Nicaragua forced the contending elites to move beyond bullets and to the ballot box to break the political stalemate and resolve national crisis. The citizens then engaged attentively in the election, assessed the candidates and context closely, reasoned thoughtfully to a vote choice, and voted for continuity or change with due consideration to long-term governing comparisons of the alternatives. Moreover, it was the lower-class citizens, poorly educated and thus often dismissed as incapable of responsible decision making, who appeared most reflective and future oriented as they reached their final vote choice and endorsed Violeta Chamorro as president.

11. Walker (1997a, 15); P. J. Williams (1994).

As Chamorro moved forward, a critical issue was how completely and for how long the masses who elected her would continue to stand with her. In supporting Chamorro, they had found wanting the future performance and promise of Ortega and the Sandinistas. They had broken with their history of revolutionary fervor and gambled on her promise and on their own judgment of her character and competence. Yet history had already shown them to be demanding of their leaders.

As both John Booth (1985) and Thomas Walker (1991a) have argued, the masses played critical roles both in social revolution and in the electoral legitimacy of Sandinismo. The new regime had responded to such mass support with egalitarian reforms that illustrated to citizens how potent their mobilized power could be. Yet despite these successes, or perhaps because of them, the masses held the Sandinistas to high standards, expecting both revolutionary change and a normalization of life. Nor were the bulk of them willing to excuse the Sandinistas by blaming the United States. They needed to believe that a stable, peaceful, reconstructed Nicaragua was possible, doubted Ortega could make that happen, and guessed that Chamorro could do better.

The Sandinista experience demonstrates, in ways reinforced by David Mayhew's analysis (2002) of U.S. politics, that partisan realignments are not won simply through mobilizing mass popular support at one or two critical moments in time, whether through bullets, ballots, or both. They must be continually re-earned through governing performance and sustained promise. New governing alignments usually fall prey to contingencies beyond leaders' control, to managerial failures, and to shifting public moods. A new regime can enjoy widespread support and fulfill its early promise, only to fall prey to new policy problems, expanding public expectations, and the normal shifts in citizens' issue focus, as documented by Bryan Jones.[12] It is thus a rare movement that solidifies its popular support, institutionalizes itself, and sustains its initial leaders and agendas across decades of dominance. Given the FSLN's massive early support, followed by sudden defeat, it was questionable whether Chamorro and democratic conservatism would do any better.

As with the Sandinistas in their heyday, Chamorro faced considerable elite dissension and turmoil while also enjoying goodwill and support from the people. Both through her prior life and in the campaign, she appeared to have earned their trust and confidence in her values and vision. In supporting her not only to remove the Sandinistas and end crisis but also to move

12. Bryan D. Jones (1994). See also Hirschman (1982); Stimson (1999); Carmines and Stimson (1989); and Green, Palmquist, and Schickler (2002, esp. chaps. 6 and 7).

toward a reconstructed nation, the masses appeared prepared to commit to a sustained experiment with the new regime, providing she could normalize national life. At the same time, in responding to her call for expanded liberties and democracy, citizens opted for a regime they and their revolutionary heroes, including Ortega, could help shape. They were giving Chamorro and democratic conservatism an opportunity to lead, not free rein to dictate the nation's future.

The immediate question was whether she would be as successful in reorienting the nation toward procedural democracy and neoliberal economics as the FSLN had been in inducing social reform and mass mobilization. The longer-term question was whether she and her successors could survive historical contingencies, their own mistakes, political challenges from the left, and public mood swings long enough and well enough to institutionalize democratic conservatism.

The story of the 1990 election thus did not end with Chamorro's inauguration. Instead, it entered a new phase as she and her regime took power. What the election had actually meant and whether it had generated a new, sustained alignment of governing forces depended now on how well the citizens had judged the candidates and context of 1990 and on the resilience and resources of leaders and followers alike. Had the election sufficiently engaged the citizens and elicited such genuine support for her regime offer that they would be attentive to Chamorro's performance in office and prepared to hold her accountable to her policy promises, should she waver from them? Were Chamorro and UNO competent to govern and reconstruct the nation, and also sufficiently committed democrats to respect the citizens and respond to them should citizens take issue with regime performance? Had the citizens embraced her vision enough to stand by her in hard times, if in fact she demonstrated good faith in efforts to fulfill her policy promise? Had Ortega and the Sandinistas learned enough from the 1980s and their 1990 defeat to behave constructively as loyal opposition, both challenging the regime to govern effectively and cooperating with it when national interest and social stability demanded? Finally, would Nicaragua move toward a governing regime more respectful of civil liberties, open to procedural and institutional democracy, and attentive to economic and geopolitical realities? And would it achieve this new maturity while retaining concern for the welfare of its citizens? This was the promise of the 1990 election. To what extent was that promise fulfilled?

PART III

Affirming the 1990 Choice:
The 1996 and 2001 Elections in Context

Chapter 7

The Post-1990 Context: Democratic Foundations and Public Choice

The 1990 election opened a new era in Nicaraguan politics. For the first time, Nicaraguans had embraced regime change through democratic elections, making a momentous shift from the radical socialism of Daniel Ortega to the democratic conservatism of Violeta Chamorro. Now at issue was how effective the nation's new leaders would be in ending the state of national crisis and instituting the new regime. Chamorro had won the election battle of 1990. Would the new regime govern sufficiently well to retain citizen approval and consolidate long-time voter support for democratic conservatism?

To explore this question we consider the governing effectiveness of the new regime, Ortega's spirited but unsuccessful challenges to rightist candidates in 1996 and 2001, and general citizen assessment of the conservative administrations as compared with the Sandinista regime. In doing so, we tell the story of the Chamorro years and highlight the democratic foundations that solidified during them.[1] We look closely at the 1996 election of Arnoldo Alemán and the fate of democracy under his administration, and evaluate the 2001 election of Enrique Bolaños. And we examine the comparative evaluations citizens offered of the revolutionary and postrevolutionary regimes, as they looked back across them following the 1996 and 2001 elections. Chapter 8 then examines citizen attitudes and vote choice in 1996 and 2001, considering the extent to which those electoral outcomes were also the result of citizen choice.

1. See also Close (1999) for an extensive assessment of the Chamorro years.

Delivering on Chamorro's Promise

The voters elected Chamorro president because they believed that she could end national crisis and move the nation forward democratically and programmatically in a more responsive manner than had come to characterize the Ortega government. Most critically, they trusted that she could pursue national reconstruction in an effective, ameliorative manner, bringing peace and reconciliation to Nicaragua's disparate factions and rebuilding the country into a more prosperous society and a more democratic polity. These prospective expectations proved particularly central to the vote decisions of the less-educated and poorer citizens who had historically formed the core of Sandinista support. Chamorro's capacity to establish a legitimate government depended on her ability to deliver on the promise that had elicited these prospective expectations.

Greatly to Chamorro's benefit and just as voters had expected, the United States ended its economic embargo as soon as she took office. She did not even need to negotiate the terms of the embargo's end. Such swift U.S. action illustrated how thoroughly the embargo had been aimed at the Sandinista regime. The United States then became an international donor for the new administration, although Chamorro did need to negotiate the new loans. Additionally, U.S. aid to the Contras also diminished and then ceased at Chamorro's continued urging.[2] Ending the war entirely, however, proved more difficult than ending the embargo.

Many Contras linked their willingness to demobilize to the return of family land that had been expropriated from them under the agrarian reform. When Chamorro indicated sympathy with that position, other Contras who had never owned land quickly linked their own demobilization and cooperation with the demand that they now receive land. Simultaneously, land reform beneficiaries defied the government to return their land to the rich or the opportunistic. Chamorro never fully resolved the issue of land. After alleviating the worst property conflict and slowly demobilizing the Contras, she turned most cases over to the courts. Some Contras received land and some Somocistas had their land returned, while some reform beneficiaries managed to hold onto what they had received during the Sandinista era. These very different individual experiences then generated conflicting regime and partisan loyalties within and across social classes. While managing a de facto end to the Contra War through such efforts, Chamorro left Nicaragua with deep, long-term divisions over land and with local tensions

---

2. Armony (1997).

that still periodically erupt in incidents of violence.[3] Ultimately Chamorro's UNO coalition disagreed within itself over the land issue, and it would become a central part of Alemán's agenda beginning in 1996.

Beyond ending the war, Chamorro also restructured the military. At the time of her election, the military was controlled by the Sandinistas and provided the strongest voting bloc favoring Ortega. Additionally, Humberto Ortega, Daniel's brother, was commander-in-chief of the armed forces. Humberto had powerful enemies among the Contras, within the new administration, and inside the United States. These groups pressured Chamorro to remove Humberto and downsize the military, simultaneously purging it of FSLN supporters and gaining conservative control over it. Chamorro yielded to some but not all of these pressures, creating another compromise surrounding the military. Within that compromise, she kept Humberto in place, indicating her appreciation of his strong support for her new government in the chaotic days of civil unrest in response to the austerity measures following the 1990 election. She did, however, reduce the size of the military. She did not systematically purge it of Sandinistas. Moreover, size reductions came gradually because Chamorro feared that fast, dramatic action would add more unemployed men to a labor market already saturated with demobilized Contras.

Chamorro's hardest task was economic reform. Like her land policy, her economic policies were controversial and met with considerable opposition. She began with the Plan Mayorga, named for her finance minister.[4] Its goals were to return property and stabilize the currency. The plan replaced the cordoba with the gold cordoba, pegged to the dollar and backed by the government. The plan devalued the currency by 100 percent without compensatory salary increases and included extensive government layoffs and increased utility fees. Simultaneously, the government moved to reduce state spending on social services drastically. Its goal in pursuing such neoliberal reforms, necessarily long term in nature, was to create a more fiscally responsible economic policy that could cut inflation, produce conditions conducive to private entrepreneurship and employment, generate sustainable economic growth, and foster a domestic consumer economy. Although the austere reforms designed to achieve these goals received strong support from external actors and financial institutions, their immediate effect was to exacerbate the domestic poverty that had reemerged in the final Sandinista years. The plan thus ignited extensive protest. The very citizens who had elected Chamorro moved to curb her policies once she was in power, with the masses

3. Jonakin (1996).
4. See "A Year of UNO Economic Policies: The Rich Get Richer," *Envio* (March 1991): 30–49.

uniting in mobilized opposition. Street fighting, strikes, and violence broke out nationwide. The country appeared poised for another civil war.[5]

The administration responded by moderating but not halting its reforms. In doing so, it worked with Sandinista leaders and elected officials who, while in the minority party, effectively pressured Chamorro to adopt less draconian measures. In deciding to respond to citizen protests and Sandinista entreaties, Chamorro demonstrated regard for the governing capital the mass citizens had accrued in so definitively supporting her election. They had trusted that she would pursue her reconstructionist agenda in a manner that fostered reconciliation and demonstrated concern for the common people of Nicaragua. Now they demanded that she be true to the caring image she had conveyed. Her failure to moderate at this critical moment would almost certainly have undermined mass belief that she truly cared about their long-term well-being and thereby would have crippled her ability to sustain their support and pursue regime consolidation. The willingness of key Sandinista leaders to support her during this period and facilitate her responsiveness was likewise critical to the maintenance of social stability and the contested crafting of the new regime.[6]

As the pace of Chamorro's reforms slowed and mobilized public opposition receded, the administration progressed toward economic stabilization. Inflation decreased from more than 13,000 percent in 1990 to 12.4 percent in 1994. The state role in the economy and employment was reduced to about one-third of its pre-1990 size, and state-owned industries were privatized. Chamorro also secured loans from bilateral and multilateral sources. Despite these developments, economic improvement came slowly. The GDP remained negative from 1991 to 1993, rising to 3.2 percent in 1994. Moreover, the austerity measures continued to take a toll on state services, funding for education, and employment.[7] The standard of living among

5. Stahler-Scholk (1995).

6. Robinson (2003, 71–86) provides a detailed discussion of the reforms of the Chamorro regime, arguing that it was continually forced to adapt its neoliberal agenda to mass popular sentiments and constraints, perhaps more so than was the case in any other Central American nation. See also Thorp (1998, 226–31). Similarly, in moving from a socialist government to a neoliberal, capitalist government, Mozambique also found it impossible to eliminate many aspects of the socialist government's interventionist policies such that the new economic program was a compromise with elements of the socialist past. See Pitcher (2002, chap. 1).

7. One of Chamorro's cost-cutting measures was decreasing state support for education. Her educational project included dismissing a large number of teachers, privatizing some aspects of education, and generally increasing cost and decreasing access. All of these are steps toward "nondemocratic" education. See Arrien (1991); Kampwirth (1997). For a discussion of democratic and nondemocratic reforms to education, see Gutmann (1987).

Nicaragua's poor majority plummeted, with rural privatization contributing to this decline.[8] Meanwhile external measures only gradually came to report improvement in Nicaragua's economic performance.[9]

Recalling Linz and Stepan's discussion of democratization, we see Nicaraguans struggling here with their own version of a dual transition. Citizens had chosen the Chamorro government and the regime it promised in part because they were tired of the socialist-managed economy in perpetual crisis and the never-ending conflict with the United States that socialism engendered. With the promises to end the war and embargo now delivered and the move to national economic reconstruction under way, Nicaraguans faced the long-term implications of their choice: the transition to a market economy and the loss of the Sandinista social safety net.

The result of Chamorro's reconstructionist policies was a return to class inequalities, with the poor again losing ground to more affluent groups. Yet despite problems and popular opposition, the Chamorro regime never lost its open, liberal democratic flexibility. In that gamble, as with their belief that she would end the embargo and war, the voters had been right about Chamorro. If they did not like her policies, at least they retained the political space for contestation against such policies. Perhaps for this reason, she herself remained popular and never became the object of widespread calls for removal from office. Such popularity could not be ascribed to other elements of her government.

Perhaps the most consequential result of the difficulties faced by Chamorro's government lay in increasingly negative assessments of UNO as a governing coalition, owing to its internal divisions. At least 40 percent of the public had seen it as highly factionalized even when UNO's positive assessments reached their highest point during the 1990 election. As the UNO government moved beyond the election to direct the ship of state, these divisions grew. As with any coalition of opposition, particularly one overriding historic animosities, UNO adherents had been better at denouncing the Sandinista regime than at agreeing on policy once they controlled the government.[10] In particular, tension grew between the president and vice-president the longer they were in office. Godoy and his Independent Liberal

---

8. Spoor (1994); Cupples (1992).

9. Banco Mundial (1993).

10. Godoy's disagreements with the Sandinistas, like Chamorro's, were fundamentally ideological but played themselves out over economic and revolutionary policy. The PLI supported capitalism and was opposed to socialism, including any economic restructuring that prioritized domestic poverty over economic productivity. See "Rebellion in the Ranks: Challenge from the Right," *Envío* (January–February 1991): 18–27.

Party (PLI) wanted free market policies and more austerity; Chamorro and the Conservatives wanted more moderate economic reform.[11]

Partisan tensions within UNO were exacerbated by an institutional lack of clarity about the political roles of Liberal and Conservative leaders within the coalition government. The constitution did not set clear responsibilities for the vice-president. Yet Godoy wanted an active role and proceeded to write his own job description. He proposed to help set land policy and resolve contradictory claims. He supported the claims of former Contras over those of agrarian reform beneficiaries and favored a decreasing Sandinista role in the military. But internal struggle centered primarily on the economic reforms. Godoy's extreme neoliberal policies were opposed by Conservative Party members of UNO. As a result, Conservatives marginalized Godoy, giving power to Chamorro family members, particularly Antonio Lacayo and Alfredo César, all Conservatives.

As the Chamorro years passed, the divisions between the Conservatives and Liberals within UNO returned to their historic intensity. By 1996, UNO was seen as a government of the Conservative Party, while the Liberals departed UNO to seek separate electoral fortunes. Godoy himself never became the heir to this Liberal separation. Toward the end of the Chamorro years, another Liberal, Arnoldo Alemán, assumed the Managua mayorship, thus giving the Liberal Party the strong political position they had lost with the marginalization of Godoy. In 1996 Alemán became the Liberal presidential candidate, running against both the Conservatives and the Sandinistas. This split within UNO helped ensure that the Chamorro regime failed to consolidate state control and thereby served to facilitate a continuing process of regime crafting through political contestation and negotiation. This open process served to aid democratization.

Democratic Foundations under Chamorro

Over the six years of Chamorro's presidency, Nicaragua moved to solidify the democratic foundations of space, class, and party that had come from history and strengthened during the revolutionary years. Political space, previously filled with secret resistance, social movements, revolution, and popular organization, now became more institutionalized. Traditional patterns of

---

11. See "UNO's Balance of Power: On a Tightrope," *Envío* (June 1990): 26–32, esp. 26–27; "Two Faces of UNO," *Envío* (July 1990): 24–37, esp. 30–31; "UNO Politics," *Envío* (August–September 1990): 26–30; "Rebellion in the Ranks: Challenge from the Right," *Envío* (January–February 1991): 18–27, esp. 18–21.

class interests resurfaced as the repercussions of UNO's policies clarified. Historic party divisions between Liberals and Conservatives reappeared, while reluctantly sharing space with Sandinismo. Although numerous smaller parties and party factions emerged and then disappeared, the three-way division of Liberals, Conservatives, and Sandinistas prevailed. The struggle for political preeminence proceeded among these three parties. With these developments we see the emergence of a new structure to Nicaraguan democracy.

Institutionalizing Political Space

During Chamorro's presidency, the political space for contestation and participation expanded to include a more meaningful role for democratic institutions. While such expansion may be an inevitable part of democratic development, it is not a process for which guidelines exist. Nor is it even, necessarily, a procedure of which participants are aware at the critical transition moments. The development of democratic state institutions can, therefore, be controversial and was in Nicaragua. Moreover, the struggle for a more institutionalized power balance was not only an effort at regime reform and state development. It was also an attempt to formalize and protect the ever-vulnerable space for pluralism that had emerged informally in past decades.

The move to broaden political space began almost immediately with Chamorro's election. From the outset she signaled her personal respect for Daniel Ortega, with whom she had worked in the provisional revolutionary government of 1979. She also made clear her acceptance of the Sandinista Party as a legitimate participant in national political life, rather than treating the FSLN as a defeated enemy, as many Contras and right-wing supporters would have preferred. Similarly, Ortega and the Sandinistas acknowledged Chamorro and her administration as the legitimately elected government, stepped down from power, and began a process of transition from a revolutionary government to a mass electoral party. These efforts by winners and losers in the 1990 election helped ensure genuine inclusiveness of opposing groups in democratic politics and an authentic contestation for power among alternative leaders and parties with diverse political agendas. In addition, despite widespread early protests against her land reforms and economic policies, Chamorro respected freedom of the press, freedom of speech, and citizen rights of petition and assembly. While Ortega and the FSLN had honored civil liberties more than Somoza had, Chamorro made respect for civil liberties a defining characteristic of her administration. Yet she was less supportive of state institutions representing popular opinion and the space for political contestation and dissent they provided.

Initial efforts to institutionalize political space came not from Chamorro's administration but from the opposition. Chamorro preferred to continue power concentration in the presidency and a family-based style of governance.[12] These old patterns of nondemocratic control dated back well before the Ortegas or Somozas to the era of traditional elite rule, when a few major families such as the Chamorros dominated national political life. The opposition pushed, instead, for genuine party-based politics and a balance of power between executive and legislature.

Chamorro's preference for concentrated executive power was facilitated by laws and structures she inherited from the Sandinistas. Under the FSLN, the presidential system subordinated the legislative and judicial branches of government to the executive, resembling "delegative democracies" elsewhere.[13] In 1979 the Sandinistas had established a sectoral legislature, the Council of State.[14] It became an elected legislature in 1984. A 1987 constitutional reform formalized the presence of the legislature and the electoral schedule but left all state institutions subordinate to the presidency.[15] With electoral victory Chamorro inherited this system. She used her unchecked presidential power for numerous decrees, solving thorny problems that would have engendered legislative debate. The Plan Mayorga, for example, was initiated by decree and never subjected to legislative discussion.

Although she had promised constitutional reform, Chamorro lacked the time, votes, and, eventually, even the interest. Apart from enjoying presidential power, UNO had only a 52-seat majority in the 92-seat legislature, not the 58 votes specified as necessary in the 1987 constitution to reform that document. With the passage of time and the struggles over policy, Chamorro began to lose even the majority support she had had in the legislature. By 1994 most legislators opposed her administration on many policy issues, including its failure to pursue constitutional reform.

---

12. Excess presidential power at the expense of a balance of power among state institutions is a problem for democratic development in Latin America. See Linz (1990); Mainwaring (1990); M. Jones (1995). Others argue that presidential systems can and do evolve into democracies. See von Mettenheim (1995).

13. O'Donnell (1994, esp. 64).

14. The sectoral legislature included members elected by organized sectors of the population: representatives from peasant unions, urban workers' unions, teachers, students, etc. These representatives had no particular geographical attachment and did not campaign.

15. There were instances where the legislature voted down an executive request, but these were rare. In 1990 legislative subordination was due in part to the fact that the majority of seats was held by UNO deputies.

In 1994 a cross-party alliance supporting constitutional reform emerged in the legislature, including UNO and Sandinista deputies but excluding both orthodox Sandinistas following Ortega and Chamorro's most devoted loyalists. The alliance agreed on the need to strengthen Nicaragua's three nonexecutive state branches: the legislature, the judiciary, and the Supreme Electoral Council. It also wanted to constrain family control of the presidency. After considerable effort at cross-class and interparty cooperation, the legislative alliance produced a constitutional reform that accomplished these goals. Facing hostility from the administration, the new constitution was passed into law in early 1995 and sent to President Chamorro for her signature.

Chamorro vetoed the new constitution. In particular, her administration resisted the effort to constrain continued family power. Chamorro's prime minister and son-in-law, Antonio Lacayo, wanted to run for the presidency in 1996 and was barred from doing so by the constitutional reform. The legislature overrode her veto with a two-thirds vote. The issue then went to the Supreme Court, which refused to decide, passing the issue of Lacayo's candidacy to Nicaragua's fourth branch of government, the Supreme Electoral Council (CSE). In the months before the 1996 campaign, the CSE ruled in favor of the legislature, and Lacayo was barred from candidacy until 2001. In the end Chamorro and the legislature reached a compromise in the form of a sunrise law. It delayed some reforms that limited the president's power until after Chamorro's term.[16]

As with other controversial issues, the battle over institutional power was not fully resolved by the end of Chamorro's administration, but enough resolution had been reached for politics and governance to proceed. In resisting the executive, Nicaraguans had moved democracy toward more balanced, institutionalized national power and away from an unchecked presidency. This movement toward democratic development, however, had come in the face of Chamorro's and Lacayo's opposition, somewhat tarnishing Chamorro's democratic image.

Despite the scandal surrounding Lacayo's use of power, Chamorro's reputation as a democrat solidified with her eventual acceptance of the new constitutional process, her continuing respect for civil liberties, and her acceptance of legislative initiative. This she tolerated without closing the chamber, arresting deputies, or staging a presidential coup d'état, responses seen in other Latin American nations in the same time period.

Asked in a late August 1996 nationwide survey to compare the Chamorro and Sandinista regimes on civil liberties and democratic performance, 57.7

16. This law became known as "La Ley Marco" or "Frame Law."

percent of interviewees indicated that the Chamorro regime was better than the Sandinista regime in respecting civil liberties, whereas only 25.6 percent rated the FSLN as better on civil liberties. Asked more generally to designate the broad characteristics that most applied to each regime, 53.8 percent designated the Chamorro regime as democratic, 5.7 percent saw it as socialist, and 15.3 percent chose an authoritarian label. In contrast, 14.2 percent saw the FSLN as democratic, 36.4 percent as socialist, and 29.3 percent as authoritarian. Clearly Nicaraguans recognized the growing space for political dissent, legislative deliberation, and political contestation that had emerged during the Chamorro years.

Restructuring Class

Despite the mass support from the poor that had elected Chamorro, her regime returned class relations to the historic configuration that had existed prior to the revolution, with the economically privileged in a position of power and the poor beneath them. It accomplished this reversal by eliminating most of the Sandinista social reforms. The Sandinista programs had redressed disparities in property; addressed health, employment, education, and welfare concerns; reduced crime; and increased social opportunity, thereby beginning to lift the poor out of their disadvantaged position. As a result of the elimination or reduction of such programs, poverty increased generally, and the size of the lowest income categories increased absolutely.

Figure 7.1 summarizes what these changes meant in terms of an income-based categorization of class in Nicaragua. These data come from DOXA's 1990 and 1996 nationwide surveys conducted during the election campaigns.[17] Since the cordoba was devalued during the Chamorro years, the income categories differ between 1990 and 1996 in absolute terms. However, these categories emerged from determinations by the same survey analysts, working in the field during both elections, as to the appropriate income range capturing class distinctions at that moment in time. The resulting comparisons of the size of the lower- and upper-income categories provide a startling portrait of class changes under Chamorro. The very poor increased dramatically in numbers under Chamorro; the very rich increased substantially; the middle-income categories declined noticeably.

The great increase in income disparity captured by the DOXA surveys across the Chamorro years parallels assessments of the changing social cir-

---

17. DOXA study, National Science Foundation grant no. SBER-9631011. See appendix.

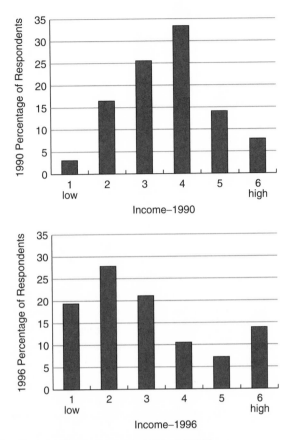

Figure 7.1 Distribution of family income in 1990 and 1996

Source: DOXA nationwide surveys in 1990 and 1996, reported in percentages of respondents.
Note: The income range for each group, in cordobas, is:
Group 1: < 300,000 in 1990; < 500 in 1996
Group 2: 300,000 to 600,000 in 1990; 500 to 1,000 in 1996
Group 3: 600,001 to 1,000,000 in 1990; 1,001 to 1,500 in 1996
Group 4: 1,000,001 to 3,000,000 in 1990; 1,501 to 2,000 in 1996
Group 5: 3,000,001 to 6,000,000 in 1990; 2,001 to 2,500 in 1996
Group 6: > 6,000,001 or outside help in 1990; > 2,500 or outside help in 1996

cumstances of Nicaraguans provided by numerous other analysts and by official national unemployment figures. According to such assessments, by 1993,
50 percent of households were below the poverty line and 19.4 percent
below the extreme poverty line. Twenty-eight percent of children under five
were malnourished. Fifty-four percent of the population had no potable
water, and 40 percent of infant mortality came from gastrointestinal

disease.[18] By 1995 unemployment and underemployment together were estimated at 50–60 percent of adult citizens.

While Nicaragua has always been among the world's poorest societies, there can be little doubt that the position of the poor worsened considerably as social services disappeared under Chamorro. The effect of this decline touched all facets of daily life and social opportunity. Literacy dropped measurably, and access to basic and higher education decreased.[19] The availability of health care declined everywhere, and clinics serving the poor decreased their services or closed. Preventable childhood diseases rose, and the country faced outbreaks of dengue and cholera. Crime skyrocketed, particularly in Managua.

With these economic developments, the structure and meaning of class changed in Nicaragua. Not only were there more poor citizens under Chamorro than during the Sandinista years, poor citizens were considerably poorer in social benefits, personal opportunities, and real-life circumstances than they had been under the Sandinistas. Simultaneously, the number of wealthy citizens had begun to grow, and remnants of the old traditional elite reemerged as powerful forces in society. Additionally, Chamorro had reduced the size of the military and state bureaucracy and eliminated financial support for students. Thus the Sandinistas' "new elite," so central to social progress and state development during the 1980s, ceased to exist as a privileged public sector vanguard of social restructuring. Instead, soldiers, bureaucrats, and students from the Sandinista era were increasingly moved out into society, spreading throughout the income class structure and disintegrating as an identifiable and cohesive class group. While in 1990 the new elite was a pivotal and distinctive participant in national electoral politics, constituting roughly 30 percent or so of the electorate and forming the solid basis of FSLN support, by 1996 it had disappeared as a distinct, identifiable, and meaningful class category.

With the disappearance of the new elite, Nicaragua shifted to a more traditional class structure defined primarily by economic status. At the bottom of this structure was the *underclass*, composed of those whose monthly family income was under 500 cordobas and who were thus destitute by Nicaraguan standards. They constituted about 19 percent of adults. Above them was the

18. Statistical indicators in this paragraph are from Dye et al. (1995) and Banco Mundial (1993).

19. Chamorro enacted a specific education agenda. It included promoting traditional Catholic values in primary schools (in violation of the 1987 constitution), portraying women and men in traditional roles of homemaker and breadwinner, and removing all references to the FSLN. See Arrien (1991) and Kampwirth (1997).

working class, with incomes between 500 and 1,500 cordobas a month, about 49 percent of adults. More than half of these had monthly family incomes from 500 to 1000 cordobas a month and were thus marginalized at the edge of working-class society. Those working-class members making more than 1,000 cordobas per month were also quite poor by the standards of affluent democracies. The *middle class* was composed of citizens with monthly family incomes between 1,501 and 2,500 cordobas per month, about 18 percent of adults. Finally, the elite had monthly family incomes above 2,500, about 14 percent of adults. We divide this elite into a *public sector elite*, composed of those employed by government, and a *private sector elite*, who worked outside the state. The former were 7.4 percent of adults and were the closest parallel under Chamorro to the new elite of the Sandinista era; the latter were about 6.5 percent of adults and were a mixture of traditional elite families and individuals from the new elite of the Sandinista era who had used their education, connections, and political experience to enter the private sector as entrepreneurs and professionals. Both the public and the private elites enjoyed an affluent lifestyle and investment capacities that had been difficult under the FSLN.

The public was well aware of the social costs and class consequences of Chamorro's government. Table 7.1 presents results of a late August 1996 survey indicating how the various classes compared the performance of the Sandinista and Chamorro regimes. On the critical social issues of employment, health, education, and welfare, and to a lesser extent on crime, a substantial plurality of every class, and in many cases a majority of a class, gave substantially higher marks to the policy performance of the Sandinista regime than to Chamorro. There was essentially no disagreement from the poorest of the poor to the wealthiest of the nation's elite that Chamorro had done much worse on social policy than had Ortega. There was also a general sense across classes that the conservative regime had been more corrupt than the socialist one.

Where substantial disagreement did exist among the classes was on the question of the economy. The underclass, working class, and public sector elite, Sandinismo's traditional support base, saw the FSLN economic performance as preferable, while the middle class and private elite preferred the Chamorro regime. The one area where all the classes evaluated the Chamorro regime more positively than the FSLN was on the question of civil liberties. Here clear majorities gave high marks to Chamorro across every group except the underclass, where she received more modest plurality support.

Finally, asked to specify the regime under which they had personally lived better, pluralities of the underclass and working class (together the

Table 7.1   Class Evaluations of Policy Performance by the Chamorro and Sandinista Regimes at the Start of the 1996 Campaign (%)

	Under class	Working class	Middle class	Private elite	Public elite
Which had a better policy for:					
Employment?					
Chamorro	16.2	17.3	17.4	20.7	18.4
Sandinistas	53.0	57.2	56.4	46.6	63.2
Health?					
Chamorro	19.2	27.1	21.0	24.1	28.7
Sandinistas	49.6	50.2	50.8	50.0	60.9
Education?					
Chamorro	21.4	27.1	33.3	37.9	37.9
Sandinistas	50.9	50.2	47.2	48.3	48.3
Welfare?					
Chamorro	22.6	19.8	20.5	24.1	24.1
Sandinistas	47.4	51.1	51.3	44.8	56.3
Crime?					
Chamorro	19.7	17.6	22.6	20.7	25.3
Sandinistas	47.4	49.7	45.6	43.1	50.6
The economy?					
Chamorro	22.2	30.2	39.0	46.6	35.6
Sandinistas	42.3	40.2	31.3	24.1	42.5
Civil liberties?					
Chamorro	45.7	57.5	66.2	69.0	64.4
Sandinistas	30.3	25.0	20.5	22.4	28.7
Which was more corrupt?					
Chamorro	39.3	46.1	39.0	32.8	40.2
Sandinistas	18.4	14.9	23.1	25.9	26.4
Under which did you live better?					
Chamorro	21.4	27.0	35.9	51.7	41.4
Sandinistas	41.5	38.7	36.4	27.6	41.4

Source: DOXA nationwide survey in August 1996.
Note: *N* for this table is 1,186, with class designations unavailable for 14 interviewees. This table presents percentages only for interviewees who chose Chamorro or the Sandinistas as preferable on a specific policy item since our purpose is to contrast the two regimes. We omit results for "neither," "both equally," and "no response" for reasons of space. The percentages given are based on all 1,186 interviewees, including those who gave any of these three designations.

majority of all citizens) chose life in the Sandinista era over life under Chamorro. The middle class and public sector elite split on this question. The private elite clearly preferred the Chamorro era.

Taken at the end of Chamorro's presidency and just as the 1996 presidential campaign was beginning, the survey reported in table 7.1 provides powerful indication of citizen concerns about the consequences of Chamorro's austere policies. Across class lines, most respondents realized that the Chamorro presidency had improved civil liberties in Nicaragua. But most also concluded that the nation had paid a high toll in social well-being to gain these improvements. Looking backward, a plurality of the lower classes that had provided the foundation of Chamorro's 1990 victory now concluded that the FSLN era had been preferable. The Chamorro administration appeared to have reinvigorated the class divisions that had initially given rise to Sandinismo, putting the presidential election at risk. While a rightist candidate might win an election focused on civil liberties, an election framed around unemployment, health, or even crime would advantage the left. As the Chamorro years ended, class had reemerged as a salient political factor in a way that could reignite the class alignments associated with the nation's political parties in the 1980s.

The Evolving Party System

As the Chamorro administration progressed, increasingly the central political issue was which traditional party, the Conservatives or the Liberals, would emerge by 1996 as the stronger opponent to the Sandinistas and thus be the party more likely to represent democratic conservatism in the 1996 presidential election. Despite Conservative Party dominance of the government, the Liberals won the battle for preeminence between the traditional parties. This was due in part to public frustration with Chamorro's social programs. Chamorro's support for Lacayo also undercut the Conservatives' ability to generate other viable candidates and to position them competitively for 1996. Additionally, the citizens of Managua, in choosing Arnoldo Alemán as mayor, placed an ambitious, skillful, and archconservative Liberal in a visible political office apart from the presidency. His success in creating a strong record as a popular, effective mayor gave the Liberals the opportunity to take advantage of the weak position of the Conservatives and emerge from the Chamorro presidency as the most viable rightist party in 1996.

Sandinismo continued throughout the Chamorro years as a strong party capable of contesting for the presidency. In the years immediately following its 1990 defeat, Sandinismo entered a period of soul-searching and self-criticism that helped it adjust to its new circumstances and participate more effectively in political life under the new regime. Most of the party acknowledged that the Sandinistas had made critical mistakes that contributed to their electoral defeat, including insensitivity to civil liberties and a strident, radical posture. Generally, the party also recognized that it would need to compete for power through electoral means and forgo revolutionary tactics. Yet despite such movement toward more mainstream politics and electoral democracy, divisions remained in Sandinismo. A more orthodox group, led by Daniel Ortega, preferred to tilt toward the party's pre-1990 vision of radical social reform, while a renovation group, led by former vice-president Sergio Ramirez, wanted policies more clearly aligned with a social democratic vision akin to that of European parties. By the 1996 campaign, Ortega had again emerged as the dominant force within the party and its presidential candidate. This insured that Sandinismo would present its more radical face to the electorate in 1996 and that the party would have to campaign by defending Ortega's record as president, both the positive and the negative aspects of it.

By late August 1996, Nicaragua's party system had begun to resemble the "two and a half party systems" that occasionally arise in established democracies. Asked for party identification, 30 percent of respondents in a 1,200-person nationwide survey identified as Sandinistas, 27.2 percent identified as Liberals, 6.9 percent identified as Conservatives, and 22.7 percent identified as independents. This made the first two the nation's dominant parties but also meant that a sizable group of unattached voters could determine an electoral outcome. This structure of partisanship meant that, should the centrist Conservatives prove unable to mount an effective campaign to regain public support, the election would be a contest between extremes of right and left. In such a contest, the Conservatives would likely receive few legislative seats and risked being relegated to increasingly marginal national status.

Ironically, while Chamorro's presidency had rekindled class concerns about social policy and regime performance and generated a newly solidified party system pitting left against right, the lower classes had not aligned themselves definitively with the left. The more affluent also had not fully aligned themselves with the right. Instead, in late August 1996 party identification cut across class lines. Both the Liberals and the Sandinistas received support from 25–30 percent of each class, except for the public sector elite, 35 percent of whom embraced Sandinismo. The Conservatives drew support from around 6–10 percent of each class. Moreover, at least 30 percent of each class was independent or undecided in its party attachments, with the working class having the largest group of unattached members. While Chamorro's presidency seemed to prime the nation for a return to traditional class politics, the connection between class and party would have to emerge in the 1996 national presidential campaign itself. It would thus depend greatly on how the contestants framed their appeals. Were the election to center on the selection of a regime devoted to civil liberties and democratic process, then all classes could unite behind a rightist candidate of democratic conservatism. By contrast, an election centering on social policies could generate a class-based result beneficial to the Sandinistas.

The Post-Chamorro Transition and Sustaining Democratic Conservatism

Outgoing president Chamorro framed the 1996 contest as a regime choice. On August 2, 1996, she officially opened the campaign with a formal speech to the National Assembly. It focused voters on liberal democratic procedures rather than on economic or social issues:

> I address you today . . . on the day formally marking the beginning of the election campaign that will lead the Nicaraguan people on the 20th October [sic] to elect the authorities who will bear the responsibility for governing the future of our country, a now democratic Nicaragua, starting in 1997. . . . I want this electoral process to be a civic and exemplary celebration . . . guaranteeing all liberties . . . by providing the political parties . . . all the necessary conditions . . . to pursue their campaigns in a way the Nicaraguan people have never experienced before. . . . Nowadays, to govern in Nicaragua means a commitment to public liberties. It is respect for all ideologies and . . . defense of the human rights of every Nicaraguan citizen.[20]

She concluded by stressing the connection between the liberal democratic accomplishments of her government and the new election, separating both from the Sandinista years.

> For all of us, this will be our first electoral process in complete freedom. The first election without any intimidation, in which the Nicaraguan people will have a chance to choose from among many candidates without any fear. . . . The world has been exceedingly generous towards Nicaragua in these elections. The world confidently observes the consolidation of democracy in these elections. Nevertheless, the most important thing is that also our children are watching us. We must give them an example of patriotism. The Nicaraguan people are already capable of settling disagreements peacefully. Let's demonstrate that we really want to give them a better homeland.

With this speech, Chamorro called on the voters who had supported her election to stand with her now in affirming the new regime. She clearly believed that she had inaugurated a new era of democracy and civil liberties distinct from the preceding period of Sandinista rule. Her suggestion was that the nation should not risk returning to a less democratic polity by again

20. BBC World News, 8/6/96.

embracing the Sandinistas. Conspicuously absent was emphasis on the serious social and economic problems that had accompanied her movement toward a more democratic polity. She was asking the voters to stay the course she had set toward a democracy, regardless of such difficulties. The question was whether the citizens who had supported her would now stay with her regime of democratic conservatism in the face of the severe social costs her regime had imposed on them.

While Chamorro sought to ignore poverty and the limits of her economic policies, the voters did not. As we have seen from survey results, most citizens appeared to want a governing regime that would combine the social awareness of the Sandinistas with the democratic credentials of Chamorro. A candidate offering such a combination would allow some of what the people needed socially and economically, while ensuring civil liberties and avoiding U.S. opposition. Another concern was to find a less corrupt administration and a president who was authoritative without being authoritarian. The absence of a serious Conservative contender made the search for compromise more difficult, since the choice was between two extremes, the right-wing Liberals and the Sandinista socialists.[21] The choices that emerged, moreover, were not only between alternative political and economic regimes but also between candidates associated by the public with the polarized extremes of contemporary Nicaraguan history: Alemán with the Somoza dictatorship his family had supported; Ortega with the revolution. Throughout the campaign each contender would seek to convince the public that he offered the ideal combination of policy responsiveness and democratic sensitivity while reminding voters of the opponent's discredited past.

The 1996 Campaign and the Alemán Victory

The Sandinistas approached the 1996 campaign divided. Disagreement between the more moderate position of Sergio Ramirez and Daniel Ortega's traditional FSLN line had caused Ramirez to leave the FSLN. His Renovationist Sandinista Movement (MRS) launched its own campaign in 1996, with little success. Sandinismo's main attention concentrated again on Ortega. Ortega tried to moderate his image, shedding combat fatigues, softening his rhetoric, and using a festive atmosphere for his stump speeches. The split within Sandinismo evidenced both a push by elite leadership toward democratization (in the moderate position of Ramirez) and the limits on such elite effort (due to Ortega's continued control of the FSLN).

<hr>

21. *New York Times*, 9/1/96, 12; Notisur, 9/6/96; *Baltimore Sun*, 10/17/96, 16A.

Reaching toward the private sector, Ortega chose businessman Juan Manuel Caldera as his running mate.[22]

The Liberal Alliance was both the newest contender on the electoral scene and the oldest player in the contemporary political game. Its candidate, Arnoldo Alemán, was new in that he had not run for national office before. But the ideas he represented and the version of Liberalism supporting him were closer to Somoza than were those of any other candidate running. In that sense his Liberal Party predated Sandinismo. However, in conducting a Managua mayorship that prioritized public works, Alemán had tried to give Liberalism a facelift that revealed a newfound public concern rather than the age-old stress on the priorities of the rich. It was an effort to evolve from premodern toward modern.[23]

Alemán also sought to unite all factions of Liberalism behind him, succeeding with all but Godoy's Independent Liberal Party. As his running mate, Alemán chose Enrique Bolaños, former head of COSEP, Nicaragua's private business organization. As a member of the Conservative Party in the 1980s, Bolaños had been a visible, vehement opponent of the Sandinista regime. Alemán's choice of him clearly stated the Liberals' position on business and class interests as well as on the Sandinista revolution. It also demonstrated an effort to reach out to voters who had historically identified with the Conservatives and pull them into the Liberal Party. Alemán also allied his campaign closely with the Catholic Church, receiving support from Managua's conservative cardinal, Miguel Obando y Bravo.

Although an important centrist voice in Nicaraguan politics, the Conservatives entered the 1996 contest deeply discredited. Their poor electoral support reflected the public attitude toward UNO, which was associated with Chamorro's austerity program and the Lacayo scandal. The Conservatives, represented by Alfredo César, still called themselves "UNO" (UNO-96) but this time made no effort at presenting a coalition. The discrediting of UNO and the Conservatives was a loss for Nicaraguan

22. The FSLN began as a party of mass mobilization. Its strengths lie in that mode of politics. Electoral politics is a very different channel of access to state power. Many tactics useful for mass mobilization are counterproductive in a campaign and vice versa. The process through which a party that began by mobilizing the poor can evolve into a viable competitor in electoral politics is a complex one and by no means certain of success. Other mass parties outside Nicaragua are also struggling with this same set of transitional problems. Consider, for example, contemporary Peronism in Argentina, which lost elections in 1997 and 1999, and the Worker's Party in Brazil, which lost repeatedly, causing internal reconsideration of tactics (Keck 1992), before finally winning.

23. For a discussion of this process in the United States and more generally, see Hofstadter (1969) and Duverger (1954).

democracy. UNO represented a centrist alternative between the FSLN and the Liberals, particularly as the major group most independent of the Somoza and Sandinista regimes and the one whose historical political position had supported democratic process.

Voters understood that the electoral contest was between the Sandinistas and the Liberals. Throughout the 1996 campaign, most respondents said they would vote for either Ortega or Alemán. By the final survey in late October 1996, nearly 80 percent (79.8) gave one of these two choices; 8.7 percent said they preferred another party; and 11.6 percent did not respond. They also understood that one of these two main contenders would win the 1996 election. By the last preelectoral survey, 46.3 percent said Alemán would win; 33.3 percent said Ortega would win.

Chamorro's strongest legacy was that of political choice, and one of Nicaragua's greatest democratic assets is its electoral contests. The 1996 campaign illustrates that citizen choice and contestation loomed central in determining the next government. Each candidate sought to present the retrospective record in the manner most beneficial to himself, while simultaneously appearing to be the more attractive prospective choice as well. As the campaign progressed, changes in the fortunes and standing of the two main contenders illustrated that the public was listening closely and thinking carefully about the alternatives.

Alemán opened the campaign in the summer of 1996, stressing his immediate retrospective mayoral record[24] and downplaying his more distant connection to Somocismo and the class loyalties behind him. He campaigned with a populist discourse that shared much with the UNO-96 and FSLN campaigns. He advocated a free market and a social safety net. He promised to invite foreign investment and to create domestic employment. He pledged public works and service. His municipal accomplishments gave him a strong governing record. In response to such a campaign position, the Sandinistas could not point toward any improvements they had overseen in the last six years. Instead, as part of the FSLN effort to present a new image, Ortega relied upon his campaign appearances themselves. The summer ended with Alemán campaigning against both the FSLN and the Chamorro governments, and August polls gave him as much as a 20-point lead over Ortega.

---

24. Alemán's retrospective focus on his accomplishments as mayor gave particular stress to his efforts at paving roads and building local plazas (Coleman and Stuart H. 1997, 171). In this regard, his retrospective focus was less on the broad performance of his government and more akin to the "constituent service" argument that Fiorina (1977) attributes to U.S. congressmen.

September 1996 brought a surprise. Ortega recovered from his trailing position, and CID-Gallup polls gave him a small lead.[25] September's press coverage focused upon a document presented to Nicaraguan politicians by the OAS, the Minimum Agenda. Supported by the Nicaraguan Catholic Church as well as by the international community, it called for cooperation among leaders to ensure governability, outlined the issues of greatest political concern, and promised to honor the 1996 electoral outcome. Of all political leaders in Nicaragua, only Alemán refused to sign it,[26] yet another example of the extent to which elite pacting appeared impossible in Nicaragua. Yet the refusal also underscored his intransigence and inflexibility, portents of his future governing style. Ortega's lead in September was also due to improvements in his campaign. He dressed in white rather than in army fatigues, stressed social policies, emphasized the failures of the Chamorro years, and reminded voters of the importance his own party had always placed on social reform.

During this period DOXA took two polls. The first, in late August, captured the tightening of the race, with Alemán and Ortega tied at around 32 percent each in vote intent. Then, in late September, in a second DOXA poll, Ortega surged ahead, leading Alemán 38.1 percent to 29.2 percent. Although initially, in the first poll, voters still expected an Alemán victory, by the second poll they were seeing either candidate as a potential winner.

In response to his decline in the polls, Alemán refocused his campaign. He stopped criticizing the Chamorro administration and started to praise it, at least its performance on civil liberties and neoliberal economics. This shift redirected his campaign attention toward the question of regime choice, underscoring the extent to which Chamorro's regime and the one he would himself offer were similar, while Ortega's regime offer was different. Alemán also sought to present a prospective image that favored himself and damaged Ortega. Taking Ortega more seriously than he had in the summer, Alemán presented his opponent as an unreformed revolutionary who would lead the nation toward political confrontation and economic disaster.[27]

Ortega fought back by emphasizing Alemán's historic record, stressing his and his family's connections to Somoza.[28] He underscored the fact that Alemán had directed a pro-Somoza student organization during the final years of the dictatorship and that his father had been a judge named to his

25. United Press International, 9/5/96.
26. Notisur, 9/6/96.
27. Agence France Presse, 9/23/96.
28. *London Guardian*, 10/11/96.

post by the dictatorship.[29] Yet, as in 1990, Ortega also made political mistakes that hurt him at precisely the time when he might have continued to pull ahead in the polls. In October he sealed a political alliance with former Contra leaders, including one known as "Mack," who had a particularly violent reputation. While moderation and compromise from Ortega appeared desirable, the alliance with Mack shocked many FSLN supporters, struck citizens as opportunistic, and decreased public trust in him.[30]

As the final campaign month began, the contest was close. The press continued to emphasize Ortega's gain in the polls but conceded that neither candidate yet had the 45 percent necessary to avoid a runoff.[31] Polls found that many voters were still undecided.[32] Ortega's rallies were estimated at four times the size of Alemán's, although after the 1990 experience, rally size received more cautious press coverage.[33] In early October, DOXA took its third survey. Mirroring press reports, it found a close election, with Alemán leading by 37.7 percent to 34.8 percent. Minor party candidates garnered 14.8 percent, and undecided was around 12.8 percent, down considerably from the 23.8 percent of the first poll, but still sizable. Yet 46.3 percent of citizens now expected Alemán to win, in contrast with 33.3 percent who expected Ortega to win and 20 percent undecided.

As the contest became increasingly close, Alemán's allies became worried. Chamorro reentered the fray, endorsing Alemán and stating that she would not turn the presidential sash over to Ortega if he won. The U.S. State Department criticized Ortega, reminding the public that the United States also had an opinion.[34] Alemán delivered a "love letter to Nicaragua," quoting biblical passages.[35] Cardinal Obando y Bravo delivered a sermon comparing Ortega with a poisonous snake from a biblical story.[36]

Election day saw six hundred international observers, including James Baker and Jimmy Carter, and four thousand Nicaraguan observers.[37] As an Alemán victory emerged from the formal ballot count, all parties other than the Liberals suspected irregularities at the polls on election day. The Sandinistas claimed electoral fraud, and Ortega refused to concede defeat.[38]

29. *St. Petersburg Times*, 10/13/96, 1A.
30. *Toronto Star*, 9/29/96; *St. Petersburg Times*, 10/13/96, 1A.
31. *Los Angeles Times*, 10/14/96, A13; Interpress Service, 10/15/96.
32. Agence France Presse, 10/14/96.
33. Agence France Presse, 10/17/96.
34. Interpress Service, 10/11/96; Agence France Presse, 10/19/96.
35. Associated Press, 10/19/96.
36. *Houston Chronicle*, 10/20/96.
37. Agence France Presse, 10/20/96; BBC World News, 10/12/96; *Washington Post* 10/13/96.
38. BBC World News, 10/23/96; Notisur, 10/25/96.

The issue was not whether Alemán had a plurality lead, but whether he had won enough votes to avoid a runoff with Ortega. The public itself doubted the integrity of the results. Only 53 percent were willing to say the election had been fair, while 37 percent believed it unfair. In response the Supreme Electoral Council conducted a second complete ballot count lasting nearly three weeks. That second count again declared Alemán the winner, and this time losing parties accepted the verdict.[39] The final election count showed Alemán with 51 percent of the vote, Ortega with 37.8 percent, and the minor parties with 11.2 percent, all based on an estimated turnout of roughly 86 percent. DOXA's final survey, taken in the week immediately following the election, reported an 88.7 percent turnout, with a 53.7 percent Alemán victory, 36.5 percent for Ortega, and 9.8 percent for the minor parties. The Liberals won a majority in the National Assembly, although the Sandinistas retained a strong legislative presence.[40] The final vote tally gave forty-six seats to the FSLN and the bulk of the remainder to the Liberals.[41]

Alemán won a major victory according to the CSE, thereby sustaining democratic conservatism and giving Chamorro the regime affirmation she had sought. The rallying of Chamorro and social elites behind Alemán, asking the citizens to remember the difficulties of the Ortega era and stay the course with regime construction, had resonated with the public. Alemán's mid-campaign move toward Chamorro allowed him to benefit from public appreciation of her. The continued reliance of the FSLN on Ortega as its standard bearer allowed the conservatives to raise the specter of renewed national crisis should he win, a fear reinforced by public doubts about the trustworthiness of his judgment. Saber rattling by the United States helped inflame such concerns. While citizens also had doubts about Alemán, his success as Liberal mayor of Managua provided just enough reassurance about his policy responsiveness to seal their movement toward him and solidify his victory. The Liberal victory kept the experiment with construction of a conservative democratic regime alive and was seen as a testament to the public's continuing faith in Chamorro.

In DOXA's postelection survey in late October, 70 percent of interviewees gave Chamorro positive marks for her performance as president, underscoring the extent to which the election was an affirmation of her and her efforts to construct a viable new regime. Most telling of all was that 43 percent of those who had just voted for Ortega were among those giving

39. Notisur, 11/1/96; Interamerican Service, 10/16/96; Interpress Service, 10/17/96; *New York Times*, 10/22/96, A2; BBC World News, 11/6/96.
40. Agence France Presse, 10/22/96.
41. Interpress Service, 11/12/96.

Chamorro high marks. Such responses illustrate the extent of Chamorro's success in reconciling contending factions and help explain her capacity to refocus citizen attention during the campaign away from issues of social justice, which could have led to the rejection of democratic conservatism, and toward reaffirmation of civil liberties and procedural democracy.[42] Yet if she and her regime appeared affirmed by the election, Alemán himself faced substantial organized opposition as he prepared to take office.

The continued opposition to Alemán was evident, both among citizens and in the National Assembly. Observers noted that he would not be able to fulfill his most extreme, anti-Sandinista promises without provoking a level of instability that even he would find unacceptable.[43] Foreign press correspondents pointed out that the bulk of Alemán's financial support had come from the Miami Cuban exile community[44] and that, postelection, Alemán would need to unify a nation he had helped polarize with a "vitriolic campaign."[45] As observers predicted, Alemán's early moves were softer and less extreme than his campaign rhetoric had been.[46] In response to the recount, Alemán declared himself a "bridge" among all parties, claiming that his "arms were open to all groups."[47]

The Alemán Years

Alemán's five-year presidency was even more clearly a government committed to the rich than Chamorro's had been, and his concentration of power in Liberal hands ostracized Conservatives as well as the Sandinistas. Yet while such polarization might have proven explosive in 1990, by 1996 Nicaragua could tolerate it nonviolently. Moreover, Alemán was never able to put in place the most extreme policies that he had threatened during his campaign. In fact, he ended up forced to respond to some of the nation's most explosive social problems. This he did because he wished to retain social and economic calm to encourage foreign investors and because his own drive for power caused him to compromise with Ortega on several occasions. At each compromise Ortega demanded social concessions in return for his own cooperation. While the institutions of liberal democracy that had generated

42. On the critical importance of issue reframing and cueing, see B. D. Jones (1994, esp. 78–133); Zaller (1992).
43. *San Diego Union Tribune,* 10/12/96; *Calgary Herald,* 11/9/96, A13.
44. *Toronto Star,* 10/26/96.
45. *Economist,* 10/26/96, 50.
46. *El Excelsior* (Mexico), 10/28/96.
47. *Calgary Herald,* 11/9/96, A13.

incremental movement forward under Chamorro suffered a setback under Alemán, he did not close down the institutions of the democratic state, launch a military coup, or engage in human rights violations. His regime was less drastic than his enemies had feared and less regressive than his friends had hoped. It also had its deeply ironic qualities.

A defining characteristic of Alemán's presidency was his effort to consolidate power in his own hands and to become the delegative president Guillermo O'Donnell (1994) has worried will emerge in nascent Latin American democracies. Yet in this effort, Alemán was less successful than he planned, illustrated not least by the fact that his presidency, originally intended to be six years, was actually shortened by a year. Alemán's first step toward power consolidation was an effort to reform the constitution away from the more balanced configuration that had been achieved at such great effort in 1995. Alemán's goal had been to shorten his term to five years in return for being allowed a second term, barred by the 1995 constitution. Instead, he achieved the first goal but not the second. He managed to change the constitution, in particular decreasing the electoral minimum required for a candidate to win. Yet he did not gain the chance to run in 2001 and was not accorded a second term. This outcome epitomizes the changes Alemán sought to achieve, those he failed to achieve, and the limitations his agenda faced.

A second characteristic of the Alemán years was the collusion between Alemán and Daniel Ortega, who sat as leader of the opposition bench in the legislature. Many aspects of Alemán's proposed legal reforms, including the changes to the constitution, would have been impossible without Ortega's acquiescence and, with him, many members of the Sandinista legislative bench. For example, as part of the constitutional reform, the two pacted to lower the winning electoral threshold from 45 percent to 35 percent. Ortega, like Alemán, thought he could win 35 percent and felt the pact increased his own presidential chances. Observers were disgusted by Ortega's agreement to the reform and other changes, and the loss of faith that Ortega experienced as a result returned to haunt him in his 2001 bid for the presidency. Yet one of the ironic by-products of Alemán's pact with Ortega was the scheduling of municipal elections for November of 2000 instead of with the presidential election of November 2001. The early scheduling allowed voters to elect the Sandinistas to most key municipal offices without attracting the international attention a national victory would have done.

A third characteristic of the Alemán years was the continued stress on the market economy, combined with gradual movement toward social responsiveness. Alemán's continued commitment to the market economy granted even greater opportunities for wealth accumulation among the rich, while the poor continued to struggle. Wealth disparity thus continued to increase. Yet noticeable improvements occurred in the lives of many citizens. These were partially caused by some improvement in the economy and a decline in extreme unemployment. They were helped by the growing availability of consumer goods made possible by the market economy and increased international trade. But improvements in daily life were also caused, in ironic ways, by Alemán's social responsiveness.

Like Chamorro, Alemán experienced extensive national protests and mass mobilization in opposition to his economic policies, but unlike Chamorro he chose not simply to moderate his austerity but also to decrease some prices and raise some wages, particularly in response to key groups of highly mobilized workers. Additionally, each pact with Ortega was purchased at the cost of one or more of Alemán's neoliberal policies, with Ortega agreeing to support Alemán's legal reforms on condition that the president roll back his neoliberal reforms. Alemán's agreement to do so ended protests that were undermining international support for Alemán's fiscal policies and improved daily circumstances for the poorest citizens. While pacting between the two leaders undermined Nicaragua's democratic institutions, it resulted in less extreme suffering for the nation's poor. It also gave more time for the economic reforms begun by Chamorro to prove themselves.

By the end of Alemán's presidency, the economy was noticeably more vibrant and citizens were enjoying the market economy. New shops had opened in metropolitan areas, selling everything from office supplies to clothes and kitchen items. Numerous international chain stores had taken up local franchises, and long lunch lines filled up Subway, Pizza Hut, and various taco shops. The available statistics confirm that the productivity of the economy and the quality of life had improved gradually. GDP had risen from 4.8 percent in 1996 to 7.0 percent in 1999, with particularly dramatic increases in construction indicators. Maternal mortality rates were now better than those of El Salvador, Guatemala, and Honduras. Infant mortality rates, at 49/1000 during the Chamorro years, had fallen to 39.5/1000 by 2000.[48] While Nicaragua was still extremely poor as a nation, and much of its citizenry was impoverished by any international standard, the country finally was making progress both on the problems with inflation and low productivity that characterized the Sandinista era and also on the worst problems with unemployment and lifestyle concerns associated with Chamorro's neoliberal austerity.

48. *Statistical Abstract of Latin America* (2002, 213, 216, 1067).

The fourth and defining characteristic of Alemán's presidency was corruption. He personally disregarded many aspects of fiscal law and encouraged his Liberal Party supporters in the National Assembly and elsewhere to do the same. For example, Alemán never paid municipal taxes to the locale where he lived throughout the first four years of his presidency. His disregard for the tax laws began to be addressed only after the 2000 municipal elections when the leadership of his locale passed from the Liberal Party to the Sandinistas. Similarly, Alemán's allies in the National Assembly engaged in numerous personal transgressions of tax, family, and importation laws. In one particularly egregious violation, a Liberal member of the legislature actually changed his name, while in office, in order to avoid child support payments. Despite testimony by his own parents that he was, in fact, the father of his children, the legislator was not required to assume his original identity or to make child payments, a court decision that could have been possible only in the context of an overall administration with scant regard for the law.

A defining moment both for the Alemán presidency and for the 2001 presidential election was the municipal elections held in November 2000. As a result of the constitutional changes made during the Alemán years, Nicaragua held separate municipal elections for the first time in its history. Previously, municipal elections had always coincided with national presidential elections. This separation of local elections from the national election so closely watched and observed abroad allowed Nicaraguans to act on their preference for many of the Sandinista social policies. It was an ideal moment for the population. Freed of the need to choose cautiously at the national level and of the concern over regime choice, citizens could vote Sandinista without producing an Ortega presidency or inflaming the United States. In the process they would generate local governments attentive to social concerns. Simultaneously, disgusted by Alemán's corruption and authoritarianism, they could punish the Liberals without risking the economic policies that finally appeared to be working or endangering the social gains made through protest and via Ortega's pacts. Pursuing this logic, Nicaraguans voted for the Sandinistas in nearly all major municipalities nationwide. This included Sandinista victories in all but two major cities and a Sandinista victory in the Managua mayoral race where Sandinista Herty Lewites won the post that many voters remembered as having been Alemán's springboard into the presidency. The Sandinista victory in Managua was a nationally visible public return of a Sandinista candidate in a key political post.

Widely seen as a commentary on the Alemán presidency, the 2000 municipal elections set the stage for Alemán's final presidential year and for the 2001 election. Subsequent to the Liberal loss of so many municipalities, Alemán was unable to consolidate power any further in his final year, and his influence on the Liberal electoral choice was weakened as well. His vice-president, Enrique Bolaños, had distanced himself from Alemán early in the presidency because of Alemán's dictatorial personal style. Bolaños then kept a low profile throughout most of Alemán's presidency and separated himself from the corruption that characterized the regime. After 2000, Bolaños increasingly emerged as the new Liberal leader and the 2001 candidate for the Liberal Party.

While the formal institutions of state weakened during the Alemán years, the democratic foundations of space, class, and party survived. Civil liberties and constitutional procedures were still honored, even if Alemán used the power of the state in corrupt and self-aggrandizing ways. Class divisions remained, as reflected in income inequality, though Alemán's social respon-siveness following mass protest and the 2000 elections complicated the dynamics of class politics. Finally, both the Liberals and the Sandinistas had established substantial governing authority across different levels of office, while the Conservatives continued to decline in national and local power. With the maintenance and strengthening of these three foundations, Downs's requisites of information, ideology, and party survived Alemán.

Similarly, Dahl's primary institutions of contestation and inclusive partic-ipation remained intact. The electoral calendar continued with relatively free and fair elections, electoral participation was high, and political fortunes continued to rely upon public opinion. Citizens continued to engage in mass mobilizations, evidence that the social capital gained in the revolution still survived. In the face of popular power, democratic conservatism continued to respect civil liberties and electoral democracy, even as the president placed a low priority on democratic institutions themselves. Critical proof of contin-ued democratic development despite the president's behavior came with the 2001 election and the transition beyond Alemán.

The 2001 Campaign and the Bolaños Victory

As Nicaragua's fourth election and second postsocialist contest, the 2001 campaign was characterized by an air of normalcy that had been absent before. Gone was the sense of economic and social crisis that had haunted the previous elections, replaced by evidence of movement forward, at least on the economic and social front. DOXA's surveys had gauged self-reported unem-ployment at 18–20 percent of the electorate during the 1996 presidential campaign. In contrast, self-reported unemployment was down to 9.5 percent in an October 2001 survey conducted by the Nicaraguan polling firm CINASE. This same survey likewise found substantial improvement over 1996 in the distribution of family incomes, as seen in figure 7.2.

The percentage of destitute citizens living at the margin of existence, defined as those surviving on less than 500 cordobas a month, had dropped from 19.4 percent toward the end of Chamorro's presidency in August 1996 down to 7 percent in October 2001. Overall, those surviving on 1,500 cordobas a month or less, whom we treated as constituting the poor mass population in 2001, now made up 54 percent of Nicaragua's electorate, down from 68 percent at the end of the Chamorro years. Simultaneously, those enjoying an affluent life by Nicaraguan standards had increased substantially, particularly the most affluent category. In fact, in 2001 almost half of those in the top income category reported family incomes in excess of 4,000 cordobas a month, with these individuals constituting 11.4 percent of overall respondents in the survey.

Even more than in 1996, Nicaragua was characterized in 2001 by income polarization, with the increase in affluent citizens coming not among middle income groups but at the high end of the income scale. This increase in the wealthy came among those who were successful business entrepreneurs in the new neoliberal economy and from the return of wealthy families who had left Nicaragua during the Sandinista years. Thus over 36 percent of the country lived on 1,000 cordobas or less a month and were quite close to the edge of subsistence, while 26 percent of the country lived in style on more than 2,500 cordobas. The growing wealth disparity was tolerable only because Alemán had relented on enough social programs to enable the poor to survive and because the improved economy was showing signs of long-term staying power.

The improvement in the economy, combined with Alemán's social concessions, raised the prospect that the normalization of Nicaraguan society that Chamorro had promised eleven years earlier was finally materializing. That hope generated an aura of expectancy and calm in 2001, with citizens beginning to sense that the long-term benefits of neoliberal restructuring were emerging and a period of social and economic stability was coming. Not yet an issue in national life was the long-term consequences of the growing wealth disparity.[49]

49. Robinson (2003, 319) argues that the growing wealth disparity that accompanied neoliberal reforms and democratization in Nicaragua and Central America at the end of the twentieth century is likely to generate "renewed social conflict," "new methods of organization in civil society," and "a fresh round of popular struggle against the prevailing social order" in the Isthmus over the coming decades.

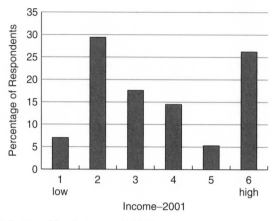

Figure 7.2 Distribution of family income in 2001

Source: CINASE nationwide survey in October 2001, reported in percentages of respondents.
Note: The income range for each group, in cordobas, is:
Group 1: < 500 in 2001
Group 2: 500 to 1,000 in 2001
Group 3: 1,001 to 1,500 in 2001
Group 4: 1,501 to 2,000 in 2001
Group 5: 2,001 to 2,500 in 2001
Group 6: > 2,500 in 2001

The sense of normalcy was reinforced by the ways in which the 2001 election resembled the 1996 contest. First, as in 1996, the split between the two traditional parties remained, with the Liberals and Conservatives each running their own candidates. The Liberals did not need a coalition to compete with the FSLN. The Conservative candidate, Alberto Saborío, proved to be as critical of Alemán and the Liberals as of Ortega and the FSLN. Second, again squashing all internal opposition within the FSLN, Ortega insisted on being the Sandinista candidate. Members of both traditional parties hoped that he would make that choice, since they considered him a lesser candidate than some other party members. Third, again as in 1996, the Conservative candidate garnered very little popular support, leaving an electoral contest that was framed as a two-party competition between Liberals and Sandinistas. Although Saborío won the respect of many observers by his electoral stance advocating liberal democracy and the rule of law and opposing corruption, he never presented any real electoral challenge. Finally, again a central issue was whether the citizens would stay with the regime of democratic conservatism, this time doing so despite Alemán's aggrandizing and corrupt behavior as president. As in 1996, Chamorro made clear her opposition to a Sandinista return to power and her desire for citizens to be patient with the regime she had inaugurated, staying the course yet again by electing Bolaños.

In response to the 2000 municipal elections, Bolaños continued to separate himself from Alemán, both in personal appearances and in policy. He did not campaign with the president and did not draw on his vice-presidential position as a campaign asset. Instead, he presented himself as a separate electoral contender, part of the Liberal Party but not of the current administration. In his platform he advocated clean government and an end to the extensive corruption that had characterized the Alemán presidency. In his demeanor he emphasized his own personal adherence to the rule of law, and he advocated a new Liberal government that would be more respectful of legal limits than Alemán had been. He proposed, in essence, to continue the economic improvements and social responsiveness that had come with the Liberal years in power while ending the corruption and authoritarian tendencies associated with Alemán personally.

Ortega also attempted to learn from past mistakes. He presented a softer image of himself than he had ever done, emphasizing "love" and "forgiveness" as campaign themes. He even eliminated the red and black Sandinista colors, substituting them with pink. He dressed in casual civilian clothes and maintained a noncombative demeanor, even on election day and when conceding victory. As in 1996, Ortega emphasized the poverty that prevailed in Nicaragua and promised a return to social reform and a prioritization of the poor. He was careful to present these promises while assuring voters that he would work with rather than against opponents.

Like the cast of characters, the course of the campaign resembled that of 1996. The three contenders opened their campaigns in September 2001 and closed them one week prior to the election on November 4, 2001. The campaign attracted less attention from pollsters and from the United States than had the 1996 and 1990 contests. United States press coverage focused on the events of September 11, leaving less space for the Nicaraguan election. Only CID-Gallup, Borge and Associates, and CINASE conducted polls, and all achieved similar results: a very close contest with both candidates making a strong electoral showing. As election day approached, the U.S. State Department issued statements critical of Ortega, and Cardinal Obando y Bravo joined Chamorro in supporting Bolaños publicly. Considered more a liability than an asset, Alemán maintained a low profile during the campaign.

Despite worries to the contrary, election day was uneventful and calm. As in 1996, the 2001 election received close international observation.

International observers came from the Carter Center, the Oscar Arias Foundation in Costa Rica, the Organization of American States, and the European Union. These observers were obvious on election day, as they all wore shirts or baseball caps identifying them with their observation organization. The 2001 election boasted the highest overall turnout that any Nicaraguan election had yet seen. Some sources placed it at 89 percent of the registered population. The Supreme Electoral Council, responsible for staffing the polling booths and providing the ballots, had not foreseen such a turnout. Some booths opened an hour or two late while staff collected the necessary ballots. Voters stood in line for hours but with remarkable patience and forbearance. Voters were also quiet and somber, engaging in little conversation. Required by law to remain open as long as a single voter stood in line, the voting stations dutifully collected ballots until all those who wished to vote had voted.

In the end, Bolaños won convincingly, while Ortega received his highest vote percentage since 1984 and the minor parties all but disappeared. The final tally from the Supreme Electoral Council showed Bolaños with 56 percent of the vote, Ortega with 42 percent, and Saborio and the minor parties with less than 2 percent. CINASE's final postelection poll estimated the turnout at 87.4 percent and showed Bolaños with 53.1 percent, Ortega with 42.5 percent, and the Conservatives/minor parties with 4.4 percent.

In an unprecedented display of legality, and in an effort to separate himself definitively from Alemán, Enrique Bolaños refused to declare himself the winner until all ballots had been counted. He affirmed, instead, that it was not up to him to do so but that declaration of the electoral outcome was the task of the Supreme Electoral Council. Both Ortega and Saborio visited Liberal campaign headquarters to concede their loss long before the Liberal victor would state publicly that he had won the election. When the CSE had counted the ballots and given him the victory, Bolaños then declared himself the new president.

Following his inauguration Bolaños moved to call Alemán to account for his corruption. Bolaños asked the legislature to remove Alemán's self-imposed immunity from prosecution. That request required a legislative vote that Bolaños lost. Most of the Liberal deputies, many of whom owed considerable favors to Alemán, voted to protect the former president from enforcement of the law. But Bolaños was not easily defeated. Having failed via institutional means to bring Alemán to account, the new president now joined with Sandinista activists to organize a massive popular march on the National Assembly to demand removal of Alemán's immunity. The march was covered by domestic and international news media and again underscored citizen involvement in Nicaraguan politics, this time in the attempted enforcement of the rule of law.[50]

Now that the legislature's role in sustaining Alemán's immunity had attracted widespread national and international attention and was no longer simply an issue on the floor of the Assembly, the deputies decided to respond. A second vote was presented to the legislators and this time Bolaños won. The legislators voted to remove Alemán's immunity and also that of his closest family and friends. Some of Alemán's family left Nicaragua immediately, fleeing to Costa Rica with their booty. Alemán, however, remained in Nicaragua to face the possibility of corruption charges and punishment minus the protection of immunity he had tried to set up for himself. When Alemán was finally brought to trial he was found guilty of extensive corruption and sentenced to prison.

The incident shows continued democratic development in Nicaragua far beyond the electoral cycle itself but, like elections, involving citizens in a central democratic role. Mobilized citizen action and institutional response together succeeded in bringing the powerful to account for illegal actions.

Evaluating the Revolutionary and Postrevolutionary Regimes: Aggregate Citizen Assessments

With the 2001 election and the inauguration of Bolaños, Nicaragua successfully completed two presidential terms in its postrevolutionary transition to democratic conservatism. These two conservative presidencies brought constitutional and regime change, neoliberal economic policies, a general reduction in social programs, improvements in civil liberties, erratic support for democratic institutions, corruption, and scandal. They also saw competitive national and local elections that generated an increasingly pluralistic distribution of governing power among parties of left and right. At the national level these contests involved two competitive electoral challenges by Daniel Ortega to candidates endorsed by Violeta Chamorro. Twice citizens reiterated their choice for the right, affirming their support of the regime of democratic conservatism espoused by Chamorro.

50. The willingness of Nicaragua's citizens to mobilize and demonstrate in favor of democracy and the rule of law fits with Nancy Bermeo's (2003) argument that average citizens support democracy more fully than studies of democratic breakdown have understood. However, in most of the cases Bermeo studies, citizens have supported democracy without necessarily mobilizing in support of it. The major exception, writes Bermeo, is the case of Spain where citizens not only mobilized but also went to war in defense of democracy. Nicaraguans have likewise shown themselves willing to take mobilized action in support of democracy and against authoritarianism.

Chapter 8 examines how voter attitudes toward candidates, the economy, and the regime shaped their reaffirmation of democratic conservatism. Before undertaking that examination let us address one final set of issues that are critical to completing our story about the eleven-year transition to democratic conservatism. Let us see how citizens assessed the different administrations of the new regime in contrast to the revolutionary era. These issues are essential for framing the discussion of vote choice and class politics in Chapter 8 and for the broader assessment of regime consolidation in Nicaragua.

We know that at the outset of the 1996 campaign many respondents had serious reservations about the Chamorro years and looked wistfully back toward the Sandinista years. What happened to these concerns? Did such reservations continue to haunt conservative candidates during the 1996 campaign and over the next five years, with the right winning despite such deep public apprehensions? Or did Chamorro's spirited defense of her regime and the aggressive assault on Ortega's record by conservative elites during the 1996 campaign resuscitate a preference for democratic conservatism and sustain the realignment of public loyalties begun in 1990? Did economic improvements and social responsiveness during the Alemán years aid the new regime? Or did corruption and authoritarianism alienate public support from it? And as the citizens developed sustained real-world experience with democratic conservatism, including the gradual improvement in the economy, did wistfulness for the revolutionary era fade away? Or did such experience, with the pressure on social programs and increases in social inequality, engender citizen appreciation still for the revolution's accomplishments and promise and a continuing desire to pursue its vision of social justice?

To examine perceptions of regime performance held by citizens during the two campaigns, we return in table 7.2 to the survey questions about the revolutionary and postrevolutionary regimes introduced in our earlier discussion of the Chamorro years. Here we consider the results of three surveys spread across the 1996 campaign and two from the 2001 campaign. These surveys allow us to look at public opinion starting in the weeks immediately following Chamorro's speech inaugurating the 1996 campaign, through the middle of the campaign, and then into the week after the 1996 election. We then look at citizen opinion a month prior to the 2001 election and the week following the election. The results of these five surveys allow us to gauge the evolution in citizen attitudes about the revolutionary and postrevolutionary regimes from the end of Chamorro's term in office to the weeks just prior to the start of Bolaños's presidency.

Table 7.2 Citizen Evaluations of the Revolutionary and Postrevolutionary Regimes during the 1996 and 2001 Presidential Campaigns (%)

	Late Aug. 1996 (N = 1200)	Early Oct. 1996 (N = 1200)	Late Oct. 1996 (N = 1200)	Late Sept. 2001 (N = 1728)	Early Nov. 2001 (N = 1600)
I. Better programs?					
Social policy					
Revolutionary era	52.5	47.4	41.0	41.9	38.8
Postrev era					
Chamorro	22.0	25.0	38.7	16.2	20.1
Alemán				25.2	29.4
Crime					
Revolutionary era	48.4	40.5	36.5	42.9	40.2
Postrev era					
Chamorro	19.5	24.0	36.6	17.1	17.2
Alemán				16.9	27.1
Economy					
Revolutionary era	38.7	34.3	29.7	28.8	24.4
Postrev era					
Chamorro	31.0	33.6	51.8	33.7	37.8
Alemán				21.0	23.4
II. Most corrupt?					
Revolutionary era	18.2	19.9	30.7	26.6	29.9
Postrev era					
Chamorro	42.6	38.3	30.8	2.0	6.9
Alemán				61.3	53.9

(continued)

Table 7.2 (cont'd)

	Late Aug. 1996 (N = 1200)	Early Oct. 1996 (N = 1200)	Late Oct. 1996 (N = 1200)	Late Sept. 2001 (N = 1728)	Early Nov. 2001 (N = 1600)
III. *Best to ensure civil liberty?*					
Revolutionary era	25.6	23.8	24.3	17.8	17.1
Postrev era					
Chamorro	57.5	59.6	65.3	47.6	48.0
Alemán				25.2	27.6
IV. *Personal preference to live under?*					
Revolutionary era	38.4	34.7	31.7	30.4	27.4
Postrev era	29.6	36.8	50.6	55.5	62.3
V. *Overall characterization*					
Revolutionary era					
Democratic	14.2	13.8	13.4	20.1	24.9
Socialist	36.4	42.4	36.9	38.9	35.2
Authoritarian	29.3	28.2	37.1	28.1	31.1
Postrev era: Chamorro					
Democratic	53.8	60.8	75.6	78.5	78.1
Socialist	5.7	3.9	1.6	9.5	10.4
Authoritarian	15.3	19.8	11.3	7.2	4.0
Postrev era: Alemán					
Democratic				42.5	49.3
Socialist				7.9	6.7
Authoritarian				37.8	35.3

Source: DOXA nationwide monthly surveys during the 1996 presidential campaign and CINASE nationwide survey in late September and early November of 2001.
Note: *N* for each survey in 1996 is 1,200, 1,728 for late September of 2001, and 1,600 for early November of 2001. All percentages are based on the entire sample and include nonrespondents in the base. In the table, the percentages for performance on social policy are averages of the percentages of positive responses given to a regime on education, employment, health, and welfare in each survey.

As the results for 1996 demonstrate, the first post-Chamorro campaign saw a dramatic shift in citizens' aggregate assessments toward the Chamorro regime and away from the Sandinistas. While the campaign opened with voters tilted toward the FSLN regime on most policy questions except civil liberties, by early October citizens were seeing Chamorro's policies in a more positive light. By the postelection survey, citizens had only a very slight preference for the FSLN on social policy, gave roughly equal marks to the Sandinista and Chamorro regimes on crime and corruption, and had shifted from a plurality preference of the FSLN on economic policy to a majority preference for the Chamorro regime. Additionally, voters tilted even more strongly toward the Chamorro regime on civil liberties than at campaign outset. Most critically, citizens moved across the campaign from a plurality preference for life during the Sandinista regime to a slight majority preference by campaign end for life under Chamorro. This shift parallels a dramatic increase in the proportion of citizens characterizing the Chamorro regime as democratic and a noticeable increase in those characterizing the FSLN as authoritarian, perceptions that she and other conservative elites sought to foster during the campaign in an effort to focus voters away from social issues.

The intense 1996 campaign clearly mattered in reshaping citizens' regime assessments as they prepared to choose between Ortega and Alemán. In pushing regime affirmation as the central concern during the 1996 election Chamorro drew on the governing capital she had earned with her forthright campaign in 1990 and her sincere efforts to deliver on national reconstruction and stabilization during her presidency. She asked citizens to affirm her accomplishments and, in the process, to stay the course with Alemán. They did so, not only electing him but embracing more positive views on the Chamorro era than they had held at campaign outset. Their shift in perspective then survived the Alemán administration and persisted into 2001, as seen in the final two surveys in table 7.2.

The perceptions of the Sandinistas during the 2001 campaign continued to roughly parallel the levels evident at the end of 1996, while the percentage of citizens preferring the postrevolutionary era on most performance items continued to grow. Voters were divided between which of the two conservative administrations—Chamorro or Alemán—they preferred on specific policy issues. But in combination these two administrations outperformed the Sandinistas across all policy areas. Separately and in combination, the two conservative administrations also outpolled the FSLN regime on issues of civil liberties, and both were seen as more democratic. Most notably, by the end of the 2001 election almost two-thirds of the citizens appeared to prefer life during the postrevolutionary period over the revolutionary era.

The glow of the postrevolutionary era was dimmed, however, by assessments of corruption and authoritarianism during the Alemán years. A clear majority of citizens in 2001 saw the Alemán administration as the most corrupt of the previous two decades. Though the effect of this development was somewhat offset by a substantial decline in perceptions of the Chamorro regime as corrupt, at campaign's end roughly twice as many citizens chose one of the postrevolutionary conservative regimes as corrupt as chose the FSLN regime. Additionally, more citizens were concerned about authoritarianism under Alemán than under the revolutionary FSLN regime. While policy performance and general life circumstances appeared to be improving during the postrevolutionary era, with the Alemán administration doing better than Chamorro especially on social policies and crime, the dark, corrupt, sinister side of politics also appeared to be growing. Moreover, the concerted campaign of the conservative elite on behalf of Bolaños in the last month of the 2001 campaign did little to alter citizen revulsion at the corrupt and authoritarian character of Alemán's administration, judging from the relatively stable attitudes on these items in our two polls.

Although the 1996 campaign greatly improved citizen evaluations of the postrevolutionary regime, and much of this improved assessment persisted into 2001, the experience with Alemán undermined citizen appreciation of democratic conservatism on the vital issues of corruption and authoritarianism. A clear and growing majority of citizens signaled a preference for life after the revolution. And more citizens characterized the Chamorro and Alemán administrations as democratic than was the case for the Ortega administration. But the corrupt and authoritarian character of Alemán created considerable public disgust and introduced tensions into the public's embrace of democratic conservatism. These tensions allowed Ortega to mount his strongest campaign since 1984 and underscore the vulnerability of the new regime to public reassessment and potential rejection should such behavior continue and expand in future conservative governments. The election of Bolaños was a testament both to his political skills in separating himself from Alemán and also to the sustained willingness of voters to stay the course with democratic conservatism awhile longer, continuing down the path they had chosen in their reasoned embrace of Violeta Chamorro and her regime offer.

Conclusion

The eleven years from Chamorro's victory in 1990 to Alemán's election in 1996 to Bolaños's victory in 2001 was a period of democratic transition and growing regime consolidation in Nicaragua. While not rivaling the drama of the 1979 revolution and the social reconstruction of the revolutionary regime, this period was an equally vital phase in the life of the nation, moving it toward liberal democracy but also greatly testing the commitment and patience of its citizens. The mass of citizens faced substantial personal reversal and family hardship during these years, and the nation at large suffered as a result of the corruption of Alemán and his cronies. In the end the citizens sustained the new regime in power and increasingly embraced it across a range of policy areas. They also came to see the postrevolutionary period as the preferred period in which to live. But these outcomes were by no means a foregone conclusion.

Both in 1996 and in 2001, complex attitudinal crosscurrents about regime performance left the door open for an Ortega resurgence, with critical concerns about the social costs of democratic conservatism evident in 1996 and widespread concern about corruption present in 2001. In both years, a sizable proportion of the public continued to appreciate contributions of the revolutionary era. This was true particularly at the outset of the 1996 campaign, when the FSLN could garner majority support for its social policies and the revolutionary era could garner plurality support as the period in which citizens preferred to live. But it was true even following the 2001 election, after two intense campaigns by Chamorro and conservative elites in behalf of regime affirmation and five years of gradual economic improvement and societal stabilization. At this point the Sandinistas could still elicit support from roughly 40 percent of the citizenry on social and crime policies, and roughly a quarter of the citizenry still looked back to the revolutionary era as having been preferable to the postrevolutionary period.

In both campaigns Ortega made a spirited effort to regain the presidency, showing signs of momentum early on in each. But both times he failed, giving the new regime more time to prove itself and consolidate public support. Why? In part the answer to this question lies in the governing capital Chamorro had accrued as candidate and president and her skillful use of that capital during each campaign in support of the conservative candidate. In part, it lies in the dynamics of each campaign and the framing of issues by the candidates and their partisans, in the strategic actions and missteps of elite actors. Perhaps particularly critical in this regard, aside from the actions of the candidates, were public criticism of Ortega by Cardinal Obando y Bravo and the U.S. State Department at critical points during the campaigns. But at a deeper level the answers lie with the citizens themselves and the reasoning they employed as they responded to Chamorro's entreaties, to the campaigns, and to national circumstances.

To understand these elections and the process of democratic transition they helped drive, we turn now to a close assessment of citizens' reasoning and vote choice during the two campaigns. We do so guided by our theory of reflective voting, with its expectation that normalization of democratic politics should produce an evolution in citizens' reasoning processes toward growing reliance on retrospection. And we do so informed by the patterns of public opinion and vote choice evident in 1990, patterns that set a high standard of citizen engagement and responsible decision making against which to assess electoral politics and democratic performance during this period of regime consolidation.

Chapter 8

Reaffirming Citizen Choice: The 1996 and 2001 Elections

As citizens approached the post-Chamorro elections, the critical question was whether they would sustain the level of political engagement and the reasoned quality of vote choice evident in the 1990 presidential election. The new regime had ended the embargo and war, as Chamorro had promised. But it had also brought increases in poverty, unemployment, and social deprivation, developments that could have generated deep disillusionment with democratic conservatism among the masses who had supported Chamorro in 1990. At issue was how citizens would respond to the difficulties associated with regime transition. We know already that they voted to keep the regime in place. But how and why did they do so, and what does the answer to this question tell us about their long-term capacities as democratic citizens?

While accepting the new regime as an instrument of societal stabilization, and seeing certain benefits to it, Nicaraguans could have become disheartened about politics as a route to improvement in their personal lives. Citizen disengagement from political life was thus a distinct possibility. Under such circumstances, attitude crystallization and differentiation would decline in surveys of public opinion about politics. Assessments of candidates, the economy, and regime would cease to shape vote intent or do so more weakly. A randomness would enter the voting process. Disillusioned voters would vote out of obligation rather than interest or commitment. General tolerance of rightist presidents could be seen as a necessity, particularly if the alternative were an Ortega-led regime that might lead to renewed conflict with the United States and a return to revolutionary experimentation at home. But it would be a tolerance bereft of engaged involvement in campaign politics and electoral choice.

Alternatively, citizens could have concluded that the new regime had brought constructive movement to Nicaragua, demonstrating citizen capacity to use elections to improve both the nation and their own life opportunities. More than ever before, civil liberties and democratic procedures were being honored, and power sharing was occurring across local and national government among parties of the left and right. In addition, gradual progress appeared under way toward a stronger national economy than had existed in the past. The immediate social price of democratic conservatism, while deeply frustrating, could be seen as worth the long-term gain and one that could be somewhat ameliorated through improved social performance by future governments. Citizens could thus seek to sustain their investment in the new regime, giving it the time, support, and encouragement to fulfill its broad promise. Such citizen response would lead voters to value electoral participation and to demonstrate substantial engagement in campaigns. Under such conditions their attitudes would evidence high crystallization and differentiation and would be closely correlated with vote intent.

A growing engagement with democratic politics combined with a relatively stable national government could generate normalization in patterns of participation. We would thus expect voters to favor increasingly retrospective assessments of candidates, since they would have some sustained governing experience with all major parties. Moreover, with a lessening of crisis, the less educated might move toward extensive reliance on retrospection. Prospection would be seen more clearly and extensively among the educated for which it was an easy and natural element of reasoning. We would also expect relatively stable and distinctive alignments between major social groups and key political parties. The repeated election of rightist candidates would reflect systematic, reasoned choice, reaffirming the direction first taken in 1990, and would evidence deepened attachment by identifiable social groups to the rightist parties.

To determine which of these alternative responses more nearly characterized Nicaraguan voters, we turn here to an examination of public opinion and vote intent in the 1996 and 2001 elections. The first part of this chapter explores the evolution of citizen assessments of the candidates, economy, and regime across the two elections, examining patterns of crystallization, differentiation, and group polarization. The second part assesses the relationship between attitudes and vote in 1996 and 2001, with special attention to comparisons of the less-educated and more-educated voters. The third part then examines the similarities and differences in group voting behavior for the two elections. Throughout the chapter we use measurement strategies and indices developed in chapters 5 and 6 and compare the results for 1996 and

2001 with those of 1990. We are thus in a position to gauge how the process of citizen choice evolved during the early years of the new regime.

Citizen Attitudes, 1996, 2001: Candidates, Economy, and Regime

Candidate Image, 1996 and 2001

To gauge retrospective assessments of candidate image in the post-Chamorro elections, we again probe evaluations of specific candidate attributes. Table 8.1 presents the results for the discrete image questions for the first and last surveys in 1996 and the postelection survey in 2001. At campaign outset in 1996, Ortega led the Liberal candidate, Alemán, on concern for the people, experience, honesty, and leadership but trailed him slightly on respect and significantly—by 27 percent—on preparedness or readiness for the job. Voters saw both Ortega and Alemán in complex ways—regarding both as leaders but distrusting both as well. Neither held a distinct image advantage: Ortega was still plagued, as in 1990, by doubts about his ability to handle the presidential job; Alemán's main disadvantage was concern about whether he was sufficiently close to the people to care about their needs. By election time, and following a heated campaign with Chamorro's endorsement of Alemán, doubts about Alemán evident in the first 1996 survey had been resolved, while Ortega still struggled with issues of untrustworthiness and preparedness and had now lost his advantage on closeness to the people. The shift toward Alemán parallels the increased citizen appreciation of democratic conservatism that emerged during the 1996 campaign, as Chamorro made her case for steady citizen support of the new regime and as Alemán moved to associate himself more closely with Chamorro. Five years later, at the end of the 2001 election, the Liberal, Bolaños, likewise led Ortega on all image assessments, though the percentage of citizens giving positive assessments to each candidate was generally lower than at the end of 1996.

Figure 8.1 explores attitude crystallization and differentiation across image assessments, following procedures for estimating citizens' image preferences presented in chapter 5. As in 1990, candidate image assessments were highly crystallized during these two campaigns, as evidenced in the low and declining nonresponse rates across the 1996 and 2001 surveys. In fact, in the final 2001 survey citizens demonstrated almost universal awareness of some attributes of the former president and vice-president.

Despite such crystallization of views, citizen engagement was less evident when one looks at response differentiation in 1996. At campaign outset, interviewees tended to be ambivalent between the two candidates. Alemán

Table 8.1 Discrete Citizen Responses on Candidate Image Questions in 1996 and 2001 (percent saying yes)

Question: Is he ...	August 1996		Late October 1996 (Postelection)		Early November 2001 (Postelection)	
	Alemán	Ortega	Alemán	Ortega	Bolaños	Ortega
Concerned about people?	46.1	56.6	59.6	48.5	51.3	43.9
Experienced?	60.8	61.9	65.5	53.3	53.5	46.4
Honest?	35.8	37.3	52.5	37.1	53.0	33.7
A leader?	63.2	65.2	71.7	61.8	50.4	46.0
Prepared (for the job)?	70.0	43.7	79.0	41.7	66.7	34.5
Respected?	58.1	57.2	67.9	52.8	55.8	41.0

Source: DOXA nationwide surveys in August and late October of 1996 and CINASE nationwide survey in early November 2001 (following the election).
Note: The percentages indicate the proportion of all interviewees (including nonrespondents) who gave a favorable assessment of a candidate. $N = 1,200$ for each 1996 survey and 1,600 for the 2001 survey.

was strongly preferred by 12.8 percent and Ortega by 10.7 percent, so only 23.5 percent of respondents strongly embraced one candidate while rejecting the other. By contrast, in 1990 a third of all respondents had held strongly differentiated views in December 1989, two months prior to the 1990 election. A surge in image differentiation came only in the last several weeks of the 1996 campaign, when the U.S. State Department expressed renewed concern about Ortega, and Chamorro and Cardinal Obando y Bravo endorsed Alemán. After being nearly tied with Alemán in image preferences in the first two polls, Ortega fell in the third poll, while Alemán's image assessments continued to improve. Then, in the last, postelection, poll, the level of differentiation reached par with that seen in 1990, with Alemán preferred on image.

Image assessments early in the 1996 campaign did not create so substantial a differentiation between candidates that retrospective candidate evaluations could dominate vote choice. In fact, the most dominant pattern that emerges from these image data is that of indecision during much of the campaign. Across the three preelectoral surveys, 59 to 65 percent of respondents held crystallized views but still failed to differentiate clearly between the two candidates, instead signaling a preference for both, for neither, or ambivalence. Only in the last, postelection, survey did this figure fall to around 50 percent. These results reinforce the sense garnered from news reports and vote intent data that the 1996 election was quite competitive early on, with voters being sufficiently open in their retrospective comparisons of the two candidates that they were willing to give considerable additional attention to such concerns as governing competence, the economy, and regime. Only toward the end of the campaign did they resolve their retrospective ambivalence about the two candidates, with a marked increase in image preferences for Alemán over Ortega.

By contrast, in 2001 we see much more extensive image differentiation. Roughly 64 percent of citizens in the final postelection survey clearly preferred either Bolaños or Ortega in image terms. This is the highest level of image differentiation for any survey from 1989 through 2001. With high differentiation, the individual image scores of the candidates on the discrete questions fall, as seen in table 8.1, because fewer citizens are scoring both candidates highly on image terms. Such high differentiation reflects the fact that the 2001 campaign was the first pitting two candidates who had already served in national office. It also reflects growing stability of citizen views about the FSLN and democratic conservatism, the growing media saturation of Nicaragua, and the extensive efforts at partisan mobilization that occurred in the 2001 election. The high level of differentiation on candidate image in 2001 points to an election in which retrospective candidate assessments were

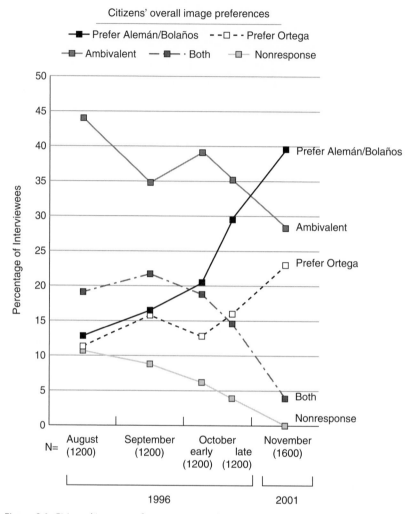

Citizens' overall image preferences

—■— Prefer Alemán/Bolaños   - -□ - - Prefer Ortega
—■— Ambivalent   —■- · Both   —■— Nonresponse

Figure 8.1 Citizens' image preferences across the 1996 and 2001 presidential campaigns, by month

Source: Nationwide surveys by DOXA in 1996 and CINASE in 2001.
Notes: "Prefer Alemán/Bolaños" indicates interviewees who gave Alemán (1996)/Bolaños (2001) four or more positive image ratings and Ortega none. "Prefer Ortega" indicates interviewees with the reverse scoring pattern. "Both" refers to interviewees who gave both Alemán/Bolaños and Ortega positive ratings on four or more items. "Ambivalent" refers to interviewees who gave both candidates at least one positive rating but who did not give both four or more positive ratings. "Nonresponse" refers to interviewees who failed to answer all six questions across both candidates. Interviewees were coded as preferring "Neither" who gave no positive ratings to either candidate, giving only negative assessments when they responded; fewer than 4.5% did so in any survey and thus these scores are omitted from the figure.

sufficiently dominant to reduce reliance on other concerns and prospective evaluations. Moreover, the growing retrospective preference for the rightist candidate, with Bolaños enjoying a 16 percent advantage over Ortega on overall image preference, makes clear that it is the right which will benefit from citizen reliance on such retrospective voting.

Candidate Competence, 1996 and 2001

To explore the extent to which citizens went beyond retrospective candidate assessment and focused on broader and prospective concerns, we examine public evaluation of the candidates' prospective governing competence. Table 8.2 presents the results of seven discrete candidate competence items across the four 1996 surveys and the postelection survey in 2001.

Considerable change occurred during the 1996 campaign. At the outset, the candidates were quite close in the percentage of citizens preferring them on the separate competence items. Alemán enjoyed a very slight advantage on five items and a 5-point advantage on local issues. Ortega had a slight advantage on health care and was tied with Alemán on education policy. In September, the percentage of citizens preferring Ortega increased and that for Alemán fell, so that Ortega gained a competence advantage across all items. Then in the last several weeks of the campaign, in the face of a strong campaign by Chamorro and other conservatives in Alemán's behalf, the preference for him soared. A postelection survey showed that Alemán led Ortega decisively on all competence concerns, with roughly a 16- to 18-point advantage on each.

At the end of the presidential campaign five years later in 2001, Bolaños maintained or improved on Alemán's 1996 postelection advantage over Ortega across each competence item. Ortega did show slight but consistent increases in competence evaluations across the two postelection surveys on six items. But on the seventh—the economy—he received his lowest competence assessment of the post-Chamorro election campaigns. Overall, the data point to stability in competence assessments for candidates from the two major parties from the end of 1996 to the end of 2001. This mirrors the stability in citizen assessments of the FSLN and democratic conservatism as governing regimes across these two elections, as discussed in chapter 7, and suggests a close similarity between the two elections. The question is whether aggregated patterns of crystallization and differentiation across the competence questions in any way qualify this conclusion.

Figure 8.2 presents the aggregated competence responses following the procedures for the Candidate Competence Index presented in chapter 5. It demonstrates that Ortega did move ahead in aggregate assessments early in

Table 8.2.   Citizens' Competence Assessments of Alemán/Bolaños and Ortega by Month
during the 1996 and 2001 Presidential Campaigns (%)

Question: Which candidate will . . .	Late August 1996	Late September 1996	Early October 1996	Late October 1996	Early November 2001
Improve economy?					
Alemán/Bolaños	36.9	33.2	38.7	50.9	54.1
Ortega	34.3	37.8	34.8	32.7	31.5
Solve unemployment?					
Alemán/Bolaños	37.3	33.6	38.0	50.1	54.0
Ortega	33.7	36.5	34.1	33.6	35.3
Improve education?					
Alemán/Bolaños	36.7	32.1	38.8	50.5	53.8
Ortega	36.8	39.1	35.9	34.1	36.4
Improve health care?					
Alemán/Bolaños	35.8	32.0	38.6	50.0	52.6
Ortega	37.3	38.3	35.5	33.9	36.8
Combat crime best?					
Alemán/Bolaños	37.6	33.3	39.0	50.5	52.3
Ortega	35.4	39.0	35.0	32.8	37.1
Combat corruption best?					
Alemán/Bolaños	36.8	32.6	39.0	50.0	52.3
Ortega	34.4	37.5	34.5	32.7	36.9
Solve local problems?					
Alemán/Bolaños	39.0	33.5	39.3	51.5	53.1
Ortega	34.4	38.4	34.9	32.7	36.3

Source: DOXA nationwide monthly surveys during the 1996 presidential campaign and CINASE nationwide survey in early November of 2001.
Note: N for each survey in 1996 is 1,200 and 1,600 for early November 2001. Percentages are based on the entire sample, including nonrespondents, and indicate the proportion seeing a candidate as more competent on a specific item. The late October 1996 survey occurred the week following Alemán's election, and the early November 2001 survey occurred the week following Bolaños's election.

the 1996 campaign, taking advantage of the severe social conditions that had arisen with the Chamorro regime and citizen desire for a candidate who could address them. Alemán then strongly rebounded at the end, as conservative elites stressed the important advances that had occurred in civil liberties and democratic process, urging citizens to stay the course awhile longer as the regime sought to make similar progress on social and economic concerns. It also demonstrates that the aggregate competence evaluations at the end of each election greatly favored the Liberal candidates. In addition, the data allow us to compare crystallization and differentiation of overall competence responses across our surveys.

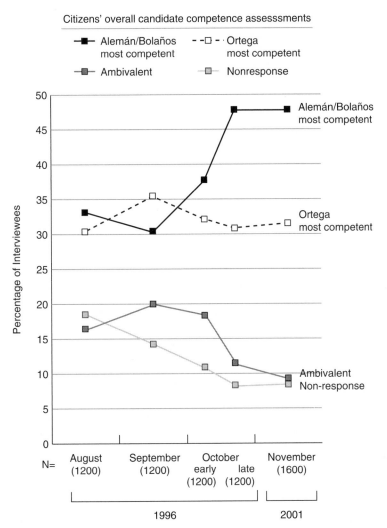

Citizens' overall candidate competence assesssments

Figure 8.2 Citizens' overall determination of the most competent candidate during the 1996 and 2001 presidential elections, by month

Source: Nationwide surveys by DOXA in 1996 and CINASE in 2001.

Notes: An interviewee's overall competence assessment of the two candidates is determined by summing the number of positive ratings given to Ortega on the seven competence questions (scored as +1 for each positive rating) and the number of positive ratings given to Alemán (1996)/Bolaños (2001) (scored as −1 for each item). When an interviewee indicates that neither is competent on an item, that response is scored as zero. Interviewees whose sum is +4 or more see Ortega as most competent, and those whose sum is −4 or more see Alemán/Bolaños as most competent. Interviewees who give neither candidate an absolute score of 4 or more are ambivalent. Interviewees who decline to rate the candidates on one or more of the eight competence questions are treated as nonrespondents in the calculation of citizens' overall competence assessments of the candidates.

In 1996 the citizenry engaged earlier in assessing and differentiating among candidates on competence questions than did citizens in 1990. In the race between Chamorro and Ortega, approximately 73 percent held crystallized views, and 61 percent clearly differentiated between the candidates two months before the election. At roughly the same point in the 1996 campaign, 81 percent of the respondents held crystallized views on the Candidate Competence Index, gauged by the number of respondents in the late August survey, and approximately 64.5 percent clearly differentiated between the two candidates, as seen in the combined percentage of those preferring either Alemán or Ortega. Early citizen engagement in prospective assessments in 1996 may have reflected greater citizen indecisiveness on retrospective assessments in 1996, which led them to look at prospective concerns earlier. It may also have reflected growing experience with citizen engagement in competitive democratic elections, an engagement reinforced by certainty that the 1996 election would actually be held, in contrast to the doubts in 1990.

As the campaign progressed, crystallization and differentiation grew. Two weeks before the election in 1996, 88.3 percent held crystallized views, and 70.9 percent clearly differentiated between the candidates, compared with the 85.2 percent crystallization level and the 74.4 percent differentiation level reached two weeks prior to the 1990 election. Finally, in the fourth (postelection) survey 92 percent held crystallized views, and 80 percent clearly differentiated between the candidates on competence issues.

At the end of the 2001 campaign, the aggregate competence assessments of the Liberal Bolaños and the Sandinista Ortega are almost identical to the patterning at the end of 1996 for Alemán and Ortega. Some 90.7 percent of the citizenry held crystallized views on candidate competence, and 81.4 percent held differentiated views. Nicaraguans were taking the elections seriously enough in both 1996 and 2001 to engage extensively in prospective candidate assessments by the end of the campaigns. Yet to clarify fully the consequences of prospective assessment, we need to examine patterns of group polarization on candidate competence, since Sniderman, Brody, and Tetlock suggest that voters are likely to act on prospection primarily when reinforced by similar attitudes among group associates.

Figure 8.3 presents the polarized competence evaluations by class, following the procedures for calculating group polarization used in chapter 5. We present the polarization scores differentiated by four class groups for the first two surveys of the 1996 campaign, the final postelection survey in 1996, and the final postelection survey in 2001. We have also examined the competence polarization scores by age and gender in 1996 and 2001.

With respect to class polarization on candidate competence, the 1996

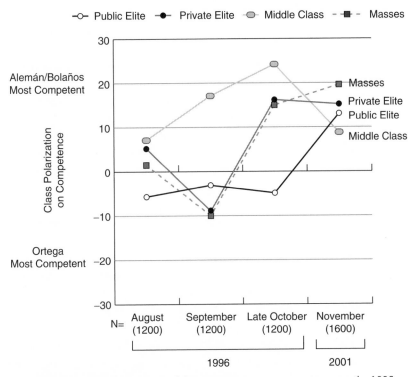

Figure 8.3 Class polarization on candidate competence assessments across the 1996 and 2001 presidential campaigns, by month

Source: Nationwide surveys by DOXA in 1996 and CINASE in 2001.
Notes: Class polarization is determined by subtracting the percentage of class members who consider Ortega to be the most competent candidate from the percentage rating Alemán (1996)/Bolaños (2001) as most competent. A positive score indicates the % tilt toward Alemán/Bolaños. A negative score indicates the % tilt toward Ortega.

campaign opened with the nation tilted very slightly toward Alemán and with modest differences among classes. As the campaign heated up in September and Ortega gained momentum, the classes polarized. The masses, alienated by the austerity of Chamorro's democratic conservatism, shifted decisively toward Ortega on competence questions, and the working class and private elite followed suit.[1] The public sector elite maintained its slight preference for Ortega. The middle class, enamored of economic reform and the growing civil liberties provided by democratic conservatism,

1. The latter group now contained elements from the new elite of the Sandinista era who had used their education and government experience to join the entrepreneurial class. These former Sandinistas, momentarily feeling the tug of previous social concerns, led this movement among the private elite toward Ortega.

went against the grain and shifted strongly toward Alemán. These patterns suggest that Ortega's momentum early in the 1996 campaign was based on broad support and linked to groups with historic political meaning.

Following the conservative attack in October 1996, the nation began shifting away from Ortega and back toward Alemán on competence assessments, with this rightward tilt led by the middle class. In the final survey (postelection), Ortega continued to show some strength among the public sector elite, remnants of the FSLN support base from the 1980s. Similarly, by the end of the campaign, Ortega's strength amidst the age and gender groups lay primarily, though modestly, in the FSLN's traditional support base of the revolutionary era—those citizens who had come of age during the revolutionary period and men. All other groups shifted decisively to Alemán. The persistence of these clear though modest group divisions in citizen differentiation on candidate competence points to continuing importance for prospective voting in 1996, with group polarization reinforcing citizens' individual views.

Five years later, the nation ended the 2001 campaign tilted even more strongly toward the conservative candidate on competence assessments than in 1996, completing a remarkable reversal in class polarization patterns from those evident early in the 1996 campaign. The 1996 campaign began with all classes bunched closely together within a 55–45 split on competence assessments of the two candidates, with neither the leftist nor the rightist candidate clearly favored. The polarized gap between the most left-leaning group, the public sector elite, and the most right-leaning group, the middle class, was only 13 percent. By the end of 1996 all classes had moved right except the public sector, but there was considerable spread among their polarization scores. At this point, the gap between the public sector and middle classes had grown to 30 percent. Six years later, as the 2001 campaign ended, all classes were bunched together again, as they had been at the beginning of the 1996 campaign, with only an 11.5 percent gap between the most left-leaning and most right-leaning groups. However, this time all groups clearly favored the rightist candidate on competence assessments.

Ironically, in 2001 the most left-leaning group was the middle class and the most right-leaning group was the masses. Alienated from the conservative regime by Alemán's corruption, the middle class gave Bolaños low marks on his capacity to control corruption and crime. The lower classes, attracted to the conservative cause by Alemán's social concessions, gave Bolaños high marks on social issues. Simultaneously, the public sector elite moved rightward in its competence assessments, no longer serving as the most left-leaning outlier. Its movement occurred particularly as a result of the strong scores it gave Bolaños on his perceived ability to deal successfully with the economy. These strong scores owed not only to the improvement in the economy but to the continuing success of the Chamorro and Alemán administrations in replacing public officials from the Sandinista era with those of a more conservative orientation.

The leftward move of the middle class on competence assessments and the move of the lower classes and public sector elite to the right, in combination, virtually neutralized class distinctions in the patterning of aggregate competence assessments in 2001. Likewise, there is virtually no gender difference in candidate assessments, with both men and women tilting to Bolaños, though women slightly more than men. The similarity in aggregate assessments across groups suggests that competence evaluations were probably muted in their power in the voting booth in 2001, since they lacked strong reinforcement from long-standing group divisions. The only notable exception was age, where Ortega nearly held his own among the revolutionary era generation, while Bolaños generated strong competence assessments among the other age cohorts.

Quite momentously for Ortega and the FSLN, the postrevolutionary generation moved from a slight tilt toward him on competence issues at the outset of the 1996 campaign to a growing tilt away from him across the postelection surveys of 1996 and 2001. While on other survey questions the postrevolutionary generation often showed positive inclinations toward the FSLN, on this central question that focused directly on Ortega's governing competence, the youngest generation has apparently taken to heart the attack on the former president mounted by Nicaragua's conservative elite. The young appear enamored of the conservatives' market economy and loath to risk a reversal in the expansion of the consumer economy that might come with Ortega's election.

Economy and Regime, 1996 and 2001

We have also examined citizens' retrospective and prospective assessments of the economy and regime during the 1996 and 2001 elections, looking at the same questions on these items that we utilized in the study of the 1990 campaign.[2] This assessment indicates that citizens became more positive about

2. While the questions asked were the same as in 1990, it is the case that the regime assessment question, asking when life was better, had three choices instead of two: before the revolution, during it, or afterward. This wording reflects a tendency that emerged during the Chamorro years of referring to the entire FSLN years as the revolutionary period and of considering the period from 1990 onward as the postrevolutionary years. The regime assessment questions here likewise differ from those explored at the end of chapter 7. There we looked solely at the contrast between the revolutionary and postrevolutionary regimes. Here, to maintain consistency with analysis of the 1990 election, we also include the prerevolutionary Somoza regime as an option.

the economy and regime change across the two campaigns, as one would expect based on the detailed discussion of economic performance and regime performance at the end of chapter 7. This shift occurred first on regime assessments. Noticeable improvements in retrospective and prospective regime evaluations of the postrevolutionary regime came in the second 1996 survey and then in the last 1996 survey, with improvement continuing into the 2001 campaign. Of these regime patterns, the most consequential has to do with retrospective regime assessment. Whereas the 1990 campaign had ended with 32.8 percent seeing life as better during the revolutionary era, the 1996 election ended with 28 percent taking this position and the 2001 election ended with only 22.2 percent saying life was better during the revolutionary regime. With respect to prospection, the 1996 campaign began with only 17.4 percent of the interviewees believing the nation was headed in the right direction, but this figure had risen to 40.1 percent by the end of the campaign. At the end of the 2001 campaign the analogous figure was 36.5 percent, a slight decrease that we attribute to concerns with Alemán's authoritarian tendencies and corruption.

Lagging behind regime assessments, aggregate attitudes about the economy shifted primarily at the end of 1996. While more than two-thirds of interviewees saw the economy as worse throughout the 1996 campaign, in the final two weeks this percentage fell to 50 percent. By the final 2001 poll, only 30 percent of the interviewees were giving a negative retrospective assessment of the economy. Similarly, while future economic assessments were erratic during the 1996 campaign, the percentage seeing a dark future dropped dramatically in the final survey, falling from 67.5 percent in late August to 51 percent in late October. Improvement in the economic assessments continued with the 2001 postelection survey, reflecting actual improvement in the economy: only 21 percent of the interviewees were giving a negative prospective assessment in the final 2001 postelection poll.

As with results on candidate image and candidate competence, the survey data on economic and regime assessments indicate serious citizen engagement in the two campaigns. Attitude crystallization was quite high across all economic and regime questions in both 1996 and 2001, with nonresponse tending to run between 5 percent and 10 percent of interviewees and well below the highest levels of 30 percent or more seen at times on some of these questions in 1990. Moreover, additional analysis of the economic and regime assessments indicates considerable consistency in retrospective and prospective responses by individual citizens, denoting high levels of attitudinal differentiation. By the end of each campaign, crystallization and differentiation approached or surpassed the levels witnessed at the end of the 1990 campaign across all attitudinal dimensions—from candidate image to candidate competence to economic assessments to regime assessments. The attitudinal engagement of citizens evident in 1990 does not appear to have been unique, but rather a harbinger of longer-term citizen desire to follow politics and assess the candidates and conditions confronting them, thereby facilitating reflective citizen choice of president. Did citizens subsequently utilize these attitudes in shaping vote choice in 1996 and 2001 as they did in 1990?

Modeling the 1996 and 2001 Vote: Attitudes and Vote Choice

To determine how well the attitudinal variables together shaped vote intent for the 1996 and 2001 elections, we present in table 8.3 logistic regression results for the seven independent variables and the dependent vote intent variable for each election. We present the results for our four 1996 surveys in order to look at vote evolution within the first post-Chamorro campaign. We present results of the postelection 2001 survey in order to gauge the evolution of vote choice across the two elections. Given the coding scheme we have employed, as presented in chapter 6, we expect a positive relationship between the dependent variable (coded 0 to predict an intended Ortega vote) and image assessments of Alemán or Bolaños (where 6 is high). All other independent variables should have an inverse relationship to the vote, since in these elections it is the economy and regime of the conservative incumbents that voters are assessing.

The seven-variable model used for predicting the 1990 vote performed well again in 1996 and 2001. The attitudinal variables account for more than 92 percent of the cases of vote choice for each survey among interviewees prepared to make a vote choice. Additionally, all variables that reach statistical significance are in the predicted direction.

The significance levels reveal that the public began the 1996 campaign with a very simple and more retrospective focus on the electoral alternatives and then moved as the campaign progressed to consider a more complex array of concerns. Early on, two retrospective concerns (Ortega's image and past economic performance) and one prospective concern (candidate competence) appeared to shape vote intent. In the second survey, as voters were doubting Alemán and giving Ortega a second look, a somewhat more complex four-variable model emerged, in which retrospective economic assessments receded as a consideration and voters looked closely at the retrospective image of both candidates, at the retrospective performance of the current regime, and again at prospective candidate competence. It was at this midpoint in the campaign that Ortega achieved his highest level in the public

Table 8.3. Modeling Vote Choice across the 1996 and 2001 Presidential Campaigns: Retrospective and Prospective Evaluations of Candidates, the Economy, and the Regime

Survey	Late August 1996	Late September 1996	October 1996	Postelection 1996	Postelection 2001
Alemán's/Bolaños's image	.072	.256***	.102	.365***	.172**
	(.091)	(.092)	(.095)	(.114)	(.080)
Ortega's image	-.213**	-.466****	-.525****	-.462****	-.672****
	(.102)	(.1)	(.099)	(.11)	(.080)
Candidate competence	-3.032****	-1.788****	-2.312****	-2.255****	-1.554****
	(.361)	(.325)	(.3)	(.381)	(.227)
Current economy	-.913***	-.157	-.884***	-.277	-.480*
	(.320)	(.243)	(.328)	(.354)	(.293)
Future economy	.36	-.014	.26	.106	-.123
	(.23)	(.239)	(.250)	(.344)	(.214)
Regime performance	-.53	-1.216***	-.661	-1.710***	-1.374***
	(.398)	(.414)	(.427)	(.553)	(.448)
Regime direction	.551	-.08	-.64	-1.452***	-.344
	(.503)	(.427)	(.506)	(.557)	(.233)
Constant	1.300	-.179	4.099***	-.648	4.930
	(1.271)	(1.192)	(1.414)	(1.597)	(.000)
N	502	604	668	785	1048
Chi square	446.839****	574.717****	668.751****	877.031****	1143.055****
Predictive strength	92.23%	93.54%	95.21%	96.82%	96.0%

Source: DOXA nationwide monthly surveys during the 1996 presidential campaign (with Ortega and Alemán as the candidates) and CINASE early November nationwide survey in 2001 (with Ortega and Bolaños as the candidates).

Note: The table utilizes logistic regression analysis. Entries are maximum likelihood coefficients. Standard errors are in parentheses.

****p <.001 ***p <.01 **p <.05 *p <.1

opinion polls. Two weeks before the election voters returned to a concern with the economy, and a simpler vote model emerged. Finally, following a heated campaign that occurred two weeks prior to the election, voters focused on precisely those factors that the combined forces of the right were emphasizing: the contrast between the candidates themselves and the regime alternatives they offered.

In the final vote model of 1996, all three candidate variables and both regime variables achieved statistical significance while evaluations of the economy receded entirely from statistical significance. The voters thus gave attention to three retrospective concerns and two prospective concerns as they shaped their final vote choice. The vote choice model is a simpler one, more focused on retrospection than in the momentous and intense 1990 election, where large numbers of voters were considering a change in historic partisan loyalties. It suggests some degree of "normalization" in the reasoning process, wherein citizens consider a more bounded and empirically grounded range of concerns. Nevertheless, amidst some considerable partisan shifting and a heated final campaign in 1996, both retrospective and prospective considerations loom large in determining the vote. In addition, in contrast to elections in established democracies, as citizens looked beyond the candidates themselves, it was regime considerations rather than economic ones that proved significant in shaping their vote.

Five years later, as evident in the results for the postelection survey in 2001, the appearance of normalization became more marked. Citizens still gave close attention to candidate image and candidate competence as they shaped final vote intent, and also remained concerned about regime performance. And, as in 1990, they considered economic performance. But in 2001, in contrast to the final surveys for 1990 and 1996, citizen concern about regime direction faded as an influence on vote choice. As a result, four of the five significant variables in 2001 were retrospective in nature. With the growing tilt to economic considerations and retrospective evaluation, aggregate patterns of vote choice in Nicaragua increasingly look like those expected in relatively established democracies, where competing parties have extensive governing records, regime direction is settled, and a primary concern is the economic performance of the governing party.

The remaining question is whether these patterns of vote choice differed among the educated and less educated. In 1990, the less educated relied more extensively on prospection than did the more educated. This pattern helped us understand why they could engage in extensive movement toward Chamorro despite her relative inexperience in government, whereas the more educated were more likely to stay with Ortega. By contrast, when we

construct separate vote models for the educated and less educated in the final
postelection survey in 1996, we find that they look roughly similar to
one another. With a significance level set at .05, both groups considered
retrospective image for the two candidates, their comparative governing
competence, and past regime performance. If we loosen our significance test
to the more modest level of .1, both groups also were looking at regime
direction. Considering the size of the maximum likelihood coefficients, however, the less educated appeared to rely more heavily on retrospective candidate image assessments than did the more educated, whereas the latter had
considerably higher coefficients for candidate competence and regime performance and slightly higher coefficients for regime direction. The model
for the educated accounts for 97.15 percent of all cases, and the model for the
less educated accounts for 97.84 percent.

While the model that explains 1996 vote choice across the entire electorate is similar to that for 1990, shifts were taking place in the attitudinal
patterning associated with vote choice among more-educated and less-
educated citizens. In 1996 the educated were relying on prospection and
looking at regime concerns more than in 1990. The less educated were relying on retrospection and candidate evaluations more than in 1990. This shift
makes sense in light of evidence from the campaign coverage and our
descriptive analysis that the educated elite were extensively engaged in
reassessment of contemporary politics and partisan loyalties in 1996, in contrast to 1990.

With the demise of the Sandinista regime, the more educated no longer
benefited from special status as members of the new elite. They were also no
longer in a strong position to pursue the goals of the Sandinistas, goals that
many of them had previously embraced and to which they had committed
their talents and energy. Now they were considering which partisan and
regime direction best served their emerging self-interest and the nation's
long-term reconstruction, within the nation's new realities. They thus
focused more on prospective and regime concerns than in 1990, when they
had been committed to staying the course with the FSLN.

Simultaneously, while some of the poor who had abandoned the
Sandinistas were now returning, many of the poor continued their support
for democratic conservatism. Thus the less educated were more retrospective and candidate centered in orientation than in 1990. With these shifts in
reasoning among the better- and less-educated citizens, the Nicaraguan electorate began to resemble those in more established democracies and periods
of normalcy, where the less educated generally vote in a more retrospective
and candidate-centered manner, and the better educated vote in a more

prospective and complex, broadly focused manner. This shift, however, appeared to reflect not simply or primarily cognitive differences between the groups but unique conditions of self-interest calculation present in the 1996 campaign. The less educated appeared prepared to reaffirm the self-interested judgments and long-term assessments they had made in 1990, which had led them to choose Chamorro and democratic conservatism. As a result, they voted more retrospectively in 1996. The more educated, in contrast, were now prepared to reconsider their earlier commitment to the FSLN and thus looked more closely at prospective considerations as they shaped their vote choice.

To consider whether this movement toward normalized patterns continued as Nicaragua entered its most stable and regularized election, we turn to the comparison of the more- and less-educated respondents during the 2001 postelection survey. This time, the less-educated citizens based their vote choice narrowly on assessments of Ortega's retrospective image, comparison of the governing competence of the candidates, and evaluations of regime performance. The less educated, in other words, had moved to a relatively simple reasoning process shaped by their reactions to the major historic development of the past two decades—the alternative regimes governing the nation. They considered the performance of those regimes, the pros and cons of Ortega's presidency, and the ability of alternative regime candidates to address immediate problems. In contrast, the more-educated citizens appeared to have a more complex calculus that also included evaluations of economic performance and Bolaños's image. The resulting model for the educated predicts 95.3 percent of all cases, whereas the model for the less educated predicts 96.0 percent.

The greater complexity of the reasoning process of the more educated in 2001 is the pattern one expects in established democracies in relatively stable times. This sense of normalization is reinforced by the fact that both the less and the more educated focused primarily on retrospective concerns. By 2001, the citizens had considerable experience with the Sandinistas and Liberals on which to base such assessments. In addition, both Ortega and Bolaños had served in national office, facilitating candidate assessments. Moreover, eleven years after Chamorro's defeat of Ortega, regime direction appeared increasingly resolved. Not only did most citizens and virtually all Liberal voters reject life during the revolution, so too did 45 percent of those voting for Ortega. Citizen concerns thus focused on immediate policies and administrative performance and on candidate attributes, more than on expectations that a vote for Ortega might produce a fundamentally new regime. The educated simply focused on a broader array of such concerns than did the less educated. The contrasts between the less educated and more educated in 2001 did appear to result primarily from cognitive differences and personal judgments, rather than from decisive contrasts in the extent to which their group interests focused their attention on retrospective or prospective concerns.

The sense that normalization of voter decision making is occurring in Nicaragua, and that it points to a deepening of democratic politics in the nation, is underscored by the broad range of developments in public opinion and vote choice between 1990 and 2001 that are consistent with this interpretation. The growing focus of citizens on retrospection points to a situation in which all major parties and candidates have governing experience, a sign of increased partisan power sharing. The growing crystallization and differentiation of citizen attitudes on questions dealing with political campaigns, public policy, and regime performance indicate a citizenry that increasingly feels comfortable following politics, that has access to the necessary information to do so, and that is interested in doing so. The increased stability in citizen assessments of the policies of the major parties, as seen in the similarity of survey results following the 1996 and 2001 elections, corresponds to the sort of attitudinal stability that McCann and Lawson (2003) see as anchoring the long-term consolidation of democratic governance. And the movement toward less complex reasoning by the less educated, with broad-gauged reflection being more the province of the educated, while troubling in normative ways, does suggest that the sense of crisis that could lead the less educated to push their cognitive limits is decreasing in the daily lives of common citizens.

Given this apparent normalization in electoral engagement and reasoning processes among voters, it is natural to wonder whether there was an analogous clarification and solidification of group alignments and partisan politics in Nicaragua. Generally analysts expect that the stability of established democracies is sustained by the existence of clear-cut and relatively continuous differences in the vote alignments of groups.[3] While often modest and cross-cutting, such group differences reflect and reinforce the different programmatic visions that give meaning to a nation's partisan conflicts and allow voters to make relatively consistent and retrospective sense out of politics across time. Eleven years into an era of democratic conservatism, is such stability in group alignments emerging in Nicaragua?

3. Lipset and Rokkan (1967). See also LaPalombara and Weiner (1966); Huntington (1968); Sartori (1976); and Mainwaring (1999).

Group Voting Behavior, 1996 and 2001

The bulk of Nicaraguan history would suggest that the lower classes would form the natural support base of the leftist Sandinistas and the more affluent would support the right-wing Liberal Party. Yet in 1990, amidst a crisis that hit them hardest, the poor abandoned the FSLN. Together with the old elite, they embraced Violeta Chamorro, while only the new public sector elite stayed with Ortega. Let us now explore what happened in 1996 and 2001.

We know from our attitudinal data that the austerity of Chamorro's social policies subsequently alienated many lower-class citizens, while the middle class, buoyed by her attention to civil liberties and neoliberal economics, were more positive about democratic conservatism. Yet we also know that Alemán's responsiveness to popular demands for social concessions generated renewed support for the right among the poor, while the middle class, alienated by his corruption, appeared more suspicious of democratic conservatism. These attitudinal shifts among classes are reflected in comparative assessments of the Sandinista and conservative regimes discussed in chapter 7 and in assessments of candidate competence in the first part of this chapter. Our concern now is to determine the patterns of group voting that emerged as individual citizens acted on their attitudinal assessments and reasoned to their preferred vote choice.

Table 8.4 presents the voting pattern for class in our final postelection surveys for 1996 and 2001. The top half indicates the percentage of interviewees in each class who supported Alemán, Ortega, or the minor parties in 1996. The bottom half presents analogous data for Bolaños, Ortega, and the minor parties in 2001. To facilitate comparison across groups and elections, we present these results in one table, with the candidates listed at the top of the table and percentages for groups summing to the right. We have also closely examined the breakdown in these voting patterns by age and gender and will report those results here as well.

The class voting data from 1996 and 2001 demonstrate that the dramatic decline that occurred between 1984 and 1990 in lower-class support for Ortega was sustained thereafter.[4] The underclass and working class tilted to the rightist candidate over Ortega in both 1996 and 2001, as they had in

4. As we demonstrated in chapter 4, roughly two-thirds of lower-class voters supported Ortega in 1984, whereas in 1990 his support among them had fallen below 35 percent. Leaving aside nonrespondents, lower-class support for Ortega (including here both the underclass and the working class) remained below 42 percent for voters in both 1996 and 2001, far below the 1984 level.

Table 8.4   Presidential Vote Choice by Class in the 1996 and 2001 Postelection Surveys (%)

| | 1996 | | | | |
CLASS	Alemán	Ortega	Minor parties	Non-response	Total
Underclass	42.0	37.0	8.8	12.2	100
Working class	46.4	31.1	8.8	13.7	100
Middle class	53.2	30.9	7.5	8.3	99.9
Private elite	58.1	32.6	7.0	2.3	100
Public elite	36.1	41.0	14.8	8.2	100.1
	2001				
	Bolaños	Ortega	Minor parties	Non-response	Total
Underclass	48.2	34.5	1.2	16.1	100
Working class	45.7	35.7	4.8	13.7	99.9
Middle class	44.3	42.0	3.9	9.8	100
Private elite	49.4	36.1	3.9	10.7	100.1
Public elite	47.7	41.1	3.6	7.7	100.1

Source: DOXA nationwide postelection survey in late October of 1996 and CINASE nationwide postelection survey in early November 2001.
Note: N for 1996 is 1,186, with class designations unavailable for 14 of the 1,200 original interviewees. N for 2001 is 1,579, with class designations unavailable for 21 of the 1,600 interviewees.

1990. Chamorro's election does appear to have broken the lower-class alignment with the left and to have generated a rightward tilt in presidential elections. Given that the lower classes constitute a majority of Nicaraguan voters and are the historic support base for the FSLN, their continued tilt to the right would seem to point to a new electoral order in Nicaraguan politics and to create severe problems for the Sandinistas at the national level.

At the same time, there does appear to be increased party competitiveness within the classes amidst this rightist tilt, particularly when we look at the vote margin between the two major contenders. Thus in 1990 the masses voted for Chamorro over Ortega by a 25 percent margin; the margin then declined to 13 percent in 1996 and to 11 percent in 2001. The public sector elite, which supported Ortega by a margin of 24 percent in 1990 (as the new Sandinista elite), supported him by 5 percent over Alemán in 1996 and then supported Bolaños by a margin of 6.6 percent over Ortega in 2001, reversing this group's previous voting pattern. The private elite, which had supported Chamorro by 37 percent over Ortega in 1990, supported Alemán by a margin of 26 percent in 1996 and Bolaños by 13 percent over Ortega in 2001. Finally, the new middle class, which in 1996 supported Alemán by a margin of 22 percent, supported Bolaños by only 2.3 percent in 2001. This general tightening within the various classes was due to apprehension within the masses about austere social policies, the growing influx of conservative public officials into the public sector elite during the Chamorro and Alemán presidencies, the growing influx of former members of the Sandinista elite into the private sector (some of whom remained supportive of the FSLN), and middle-class apprehension about Alemán's corrupt and authoritarian tendencies (which then hurt the campaign of his vice-president, Bolaños).

Amidst this tightening, perhaps the most intriguing development was the way in which classes shifted positions across time in the ordering of their rightist or leftist support. In 1996, the private elite and the middle class provided Alemán his strongest class support, while the lower classes had moved somewhat back toward Ortega and the public sector elite continued to support him by a slight margin. At this point, following Chamorro's austerity, the electorate appeared to be returning to a traditional ordering of class voting. The rich clearly supported the right; the poor were more likely to be open to a leftist appeal; and the public sector elite led the way for them. But in 2001, following Alemán's corrupt but somewhat socially responsive presidency, the middle class had become Ortega's strongest class support group, whereas the public sector elite had swung to the right, voting more conservatively than the middle class. Simultaneously, the private elite had become less hard-core in its rightist support, while the masses maintained the moderate rightward tilt they had evidenced in 1996, so that the vote margin of the masses in behalf of Bolaños approximated that of the private elite in 2001. While no class gave Ortega a plurality of support in 2001, the middle class came close, with 42 percent voting for him and 44.3 percent voting for Bolaños. In contrast, the underclass, which had been one of Ortega's two strongest groups in 1996, joined the private elite as one of his two weakest groups in 2001.

Such fluidity is also seen in voting by age. In 1996, the left had seemed poised to solidify virtually as much support among the postrevolutionary generation (those under 25 years of age) as it received among the revolutionary era cohort (those aged 25 to 44), with Ortega trailing Alemán by 11 percent among the former, 9 percent among the latter, and 35 percent among the prerevolutionary generation (those 45 or older). In 2001, with the greater success of Alemán in fostering the market economy, the postrevolutionary generation (those 30 and under) voted more strongly for Bolaños while the revolutionary era generation (those 32 to 51) swung strongly toward Ortega, doing so in response to Alemán's rightist authoritarian tendencies. Thus Ortega trailed Bolaños by 13 percent among the young, 1.3 percent among the revolutionary era generation, and 20 percent among the prerevolutionary era group (those 52 years of age or older in 2001). Like the revolutionary era group, some among the older voters were taken aback by Alemán's behavior, perhaps remembering the Somozas and voting less strongly rightist than in 1996.

Simultaneously, the gender gap in voting narrowed in 1996 and virtually disappeared in 2001. In 1990, the margin of female support for Chamorro exceeded the margin of male support for Ortega by 18 percentage points. In contrast, the margin of support for Alemán over Ortega among women in 1996 was only 7 points greater than the right-left margin among men that year. By 2001 the margin of support for Bolaños over Ortega among women was only 3.5 points greater than the margin among men.

To gauge the statistical power of groups to predict vote intent, we again use logistic regression. In doing so, we create two binary measures of class. The first, class 1, is based on the history of lower-class support for Sandinismo. It combines the public sector elite with the underclass and the marginalized working class into one class group, with a historical inclination to support the FSLN, pitted against the middle class and private sector elite. The second, class 2, is designed to gauge the lower-class opposition to the FSLN that emerged in 1990; it pits the underclass and working class against the middle class and elites. In a bivariate logistic model predicting vote intent (Ortega versus the opposition), class 1 was significant in 1996, but neither was significant in 2001. When we combine class 1 with age and gender in a multivariate logistic regression model for presidential vote in 1996, class 1 and age were significant, and together account for 63.2 percent of the cases. In this analysis, age was coded with the revolutionary generation as 1, the postrevolutionary generation as 2, and the prerevolutionary generation as 3, an ordering that captures the tendency of the vote inclinations of the postrevolutionary generation to fall between that of their revolutionary era parents and their prerevolutionary grandparents. For gender, men are coded as 1 and women as 2. For 2001, in a logistic regression analysis of presidential vote using class 2, age, and gender, only age was significant. In a bivariate model, it accounted for 57.7 percent of the cases, with a maximum likelihood coefficient of .261.

The shifting class dynamic across the two elections suggests that the way issues and events frame an election in Nicaragua is proving quite powerful in eliciting different dimensions of class response. Austere programs by conservatives, as with Chamorro, bring forth traditional class opposition to the right by the poor and activist social elites. Simultaneously, neoliberal reforms, limited corruption, and observance of civil liberties can solidify support for the right among the affluent. The result will be a modest degree of traditional class voting, as evident in 1996.

By contrast, more responsive social programs by conservatives may diffuse lower-class opposition to the right and limit class voting. When social responsiveness to the poor combines with political corruption that alienates the middle class, traditional class divisions may dissipate. Thus, following Alemán's corrupt but socially concessionary administration, his former vice-president gained more support from the poor than the right had following upon Chamorro's administration but lost ground among the middle class. Alemán's behavior thus succeeded in generating a class-neutral pattern of group voting, at least for that election, in a nation that is one of the world's most class-conscious societies. By inference, a corrupt conservative administration that also failed to respond to social concerns could face serious problems with the electorate, while a conservative administration that avoided corruption, honored civil liberties, and demonstrated social responsiveness amidst economic progress could consolidate a strong electoral following. Overall, across the 1996 and 2001 elections, group politics did shape vote intent, as it did in 1990. Inattentiveness to group concerns would be political suicide in Nicaragua. Certainly Alemán helped the Liberal cause by negotiating with the left on social reforms. Yet these traditional groups are not determinative of political attitudes or the vote. Considerable internal division exists within groups, with such divisions likely shaped by different individual experiences during the previous decades of dictatorship, revolution, socialist reform, civil war, and conservative retrenchment.

The political role of traditional social groups clearly has changed and weakened over the past two decades in Nicaragua. The strong ordering of class and partisan voting seen in 1984, or of gender and partisan voting seen in 1990, has dissipated. Today, if any group voting pattern seems persistent, it is the tendency of the prerevolutionary and postrevolutionary generations to tilt increasingly right, while the revolutionary era generation remains more open to the FSLN. While modest patterns of group voting can emerge in a specific electoral context, Nicaraguans today appear more characterized by individuality in voting than by group patterns of voting.

The electorate as a whole evidences strong support for the right in national elections, a substantial alteration in partisan and ideological alignments from 1984. But within that broad shift rightward, the ordering of group voting election by election is fluid. Which groups will support the right and the left depends on governing performance. In so far as stable and distinct group alignments are a sign of maturing democracy, Nicaragua falls short of that mark. Moreover, as in 2001, the FSLN cannot assume that experience with democratic conservatism will automatically regenerate its lower-class base. Similarly, the right cannot assume the loyalty of the affluent and middle classes in the face of corruption or authoritarianism from a conservative administration.

What is not clear is how entrenched this new order is, particularly as Ortega has been the FSLN candidate in the three presidential elections. While the rightist tilt of the electorate has now been sustained across the elections, and clearly entails some strong support for the liberal democratic regime that Chamorro's conservatism initiated, it is unclear whether the size of the presidential vote in 1996 and 2001 owes substantially to a preference for a conservative president or also reflects continued concern about Ortega himself. Across time, citizens have shown increased retrospective concerns about Ortega, as seen in the steady decline in his retrospective image scores presented earlier in table 8.1. In particular, while the citizens' retrospective assessments continue to demonstrate a residue of appreciation of him, they also indicate widespread concern over whether he is honest and is truly up to the job of president. This mixed retrospective assessment of Ortega has continued to shape citizens' vote decisions in the 1996 and 2001 elections, as it did in 1990. But the true import of these retrospective assessments for overall vote margin is more difficult to estimate. Unless and until the Sandinistas present a credible presidential candidate other than Ortega, we cannot know if citizens are voting against Ortega but are prepared to consider a Sandinista candidate less tied to the past, or whether they are truly voting against the party, irrespective of its presidential candidate, with the retrospective concerns about Ortega merely reinforcing this inclination.

It is possible that the FSLN could produce a new and attractive candidate devoted to social reform and willing to operate within the broader confines of today's democratic procedures. Such a candidate would be less tied to the old regime, more in tune with the young, postrevolutionary generation, but also capable of rallying the party's revolutionary era loyalists. Herty Lewites, Managua's Sandinista mayor, exemplifies such a person but is unlikely to become a presidential candidate for reasons of age and health. Yet a younger leader who shares many aspects of Lewites's personality and style might bring an FSLN victory in a future presidential election.

The election of such a candidate would be easier if the right were hindered by voters' concerns over Liberal corruption or by renewed strength among Conservatives that weakened the Liberal dominance among right-center voters. The possibility of such a victory is supported by the Sandinistas' 2000 municipal victories, including Lewites's success in Managua, and by the party's continuing ability to elect a sizable group of legislators to the National Assembly. These successes not only demonstrate the party's continuing electoral power but provide it a substantial group of experienced political leaders from whom to select a national presidential candidate. A possible non-Ortega FSLN victory also finds support in public opinion polls supporting many FSLN social policies and in citizen concerns about corruption under the Liberals. It is heightened by the persistence of a substantial body of citizens who are independents (about 18 to 20 percent in the 2001 surveys by CINASE) or Conservative identifiers (around 9 to 10 percent in 2001). These independents and Conservative identifiers could provide potential supporters for an attractive FSLN candidate in a close race with a problematic Liberal standard-bearer. And future FSLN victory is made possible by the party's sustained willingness to respect civil liberties and democratic process at the local level and to play a constructive role in legislative policy making at the national level. These efforts serve to reduce apprehension that the FSLN in power would immediately revert to its more oppressive tendencies witnessed in the late 1980s.[5]

A victory for the Sandinistas, if combined with responsible performance in power and with respect for Nicaraguan democracy by the international community, particularly the United States, would be a moment of historical importance in the evolution of Nicaraguan democracy, on a par with the election of Chamorro in 1990. It would signal the capacity of the nation to engage not only in power sharing between right and left across local and national offices. It would demonstrate its capacity to embrace power alternation between the right and the left—twice—through national elections. Such an FSLN victory, combined with its governing success, could also establish Sandinista candidates as true alternatives to rightist presidents, thereby constraining the temptation of rightist governments to engage in corruption and authoritarian behavior, lest such behavior lead to loss of control of government.[6] A strong governing performance by the Sandinistas might also serve to regenerate attachment from some of their natural supporters, who have thus far remained relatively fluid in their partisan support and voting behavior, thereby fostering greater stability and class structuring to the nation's party system.

Should power alternation occur and be respected by the United States, it would signal a deepening of democracy in Nicaragua. Yet such developments

5. The potential for the resurgence of a moderated FSLN also would seem supported by Coppedge (2001, 199). He argues that broad environmental changes are under way throughout Latin America in the early twenty-first century, as a result of which "we can expect to see different sorts of parties favored in future elections. In particular, the environment seems to favor the center-left over the center-right." See also Coppedge (1998).

6. For a study arguing that moderate behavior by leftist parties helps to reassure the right, offset authoritarianism, and foster democratic consolidation, see Alexander (2002).

are not guaranteed. Bolaños's willingness to bring to justice a member of his own party and of his own wealthy old elite class is a positive signal, while future efforts to pardon or release Alemán, or to unseat the Bolaños government as political payback for Alemán's prosecution, could undermine democratic progress. Similarly, movement inside the FSLN away from Ortega could signal democratic progress. Only a major political crisis, perhaps together with the splintering of the right-center presidential vote, would seem to allow Ortega himself to regain the presidency. This development would require great skill on his part in reassuring opponents about his commitment to democratization.

Conclusion

The high civic engagement by Nicaraguans in the 1990 presidential campaign continued during the post-Chamorro era. With this engagement came competitive elections whose outcomes served to reaffirm citizens' 1990 choice of democratic conservatism and also to sustain Sandinista influence in the crafting of the new regime. The commitment of the masses to Chamorro and her vision of a reconstructed Nicaragua that emerged during the 1990 campaign was apparently quite real, generating substantial mass support for subsequent presidential candidates she endorsed, even in the face of the severe social problems generated by her austere neoliberal policies. Yet many citizens continued to support Ortega and to elect a large bloc of Sandinistas to the National Assembly, giving Ortega and the party influence over constitutional reform and policy change.

The main electoral shift that occurred in the post-Chamorro years was the willingness of the more educated to move rightward, following the demise of the FSLN regime. This completed a two-stage realignment of class loyalties, begun with the shift of the masses to Chamorro in 1990. By November 1996 the entire class structure had moved substantially to the right, when voting patterns that year are contrasted with those of 1984. Yet citizens continued to remain open to the Sandinistas, particularly in municipal elections but also, to a lesser extent, for the presidency and National Assembly. This openness allowed Ortega to mount serious election challenges and meant that citizens were continually reassessing partisan loyalties during the 1996 and 2001 elections. Neither election was a foregone conclusion. Amidst Nicaragua's extensive poverty, the FSLN's social policies continued to attract support and generate attention to Ortega's candidacy. He showed momentum in both campaigns, pushing citizens to think about the elections and their vote choice.

As in 1990, citizens took their responsibility as voters seriously. In doing so, they demonstrated a sustained capacity to fulfill the roles of democratic citizenship in the face of serious personal reversals, complex policy problems, and slow if steady progress in national reconstruction. Despite the difficulties attendant on the transition to neoliberal economics, which could have generated deep voter disengagement and apathy, they continued to engage in electoral politics and reasoned carefully to their vote choice. Attitude crystallization and differentiation approached or surpassed those witnessed during Chamorro's election. Similarly, attitudes closely shaped vote decisions, indicating that the election outcomes and the reaffirmation of democratic conservatism were conscious, reflective choices. Moreover, citizen reasoning evolved across the elections in ways that point to responsible citizen choice and that also reflect growing experience with a range of governing parties and candidates. Thus, in 1996, as they considered a shift rightward, the educated engaged more extensively and consequentially in prospective reasoning than in 1990. By 2001, confronted by candidates and parties with substantial experience in national government, the entire electorate shifted toward retrospective voting. This shift was consistent with Fiorina's argument that electorates in established democracies rely on retrospection.

These patterns point to a normalization of electoral politics in Nicaragua, with citizens having sufficient experience with candidates and parties in 2001 to rely on past performance in assessing them. Within this retrospective orientation, in ways proposed by Sniderman, Brody, and Tetlock, it was the educated who reflected more fully across retrospective and prospective concerns. The less educated relied more on retrospection. Insofar as voter reflection across both would appear desirable even in more normal times, this finding reinforces the argument of Sniderman and his co-authors: democratic nations must continually aspire to provide and improve mass education if they wish to have broadly informed and reflective citizens, a task that the Sandinistas took to heart.

The move toward normalized processes of voter decision making, unfortunately, was not accompanied by a stable and distinctive alignment between social groups and political parties.[7] As a result, Nicaraguan politics continues

---

7. For a set of case studies and interpretive essays suggesting that parties worldwide are struggling to mobilize, represent, and serve the interests of their natural group allies, see Diamond and Gunther (2001). See also Gunther, Montero, and Linz (2002). For case studies demonstrating a weakening in the social bases of parties in advanced industrial democracies, see Dalton and Wattenberg (2000); and for a challenge, see Mair (1997). At issue across these books is the extent to which weak or weakening linkages between social groups and parties are undercutting democratic government. As a general rule, they suggest that parties in parliamentary regimes and well-established democracies may suffer less from the weakening of their social anchorage, whereas presidential regimes and new democracies may suffer more. The latter is the fear in the Nicaraguan case.

to be characterized by considerable fluctuation and openness in group voting. To some extent, such fluctuation is a sign of serious citizen choice, election by election. On the other hand, the ability of social groups to know and pursue their interests in sustained ways is generally aided by their close association with specific mass political parties. When such parties take seriously their responsibility to work for and represent supportive groups, they fulfill a variety of roles essential to democratic politics. In particular, they keep their support groups informed of ongoing political and policy developments, lobby for them in the corridors of power, and mobilize them in behalf of vital interests. In doing so, they ensure that democracy has real policy substance. They also help ensure that democratic institutions, particularly legislatures, realize their policy-making potential and constrain and guide executive power.[8]

At the height of its power and promise in the early to mid 1980s, the FSLN performed the roles of a responsible mass party in classic manner, aiding the poor in critical ways. It also did so during the constitutional reform under Chamorro and on behalf of social reform during the Alemán years. Yet it remains to be seen if a well-developed party system, composed of distinct mass parties grounded in support from distinct social groups and willing to play their representational roles in a responsible, sustained manner, will solidify in Nicaragua. In the absence of strong and distinctive attachments between specific social groups and the mass parties, it is unclear how far the current democratization process will proceed. In particular, it is not clear whether Nicaragua can generate a stable and truly competitive national party system in which the party of the left—as well as the party of the right—can compete for the presidency with a real chance to win and govern. With such a party system, and the strengthening of democratic governing institutions it could help generate, Nicaragua may become increasingly immunized to the return of authoritarianism, a return that looked distinctly possible with the presidency of Arnoldo Alemán. Without it, Nicaragua's budding democracy may well remain a fragile and vulnerable one.

Thus, as we end our empirical assessment of Nicaragua's elections, we join Thomas Walker in urging observers to look at Nicaragua "without illusions."[9] Certainly if one contrasts its politics in the early twenty-first century

8. See Epstein (1980); Beck and Sorauf (1992); Ware (1996); Gunther, Montero, and Linz (2002). The classic study of the weakness of democratic government without competitive parties is Key (1949). For qualifications about the benefits of strong parties in Latin American contexts, see Coppedge (1994).

9. See Walker (1997b) and Dye (2000).

with the mid-1970s, much has been accomplished. Few would deny that it is today a less repressive, more responsive, egalitarian, hopeful, pluralist nation than then, owing both to the revolution and Sandinista reforms and to the expansion of civil liberties and democratic processes since 1990. Yet it is neither the pure, egalitarian socialist democracy that many dreamed it would become, demonstrating the people's power to right the wrongs of centuries of exploitation, nor the vibrant, affluent democracy Chamorro envisioned. It is a world of poverty as well as neoliberal promise, a world of Alemán, corruption, and political irresponsibility as well as engaged, responsible citizens and earnest leaders like Chamorro, Ortega, and Bolaños. It is a politics in the making, with much potential but also sufficient cause for alarm. Its evolution remains a fascinating and frustrating experience to observe, fully a testament to the difficulties and the promise of democracy.

Chapter 9

Learning Democracy In and From
Nicaragua: Concluding Perspectives

We conclude our study of Nicaraguan democratization here, knowing that this is neither the end of the story nor the confines of its meaning. As this book closes, Nicaraguan democratic development remains open, incomplete, uncertain, and insecure. The fact of an Alemán presidency and all the questions about democratic loyalty such an event entails, combined with the admonitions of democratic theory, cannot help but leave us cautious as this book ends. And yet, in four elections across two decades, Nicaragua has engaged in electoral process and respected democratic procedure. Nicaraguans have elected the presidential candidates of three different parties, representing diverse ideological and historical traditions. Those choices have brought momentous shifts in the nation's governing regime. Citizens and leaders have increasingly abided by the electoral results and taken their disagreements into the National Assembly, the press, peaceful protests, the court system, and subsequent elections rather than to the battlefield. Nicaragua appears to be evolving into an inclusive, constitutional democracy.

Whatever surprises and reversals the future may hold, initial steps to democracy appear undeniable and require explanation. How can one account for this remarkable use of democratic procedures to make momentous regime choices in so unlikely a setting as Nicaragua? It is, after all, an impoverished nation that fits few of the "requisites of democracy" that democratization theorists emphasize. It is to this puzzle that we now turn, first by addressing the meaning that the elections have for the puzzle itself.

The Puzzle of Nicaraguan Democratization

The puzzling nature of democratization in Nicaragua lies in the arrival of regular elections in a setting that contemporary theories describe as hostile, if not fatal, to democratization. Such theories argue that serious democratization requires domestic affluence, or cohesive domestic leadership, or widespread norms of participation gained through generations of associational membership, or a history of gradualist development and free market economics devoid of social revolution and socialist experimentation. Nicaragua meets none of these criteria. It is deeply poor, is characterized by severe and continuing elite conflict, lacks any sustained history of associational membership, and experienced a socialist revolution. Then why democracy?

Some analysts reply that there is really no puzzle at all here and that the move to democratization in Nicaragua is more illusion than reality. This perspective relies on one or more of several interpretations of the 1990 election: confused and disengaged citizens inadvertently embraced an appearance of democratic politics when, in truth, they preferred socialism; citizens used elections to repudiate the despised Sandinistas but not necessarily to embrace democracy; citizens actually supported one-party Sandinista rule and sought merely to constrain the party, not renounce it or institute procedural democracy; or, finally, citizens were and are capitulating to the United States, not embracing a new regime direction because of its vision. The evidence in this book argues otherwise.

Nicaragua's democratization process has been complex, giving rise to concerns about its authenticity. At times, citizens have looked apathetic or confused. This appearance has been heightened by the failure of visible pollsters to predict the 1990 election correctly and by subsequent explanations for that failure that attribute it to voter ineptness and fear. There is a minority of citizens who oppose the Sandinistas under any conditions, blame them for all problems, and refuse to consider them as a governing option. There were also periods of cynicism when some citizens doubted whether the Sandinistas would hold or honor free elections, so insincere voting might have seemed an option. Many citizens have been concerned about the FSLN's ability to reach accommodation with the United States, while having greater confidence in the conciliatory capacities of Chamorro and her successors. Moreover, the Panama invasion in the middle of the 1990 campaign underscored U.S. willingness to intervene militarily in Central America. Thus one might conclude, in the absence of public opinion data, that Nicaraguans simply capitulated to the United States in electing Chamorro, driven to this decision by fear that otherwise they risked invasion. Yet these observations and conclusions are only a small and misleading part of the story.

Close assessment of electoral decisions among Nicaraguans and of contemporary political history questions these interpretations. While voters showed signs of apathy early in the 1990 campaign, and some visible international pollsters mispredicted the outcome, the widely reported mispredictions came primarily from U.S. pollsters who lacked experience in the special conditions and poverty of Nicaragua. Such errors underscore the need for contextually sensitive polling more than a dearth of democratic capacity among Nicaraguans.[1] Reputable, if less well-known, Latin American pollsters who did have contextual experience accurately called the 1990 election and those thereafter. Their data show that Nicaraguans moved rapidly in 1990 to engage in the electoral contest, once it became clear that the contest would be genuine. Moreover, citizen engagement, particularly support for Ortega, increased following the Panama invasion. Voters then maintained their high levels of political involvement through the 1990 election and demonstrated similar involvement in the 1996 and 2001 campaigns as well. In addition, both in 1990 and thereafter many citizens were open to candidates of both right and left, respecting and considering each rather than ruling out one without consideration.

Across all three elections, citizens reasoned their way to final vote choices in an engaged, attentive and responsible manner that accorded closely with the expectations of our theory of reflective voting. In doing so, they drew from the beginning of each campaign on both retrospective and prospective assessments of the candidates, the economy, and the regime. These assessments closely shaped the vote decisions of both the educated and less educated, doing so in sensible ways that appear reasonable within the context the citizens confronted at the time. There is little if any evidence of insincere or disingenuous voting in any of the elections studied here. Similarly, the polls do not show significant evidence of citizen capitulation to the United States following the Panama invasion. If anything, the invasion increased support for Ortega, a defiant popular reaction that is in keeping with Nicaraguan history. Moreover, particularly in 1990, the connection between attitudes and vote choice points toward a thoughtful, farsighted, prospective consideration of future paths associated with the two candidates. In the end, citizens supported Chamorro more out of a belief that she could lead the country forward than out of a belief her election would lead to a cessation of U.S. Contra support. It was this belief in her ability to lead toward reconciliation and

---

1. Anderson (1992, 1994a).

reconstruction that best accounts for her growing mass support. Thereafter, it was the respect for civil liberties and the move toward democracy that citizens saw as her greatest accomplishments. The fact that 70 percent of respondents gave her a positive overall evaluation as she departed office, with considerable support coming from Ortega voters as well, suggests that neither her election nor her presidency was rejected by the citizens.

Yet Chamorro's election and the sustained movement toward democratic conservatism do not appear to constitute a rejection of Sandinismo either. In 1990 and subsequently, many citizens supported the idealism and vision of the Sandinista Party, particularly the commitment to social justice and the view of state responsibility for it. Moreover, a substantial proportion of the electorate has supported Ortega in each of these elections. Retrospective disappointment with Ortega's presidency did hurt the FSLN in each election, as one would expect when a leader's incumbency yielded severe economic deterioration and governing crisis. Yet substantial support for the party's social program remains, as does respect for Ortega and acceptance of his and his party's participation in national political life. If anything, Ortega's continued capacity to draw 40 percent or more in electoral support is one of history's stronger performances by a leader under whom a nation suffered calamity and underscores sustained popular support for the FSLN.[2] While it may now be time for the party to move beyond Ortega as its presidential standard-bearer, this is due less to a long-repressed citizen repudiation of him than to a need for new leaders in new times.

As the citizens engaged in choosing between Ortega and three successive rightist candidates, their process of vote decision making evolved election by election, again much as the theory of reflective voting argues. Early in the democratization process, in the momentous 1990 campaign, citizens closely considered both retrospective and prospective assessments of the candidates and context and voted according to these assessments. The less educated proved at least as sophisticated in their reflective reasoning processes as did the more educated. In fact, in 1990 the less-educated and lower-class citizens showed greater complexity and a more prospective tilt as they reasoned toward dominant support of Chamorro than did the more educated elite citizens as they reasoned toward dominant support for Ortega. In addition, the less-educated and poorer citizens, who were the voters most responsible for Chamorro's election, demonstrated foresightful attention to her ability not only to end the nation's state of crisis but to bring about national reconciliation and reconstruction. In providing majority support for Chamorro in

2. Hill (1988).

1990, these less-educated and poorer voters broke with their historic support of the left, as seen in the 1984 presidential vote, and moved rightward in a classic demonstration of the capacities of citizens to refocus their issue priorities and alter their partisan voting alignments.[3]

In the two elections following Chamorro's victory, voters showed signs of increased reliance on retrospective voting along lines Fiorina and others have shown for established democracies. Such patterns point toward the presence of a competitive, democratic system wherein a range of parties are gaining governing experience, enabling voters to rely more on retrospection in their electoral evaluations. Such retrospection grounds voter choice in real-world events and performance and helps ensure that voters are using informed reasoning. Yet Nicaraguans also can look beyond retrospection to reflect on possible future contributions by candidates and parties, a capacity that seems essential for a developing nation with severe poverty, deep problems, and difficult decisions to make regarding those problems.

Nicaraguans see their elections as fundamentally free and fair, including the 1984 election. Moreover, the case for democratization looks well beyond elections to include evidence of the construction of democratic rules, procedures, and institutions. This includes power sharing across parties, institutions, and levels of government; respect for civil liberties and legal process; and multiple avenues for citizen participation. The multiple avenues for citizen participation include not only elections but mass protests and the lobbying of legislators, both of which have allowed citizens to hold the regime accountable for its policy promises and to assert new policy demands. The ongoing movement toward legal procedure is evident in the efforts to hold Alemán and his consorts accountable for theft and corruption during his presidency. With these developments, citizens increasingly give positive assessments to the policy performance and democratic practices of the governments of democratic conservatism while feeling free to oppose and rally against austere social policies, political corruption, and authoritarianism. Clear preference for life during the post-Sandinista regime appears to be growing, even among Sandinista voters.

The puzzle of democratization in Nicaragua appears real. Citizens are participating in a democratic polity in meaningful ways and respecting participatory and institutional mechanisms of democracy. They are doing this, moreover, despite poverty, without sustained elite guidance, without long-term civic experience, and after a socialist revolution. How is this possible?

3. B. D. Jones (1994, esp. 155–56).

Answering this question requires analysts to reassess the literature on democratic requisites.

The existing theories about democratic requisites provide a helpful starting point for considering the circumstances that facilitate democratization. But particularly in light of the Nicaraguan experience, that literature may have rushed too quickly to identify specific substantive conditions as essential to democracy. There may be core mechanisms and processes that are central to democratization, as the literature on democratic requisites implies. And affluence, elite guidance, civic associations, or the gradual emergence of capitalist democracy may have helped generate such mechanisms and processes among North Atlantic nations. But perhaps other substantive conditions could well generate such core requisites in other times and places.

The concern is to identify the core mechanisms and processes of democratization, and to consider the range of functionally equivalent conditions that may give rise to them. In this regard, as Charles Tilly suggests, democracy may be like a lake, able to form in a myriad of ways and circumstances.[4] The precise conditions that give rise to a lake in an arid desert may be diametrically opposed to those generating a lake in a mountainous rain forest. But both lakes may water gardens and sustain life all the same and share some central core requisites—sources of water, mechanisms for circulation and replenishment, a terrain that can contain the lake, and so forth—that are necessary to their creation and sustenance.[5] Those core requisites will simply not be obvious based on similarities or differences in the lakes' visible circumstances. Rather, underground streams may provide water for a desert lake, which observers might never have expected from the concentrated study of rain forests.

Much as with a lake, the true requisites of democracy may not depend on the precise material or substantive circumstances that have given rise to specific democracies, but on the core underlying processes and mechanisms of democratization that those conditions helped facilitate. Quite different substantive conditions could well generate those same core requisites. The emergence of democratization in Nicaragua would then be understood as resulting from the ability of its substantive conditions to yield such core

4. Tilly (1997, esp. chap. 8). A similar conclusion about multiple paths to democracy is seen is Rose, Mishler, and Haerpfer's (1998, 224) analysis of regime transitions in postcommunist societies. See also Flanigan and Fogelman (1971a, b).

5. Di Palma (1990, 17) makes a similar argument from a general perspective.

requisites, even if they have been generated differently in other nations. At issue is what those core requisites are.

We see four processes and mechanisms as playing critical, if not essential, roles in democratization, with all four being evident both in the literature on democratic requisites, which derives largely from the study of the North Atlantic nations,[6] and in the real-world experience of Nicaragua. These four core requisites are: (1) widespread resources for democratic citizenship, (2) national readiness for democracy, (3) citizen capacity for civic action, and (4) a developmental path that facilitates democratic learning. The presence of these core requisites in Nicaragua explains why the nation has been able to move toward democratization, despite the absence of the material conditions stressed by democratization theorists. These core requisites were generated by a different set of historical experiences and substantive conditions from those evident in the North Atlantic democracies, but their value to democratization is no less real.

The Resources of Democratic Citizenship

At the heart of the democratization literature, particularly those approaches stressing affluence and a civic culture, is the suggestion that citizens need cognitive and substantive resources that enable them to participate and function constructively as democratic citizens.[7] Affluence and its associated experiences generate these resources, so the argument goes, making it and its byproducts essential to democratization. Thus, affluent societies generate high education levels that produce the political knowledge and systematic reasoning capacities essential for citizens to engage in democratic decision making. They expand leisure time to allow for civic participation and democratic learning through such participation. They produce material comfort that moderates the level of conflict by giving citizens a stake in maintaining the social order. And they provide a base level of equality in which most citizens have some degree of economic and social autonomy in their private lives. Such autonomy then allows them to participate in politics more freely and to believe that their participation can make a real difference in political and policy outcomes.

We have no direct quarrel with the argument that affluence may foster cognitive and substantive resources in ways that facilitate citizen engagement

---

6. The phrase is from Habermas (1996, 2). Moreover, the lessons attributed to the "North Atlantic" nations may not be homogeneous or decisive even among them; see Dahl (1966); Powell (1982); Lijphart (1984); and Dodd (1976).

7. For a probing discussion, see Verba, Schlozman, and Brady (1995).

in democratic politics. Our question is whether affluence is necessary to the existence of such resources, and whether the conditions that seem to manifest democratic citizenship in affluent societies are the appropriate and universal measure for gauging democratic citizenship everywhere. In affluent societies such conditions might include possessing highly refined knowledge about politics or refraining from immoderate forms of political participation. But these might not be appropriate elsewhere. There are substantial reasons to question the necessity of affluence and to look to other manifestations of democratic citizenship aside from those seen in affluent nations. The remainder of this chapter highlights various of these reasons. But we begin by offering three perspectives on the true resources of democratic citizenship that together suggest that citizens throughout most of the contemporary developing world, as in Nicaragua, may be far better prepared for democratic participation than is generally realized.

The Capacity to Reason and Learn

Citizens in many different contexts can learn to participate in democracy, first because the capacity to assess social reality and to know one's immediate and long-term interests precedes wealth, education, and national development. Students of the poor and marginalized have long realized that average people know very well what their interests are and can make savvy choices in pursuit of those interests. Students of peasants and workers, for example, know that such citizens can often outguess and outwit those with more affluence, power, social standing, intellectual refinement, or economic resources. And they can engage in sustained collective action in pursuit of such interests, from everyday resistance to social revolution.[8] But scholarly knowledge about the reasoning capacities of the poor has not penetrated the mainstream study of democracy because scholarship on democratization and elections has focused almost entirely on the North Atlantic experience and the presence of affluence and education that that fortunate experience included. Scholarship of democracy and elections has ignored the political capacities and learning potential of people who live in the world's nondemocracies. Therefore, the capacities of citizens who lack education and affluence do not enter into theories about democratic development.

Nicaragua shows that poor citizens can learn the mechanics and reasoning processes of democracy and do so quickly if crisis and the need to save themselves and their nation demand it. These learning capacities were

8. Scott (1976, 1985); Popkin (1979); Tsing (1993); Anderson (1994b).

underscored by the nature and conditions of the 1990 election. Logistically, the election was far more complex than those in most established democracies. Nearly all Nicaraguan voters are registered to vote in the town or village where they were born since birth records are easier to maintain than are records about immediate residence and do not change. If they have moved as adults, almost all voters travel back to their place of origin to vote. Such travel itself imposes obstacles to voting, given the poor roads, inadequate transport, and low income levels of Nicaragua. Nicaragua also lacks an efficient mail service to deliver voter registration cards and instructions about voting locations, so voters must take special care to have the necessary cards and information required to vote. And once citizens arrive at the voting station, the antiquated procedures for voting and the limited number of voting booths mean they must stand in long lines on election day just to cast their ballots. For many voters, to vote on that Sunday is all they get done the entire day, or even the entire weekend if they are forced to travel overnight in order to reach their assigned voting station.

In 1990 voting proceeded not only amidst procedural complexity and occasional confusion, but during a civil war, severe economic deterioration, and a debate over regime direction. Yet, despite such adversity, in 1990 well over 80 percent of the nation voted. Thereafter, despite concerns about vote fraud in 1996 and hurricane devastation in 2001, leaving the Atlantic region under four to five feet of water on election day, voter turnout actually increased. In each of these elections, the voting and electoral procedures met the expectations of international observers; the election outcome was certified as resulting from free and fair voting processes; and, as this book shows, most citizens carefully reasoned their way to their vote choice.

These citizens did not have decades of experience in voting, extensive instruction in voting procedures, or other advantages of affluence. The ability of more than a million and a half voters to comprehend the elaborate rules confronting them, proceed over a weekend to assigned voting stations, vote, and return home to work by Monday morning should speak volumes about the capacity of inexperienced citizens to learn democratic process in a rapid manner and about their desire to do so. While a variety of circumstances facilitated this learning, this grasp of democratic process and the complex reasoning Nicaraguans utilized certainly suggest that poor citizens amidst poverty possess learning and reasoning capacities that theorists need to recognize and respect.[9]

9. This call for attention to the reasoning capacities of voters is reinforced by the findings and arguments in Popkin (1991).

The Empowering Benefits of Primary Education

Second, democracy can develop in many contexts because of the empowerment that comes with even meager levels of education and literacy.[10] Given some basic human capacities for reasoning and learning, education brings this capacity forward so that relatively modest educational levels can activate democratic engagement. The question is where to draw the line in the hierarchy of educational training, below which citizens are truly incapable of selecting their government. The Nicaraguan experience speaks directly to this issue.

In Nicaragua in 1990 the major dividing line in civic engagement appeared to be between those citizens who were illiterate and those who had received at least some formal education or job training. The illiterate were substantially less likely to respond to survey questions and less likely to indicate a desire to vote. In addition, they were the only education group among the underclass who did not significantly reassess their support for Ortega. As one looks beyond the illiterate, attitude crystallization jumped markedly, the report of vote intention increased, and citizens were more likely to share their vote intent. Most critically, when we look at the less educated as a group in 1990, and to a lesser extent thereafter, their reasoning patterns look much like the complex and sophisticated processes ascribed to highly educated American voters by Sniderman, Brody, and Tetlock. The less educated assessed and reassessed both candidates in 1990. Reflecting across retrospective and prospective concerns, they made the difficult decision to change governing regimes, showing faith in their own judgment and abilities as they did so. They also demonstrated a more savvy awareness of the electoral problems facing Ortega than did better-educated neighbors and many pollsters. It was the less educated who early on reported seeing a Chamorro victory.

The evidence from Nicaragua should force theorists to rethink the level of education at which democratic politics becomes possible and to broaden the range of circumstances that may be amenable to democratic citizenship. The critical issue here is not whether advanced education helps citizens become more engaged and informed in democratic politics, and to do so more rapidly, than does limited education. Obviously it does, as the data on attitude crystallization and vote participation in Nicaragua demonstrate,

10. On the personal empowerment that comes with literacy, see Milner's (2002) cross-national analysis of the influence of functional literacy on democratic participation in Scandinavian, North Atlantic, and British Commonwealth democracies. The importance of the Nicaraguan case is to indicate that the move from illiteracy to literacy may contribute to widespread citizen participation not only in the "developed world," as documented by Milner, but also in impoverished third world contexts, helping make democracy possible there as well.

paralleling results from a long line of studies in established democracies.[11] The pressing question, instead, is the point of education below which citizens become incapable of choosing their government. To this much more important, difficult, and poorly studied question, the Nicaraguan experience provides a powerful answer: even modest education may prepare citizens to utilize their reasoning capacities and participate effectively in the selection of governments and regimes, doing so far better than theorists have realized. This possibility, moreover, has ramifications not only for developing democracies but for established ones as well.

A major reason that students of democracy show limited concern with the low participation rates, political disengagement, and inadequate reasoning processes of poorer and less-educated citizens in the developed world is the assumption that they lack the real capacities for genuine civic engagement. The evidence from Nicaragua suggests that poorer and less-educated citizens may not be as incapable of meaningful civic participation as students of established democracy assume, thereby raising questions about whether the lack of participation and sophisticated reasoning among the underclass in such democracies flows from their inherent incapacity to do so. Alternatively, their poor participation and reasoning could arise from inegalitarian social structures and elite-dominated political institutions that convince them that their voices will go unheard.

Nicaragua's experience suggests that democratic theorists need to look more closely at the contributions that primary education and modestly educated citizens can make to democratic participation and civic life. This is certainly a pressing issue for the developing world. Widespread advanced education is decades away for most such nations, in the best of scenarios. Yet attention to modest levels of mass education so that all citizens are literate and that most have primary education may go a long way in ensuring that such citizens can utilize their inherent intelligence and reasoning capacities to participate effectively in national self-governance, particularly in egalitarian societies. The literacy and education programs of the Sandinistas provided precisely this kind of close attention to mass education, while their social programs pushed the nation toward greater egalitarianism. Together these developments then helped activate citizen capacity for reasoning and self-government, a capacity that allowed them to move beyond the FSLN regime.[12]

11. For discussion of this literature, see Schlozman (2002).

12. Relatedly, Polletta (2002) argues that participatory democracy itself can help marginalized citizens learn political skills, in ways analogous to the role of political mobilization by the Sandinistas. Such mass mobilization was yet another accomplishment of the FSLN that empowered common citizens to engage in the reasoned choice that moved Nicaragua beyond the FSLN regime.

The Resourcefulness of the Common Citizen

Democracy can develop against the odds, third, because common citizens are more resourceful than democratic theorists realize. They can turn their domestic circumstances into opportunities for change, regardless of whether similar circumstances and processes proved vital to established democracies.[13] Perhaps the most telling example of this during the 1990s is the role citizens played in elevating Violeta Chamorro to the presidency.

Despite the advent of the UNO coalition, in 1990 the citizens had numerous potential candidates to support and many presidential aspirants who had not joined UNO. Yet the name that had the most public resonance was Violeta Chamorro. Whatever her differences with Sandinismo, she was not a right-wing devil. Her husband had died defying the Somoza dictatorship. She had herself once been part of the revolutionary junta, and her family epitomized Nicaragua's struggle for civil liberties and press freedom. While a Conservative like her husband, she was no Somocista.[14] Neither was she a Contra hero or a U.S. tool. Rather, she demanded an end to U.S. Contra support while campaigning for the presidency. She was a conservative democrat in the tradition of her party, committed to bringing democratic liberties and a market economy to Nicaragua and, in doing so, prepared to work with the United States, without simply following U.S. dictates.[15]

13. On the resourcefulness of the common people in developing societies, see J. Diamond (1997). He argues (20–22) that evolutionary factors led third world peoples to develop at least as much intelligence as citizens in developed nations. Third world peoples appear to be "backward" only because geographical factors inhibited the native development of food production and animal domestication in such societies. Once food production systems and related developments are introduced to these settings from dominant nation-states, the people prove rapidly able to learn to use them to good effect, adapting them to special local conditions in creative and resourceful ways.

Our suggestion here is that this same intelligence and resourcefulness can enable the common people of developing nations to embrace the procedures of democratic self-government found in the world's dominant nation-states, and to show great resourcefulness in how they pursue and utilize such procedures. They can even combine mass elections, popular mobilization, violent protests, support for civil liberties, revolution, judicial proceedings, rapid shifts in ideological loyalties, socialist reforms, and intense struggles over regime construction in ways that confound contemporary theorists of democratization but nevertheless foster democratization and self-government.

14. In fact, as Norsworthy (1997, 288–89) reports, one of Chamorro's most difficult personal moments early in her presidency came when anti-Sandinista elements of the La Prensa staff forced her daughter to resign as editor and engineered Violeta Chamorro's removal from the board. The staff moved against mother and daughter because of their support for the government's policy of national reconciliation, a policy "seen by the Right as an unnecessary concession to the Sandinistas."

15. Thus Walker (1997d, 298) notes that, in pursuing national reconciliation, Chamorro was defying not only the right in Nicaragua but also the Bush and early Clinton administrations. Similarly, her decision to retain Humberto Ortega as commander of the armed forces "met strenuous objections from Washington." It nevertheless proved a "brilliant move" in reassuring the FLSN of her good intentions and inducing their cooperation with her in regime transition.

Chamorro became Ortega's most important challenger because of popular support for her in the summer and early fall of 1989, when her effective leadership of UNO was not yet certain, and the coalition's campaign coffers were still low. While the United States certainly wanted Chamorro to win, it is difficult to believe that her victory came as a result of skillful U.S. action in choreographing her victory. Her campaign itself was disorganized, fractious, and inept, particularly in comparison to Ortega's effort, and early on she had to spend precious time traveling to Washington and seeking financial assistance rather than campaigning at home. The United States proved slow in providing campaign aid, which arrived well after Chamorro had taken the lead in surveys by DOXA and CID-Gallup. The United States was also foolhardy in its invasion of Panama, if a secondary reason for that invasion was to intimidate Nicaraguans into repudiating Ortega. The invasion was, in fact, the one development during the campaign that sparked an Ortega resurgence and might thereby have propelled him to victory.[16]

It is possible that Bush and the State Department, reading U.S. polls and aware of the confusion and ineptness within the Chamorro campaign, simply did not realize how popular she was, and thus risked slow provision of aid and the Panama invasion because they saw her as having little chance to defeat Ortega anyway. Certainly her election caught the administration by surprise. Two days after the election the White House admitted that neither the CIA nor the administration's polls had foreseen the Chamorro victory and thus President Bush had prepared no contingency plans for the transition to a Chamorro administration.[17] In the end, Chamorro won, we suggest, not because of secret or skillful machinations by the U.S. government, though undoubtedly it was tempted to engage in such actions, but because of her own aggressive and telling attack on Ortega and his regime, because of her reconstructionist vision, and because voters assessed her character, values, vision, and governing potential as being better for Nicaragua.

In supporting Chamorro early and in ever-increasing numbers, Nicaraguans believed they had found a path out of crisis and toward a peaceful, democratic future. But it was common citizens and not observers who saw this possibility. Most journalists prepared to report a swift Ortega victory, and the U.S. administration seemed resigned to the same. It was

16. This possibility, in fact, was reported by NBC's Ed Rabel from Managua on February 21, 1990, prior to the election: "The election observers say the Bush administration may have itself to blame for Daniel Ortega's rise in popularity among the voters. The reason, they say, is the military invasion in Panama. . . . It was a close race until the U.S. invaded." Mike Feinsilber, "The Landslide That Slid the Other Way," Associated Press, 2/28/90.

17. See *Washington Times*, 2/27/90, A1; and *New York Times*, 2/26/90, A6.

the Nicaraguan masses who saw the promise of national reconciliation Chamorro offered and then pursued once in power, and it was these same citizens who evaluated her highly as she left office, despite the many problems of her administration. Whatever the social consequences of Chamorro's presidency, it also began a period of potential in which the nation could move to pluralist power sharing and a contested process of national reconstruction, freed to some extent from U.S. meddling and assault. More than observers have acknowledged, this accomplishment is owing to the electoral engagement and choice of average citizens rather than to any elite group, and is powerful testimony to their resourcefulness and judgment.

Citizens again showed resourcefulness and a willingness to engage in self-correction in their response to Alemán's presidency. When he and his administration proved less responsive and more high-handed than many voters had expected, the public responded in decisive ways. They took to the streets in protest and helped moderate Alemán's social programs. They awarded control of most municipalities to the Sandinistas one year before he planned to run for the presidency again, destroying his reelection ambitions and checking the aggrandizing behavior of his administration. After he left office they campaigned for his trial for corruption, pressuring even the Liberal-dominated National Assembly to repeal the immunity he had brazenly bestowed upon himself. Thus, not only were citizens learning to use a range of democratic processes in shaping their nation's regime and limiting authoritarianism, drawing on the "governing capital" they had accrued in their extensive and responsible engagement in contemporary presidential elections, but they were showing great savvy in doing so.

As a final illustration, the citizens showed considerable resourcefulness when they embraced the Sandinistas from the late 1970s onward and empowered the party and Ortega to lead their country out of the depths of authoritarian repression and toward social justice. Whatever mistakes the Sandinistas made in that mammoth and difficult task, they were and are genuinely committed to popular empowerment and social justice. With popular support, they fundamentally reoriented Nicaragua toward the social concerns of the masses and then respected the decision of the masses that they should leave office. They then accepted some considerable responsibility for their own errors and redoubled their efforts on behalf of social justice within the confines of a constitutional democracy.

In embracing Ortega and the FSLN in 1979, giving Ortega electoral legitimacy in 1984, and supporting the party's continued involvement in national life after 1990, the citizens supported social activists and leaders who proved to be constructive revolutionaries as well as responsible, adaptive political realists. As with their support for Chamorro in 1990, citizens' early and sustained embrace of the FSLN suggests judgment and resourcefulness vindicated by the critical contributions the Sandinistas made to social liberation and democratic transition in Nicaragua.

The ability to learn and to reason, the capacity to use modest education to empower themselves, the capacity for savvy resourcefulness and self-correction when faced with severe problems—these are the fundamental resources of democratic citizenship that democratization theorists need more fully to appreciate. Moreover, they provide foundations for democratization that may be present throughout much, if not most, of the developing world today. The question in such settings then is whether additional core requisites of democratization exist to enable citizens to utilize these resources fully. Chief among these requisites is a nation's readiness for democracy.

Readiness for Democracy

A second suggestion of democratization theory is that a viable transition process depends on whether a citizenry is "ready" for democracy, a state of being that theorists believe requires considerable guidance from pacted, cohesive elites and the moderated levels of conflict that elite cohesion generates. Elite guidance helps ensure that citizens are prepared to understand and respect democratic processes and abide by the results of free elections. A moderated level of conflict encourages citizens to trust in democratic processes and engage in learning how to use them without fearing that support for a defeated party will lead to political and social recrimination. It also reduces citizens' tendency to take to the streets or to the battlefield in violent, destructive response when elections go against their preferences. In its most restrictive form, as witnessed in the writing of Samuel Huntington, this argument on behalf of elite guidance and moderated conflict suggests that mass citizens should not be involved, mobilized, or activist, much less contentious or revolutionary, unless and until institutions are fully established and capable of absorbing popular participation so that contestation does not cause disorder.

We have no quarrel with the possibility that readiness for democracy is an important component of successful democratization. But we do question whether reliance on domestic elites and careful institutional engineering, all the while silencing the masses, is the only path, the best path, or even a productive path to democratic readiness. Some mechanisms that can facilitate and ensure meaningful, inclusive democratic contestation may well be essential before citizens are ready for democracy. But the Nicaraguan experience questions whether such conditions depend on guidance from a cohesive domestic elite, the gradual elite crafting of democratic institutions, and the passivity of the masses until the magic democratic moment arrives.[18] Rather, readiness for inclusive contestation may come from freewheeling conflict among contentious elites; from the heated and even violent struggles by citizens for political space, class consciousness, and partisan structures necessary to the articulation of political differences; and from an international community prepared to support authentic movement toward democracy.

The Value of Elite Contestation

Given the story told in this book, there should be no doubt that democratization in Nicaragua has proceeded in the face of extensive conflict among domestic elites. During the Somoza era elite cohesion was absent, and the revolution was partly the result of conflict between pro- and anti-Somoza elites. Following Somoza's ouster, the Sandinista regime was not composed of committed liberal democrats leading the nation toward constitutional democracy. Their goal was social restructuring and equality, mass mobilization but not liberal democracy. As the Sandinistas became elites themselves, their reforms directly challenged the traditional elite, both those who had been Somocistas and those who had opposed Somoza. In response, the traditional elite who originally supported the revolution and joined the revolutionary government departed it early in the 1980s and remained outside it through the 1980s; some even supported the Contra War against Sandinismo right up to the 1990 election. Elite division rendered the right noncompetitive in the 1984 election, and even in 1990 Chamorro had trouble holding the UNO coalition together.

In the behavior of Nicaragua's elites, there is little hint of democratic commitment to guiding a recalcitrant, unready citizenry into democracy while avoiding divisive issues. Rather, elites on both sides opted for violence against each other, a pattern that preceded and continued with the Sandinista revolution. Moreover, elite commitment to electoral politics was uncertain; preelectoral doubt existed that the Sandinistas would honor an electoral defeat or that conservatives would cease their Contra support should Chamorro lose.[19] Doubts about elite commitment to democracy persisted

18. Yashar's (1997) study of elites in Costa Rica and Guatemala likewise questions the reliance on elite cohesion, arguing that division within elites is more conducive to democratization, as in Nicaragua.

19. For this perspective, see *New York Times*, 11/2/89, A12; 11/2/89, A12; 11/5/89, A10; 11/7/89, A10.

during Chamorro's presidency as Lacayo tried to use state power to capture the presidency through traditional elitist nepotism.

This pattern of deep elite conflict more nearly reflects reality in developing nations than does pacted elite cooperation. In societies subjugated by colonial experiences or by exploitative class relations, it is not surprising that elites who benefit from such systems will contend with elites who oppose them. In such settings, the rise of a moderate, cohesive elite reflecting a range of ideological positions is a daunting expectation. Generating cohesion in such settings may well require the silencing of major groups and impose an artificial dampening of conflict that can subsequently explode. The Somoza regime exemplified such a constructed and artificial outward cohesion and the eventual explosion in response. It is the contestation in response to Somoza and Sandinismo rather than elite cohesion that generated today's democratization. The turn of this contestation toward democratic means was then facilitated by the presence of space, class, and party, whose existence was owing to the long history of conflictual and often violent contestation within Nicaragua.

The Role of Space, Class, and Party

Chapters 2 and 7 show in great detail how elite contestation and mass protests created space for political dissent, fostered class consciousness, and generated a party system representing differing perspectives. The early stages of contestation came prior to the Somoza era, with elites contending over alternative visions of the market economy and over constitutional liberties. Moments of protest, as with the Sandino affair and Pedro Joaquin Chamorro's press campaign, sustained and broadened contestation efforts. The revolution then brought the poor and their advocates fully into the political struggle. Altogether, this history generated alternative visions of politics and society, argument over those alternatives, and communication outlets such as newspapers that represented different perspectives and provided information to citizens. Out of such arguments came simplifying ideologies that helped citizens understand politics and build opinions around those ideologies.

The tradition of political contestation, the link between political positions and ideologies, and the association of ideologies with political parties gave citizens a simple framework within which to comprehend democratic competition and make individual choices. Yet the emergence of space, class, and party came precisely from domestic elite *contestation* rather than elite cohesion and guidance, and from mass protest and revolt rather than from mass silence and passivity. Moreover, the broad relevance of space, class, and party to the citizens came not from moderation or gradualism but from social revolution, which expanded the range of ideologies that then came to the fore in electoral contestation.

In sum, it was contestation and division, including violent and revolutionary action, that helped make Nicaraguans ready for democracy, with such behavior seen among both the elite and the masses. Certainly it was not unity among domestic elites and their careful guidance of mass citizens toward democracy that led to democratic readiness. This is not to say that some type of elite oversight of Nicaraguan democratization was not present and valuable. But it was not *domestic* elite oversight. Insofar as guidance from elites played a role in Nicaragua's democratic experiment, it came from the international community.

The Importance of International Support

The ability of Nicaraguans to have a decisive influence on the future of their nation in the 1980s and thereafter was aided by growing international attention to democratization and human rights worldwide. This movement included institutionalized oversight from organizations like the Carter Center and systematic electoral observation by multiple international organizations from Europe, Latin America, and the United States. Moreover, by the late 1980s, the international community was relatively cohesive in support of elections, with even Mikhail Gorbachev joining leaders from Western Europe and the United State in advocating democratic elections.

From 1984 onward, international observers provided extensive electoral assistance to Nicaragua. In 1990, observers trained a spotlight on Nicaragua's electoral process, making it difficult for any elite faction to rig the election. On election day they spread throughout the country to ensure citizen access, a secret ballot, and accurate ballot counting. Afterward international election officials assessed the fairness of the election and the validity of its outcome. Moreover, the range of organizations fielding observation teams helped ensure that international oversight did not favor one group of elites or another.

There can be no doubt that this international oversight mattered. In 1984, the certification of a free and fair election by all international observers except the U.S. government helped protect Nicaragua from even greater intervention by the Reagan/Bush administration and allowed the Sandinistas to continue their movement toward democratization of Nicaraguan society. Ortega's willingness to accept the 1990 election also owed something to international pressure from the democratization movement, in this case particularly from his Central American neighbors. Finally, the Sandinistas were able to take their legislative seats and use them as an effective opposition bloc after 1990 partly because of Chamorro's commitment to pluralism and partly because of international observers' certification that the Sandinistas themselves had played fair in 1990 and won their seats honorably.

Similarly, international oversight in 1996 helped scrutinize suspicious circumstances surrounding Alemán's victory, so that he and his Liberal Party realized that brazen violations of democratic process were not possible. Such oversight then helped ensure that the Liberal Party would respect Sandinista municipal victories in 2000, forced Alemán to hold the 2001 elections, and ensured that he departed the presidency then rather than attempting an electoral coup. It also may continue to be needed in the future.

The strong role of the international community over these past twenty years helps make clear that elite oversight as well as citizen engagement can be vital for successful democratization. But elite oversight need not be domestic. The international community can create conditions and processes facilitative of democracy, just as they can sabotage it. This realization should lead scholars to recognize that democratization may prove possible even in societies that lack cohesive elite commitment to democratization. This should free all concerned, both domestically and internationally, to accept a greater degree of serious domestic contestation among elites, rather than to stress the need for elite cohesion. Giving freer rein to internal conflict and relying more on international oversight than on domestic moderation may better prepare a nation for democracy and better empower citizens to play key roles at the moment of choice. The Nicaraguan experience shows how well citizens can take advantage of such an opportunity, provided they have a capacity for civic engagement. It also demonstrates that the development of such a capacity can come in ways almost diametrically opposed to the conditions outlined in prevalent theories of democracy.

The Capacity for Civic Engagement

A third suggestion of theories about democratization is that citizens must have a well-developed capacity for civic engagement. This argument was introduced by Alexis de Tocqueville in *Democracy in America*, where he noted the widespread tendency of Americans to form associations "of a thousand different types"[20] and to engage in such associations as a central part of their intellectual and moral life. Such experience then provided key foundations

---

20. Cited by Putnam (1993, 48).

for their ability to understand the value and norms of participation in the public sphere. Gabriel Almond and Sidney Verba's *The Civic Culture* and Robert Bellah's *Habits of the Heart* both build on Tocqueville as a basis for understanding the foundations of democratic citizenship. But by far the most influential contemporary statement of this argument as it would apply to democratic development is Robert Putnam's *Making Democracy Work*, a book focused on an established democracy in the industrialized world.

Putnam seeks to understand why northern Italy has appeared more responsive to political reforms over the past several decades than has southern Italy. He suggests that the answer to this puzzle lies in the differential experience of citizens in the two regions with private civic associations, an experience that is far more widespread in the north than in the south. Like Tocqueville, Putnam argues that citizens take the norms of civic participation that they learn in private associations and draw on them in the public sphere as an underpinning of engagement in democratic politics. What he adds to Tocqueville is the emphasis of contemporary political science on the critical role of path dependency in political development, wherein the way in which contemporary politics proceeds is rooted deep in path choices and developmental experiences across centuries. Thus it is the divergent paths taken by northern and southern Italy across several centuries, with citizens experiencing far more widespread historical involvement in civic associations in the north than in the south, that have proven crucial to the recent differences between the regions in successful political and administrative reform. The inability of the south to respond effectively to the reformist movement in Italy is then augmented by the strong presence of the Catholic Church in the south, a factor that serves to create a hierarchical perspective on politics and thereby to inhibit the creation of civic norms and citizen engagement in participatory democracy.

In contrast to the advanced, industrialized society Putnam studies, Nicaragua is an impoverished, agrarian nation where the long-term, widespread associational life he describes for northern Italy was mostly absent until after 1979, except among a small, privileged elite. This absence would seem to foreclose the capacity of mass citizens to grasp the norms and procedures of democratic politics, much less to engage in the momentous and sustained processes of democratic choice witnessed over the past two decades. There simply has not been the time since the revolution of 1979 for citizens to experience the gradualist process of democratic learning that Putnam sees as critical to democracy, a fact that he acknowledges to be demoralizing for contemporary efforts at the rapid creation of a democratic culture even within Italy. Within Putnam's framework, the contemporary Nicaraguan experiment would seem essentially impossible. His emphasis on the deleterious influence of the Catholic Church in southern Italy then reinforces such skepticism, since Nicaragua is a deeply Catholic society akin to southern Italy.

Despite the skepticism that would result from a purist reading of Putnam's work, Nicaragua has engaged in civic learning and democratic transition all the same. It has, in fact, evidenced a strong capacity for civic engagement in the public sphere over the past quarter century, with this proving critical to democratization. Yet this capacity does not appear to result from gradual learning through private associational life but has come only recently and in quite different ways. Why?

Many factors have contributed to this outcome, some of which we will discuss with respect to the nation's developmental path. But three seem particularly relevant to the debate over civic learning that we wish to emphasize here. These deal with the experience of political mobilization during and after the revolution, the availability of models of democracy in the international community, and the psychology of social learning.

The Revolutionary Experience with Political Mobilization and Popular Empowerment

Nicaraguans were prepared for contemporary civic engagement, first and foremost, because of their experiences during and following the 1979 revolution. It was a genuine mass insurrection that capitalized on organized and spontaneous citizen participation throughout the country. During the late 1960s and mid-1970s, popular participation came through clandestine support for Sandinista guerrilla activity. As protest against the Somoza regime gained momentum, insurrectionary citizen groups came to include organizations of rural and industrial workers, peasants, and neighborhood organizations as well as organized participation from university campuses, high schools, businessmen's organizations, and the church. In addition, women and children provided critical clandestine support for the insurrection. The assassination of Pedro Joaquin Chamorro in January 1978 then provoked mass protests in Managua. In response, the revolt against Somoza gained momentum nationwide and became a mass military movement. Organized by the Sandinistas, citizens formed four military fronts that converged upon Managua from the north, south, east, and west. Somoza's fall in 1979 came directly as a result of domestic insurrection that demonstrated to citizens the power of organization and mass political participation.

After the military victory in July 1979, the Sandinistas helped encourage civic participation to channel itself into mass organizations. These included organized unions of peasants, agrarian workers, industrial laborers, women, and university and high school students and the informal sector of taxi drivers and market or street vendors.[21] In addition, many citizens formed neighborhood associations. Some of these early mass associations had originated with the military insurrection; others formed after July 1979. All of these early civic groups were organizations of the poor. The new Sandinista government gave official recognition to these mass associations by granting them sectoral representation in the national legislature.

Once it became clear how effective the mass associations could be in promoting the interests of the poor, other, more affluent members of Nicaraguan society also mobilized in similar manner. These later organizations included unions and associations of professionals, teachers, doctors, nurses, and university professors. Soon Nicaragua's wealthy classes also organized themselves into unions of landowners, cattle ranchers, coffee growers, cotton plantation owners, and private businessmen's organizations. Within a few years of the revolutionary victory, most of Nicaraguan society was mobilized, with many citizens belonging to more than one association and feeling empowered by each. Citizens then learned to work with each other and use the associations to press their own political and social concerns. From these mobilizational activities citizens also learned that risk could be beneficial and bring positive results, producing a citizenry possibly more willing to embrace risk than one that had never learned political capacity through revolution.[22]

Another source of lessons in civic learning was the Nicaraguan Catholic Church prior to 1979. In contrast to southern Italy, many Nicaraguan clerics were influenced by liberation theology. This made them sympathetic to the goals of social justice that the revolution advocated. The clergy organized Bible study meetings that taught the Bible to citizens in a manner that stressed the poverty of Christ and his sympathy with the poor.[23] Such messages fit closely with the Sandinista revolutionary message. In return, the

21. Many scholars have explored the role of popular organizations in revolutionary Nicaragua and the development of policy for the benefit of the poor and in response to popular demands. For a few examples, see Collins (1986); Enriquez (1991); Luciak (1995); and Ruchwarger (1987). For a study of associational experience and learning in the Cuban revolutionary context, see Fagen (1969).

22. Awareness of the role of learning in politics owes to the pioneering work of Heclo (1974). Bermeo (1992) has introduced the concept into the comparative study of democratization, specifically of redemocratization in Eastern Europe. Both she and Linz and Stepan (1996) refer to elite learning, Bermeo to elites who learn from mistakes they have made in the past, Linz and Stepan to elites who learn from mistakes made by elites elsewhere. Both uses capture part but not most of what we are referring to as "learning."

23. Berryman (1987); Lernoux (1982).

Sandinistas were never hostile to Catholicism or to religion in general, and many were devout Catholics. Through the church, religiosity provided another connection to the struggle for social justice and another lesson in civic engagement. While the church hierarchy, notably Cardinal Obando y Bravo, turned against the revolution after 1979, the Nicaraguan people were sufficiently resourceful to retain the lessons in civic engagement that they had learned from the church, even if they directed such capacities elsewhere.

Yet another manner in which the revolution empowered citizens was through the spread of primary education.[24] While Nicaragua was a largely illiterate society in 1979, the Sandinistas soon launched a nationwide literacy campaign modeled on the Cuban example. University and high school students went to live in the countryside for several months to teach adults to read. Subsequently, the Sandinistas poured resources into constructing primary schools in every corner of the country. Initially, while Nicaraguans were still being trained, the schools were staffed by teachers from Cuba. Later, as the Nicaraguan teacher-training program produced newly trained teachers and also in response to U.S. hostility to any Cuban involvement in Nicaragua, the Cuban teachers were gradually sent home and replaced by new Nicaraguan teachers. Ironically, this emphasis on education, including of adults, helped activate citizens' capacity to reason, think prospectively, and imagine regime change, all of which contributed to the popular vote for Chamorro in 1990 and the Sandinista fall from power.

In the absence of a long experience with civic associations and the gradualist inculcation of participatory norms, other viable paths exist to the necessary norms and participatory experiences. In particular, genuine social revolution and an authentic effort by a revolutionary government to mobilize mass political participation can induce rapid learning of the possibilities and power associated with civic engagement, thereby laying critical foundations for a democratic transition.

We embrace Putnam's emphasis on civic norms and social capital as foundations of democracy, but we believe that the conditions that can generate them may be more varied than his discussion of path dependency and associational learning indicates. Citizens can learn to value and participate in politics, and to cooperate in pursuit of "self-interest rightly understood," as Tocqueville so eloquently put it,[25] through intense personal experiences that underscore the value of collective action in their personal lives. This is, of course, a lesson not solely for the developing world but for established democracies that contain large

24. Brandt (1985) and Kampwirth (1997, esp.120–23).
25. Cited by Putnam (1993, 118).

pockets of citizens or regions that have lacked the gradualist evolution of associational life. Moreover, such personal experiences may include substantial engagement with mass protests and organized mobilization, including social revolution in settings unresponsive to the concerns of disempowered citizens.

The Availability of Models of Learning

A second factor that has helped citizens in contemporary Nicaragua grasp the nature and importance of civic engagement is having models of how democracy works among Central American nations such as Costa Rica and in the broader international community.[26] Even in the authoritarian Somoza era, awareness of civic life elsewhere in the world penetrated Nicaragua and brought a vision of democratic life. Pedro Chamorro's demand that Somoza respect liberties like press freedom and public involvement in politics made his life and his assassination powerful symbols that galvanized the people against the dictator. The position of Pedro Chamorro was reinforced by a steady flow of Nicaraguans who traveled abroad, often for education. With the revolution, the exchange between Nicaragua and the outside world increased. Many U.S. and Western European citizens visited Nicaragua to help with development work, to become involved with religious NGOs, or to study Spanish. The U.S. academic community also sent many scholars to Nicaragua. At the same time, some wealthy Nicaraguans, particularly those supportive of Somoza, left Nicaragua to live in Miami. With a Nicaraguan community living in Miami and relatives traveling between the United States and Nicaragua, international contact increased still further. Similarly, electronic and media communication in the late twentieth century brought Nicaraguans images of affluent life in established democracies. Those images served as incentive toward democratization.[27]

Much of the Nicaraguan movement toward a constitutional structure in the 1980s and 1990s fit with similar movements in many places worldwide.[28]

---

26. Nicaraguan citizens, unlike citizens in democracies that developed earlier, also have the advantage of knowing that alternation in power as a result of an electoral outcome constitutes normal politics in many other nations. In this sense they can look to the example of other democratic nations and learn about democratic practice more rapidly than they would do if the entire concept of elections were new worldwide. This example thus contributes to the "fast-forward" learning we are describing here.

27. Rosenau (1997) argues that the mass communications revolution facilitates transmission and learning of skills in a manner never seen previously. People are able to learn more information and skills more rapidly than ever before.

28. Di Palma (1990, esp. chaps. 2 and 9), in particular, has an optimistic outlook on global democratization because of diffusion effects.

The division of government into three branches and the use of parties and elections to change governments could be understood by reference to politics elsewhere.[29] Yet learning by international modeling was complex. As a result of their observation of problems with election fraud and political corruption elsewhere and of their own efforts to insure the legitimacy of domestic elections, Nicaraguans concluded that a fourth branch to oversee elections might prove useful and instituted one for themselves, thus both learning from and moving beyond dominant models of constitutional democracy such as the United States. These various experiences and modeling opportunities helped facilitate a fast-forward learning in Nicaragua that is underestimated by concentrating on how democratization arose gradually in the first North Atlantic democracies. Such learning can then be supported by conditions that reinforce the motivation of citizens in developing societies to focus their attention on politics and follow it closely. Chief among such conditions is a tendency toward political and societal crisis.

The Role of Crisis

As George E. Marcus and Michael B. MacKuen and others suggest, based on studies in established democracies, crisis can facilitate a heightened level of citizen attentiveness and focus on politics, making voters more open to new ideas and to the possibilities of political change.[30] While under some conditions social crisis can orient citizens toward destructive authoritarian and antidemocratic movements, topics that scholars have explored extensively, the work of Marcus and MacKuen and other learning theorists suggests that crisis can also engender in citizens an openness to experimentation with popular empowerment, democratic process, and constructive political change. We believe this is part of what happened in Nicaragua, somewhat offsetting a lack of deeply ingrained civic culture.

The exploitative, repressive nature of Somocismo in the 1970s generated a systemic crisis so severe that citizens eventually took to the battlefields and to the streets, exhibited revolutionary leadership, and moved against the regime. With this choice, they embraced a belief that they could participate in changing their government and society for the better. The new regime they brought to power moved a considerable distance toward delivering on that vision, even if it also became mired in global and domestic conflict. The

---

29. Keck and Sikkink (1998) argue that international pressures have affected far more than elections.

30. Marcus and MacKuen (1993); Marcus, Neuman, and MacKuen (2000); Dodd (1994).

systemic crisis Nicaraguans again faced in 1990 then forced citizens as well as many elites into another fast-forward learning mode. In the process they drew on participatory experiences during the revolution, benefited from the social, political, and constitutional reforms of the revolutionary government, patterned their behavior after democratic models in other nations, and accomplished in a short time what citizens in older democracies learned in a more gradual fashion across a number of generations.

Facing severe crisis, the voters in 1990 believed they would be greatly affected by whatever outcome the election produced. Given two choices about how to end the crisis and move toward national reconstruction, Nicaraguans took the election seriously and used their best judgment. They did so with quite limited prior experience with such procedures and choices and with only 1984 as a domestic electoral example. Moreover, neither the 1990 election nor any other election visible in Central America or developed democracies provided quite an analogous situation of momentous regime choice. As a result, anxiety resulting from crisis was magnified by anxiety over the election's potential consequences, reinforcing their efforts to focus on the campaign, master the processes it entailed, and give it their best call.[31]

Whatever one may think personally or politically about the citizens' choice, one surely cannot doubt that they showed themselves open to the democratic opportunity of the moment and took responsibility for the nation's future. As they did so, they generated one of the most powerful exemplars of partisan realignment in contemporary political history, simultaneously demonstrating the capacity of electoral revolution to defuse crippling crisis and transform a nation's political landscape. In the process, they embraced an expanded democratic vision for the nation, thereby demonstrating a deep belief in themselves and in their capacity for democratic citizenship. This leap into the unknown and the surprising capacities for reasoning and change they demonstrated in 1990 resulted from a state of crisis, not one of moderation. The capacity for reasoning and change then continued in 1996 and 2001, both elections under conditions that, while less threatening than those of 1990, still rank as difficult electoral circumstances in the contemporary world. Across the 1990, 1996, and 2001 elections, the citizens of Nicaragua provided a critical and sustained demonstration, of a sort perhaps never before documented in such a striking, public, and consequential

---

31. Similarly, Dominguez and McCann (1996, 75) found that Mexico's economic crisis of the 1980s, while not as severe as the situation in Nicaragua, generated close attentiveness by voters: "The decade-long economic hardship focused [Mexicans'] attention, not unlike the prospect of a hanging."

manner, that common citizens can engage in reasoned choice even in the face of crises far more severe than those experienced by contemporary established democracies. In doing so, they underscored the need for analysts to broaden the conditions under which democracy can be expected to flourish.[32]

Theories of democratization that stress stability, moderation, and avoidance of conflict miss the degree to which crisis makes citizens open to rapid democratic learning, able to focus on the roles of democratic citizenship, and ready to embrace democratic process. Of course, such conditions historically have also helped generate totalitarianism and authoritarianism. But such nondemocratic outcomes need not become foregone conclusions. In a world of international democratization and international oversight of elections, more willingness to accept domestic tensions and crisis in developing nations, trusting to citizens and elites to craft solutions amidst crisis, may be a viable way toward democracy.

The Importance of a Facilitative Developmental Path

A final suggestion of contemporary democratization theory is that a nation's previous regime experience largely determines its capacity for democratization. Of course, the idea that previous social and political developments may be critical to democracy is central to the democratization literature. This perspective is evident in theorists' stress on the importance of societal affluence, a democratically committed and cohesive domestic elite, and a history of widespread citizen involvement with civic associations. Each of these perspectives is also a kind of path-dependent theory, as is the emphasis on previous regime. Yet each is a limited perspective, stressing one particular condition, and a perspective that to some degree identifies a substantive situation that is subject to contemporary adjustment. Thus, if a nation lacks affluence, it may create it. If it lacks a cohesive elite, it may nurture one. And if it lacks civic associational life, it may foster conditions that will generate it. Such developments may take time, but they appear to be discrete enough to

---

32. On the lack of studies of citizen reasoning and vote choice amidst severe crisis, see Marcus, Neuman, and MacKuen (2000, 95 n. 1). The authors call for serious empirical investigation of elections in circumstances characterized by severe crisis in order to clarify citizens' capacity to engage in reasoned democratic choice in such settings. Our study of Nicaragua would seem to provide precisely such evidence. In doing so, it strongly suggests that democratic elections need not be limited to the relatively moderate range of circumstances that have characterized affluent established democracies during the post–World War II era but can be employed to elicit the reasoned judgment of citizens even amidst severe crisis, and even among mass citizens, particularly if a range of other supportive conditions such as free and fair elections and a history of "space, class, and party" exist.

be possible and thus can be made the basis of policy prescriptions, even if one does not accept our argument that stressing such conditions underestimates the range of circumstances that can facilitate democratization.

The regime path argument is different in kind from the arguments about other democratic requisites. It stresses the salutary or deleterious effects of specific regime paths that are broadly consequential in their results and seemingly irreversible in nature, particularly in the sense that a negative experience may cripple a nation's democratic potential. Thus Linz and Stepan argue that democratization is easier amidst a capitalist, free market economy, even if the previous regime has been authoritarian. The North Atlantic nations exemplify the salutary nature of capitalism. In contrast, a previous history of revolution and socialism is so destructive of individualism, civil society, and participation as to make democracy virtually impossible. They sustain this argument by comparing cases in Eastern Europe and Russia with those in southern Europe and Latin America. In doing so, they highlight the devastating consequences that Soviet totalitarianism had for democratization, attributing these to the revolution and subsequent socialist regime. The cautionary moral is that once the path to revolution and socialism is taken, the possibility for democracy is greatly curtailed, if not circumscribed altogether.

We have no quarrel with critiques of Soviet totalitarianism, nor do we oppose nonviolent experiences with democratization. We also agree that the previous regime matters. Yet are the Russian or Eastern European experiences appropriate models for assessing the effects of social revolution and socialist reforms in contemporary developing nations? Concentrating on the Soviet experience may provoke such ideological blinders as to prevent us from recognizing a range of promising paths toward democracy available to the developing world today, including social revolution and socialist reform.

Comparing the Soviet and Nicaraguan Experiences

The applicability of the Soviet experience is limited because of the unusual circumstances of the Russian Revolution. It took place at a time of world war in a vast, ethnically and religiously heterogeneous nation. It came to a nation crushed under entrenched czarist bureaucratic rule, in which little meaningful space existed for dissent, class consciousness, or political parties. It came at a time when utopian communism appeared new and possible. With respect to Eastern Europe, its socialist experience was primarily driven not by domestic factors at all, but by Soviet occupation.

In Russia the revolution was meant to be liberating but rapidly failed. Confronted with the demands of war and the governance of a huge empire, the revolutionary regime soon enacted domineering strategies of state control that quickly made it resemble the imperial autocracy it had replaced. The totalitarian regime then remained entrenched for decades, installing a fully command economy, crushing dissent, and proving impervious to international influences until late in the twentieth century. To aid its survival and increase further its isolation from the West, it occupied Eastern Europe after World War II and imposed totalitarianism there as well. In Eastern Europe "revolution" was never meant to be domestic liberation but rather Stalinist domination. In pursuit of such domination, the Soviet regime became an international pariah that imposed control at home and in Eastern Europe through a secret police, military domination, and isolation of its citizens from international influences. It fostered fear, inhibited individual participation in government, and stifled capacities for mass revolt by disintegrating civil society and turning everyone against everyone else. When change came, it came through elite choice, not through mass insurrection.

As with much of the developing world, Nicaragua's social and political struggles during the postwar era have occurred in strikingly different circumstances. A small, poor nation with a more homogeneous population, it had a tradition of space, class, and party, and its revolution came amidst a world community increasingly preoccupied with human rights and democratization. Support for the revolution was widespread and combined calls for social justice and egalitarianism with a desire for human rights. Moreover, rather than isolating itself, Nicaragua's revolutionaries appealed to the United States and Western Europe for help and took their international concerns to the World Court in The Hague. The Sandinistas never developed a KGB or a capacity for state terror. Indeed, the poverty and disorganization that characterized Nicaraguan underdevelopment would have made such an apparatus virtually impossible. Rather than seeking totalitarian control, they focused on alleviating poverty and mobilizing the masses for sustained political engagement.

Nicaragua's experience suggests that socialist revolution in developing countries today need not replicate the Soviet experience and, in fact, can have constructive consequences that help end tyranny, promote social justice, and facilitate popular participation. While Sandinismo in power did begin to develop some elements of a domineering state and elitist control, Sandinista opponents battled these tendencies in an open press and ended them entirely with the 1990 election. Far from being totalitarian or the result of foreign domination, the Nicaraguan revolution fought against foreign domination, ended authoritarian control by a domestic tyrant, and left power before the temptations associated with state control led them down a more repressive path. As a result the revolution freed and revitalized civil society rather than undermining it.

As with Russia, the Nicaraguan case may not be relevant everywhere. Nicaragua's socialist revolution and its democratization process were also shaped by the particulars of context. Thus, despite the positive aspects of Nicaragua's socialist revolution, even within the contemporary developing world experiences with socialism can be quite varied. Consider, for example, Anne Pitcher's portrait of Mozambique, where an elite-driven socialist revolution resulted in a much more repressive state than did the popular socialist revolution in Nicaragua (2002, 101–24). Similarly, we recommend caution in assuming from the Nicaragua case that the removal of dictators and coming of rebellion lead easily and naturally to democracy. In Iraq, for example, while resistance to long-term U.S. occupation and the early move toward Iraqi sovereignty demonstrate a desire by citizens and elites to govern their own nation, the creation of a viable democracy does not follow automatically from such resistance and rebellion, or from the interventionist removal of a long-term tyrant.

We do believe that mass citizens worldwide have innate capacities for reasoning that can facilitate transitions to democracy. Similarly, the conditions that foster popular involvement in democratic transitions are much broader than the classic requisites of democracy indicate. At the same time, the flourishing of citizens' innate capacities can be inhibited by a variety of adverse circumstances that must be taken seriously. These would include widespread illiteracy that goes unaddressed; deeply engrained social and political inequities that discourage citizens from believing that they can truly influence their government; a culture that opposes the space for open deliberation and dissent; religious beliefs that repress expression of vital personal and group interests; or an experience with external invasion and occupation that leaves disorder, distrust, and social breakdown in its wake. While democratization may proceed in the face of such conditions, if counterbalanced by other facilitative conditions such as international support and rapid citizen learning, its success cannot be naively assumed, but will come only with hard work, sacrifice, and contestation among a nation's mass citizens and elite actors.

As third world nations face the difficult task of democratization, the vital lesson of Nicaragua lies not in fostering a belief that democratization is easy, but in demonstrating that such nations have a more varied range of developmental paths by which to pursue democracy and self-governance than analysts have realized. In particular, revolutionary action and socialist experimentation may have advantages for the democratization process in small and homogenous nations where a highly authoritarian government is in league with an exploitative economic class and when a nation has some reasonable tradition of space, class, and party that encourages socialist revolutionaries to move toward procedural democracy, particularly when such encouragement is reinforced and supported by the international community. The Nicaraguan case thus reminds us of what Soviet entrenchment caused us to forget: nations need not remain mired in a history of social exploitation and repression but have the right and the opportunity to rebel. The act of revolution, moreover, is not just a destabilization of local, regional, or international order but can also be liberating, a vehement popular rejection of tyranny. That lesson had already been learned in the United States and France, but has been forgotten or clouded over by the Soviet disaster. Perhaps we can better remember revolution as liberating by reconsidering the role that social revolution played in France and the United States.

Remembering the Role of Revolution: France and the United States

Lest political analysts forget, the worldwide movement toward human rights and democratization started not in the 1970s and 1980s but in the two great social revolutions of the late eighteenth century. The American Revolution of 1776 demonstrated the capacities of common citizens to overthrow an occupying colonial power viewed as tyrannical, to justify their actions through appeal to the inalienable rights of all men, and to govern themselves thereafter through liberal democratic means.[33] They did so, moreover, without an extensive history of civic associations.[34] In fact, extensive associational life emerged, in Skocpol's phrase, only "as the colonies roused themselves to separate from Britain" (1999, 37). Voluntary popular associations then proliferated, as she and others document, in the decades following the revolution. Moreover, the popular energy the revolution unleashed over the following several decades swept away the social and political controls the revolutionary leadership tried to establish immediately after 1776. As part of this process, the citizens defeated the Federalist fathers in the electoral revolution of 1800, just twelve years following the advent of popular elections, and turned the presidency over to the great Republican supporter of the

33. Wood (1969) and Elkins and McKitrick (1993).

34. According to Skocpol (1999, 36–37), "Despite [the] socioeconomic potential, relatively few voluntary groups were created during colonial times. As Brown's statistics show, before 1760 there were only a few dozen voluntary groups apart from churches in all of Massachusetts/Maine." The reference is to Brown's (1973, 1974) data on the growth of voluntary groups in Massachusetts in the colonial, revolutionary, and postrevolutionary period.

French Revolution, Thomas Jefferson.[35] Free of elitist controls, an individualist, egalitarian nation emerged and moved rapidly westward as citizens pursued a new life in a boundless new world—with citizens creating civic associations or expanding them into the American heartland as they went.[36] With this energized popular crafting of a new society came the mass political participation and civic life Tocqueville so admired as the foundational strength of American democracy.[37]

Similarly, the French Revolution of 1789 demonstrated the capacities of a mass social revolution to sweep aside the ancien régime deeply embedded in domestic soil and create a new vision of politics.[38] With the Revolution came the creation of political associations throughout France in the 1790s, preparing Tocqueville to recognize the power of associational life when he visited America forty years later.[39] Also with the French Revolution came the rise of essential elements of democracy, such as ideological contention, mass political participation, party organization, and an international model of mass direct rule and citizen rights.[40] Perhaps most critically, the French Revolution embodied the Rousseauean idea that a new kind of politics could create a new kind of citizenry capable of self-government.[41]

The roots of democracy lie not in gradualist evolution but in revolutionary upheaval.[42] It was this upheaval that demonstrated the ability of common citizens to assert their rights, reason to new forms of government, and rapidly learn to organize and act. It was this upheaval that gave the world its initial models of mass popular participation and democratic self-government. It was this upheaval that created the contemporary language of civic engagement and democratic citizenship. And it was this upheaval that pointed toward the importance of mass experiences with civic associations in

35. On the growing "democratic" character of politics in late-eighteenth-century America and its role in the decline of the Federalists and the turn to Jeffersonian Republicanism, see Elkins and McKitrick (1993, 451–88).

36. Wood (1992); Skocpol (1999, 39–47).

37. Wood (1992, 1974).

38. Moore (1966, 108) argues that the French Revolution marked a critical step toward democratic development in that country by sweeping aside the ancien regime and its upper classes who were so hostile to democracy.

39. Woloch (1994, 91–92).

40. Even electoral studies in France emphasize ideology related to social class and deep social cleavages as a result of the impact on democracy of the French Revolution. The study of social cleavage, of course, is also of European origin. See Lipset and Rokkan (1967); Rokkan (1970).

41. Hunt (1984).

42. Thus Tilly (1998, 65) writes that the decisive move toward an international model of mass direct rule and extensive citizen rights came with the French Revolution

the life of a vibrant democracy. Thus the understanding of associations as a basis of democracy comes, in part, from the study of the connection between revolution and democracy. Both in France and in the United States, as in Nicaragua, it was revolution that generated popular mobilization, energized citizens to create mass civic associations, and engendered a democratic political culture. Tocqueville, noting the vibrancy of civic associations and participatory norms as foundations of democracy in America in the 1830s, was documenting a world made possible by the revolutions of the 1770s and 1780s and the social energy they released among citizens.

The critical role of revolution in democratization, as seen in the histories of France and the United States, is reinforced by the findings of Mary Ellen Fischer in her examination of democratization experiences across eight nations. Fischer's study argues that some form of crisis in an old regime, followed by political struggle, is common in the establishment of democracy. Nations emerging from such crises are characterized less by a mass of democratic citizens who adhere to long-nurtured norms of civic participation than by a population in the process of learning democratic citizenship. Solidification of participatory norms and democratic citizenship follows crisis and democratization rather than preceding it via associations. Such democratization processes, she suggests, may be particularly open to rapid learning and solidification in the aftermath of popular revolt if effective models of democracy exist for a nation to draw upon. Foreign support or examples can then substitute for some of the traditional requisites for democracy, particularly when basic procedural foundations for democracy already exist.[43] This is precisely what we have argued happened in Nicaragua, yielding democratization even in the most seemingly unlikely circumstances.[44]

The Democratic Legacy of the Nicaraguan Revolution

The historical literature on the French and American Revolutions, combined with Fischer's broad comparison, provides substantial evidence in support of the capacity of social upheaval and citizen mobilization to facilitate democratization. Fortuitously, the conditions Fischer stresses were present

43. See Fischer (1996, conclusion). Di Palma (1990, chaps. 2 and 4) also focuses on foreign influence in encouraging democratization.

44. On the relationship between revolution, popular associational life, and democratic development in France and the United States, see Wolin (1994).

In the case of Nicaragua, P. J. Williams (1994) has argued that the revolutionary experience enhanced electoral participation.

in Nicaragua over the past quarter century, including a crisis in the Somoza regime, an effective, widely supported challenge to it, international support for democratization following the fall of the regime, and learning from other democratic models. With these developments came (1) educational reform, which helped prepare citizens to reason and participate effectively as they reshaped their governing regime, (2) an expansion in political space, class consciousness, and partisan contestation that helped ready them for an inclusive political contestation, and (3) mass mobilization that helped orient citizens toward sustained civil engagement. In addition, the social revolution that sparked these developments generated one additional accomplishment, perhaps its most momentous one and the one most vital to developing nations: an emphasis on equality.

Once in power, Sandinismo broke the inegalitarian structure of Somocista society and replaced it with a more egalitarian one, thereby facilitating the capacity of all citizens to aspire to a decent life and have meaningful influence in choosing those who would govern them. The justification it gave for such dramatic reform was so convincing that many elements of society, including those elites who stayed in Nicaragua, came to believe in the justice of such change. The leveling process included moving the poor upward as well as bringing the rich down. Thus, Sandinismo reduced illiteracy, provided primary education, and encouraged civic engagement and associations. It provided social benefits to all Nicaraguans and tried to provide employment. Most important, it redistributed the nation's most important resource, land, in ways designed to spread property widely among the poor.[45]

Dahl has written that democratic institutions tend to develop where a society has a "logic of equality," such that many members feel they deserve a say in governance and have a genuine stake in decisions.[46] While Dahl's consideration of the subject underscores how the logic of equality can develop inadvertently (in agrarian settings, in places of small geographic size, on an island), the Nicaraguan experience suggests that the logic of equality can also

45. On prerevolutionary poverty, especially in Managua, see Téfel (1978). On the egalitarianism that came with Sandinista reforms, see Kaimowitz (1986); Collins (1986); and Enriquez (1991).

46. Dahl (1998, esp. chap. 2, pp. 10, 20). Tocqueville, he argues, found in 1830 a society where a logic of equality had been created by a rich associational life (63). See also Dahl (1971, esp. chap. 7). Moore (1966) argues that a market economy that spreads resources widely was essential to democratic development in Britain and France. Similarly, Lipset (1960) contends that relatively equal distribution of economic resources across citizens is essential to democracy because it equalizes access to power and participation. Tracing mutual experiences throughout the life cycle, Shapiro (1999) illustrates how such experiences can be incorporated into daily life.

be deliberately created by human agency. The Sandinista revolution did just that. It taught and encouraged civic life, moved to equalize society, and then left power long before popular civic organizations could be entirely turned toward a purpose of state domination.

While leveling society, Sandinismo also initiated democratic institutions and procedures, doing so, in part, in response to pressure from the United States and Western Europe, but also in response to the egalitarian logic of the revolution itself. A mass citizenry capable of overthrowing tyranny and liberating itself would seem to have an inherent right to self-governance, a right the Sandinistas themselves acknowledged in the early 1980s by creating a sectoral National Assembly. Thereafter the Sandinistas implemented an electoral calendar and faced national elections in 1984, becoming the first socialist revolutionary regime to do so. In addition, while falling short of the record of civil liberties generally seen in established democracies, they provided for press freedom, free speech, and freedom of assembly to a greater extent than ever seen before in Nicaragua. As they moved to ensure such liberties, their shortcomings resembled those of young democracies like the United States and France, both of which had great blemishes in their pursuit of universal human rights and civil liberties, early in their democratization experience and later during periods of civil strife.[47]

With the 1990 election Nicaragua's egalitarian reforms yielded a great paradox: It was social revolution and its reforms that enabled citizens to embrace democratic transition and elect to move beyond revolution. When the election arrived, the same generation who remembered the revolutionary lessons of civic engagement now went to the polls with the experience of popular power still fresh in their minds. Education and mobilization allowed them to believe that they could participate in politics with self-confidence and could realistically control their own destiny, while social egalitarianism gave them a considerable stake in national reconciliation and reconstruction. As a result, citizens embraced democracy as part of a conserving and consolidating movement, not a radical or reactionary one. Nicaraguans were thus able to accomplish a feat rare in the history of social revolution: they integrated the revolutionaries and much of their vision into the new order. While the postrevolutionary era has failed to pursue the most visionary elements of the Sandinista social agenda, contemporary Nicaragua is a more

---

47. On civil liberties in Nicaragua during the Sandinista era, see Linfield (1991). On civil liberties as the founding fathers sought to implement constitutional democracy in the United States, see the discussion of the Alien and Sedition Laws in Elkins and McKitrick (1993, 590–93). For a discussion of civil liberties during the U.S. Civil War, see McPherson (1990, esp. chap. 3). On civil liberties in the revolutionary era in France, see Moore (1966, esp. chap 2).

civil, less repressive, more egalitarian, and less exploitive society than was prerevolutionary Nicaragua.[48] A concern with human rights and social justice remains present in politics today, and citizens of left and right have embraced civil liberties and democratic process. Most remarkably, the Sandinistas themselves remain active and broadly influential as one of the world's most radical electoral parties, working in behalf of social justice from within the National Assembly and as municipal leaders nationwide.

The 1979 revolution produced a sufficiently egalitarian structure that citizens chose in 1990 to conserve the revolutionary gains rather than to push the edge of revolutionary possibility. Even the revolutionaries, in the end, chose to join the imperfect democratic fray rather than to pursue idealism against democracy. Much was lost with the conservative thrust of the election that disappointed observers and citizens alike. The new regime of democratic conservatism lessened state support for ameliorative social reforms and introduced a harsh neoliberal austerity into public policy and social life. In contrast, with time, renewed electoral legitimacy, and international support, the Sandinista regime might have institutionalized an even more egalitarian society and a functioning socialist economy that would have raised the standard of living for all and incorporated popular self-government. We will never know. But we do know that the revolution went considerable distance in ending repression, inducing egalitarianism, and fostering mass participation. It did so even in the face of the U.S. embargo and the Contra War. In combination with the worldwide movement toward human rights and international support for and oversight of elections, the revolutionary reforms fostered the emergence in Nicaragua of a democratic citizenry capable of sustained and informed civic engagement and reasoned electoral choice.

That such a decisive move toward democracy would occur following revolution and egalitarian restructuring should surely give pause to those concerned to understand the requisites of democracy, reminding us to probe deeper into history to envision the variety of models of democratization that may be viable today. Just as the sweeping away of the upper classes and their entrenched power was essential to democracy in France, and just as the American Revolution was critical to an egalitarian social structure and mass democracy in the United States, so too may revolutionary upheaval and egalitarian reform be critical and constructive in certain contexts within the contemporary world. In Nicaragua we see the revolutionary restructuring of

48. See, for example, the discussion throughout Walker (1997b, esp. 297–304). See also Selbin (1993).

society as a vital element in the subsequent citizen capacity to embrace democracy. Additionally, social egalitarianism allowed citizens to play a critical role in shaping and constraining the new regime, pushing social issues forward and limiting the authoritarian tendencies of new leaders.

In societies where broad mass affluence is but a distant dream, perhaps egalitarianism is the more viable and powerful requisite of democracy. If so, then greater attention is required to those conditions and processes that might foster egalitarian reform, even including social revolution. Today, as in the late eighteenth century, revolutionary upheaval may prove critical to the egalitarianism that can make a democratic future possible. Thereafter the pressing issue is whether democracy can flourish amidst the inegalitarianism that so often attends the competitive individualism and market economies accompanying contemporary moves to democracy.

Looking to Nicaragua's Future

With basic democratic institutions and procedures at hand, Nicaragua's challenge today is to consolidate and sustain democracy amidst the social pressures and inegalitarian tendencies that democracy and the free market themselves unleash.[49] This task is made harder by potential shifts in the environmental context that helped foster social restructuring and the move to democracy, and by the deep social problems that made revolution necessary.

The cruelty and inequity of the Spanish conquest and postindependence years, to say nothing of Somocista exploitation and repression, left deep social inequities and widespread poverty. The 1979 revolution and the revolutionary government went some distance in recognizing these injustices and providing initial social reform. Yet Nicaragua remains a poor nation, so that the existence of substantial egalitarianism means that democratic politics proceeds amidst a population struggling with the daily necessities of life and now doing so within a regime committed to free market economics, indi-

---

49. Dahl (1998, 166, 173) argues that capitalism and democracy have an inherently conflictual relationship, rather like a contentious marriage that works poorly but that neither partner is prepared to leave. See also Chua (2003). She argues provocatively that the extension of free market democracy beyond established, affluent democracies is likely to generate ethnic hatred, a backlash against democracy, and global destabilization, owing to the tensions between "market dominant" ethnic minorities and underclass ethnic majorities. She applies this argument explicitly in chapter 2 to all of Latin America, save Argentina, Uruguay, and Chile. Chua concludes that the prevention of the serious problems she details requires attention to various strategies for spreading the wealth in third world nations, so that the masses have a stake in the benefits of a market economy. Interestingly, Nicaragua's social revolution was precisely such an effort, though not one that she explicitly discusses. For a related argument, see De Soto (2000).

vidual initiative, and limited provisions for social welfare. In this setting, the advantages that some citizens have in terms of education, family wealth, and previous experience are translating into an entrepreneurial success that is passing others by, leading to a growing gap between the poor and the more affluent. Simultaneously, the market economy is introducing a broadening array of consumer goods that are available to the emerging middle and upper classes but just out of reach of the poor. While today's economic elite does not have the entrenched wealth of the prerevolutionary era, democratic conservatism is recreating a clearly etched economic class structure and generating visible differences in lifestyle within a nation of great poverty.[50]

As we have seen, the reemergence of extensive differences in life opportunities among economic classes is introducing a complex dynamic into Nicaraguan politics. Following the austerity of the Chamorro presidency, the lower classes moved away from support for the right, while the more affluent swung to the right. With Alemán's calculated responsiveness on key social issues, the lower classes swung back to the right in 2001, while the affluent, alienated by Alemán's corruption and authoritarianism, became more open to the left. Although support for civil liberties and democratic processes exists across classes, Nicaragua's social problems remain deeply ingrained and now are regaining such sharp salience that mass support for authoritarian leadership that also offers social reforms is a possibility. This threat is more troubling in view of the Sandinistas' continuing inability to mount a viable national campaign with a forward-looking candidate who speaks to the poor but can also build a broad-based governing mandate. Their failure only increases the openness of the lower class to rightist candidates who combine social programs with authoritarianism.

Concern about democracy's future in Nicaragua is then reinforced by the shift in the focus of world attention away from democratization and toward terrorism and by the U.S. war on drugs in Central America. Already in the November 2001 election, the international concern with terrorism had worked its way into Nicaragua's presidential election. During the last weeks of that campaign comments emerged from the United States government suggesting that Ortega might have close ties with the terrorists of September 11. Such rhetoric only purchases greater license for U.S. aggression, while the drug war again introduces "military advisors" into Central America.

Democracy in Nicaragua is sufficiently fragile and the history of U.S. intervention sufficiently recent that such developments are cause for alarm.

---

50. Robinson (1997, 27–30; 2003, 81–86). Another problem is the continuing struggle over land in Nicaragua. See Jonakin (1996).

At the very least, the shifting attention of the international community could deprive Nicaragua of electoral oversight to ensure democratic procedures during elections. More ominously, the shifting international environment could make Nicaragua yet again a hostage to international conflicts and great power machinations of the sort that gave rise to Somoza in the first place.

In the face of domestic potentialities for populist authoritarianism and international pressures that could undermine Nicaragua's budding democracy, the citizens remain Nicaragua's best safeguard and strongest asset in its democratic experiment.[51] The democratic consciousness of the electorate, including the extensive popular organizing that took place during the revolutionary years, may brake the worst excesses of nondemocratic behavior by any popularly elected leader. In making this argument we join Nancy Bermeo who argues that citizens stay the course with democratic institutions and support the democratic center, even in times of crisis, much more fully and widely than previous studies have understood.[52] Certainly this was evident in popular response to Alemán's authoritarianism and corruption. Similarly, citizen support for the 1979 revolution, for Ortega's 1984 election, for Chamorro in 1990, and for the left's municipal victories in 2000, taken together, point toward a populace with the courage and judgment to adapt to new contexts in ways that support national autonomy and domestic progress.

Nicaragua's developing democratic institutions also provide growing safeguards. The legislature, pressured by mobilized protests, has moved against Alemán's democratic disloyalty and corruption.[53] While Alemán tried to weaken this branch so that it could never challenge him, he could not undo the learning that emerged from the confrontation during the Chamorro years. As his hold on power weakened, it rose to thwart him and forced him to stand trial. Moreover, the public has learned and remains aware that the legislature can present a powerful check on executive power, and it was to the legislature that the anti-Alemán demonstrations were directed. The fact that the move against Alemán was encouraged by Bolaños indicates that the executive, at least momentarily, also represents a voice

51. Our faith in average citizens' ability to promote democratization finds support in Tilly's (1995) study of democratization in Britain. He demonstrates that during more than seven decades popular contentious politics pushed the British polity toward democracy, including greater public reference to parliamentary representatives and other national leaders, an increasingly national rather than parochial perspective, growing recourse to dialogue and negotiation, and declining use of violence. See also Thompson (1966, 1971, 1975, 1991).

52. Bermeo (2003). Quantitative studies of popular support for democracy in times of crisis appear in Muller, Jukam, and Seligson (1982) and Seligson and Muller (1987).

53. The notion of disloyal or semiloyal elites who have no commitment or an imperfect commitment to democracy is used by Valenzuela (1978) and in Linz and Stepan (1996).

against corruption and unrestrained power. And even the judiciary has now had the courage to apply the law and imprison Alemán. If these developments are respected by future governments and court decisions, then progress has been made.

Another safeguard is the existence of a viable electoral opposition, something Alemán also failed to undermine. Opposition to him now comes from within his own party, as well as from the FSLN. Furthermore, as 2000 has shown, when Ortega is not running the public is perfectly ready to vote for Sandinismo. If Ortega can be convinced to remove himself from candidacy in the future, the FSLN's electoral competitiveness could increase and even help foster party alternation in national government. Such greater competitiveness and partisan alternation would greatly strengthen democracy in Nicaragua. The biggest obstacle to this is Ortega's insistence on continued control of the FSLN and on being its presidential candidate. While the Sandinistas' social policies have great attraction to much of the public, and Alemán's behavior provided the FSLN a basis of appeal to the affluent, it is doubtful that the voters will again elect Ortega president in light of concerns about his erratic performance as president and the difficulties that attended his decade in power. The potential continues to exist for a Sandinista resurgence, should the public refocus on the pursuit of social justice and away from preoccupation with democratic consolidation and economic stabilization. But such a refocusing probably requires reassurance that an FSLN victory would not lead to a reversal in democratic liberties or in the availability of consumer goods, a reassurance that Ortega might find difficult to provide in convincing fashion.

Despite these caveats and qualifications, Nicaraguans are learning the basics of democracy, and democracy is fumbling forward in an imperfect but genuine manner. In making this claim, we define Nicaraguan democracy broadly, focusing not only on elections while allowing that elections are crucial. In evaluating democracy, we look also at the creation of democratic institutions, respect for civil liberties, the existence of inclusive contestation, the spread of power across parties of right and left, and processes that impose the rule of law on the powerful as well as the weak. A viable democracy requires all these ingredients. While Nicaragua's development in these regards is uneven, it is proceeding on all fronts. Moreover, it is doing so through the engagement and reasoned choice of the nation's citizens. Whether it be amidst poverty or affluence, this is no small achievement.

Appendix

This appendix describes the data sources for this book. These include three sets of surveys for the three electoral years, 1990, 1996, and 2001, and a content data analysis set examining newspaper coverage during the 1990 election campaign. The first two sets of surveys were gathered by the Venezuelan public opinion firm DOXA, while the 2001 survey data were collected by the Nicaraguan polling firm CINASE. The content analysis focused on two newspapers, *El Nuevo Diario* and *La Prensa*.

The National Surveys

Each survey reported in this book was representative of population density by geographical area and probed a wide variety of questions on candidate image and competence, views of the nation's economy, evaluations of governing regime, and vote intention. Selected surveys also probed other issues and political developments relevant to the particular election or to the comparison of the governing performance of the Sandinista and Chamorro era regimes. All surveys probed such demographic characteristics as age, gender, education, and employment. The combined surveys for each year allow us to trace the shifting political attitudes during each campaign and to link those attitudes with evolving vote intention. Comparative analysis of surveys across the elections allows us to trace the evolution of attitudes and vote choice in Nicaragua from 1990 through 2001.

In conducting these surveys, DOXA and CINASE worked hard to obtain extensive interviews and to conduct interviews throughout Nicaragua. They sought small town coverage in lesser provinces as well as the major cities.

They sought to balance the urban barrios and shantytowns where unemployment is higher. Additionally, by conducting house-to-house random sampling, they incorporated many women in the respondent pool, including domestic workers and female heads of households following a war-related death.[1]

The DOXA Surveys

DOXA is a polling firm with deep roots and extensive experience in Latin America, and specifically in Central America. Located in Caracas, Venezuela, DOXA is the full name of the organization and is not a set of initials standing for a longer name. The word *doxa* refers to the Greek word "to know." DOXA is the firm involved in conducting the ongoing Latinobarometro study and also was selected by the Venezuelan government to conduct its national census.[2] It also had repeatedly conducted polls in other Central American countries such as El Salvador and Panama at times when elections were tense and the population inexperienced, timid, and reticent. This helped its survey team understand the language, culture, and special election dynamics of a poor Latin nation like Nicaragua where democracy was only just emerging. But DOXA was not a Nicaraguan firm and was not engaged in the partisan struggles within Nicaragua. It could recruit interviewers from a variety of partisan and nonpartisan backgrounds and report "disappointing" results without concern for raising the ire of partisan financiers or weakening the political position of partisan allies.

In addition, DOXA's director, Gustavo Mendez, had been trained in survey research at the University of Michigan and thus had a professional and systematic approach to survey research. He had spent his career before and after graduate school immersed in survey analysis of Latin America. He was thus close enough to draw upon extensive contextual experience but distant enough to avoid partisan influence. This was particularly important during the 1990 election, which so many polling firms failed to analyze accurately.

1. Since these surveys were nationwide and rural as well as urban, they included at least some former Contras, particularly the rural surveys of the interior departments (Zelaya, the Segovias, Boaco). However, the survey instrument deliberately excluded questions about former Contra activity in the effort to remain nonpartisan and unthreatening and to increase response rates. We do not know which respondents were former Contras, although they could not have been more than a tiny minority.

2. The Latinobarometer models the Eurobarometer, spearheaded by the work of Ronald Inglehart and designed to probe for values and value changes within the European community. The Latinobarometer does the same for Latin America, testing, in particular, for the rise and health of democratic values and other attitudes supportive of political pluralism.

The Nicaraguan polling firms, like the newspapers, had a partisan position that made it difficult to recruit objective interviewers and may have evoked citizen concerns about how the data would be used. Partisanship also tended to elicit subtle inclinations about how the data were interpreted and reported. Thus Nicaraguan polling firms proved unreliable in their election analysis, as did firms from the United States. The greatest success came from Latin American firms outside Nicaragua, including DOXA, Mora y Aruajo, and CID-Gallup.[3]

An example of the care DOXA took in its surveys was the manner in which it created its survey samples. Using the voting precinct lists from the1984 election, it chose a random sample of precincts, a random sample of households within precincts, and a random choice method for surveying voting-age residents of each household. In addition to the precinct lists, DOXA accessed school records in order to add to the sample an appropriate representation of young voters who might not have voted in 1984. The voting age in Nicaragua is sixteen, and DOXA included this age group in the sample.

All DOXA interviews were conducted in person in or near the interviewee's home and always in his/her neighborhood of residence. Interviewers wrote responses on a form provided them by DOXA. No names were recorded on the responses, and all responses were kept anonymous. When respondents were given a choice of responses in a closed-ended question, they were handed a small, cardboard disk on which the various response options were listed in equal-sized "pie pieces" of the disk. In this fashion there was no bias in the order of priority of the response possibilities. When a respondent was illiterate, the interviewer read the responses off the disk for the interviewee.

Interviewers wore no particular color associated with any party and did not use color-coded pens or pencils. They informed respondents that they were working for a Venezuelan polling organization and told interviewees that their responses would be kept confidential. DOXA finished its final survey on February 10, 1990, two weeks prior to election day, February 26, 1990. This was in accordance with Nicaraguan law as mandated under the Sandinista regime: all surveys were to be concluded two weeks prior to the election, and no further data collection was permitted during the last two weeks of the campaign. In 1996 DOXA again finished its last preelection survey two weeks prior to the election, and then conducted a postelection survey immediately following the election.

---

3. Mora y Aruajo was Argentine. CID-Gallup was Costa Rican. Both predicted an UNO win. P. V. Miller (1991).

Such careful procedures allowed DOXA to conduct unusually good surveys in Nicaragua in 1990 and also in 1996. The 1990 DOXA study was
funded by Venezuelan sources and by DOXA itself. The data were later
released by Mendez to Leslie Anderson. The surveys were conducted during
the four months prior to the 1990 election, beginning in November 1989
and continuing through mid-February 1990. During those months DOXA
conducted a pilot study in early November and then five national surveys.
The pilot study and each of the surveys were national samples including
respondents from every Nicaraguan department (state) excluding Rio San
Juan. The 1996 DOXA study was funded by a National Science Foundation
grant to Leslie Anderson (SBER-9631011) and based on methodology used
by DOXA in 1990. In 1996 DOXA conducted three national surveys prior to
the election and one postelection survey. The election was on October 26,
1996.

DOXA's final 1990 survey forecast a 49.6 percent vote for Chamorro and
a 39.8 percent vote for Ortega. In the election she received 53.7 percent
of the vote and he received 40.8 percent. DOXA forecast a 9.8 percent
Chamorro lead whereas in the election she won by 13 percentage points.[4]
DOXA's final 1996 postelection survey estimated 53.7 percent for Alemán,
36.5 percent for Ortega, and 9.8 percent for the minor parties; the formal
electoral results were 51 percent, 37.8 percent, and 11.2 percent.

DOXA published a newspaper advertisement and rented a room in
Managua where young people could respond to the advertisement. From the
advertisement, DOXA staff members interviewed and selected about fifty
Nicaraguan citizens as potential interviewers. All of these had a high school
education, and many had some university education. DOXA then asked all
potential interviewers to attend a one-week training clinic in which they
were taught DOXA's interviewing expectations, trained to interview, and
practiced interviewing each other. The clinic was staffed by numerous
DOXA staff members, and personal oversight was available for each interviewer. After one week of training, DOXA then dropped about 20 percent of

4. We have also investigated several other data sets and the possibility of obtaining the
CID-Gallup data and the Mora y Aruajo data, surveys that also accurately predicted an UNO
win in 1990. To the best of our knowledge, the Mora y Aruajo data have never been released,
but Anderson has discussed the UNO prediction with Felipe Nogera, Mora y Aruajo's partner.
(Interview, Buenos Aires, May 1993). The CID-Gallup data can be purchased from the Roper
Institute but are much less extensive than the DOXA data. For a complete discussion of the
1990 polls and their dates see Barnes (1990).

Most of the 1990 surveys were conducted between November 1989 and February 1990.
A few organizations conducted single surveys before October 1989. One was Itztani, whose
surveys began in August 1990. Anderson (1990) has analyzed the Itztani data.

those who had been trained, ending up with a total number of interviewers of about forty, excluding supervisors. From these forty interviewers, DOXA created its interviewer teams.

For each survey DOXA used several teams of interviewers. Each team had a field supervisor, also a Nicaraguan, on the ground with them who spot verified interviews after they were conducted. By using several teams, DOXA was able to cover most of Nicaragua's departments within a seven- to ten-day period. By sending teams to interior departments while having other teams working in Managua and other large central cities, DOXA was able to survey central and more distant regions over the same time period.

The CINASE Surveys in 2001

By 2001, polling had become more professional and less partisan in Nicaragua, and DOXA had withdrawn from election polling there. The Nicaraguan firm CINASE replaced DOXA as our polling firm. CINASE is a set of initials that stands for Centro de Investigacion Social y Economica (Center for Social and Economic Investigation).

CINASE is directed by Sergio Alberto Santamaria, an experienced Nicaraguan pollster who also collects data for various development projects funded by NGOs. These include the United Nations and the Nicaraguan NGO INPRU (Instituto para la Promoción Humana). These data are then used to make policy and investment decisions about development projects throughout Nicaragua. CINASE also regularly conducts preelectoral polls for political parties and the media in Nicaragua.

As public opinion polls and professional surveys have become more common within Nicaragua, CINASE has led the way in developing multiple strategies to maximize citizen cooperation and response rates. For example, CINASE pollsters carry with them a small ballot box, designed to look like a miniature version of the ballot boxes used at voting booths nationwide on election day. The question about vote intent is the last question CINASE pollsters ask. At the bottom of the survey sheet on which they have marked all previous answers is a color photograph of the face of each of the main candidates for the three principal parties: the Sandinistas, the Conservatives, and the Liberals. On the chest of each candidate is a large, white circle. Respondents are handed the survey sheet, a pen, and the ballot box. Out of view of the interviewer, the respondent makes his/her candidate choice on the survey sheet, folds the sheet as if it were a ballot, and places it in the slot at the top of the miniature ballot box. This helps to reassure the respondents that they are free to give their honest vote intent.

This action, closely resembling the real act of voting, is repeated for every respondent in the survey. The 2001 data for this study were collected in this manner.

Using survey techniques similar to those employed by DOXA, CINASE achieved balanced survey results in 2001 that closely reflected the election outcome. The collection of the 2001 data was funded by the Manning Dauer Chair, held by Lawrence Dodd, at the University of Florida. The instrument was written by Anderson and Dodd to incorporate questions from 1990 and 1996, making the 2001 data comparable to the previous two data sets. The final tally from the Supreme Electoral Council showed Bolaños with 56 percent of the vote, Ortega with 42 percent, and Saborío and the minor parties with less than 2 percent. CINASE's final postelection poll estimated the turnout at 87.4 percent and showed Bolaños with 53.1 percent, Ortega with 42.5 percent, and the Conservatives/minor parties with 4.4 percent.

Content Analysis of Newspapers

In order to create a data base that would reflect the domestic political context in which the 1990 election was held, we used content analysis of Nicaragua's two largest-circulating newspapers, *El Nuevo Diario* and *La Prensa*. A CID-Gallup poll conducted prior to the 1990 election found that newspapers were the most trusted source of news in Nicaragua. The percentages were as follows: newspaper 35.8 percent; radio 28.7 percent; TV 22.7 percent; no source/DK/NR: 12.8 percent ($N = 1,226$). That same poll also found that *La Prensa* and *El Nuevo Diario* were the two leading newspapers in Nicaragua. Among respondents, 26.5 percent said *La Prensa* was their first- or second-choice newspaper; 25.1 percent said the same of *El Nuevo Diario*. *Barricada*, Nicaragua's only other daily, and the official voice piece of the Sandinista Party, was chosen as first or second choice by only 17.9 percent of respondents to the CID-Gallup poll. Because of its official relationship to one of the two major electoral parties and because of its lesser circulation and popularity we chose not to code articles from *Barricada*.

The articles analyzed for the content analysis data base corresponded to the time period of the 1990 DOXA study. Accordingly, we analyzed articles beginning November 1, 1989, and terminated the analysis with February 15, 1990. Newspaper coverage in Nicaragua is highly partisan. In an effort to obtain perspectives from opposing sides, we used *El Nuevo Diario* and *La Prensa*. Taken together they represented the two sides of the campaign, but neither was an official party newspaper. In order to make the recording of the data manageable under limited resources, we coded the articles from the Wednesday and Sunday editions of each week.

For the content analysis we used a team of four coders. One coder was Leslie Anderson; the other three were graduate students in the Political Science Department and Center for Latin American Studies at the University of Florida. All four coders were fluent in Spanish. In preparation for coding, both authors met repeatedly with the three graduate students to explain what we were doing. We were guided in our content analysis effort by Professor Leonard Tipton of the School of Journalism at the University of Florida and by various texts he made available to us on content analysis. We began the effort by reading the newspapers with all four coders reading the same issues of both newspapers in their entirety. We then met at length to share our summaries of the articles and to discuss the range of subjects they covered. We then debated how best to categorize each subject until we had reached agreement and could create a coding scheme that everyone understood.

Once we had reached agreement on a set of specific categories covering all aspects of electoral reporting by both newspapers, we then divided the four coders into two teams of two coders each. Each team then read two weeks of articles from both newspapers, with each individual coder reading and working separately. Each coder on each team coded the subject matter of the articles according to the coding scheme we had developed in meetings, seeking to determine the *primary topic of each article*. Each team of two coders then met and compared how they had individually coded the various articles. Where there was disagreement on coding between the two team members, they discussed their reasoning until they could agree upon one code as better. Each team of two coders repeated this process until they were 90 percent in agreement on the coding of the primary topic of every article. Where unresolvable disagreement arose, the entire coding team of graduate students met with both authors to resolve the differences until everyone was coding the same way.

Once each team was coding 90 percent the same, the two teams were switched so that, if coder A and B had worked together while C and D did likewise, now coders A and C worked together and B and D were paired. We then began the process over again, coding, comparing codes, discussing, meeting, and recoding until the second set of teams was also coding 90 percent in agreement.

When we had reached a point where the coding was 90 percent the same across all four coders and all questions and differences had been resolved, we then began coding the newspapers for the four months of the campaign. For each article of each newspaper, at least two different coders coded it and any differences were then discussed and resolved. In this manner we created a data base that was the same across all four coders and provided *a numerical estimate of the primary campaign topics covered weekly by both newspapers across the four campaign months*.

Bibliography

Abramson, Paul R., John H. Aldrich, Phil Paolino, and David W. Rohde. 1992. "'Sophisticated' Voting in 1988 Presidential Primaries." *American Political Science Review* 86: 55–69.

Abramson, Paul R., John H. Aldrich, and David W. Rohde. 1994. *Change and Continuity in the 1992 Elections*. Washington, D.C.: Congressional Quarterly Press.

———. 1998. *Change and Continuity in the 1996 Elections*. Washington, D.C.: Congressional Quarterly Press.

———. 1999. *Change and Continuity in the 1996 and 1998 Elections*. Washington, D.C.: Congressional Quarterly Press.

———. 2002. *Change and Continuity in the 2000 Elections*. Washington, D.C.: Congressional Quarterly Press.

Alesina, Alberto, John Londregan, and Howard Rosenthal. 1993. "A Model of the Political Economy of the United States." *American Political Science Review* 87: 12–33.

Alexander, Gerard. 2002. *The Sources of Democratic Consolidation*. Ithaca: Cornell University Press.

Alford, Robert R. 1963. *Party and Society: The Anglo-American Democracies*. Chicago: Rand McNally.

Almond, Gabriel A., and Sidney Verba. 1963. *The Civic Culture: Political Attitudes and Democracy in Five Nations*. Boston: Little, Brown.

———. 1989. *The Civic Culture Revisited*. Newbury Park, Cal.: Sage.

Anderson, Leslie E. 1990. "Post-Materialism from a Peasant Perspective: Political Motivation in Costa Rica and Nicaragua." *Comparative Political Studies* 23: 80–113.

———. 1992. "Surprises and Secrets: Lessons from the 1990 Nicaraguan Election." *Studies in Comparative International Development* 27: 93–119.

———. 1994a. "Neutrality and Bias in the 1990 Nicaraguan Preelection Polls: A Comment on Bischoping and Schuman." *American Journal of Political Science* 38: 486–94.

———. 1994b. *The Political Ecology of the Modern Peasant: Calculation and Community*. Baltimore: Johns Hopkins University Press.

———. 1995. "The Legislature as a Reflection of Democracy:" *Extension of Remarks, Legislative Studies Newsletter.* Washington, D.C.: American Political Science Association. July.

———. 1997. "Between Quiescence and Rebellion among the Peasantry: Integrating the Middle Ground." *Journal of Theoretical Politics* 9: 503–32.

———. 2002. "Of Wild and Cultivated Politics: Conflict and Democracy in Argentina." *International Journal of Politics, Culture, and Society* 16: 99–132.

———. 2005. "Horizontal and Vertical Accountability in a New Democracy: A Nicaraguan Perspective." *Latin American Politics and Society,* unpublished manuscript.

Anderson, Leslie, and Lawrence C. Dodd. 2002a. "Comportamiento electoral y democracia en Nicaragua: 1990–2001." *America Latina Hoy* (Salamanca) 30 (April): 205–30.

———. 2002b. "Nicaragua Votes: The Elections of 2001." *Journal of Democracy* 13: 80–94.

———. 2004. "Démocratie envers et contre tout: Comportement Electoral et démocratie au Nicaragua, 1990–2001." *Revue Le Banquet* (Paris) 21 (October): 293–323.

Anderson, Leslie, Michael Lewis-Beck, and Mary Stegmaier. 2003. "Post-Socialist Democratization: A Comparative Political Economy Model of the Vote for Hungary and Nicaragua." *Electoral Studies* 22: 469–84.

Ansolabehere, Stephen, and Shanto Iyengar. 1994. "Riding the Wave and Claiming Ownership over Issues: The Joint Effects of Advertising and News Coverage in Campaigns." *Public Opinion Quarterly* 58: 335–57

Armony, Ariel C. 1997. "The Former Contras." In Thomas W. Walker, ed., *Nicaragua without Illusions: Regime Transition and Structural Adjustment in the 1990s,* 203–18. Wilmington, Del.: Scholarly Resources.

Arrien, Juan Bautista. 1991. "The Transformation of Education: UNO's Political Project." *Envio,* September.

Axicri, Max. 1985. "Relations with Latin America." In Thomas W. Walker, ed., *Nicaragua: The First Five Years,* 499–520. New York: Praeger.

Banco Mundial. 1993. *The Who, What, and Where of Poverty in Nicaragua.* Managua: Banco Mundial.

Banks, Arthur S., and Thomas C. Muller, eds. 1998. *Political Handbook of the World.* Binghamton, N.Y.: CSA.

Barnes, William. 1990. "Pre-Election Polling in Nicaragua." In *Interamerican Public Opinion Report.* Washington, D.C.: Interamerican Foundation. January.

———. 1992. "Rereading the Nicaraguan Election Polls." In Vanessa Castro and Gary Prevost, eds., *The 1990 Elections in Nicaragua and Their Aftermath.* Lanham, Md.: Rowman and Littlefield.

Baumeister, Eduardo. 1991. "Agrarian Reform." In Thomas W. Walker, ed., *Revolution and Counterrevolution in Nicaragua,* 229–45. Boulder, Colo.: Westview Press.

Beck, Paul Allen, and Frank J. Sorauf. 1992. *Party Politics in America.* New York: Harper Collins.

Bellah, Robert N., Richard Madsen, William M. Sullivan, Ann Swindler, and Steven M. Tipton. 1985. *Habits of the Heart: Individualism and Commitment in American Life.* New York: Perennial.

Berelson, Bernard, Paul R. Lazarsfeld, and William N. McPhee. 1954. *Voting: A Study of Opinion Formation in a Presidential Campaign.* Chicago: University of Chicago Press.

Berman, Sheri. 1997. "Civil Society and the Collapse of the Weimar Republic." *World Politics* 49: 401–29.

Bermeo, Nancy. 1992. "Democracy and the Lessons of Dictatorship." *Comparative Politics* 24: 273–92.

———. 2003. *Ordinary People in Extraordinary Times: The Citizenry and the Breakdown of Democracy.* Princeton: Princeton University Press.

Bernstein, R. B. 2003. *Thomas Jefferson.* New York: Oxford University Press.

Berryman, Philip. 1987. *Liberation Theology: Essential Facts about the Revolutionary Movement in Latin America—and Beyond.* Philadelphia: Temple University Press.

Bischoping, Katherine, and Howard Schuman. 1992. "Pens and Polls in Nicaragua: An Analysis of the 1990 Pre-election Surveys." *American Journal of Political Science* 36: 331–50

Booth, John. 1985. *The End and the Beginning: The Nicaraguan Revolution.* 2nd ed. Boulder, Colo.: Westview Press.

Bossert, Thomas John. 1982. "Health Care in Revolutionary Nicaragua." In Thomas W. Walker, ed., *Nicaragua in Revolution*, 259–72. New York: Praeger.

Brandt, Deborah. 1985. "Popular Education." In Thomas W. Walker, ed., *Nicaragua: The First Five Years*, 317–45. New York: Praeger.

Brown, Richard D. 1973. "The Emergence of Voluntary Associations in Massachusetts, 1760–1830." *Journal of Voluntary Association Research* 2 (2): 64–73.

———. 1974. "The Emergence of Urban Society in Rural Massachusetts, 1760–1820." *Journal of American History* 61 (1): 29–51.

Burnham, Walter Dean. 1970. *Critical Elections and the Mainsprings of American Politics.* New York: Norton.

———. 1976. "Revitalization and Decay: Looking toward the Third Century of American Electoral Politics." *Journal of Politics* 38 (August): 146–72.

———. 1994. "Pattern Recognition and 'Doing' Political History: Art, Science, or Bootless Enterprise?" In Lawrence C. Dodd and Calvin Jillson, eds., *The Dynamics of American Politics*, 59–82. Boulder, Colo.: Westview Press.

Burns, Nancy. 2002. "Gender: Public Opinion and Political Action." In Ira Katznelson and Helen V. Milner, eds., *Political Science: The State of the Discipline.* New York: W. W. Norton. 462–87.

Burns, Nancy, Kay Lehman Schlozman, and Sidney Verba. 2001. *The Private Roots of Public Action: Gender, Equality, and Political Participation.* Cambridge, Mass.: Harvard University Press.

Burton, Michael, Richard Gunther, and John Higley. 1992. "Elites and Democratic Consolidation in Latin America and Southern Europe: An Overview." In John Higley and Richard Gunther, eds., *Elites and Democratic Consolidation in Latin America and Southern Europe.* Cambridge: Cambridge University Press.

Butler, David, and Donald Stokes. 1969, 1974. *Political Change in Britain: Forces Shaping Electoral Choice.* London: Macmillan.

Butler, Judy. 1997. "The Peoples of the Atlantic Coast." In Thomas W. Walker, ed., *Nicaragua without Illusions: Regime Transition and Structural Adjustment in the 1990s*, 219–34. Wilmington, Del.: Scholarly Resources.

Cain, Bruce, John Ferejohn, and Morris Fiorina. 1987. *The Personal Vote: Constituency Service and Electoral Independence.* Cambridge: Cambridge University Press.

Calvert, Randall L. 1985a. "Robustness of the Multidimensional Voting Model: Candidate Motivations, Uncertainty, and Convergence." *American Journal of Political Science* 29: 69–95.

———. 1985b. "The Value of Biased Information: A Rational Choice Model of Political Advice." *Journal of Politics* 47: 530–55.

Campbell, Angus, Philip E. Converse, Warren Miller, and Donald Stokes. 1960. *The American Voter*. New York: Wiley.

Carmines, Edward G., and James A. Stimson. 1989. *Issue Evolution: Race and the Transformation of American Politics*. Princeton: Princeton University Press.

Casper, Gretchen, and Michele M. Taylor. 1996. *Negotiating Democracy: Transitions from Authoritarian Rule*. Pittsburgh: University of Pittsburgh Press.

Chavarria, Ricardo. 1982. "The Nicaraguan Insurrection." In Thomas W. Walker, ed., *Nicaragua in Revolution*, 25–40. New York: Praeger.

Chua, Amy. 2003. *World on Fire: How Exporting Free Market Democracy Breeds Ethnic Hatred and Global Instability*. New York: Doubleday.

Chubb, Jerome M., William H. Flanigan, and Nancy H. Zingale. 1980. *Partisan Realignment: Voters, Parties, and Government in American History*. Beverly Hills, Cal.: Sage.

Chuchryk, Patricia M. 1991. "Women in the Revolution." In Thomas W. Walker, ed., *Revolution and Counterrevolution in Nicaragua*, 143–65. Boulder, Colo.: Westview Press.

Clarke, Harold D., Allan Kornberg, and Peter Wearing. 2000. *A Polity on the Edge: Canada and the Politics of Fragmentation*. Toronto: Broadview Press.

Close, David. 1999. *Nicaragua: The Chamorro Years*. Boulder, Colo..: Lynne Rienner.

Coleman, Kenneth M., and Douglas Stuart H. 1997. "The Other Parties." In Thomas W. Walker, ed., *Nicaragua without Illusions: Regime Transition and Structural Adjustment in the 1990s*, 165–84. Wilmington, Del: Scholarly Resources.

Collins, Joseph, with Frances Moore Lappé and Nick Allen. 1986. *Nicaragua: What Difference Could a Revolution Make?: Food and Farming in the New Nicaragua*. 1st ed. New York: Grove Press.

Conroy, Michael E. 1985. "Economic Legacy and Policies: Performance and Critique." In Thomas W. Walker, ed., *Nicaragua: The First Five Years*, 219–44. New York: Praeger.

Converse, Philip E. 1964. "The Nature of Belief Systems in Mass Publics." In David E. Apter, ed., *Ideology and Discontent*. New York: Free Press.

Converse, Philip E., and Roy Pierce. 1986. *Political Representation in France*. Cambridge, Mass.: Belknap Press of Harvard University Press.

Conway, M. Margaret. 1994. *Political Participation in the United States*. Washington, D.C.: Congressional Quarterly Press.

Conway, M. Margaret, Gertrude A. Steuernagel, and David W. Ahern. 1997. *Women and Political Participation: Cultural Change in the Political Arena*. Washington, D.C.: Congressional Quarterly Press.

Cook, Timothy E. 1998. *Governing with the News: The News Media as a Political Institution*. Chicago: University of Chicago Press.

Coppedge, Michael. 1994. *Strong Parties and Lame Ducks: Presidential Partyarchy and Factionalism in Venezuela*. Stanford: Stanford University Press

———. 1998. "The Dynamic Diversity of Latin American Party Systems." *Party Politics* 4: 547–68.

———. 2001. "Political Darwinism in Latin America's Lost Decade." In Larry Diamond and Richard Gunther, eds., *Political Parties and Democracy*. Baltimore: Johns Hopkins University Press.

Cox, Gary W. 1997. *Making Votes Count: Strategic Coordination in the World's Electoral Systems*. New York: Cambridge University Press.

Cupples, Julie. 1992. "Ownership and Privatization in Post-revolutionary Nicaragua." *Bulletin of Latin American Research* 11: 295–306.

Dahl, Robert A. 1956. *A Preface to Democratic Theory*. Chicago: University of Chicago Press.

———, ed. 1966. *Political Oppositions in Western Democracies*. New Haven: Yale University Press.

———. 1971. *Polyarchy: Participation and Opposition*. New Haven: Yale University Press.

———. 1998. *On Democracy*. New Haven: Yale University Press.

Dahl, Robert A., and Edward R. Tufte. 1973. *Size and Democracy*. Stanford: Stanford University Press.

Dalton, Russell J. 1996. *Citizen Politics: Public Opinion and Political Parties in Advanced Industrial Democracies*. 2nd ed. Chatham, N.J.: Chatham House.

———. 2002. *Citizen Politics: Public Opinion and Political Parties in Advanced Industrial Democracies*. 3rd ed. New York: Chatham House.

Dalton, Russell J., and Martin Wattenberg. 1993. "The Not So Simple Act of Voting." In Ada Finifter, *Political Science: The State of the Discipline II*. Washington, D.C.: American Political Science Association.

———, eds. 2000. *Parties without Partisans: Political Change in Advanced Industrial Democracies*. New York: Oxford University Press.

De Soto, Hernando. 2000. *The Mystery of Capital: Why Capitalism Triumphs in the West and Fails Everywhere Else*. New York: Basic Books.

Diamond, Jared. 1997. *Guns, Germs, and Steel: The Fates of Human Societies*. New York: W.W. Norton.

Diamond, Larry. 1999. *Developing Democracies: Toward Consolidation*. Baltimore: Johns Hopkins University Press.

Diamond, Larry, and Richard Gunther, eds. 2001. *Political Parties and Democracy*. Baltimore: Johns Hopkins University Press.

Diamond, Larry, and Marc F. Plattner, eds. 2001. *The Global Divergence of Democracies*. Baltimore: Johns Hopkins University Press.

Dietz, Henry. 1992. "Elites in an Unconsolidated Democracy: Peru during the 1980s." In John Higley and Richard Gunther, eds., *Elites and Democratic Consolidation in Latin America and Southern Europe*. Cambridge: Cambridge University Press.

Di Palma, Giuseppe. 1990. *To Craft Democracies: An Essay on Democratic Transitions*. Berkeley: University of California Press.

Dodd, Lawrence C. 1976. *Coalitions in Parliamentary Government*. Princeton: Princeton University Press.

———. 1994. "Political Learning and Political Change." In Lawrence C. Dodd and Calvin Jillson, eds., *The Dynamics of American Politics*, 331–64. Boulder, Colo.: Westview Press.

Dodson, Michael. 1991. "Religion and Revolution." In Thomas W. Walker, ed., *Revolution and Counterrevolution in Nicaragua*, 167–84. Boulder, Colo.: Westview Press.

Dominguez, Jorge. 2004. "Conclusion: Why and How Did Mexico's 2000 Presidential Election Campaign Matter?" In Jorge Dominguez and Chappell Lawson, eds., *Mexico's Pivotal Democratic Election: Candidates, Voters, and the Presidential Campaign of 2000*. Stanford: Stanford University Press.

Dominguez, Jorge I., and Chappell Lawson, eds. 2004. *Mexico's Pivotal Democratic Election: Candidates, Voters, and the Presidential Campaign of 2000*. Stanford: Stanford University Press.

Dominguez, Jorge I., and Marc Lindenberg, eds. 1997. *Democratic Transitions in Central America*. Gainesville: University Press of Florida.

Dominguez, Jorge I., and James A. McCann. 1996. *Democratizing Mexico: Public Opinion and Electoral Choices*. Baltimore: Johns Hopkins University Press

Dominguez, Jorge I., and Michael Shifter, eds. 2003. *Constructing Democratic Governance in Latin America*. Baltimore: Johns Hopkins University Press.

Dore, Elizabeth. 1985. "Culture." In Thomas W. Walker, ed., *Nicaragua: The First Five Years*, 413–22. New York: Praeger.

Downs, Anthony. 1957. *An Economic Theory of Democracy*. New York: Harper.

Duverger, Maurice. 1954. *Political Parties: Their Organization and Activity in the Modern State*. Trans. Barbara North and Robert North. London: Methuen.

Dye, David, with Jack Spence and George Vickers. 2000. *Patchwork Democracy: Nicaraguan Politics Ten Years after the Fall*. Cambridge, Mass.: Hemisphere Initiatives.

Dye, David, et al. 1995. *Envio*, November.

Easton, David, 1976. "Theoretical Approaches to Political Support." *Canadian Journal of Political Science* 9: 431–48.

Edmisten, Patricia Taylor. 1990. *Nicaragua Divided: La Prensa and the Chamorro Legacy*. Pensacola: University of West Florida Press.

Edwards, George C., III, William Mitchell, and Reed Welch. 1995. "Explaining Presidential Approval: The Significance of Issue Salience." *American Journal of Political Science* 39: 108–34.

Elkins, Stanley, and Eric McKitrick. 1993. *The Age of Federalism*. New York: Oxford University Press.

Enriquez, Laura. 1985. "The Dilemmas of Agroexport Planning." In Thomas W. Walker, ed., *Nicaragua: The First Five Years*, 265–80. New York: Praeger.

———. 1991. *Harvesting Change: Labor and Agrarian Reform in Nicaragua, 1979–1990*. Chapel Hill: University of North Carolina Press.

Epstein, Leon D. 1980. *Political Parties in Western Democracies*. New Brunswick, N.J.: Transaction Books.

Everingham, Mark. 1996. *Revolution and the Multiclass Coalition in Nicaragua*. Pittsburgh: University of Pittsburgh Press.

Fagen, Richard R. 1969. *The Transformation of Political Culture in Cuba*. Stanford: Stanford University Press.

Ferejohn, John A., and James Kuklinski, eds. 1990. *Information and Democratic Processes*. Urbana: University of Illinois Press.

Finifter, Ada W. 1996. "Attitudes toward Individual Responsibility and Political Reform in the Former Soviet Union." *American Political Science Review* 90: 138–52.

Finifter, Ada W., and Ellen Mickiewicz. 1992. "Redefining the Political System of the USSR: Mass Support for Political Change." *American Political Science Review* 86: 857–74.

Fiorina, Morris P. 1977. *Congress: Keystone of the Washington Establishment.* New Haven: Yale University Press.

———. 1981. *Retrospective Voting in American National Elections.* New Haven: Yale University Press.

Fischer, Mary Ellen, ed. 1996. *Establishing Democracies.* Boulder, Colo.: Westview Press.

Flanigan, William H., and Edwin Fogelman. 1971a. "Patterns of Democratic Development." In John V. Gillespie and Betty A. Nesvold, eds., *Macro-Quantitative Analysis: Conflict, Development, and Democratization.* Beverly Hills, Cal.: Sage.

———. 1971b. "Patterns of Political Development and Democratization: A Quantitative Analysis." In John V. Gillespie and Betty A. Nesvold, eds., *Macro-Quantitative Analysis: Conflict, Development, and Democratization.* Beverly Hills, Cal.: Sage.

Funk, Carolyn L. 1996. "The Impact of Scandal on Candidate Evaluations: An Experimental Test of the Role of Candidate Traits." *Political Behavior* 18: 1–24

Geddes, Barbara, and John Zaller. 1989. "Sources of Popular Support for Authoritarian Regimes." *American Journal of Political Science* 33: 319–47.

Gelman, Andrew, and Gary King. 1993. "Why Are American Presidential Election Campaign Polls So Variable When Voters Are So Predictable?" *British Journal of Political Science* 23: 409–51.

Gerber, Alan, and Donald P. Green. 1998. "Rational Learning and Partisan Attitudes." *American Journal of Political Science* 42: 794–818.

Gibson, Bill. 1991. "The Nicaraguan Economy in the Medium Run." *Journal of Interamerican Studies and World Affairs* 33: 23–51.

Gilens, Martin. 1988. "Gender and Support for Reagan: A Comprehensive Model of Presidential Approval." *American Journal of Political Science* 32: 19–49.

Gillespie, John V., and Betty A. Nesvold, eds. 1971. *Macro-Quantitative Analysis: Conflict, Development, and Democratization.* Beverly Hills, Cal.: Sage.

Glenn, Norval D. 1974. "Aging and Conservatism." *Annals of the American Academy of Political and Social Science* 415: 176–86.

Green, Donald, Bradley Palmquist, and Eric Schickler. 2002. *Partisan Hearts and Minds: Political Parties and the Social Identities of Voters.* New Haven: Yale University Press.

Guchteneire, Paul de, Lawrence LeDuc, and Richard G. Niemi. 1985. "A Compendium of Academic Survey Studies of Elections around the World." *Electoral Studies* 4: 159–74.

———. 1991. "A Compendium of Academic Survey Studies of Elections around the World: Update 1." *Electoral Studies* 10: 231–43.

Gunther, Richard, José Ramón Montéro, and Juan J. Linz. 2002. *Political Parties: Old Concepts and New Challenges.* Oxford: Oxford University Press.

Gutmann, Amy. 1987. *Democratic Education.* Princeton: Princeton University Press.

Habermas, Jürgen. 1979. *Communication and the Evolution of Society.* Trans. Thomas McCarthy. Boston: Beacon Press.

———. 1996. *Between Facts and Norms: Contributions to a Discourse Theory of Law and Democracy*. Trans. William Rehg. Cambridge, Mass.: MIT Press.

Hagopian, Frances. 1996. *Traditional Politics and Regime Change in Brazil*. New York: Cambridge University Press.

Hartlyn, Jonathan. 1988. *The Politics of Coalition Rule in Colombia*.. Cambridge: Cambridge University Press.

Hartz, Louis. 1955. *The Liberal Tradition in America: An Interpretation of American Political Thought since the Revolution*. New York: Harcourt & Brace.

Heclo, Hugh. 1974. *Modern Social Politics in Britain and Sweden: From Relief to Income Maintenance*. New Haven: Yale University Press.

Hibbs, Douglas A., Jr. 1981. "Economics and Politics in France: Economic Performance and Mass Political Support for Presidents Pompidou and Giscard d'Estaing." *European Journal of Political Research* 9: 133–46

———. 1987. *The American Political Economy: Macroeconomics and Electoral Politics*. Cambridge, Mass.: Harvard University Press.

Hibbs, Douglas A., Jr., and Heino Fassbinder, with the assistance of R. Douglas Rivers, eds. 1981. *Contemporary Political Economy: Studies on the Interdependence of Politics and Economics*. Amsterdam: North-Holland.

Hibbs, Douglas A., Jr., R. Douglas Rivers, and Nicholas Vasilatos. 1982. "On the Demand for Economic Outcomes: Macroeconomic Performance and Mass Political Support in the United States, Great Britain, and Germany." *Journal of Politics* 44: 426–62.

Hibbs, Douglas A., Jr., and Nicholas Vasilatos. 1982. "Economic Outcomes and Political Support for British Governments among Occupational Classes: A Dynamic Analysis." *American Political Science Review* 76: 259–79.

Higley, John, and Michael G. Burton. 1989. "The Elite Variable in Democratic Transitions and Breakdowns." *American Sociological Review* 54: 17–33.

Higley, John, and Richard Gunther. 1992. *Elites and Democratic Consolidation in Latin America and Southern Europe*. Cambridge: Cambridge University Press.

Hill, Kim Q. 1988. *Democracies in Crisis: Public Policy Responses to the Great Depression*. Boulder, Colo.: Westview Press.

Hirschman, Albert O. 1982. *Shifting Involvements: Private Interests and Public Action*. Princeton: Princeton University Press.

Hofstadter, Richard. 1969. *The Idea of a Party System: The Rise of Legitimate Opposition in the United States, 1780–1840*. Berkeley: University of California Press.

Hunt, Lynn. 1984. *Politics, Culture, and Class in the French Revolution*. Berkeley: University of California Press.

Huntington, Samuel P. 1968. *Political Order in Changing Societies*. New Haven: Yale University Press.

———. 1991. *The Third Wave: Democratization in the Late Twentieth Century*. Norman: University of Oklahoma Press.

Inglehart, Ronald. 1977. *The Silent Revolution: Changing Values and Political Styles among Western Publics*. Princeton: Princeton University Press.

———. 1990. *Culture Shift in Advanced Industrial Society*. Princeton: Princeton University Press.

Isbester, Katherine. 2001. *Still Fighting: The Nicaraguan Women's Movement, 1977–2000*. Pittsburgh: University of Pittsburgh Press.

Jackson, John E. 1975. "Issues, Party Choices, and Presidential Votes." *American Journal of Political Science* 19: 161–85.

Janos, Andrew C. 1992. "Political Dynamics of the Post-Communist Transition: A Comparative Perspective." In Nancy Bermeo, ed., *Liberalization and Democratization: Change in the Soviet Union and Eastern Europe*. Baltimore: Johns Hopkins University Press.

Jonakin, Jon. 1996. "The Impact of Structural Adjustment and Property Rights Conflicts of Nicaraguan Agrarian Reform Beneficiaries." *World Development* 24: 1179–91.

———. 1997. "Agrarian Policy." In Thomas W. Walker, ed., *Nicaragua without Illusions: Regime Transition and Structural Adjustment in the 1990s*, 97–113. Wilmington, Del.: Scholarly Resources.

Jones, Bryan D. 1994. *Reconceiving Decision-Making in Democratic Politics: Attention, Choice, and Public Policy*. Chicago: University of Chicago Press.

———. 2001. *Politics and the Architecture of Choice: Bounded Rationality and Governance*. Chicago: University of Chicago Press.

Jones, Mark P. 1995. *Electoral Laws and the Survival of Presidential Democracies*. Notre Dame, Ind.: University of Notre Dame Press.

Kahneman, Daniel, and Amos Tversky. 1979. "Prospect Theory: An Analysis of Decision under Risk." *Econometrica* 47: 263–92.

Kaimowitz, David. 1986. "Nicaraguan Debates on Agrarian Structure and Their Implications for Agricultural Policy and the Rural Poor." *Journal of Peasant Studies* 14: 100–170.

Kampwirth, Karen. 1997. "Social Policy." In Thomas W. Walker, ed., *Nicaragua without Illusions: Regime Transition and Structural Adjustment in the 1990s*, 115–29. Wilmington, Del.: Scholarly Resources.

Karl, Terry Lynn. 1986. "Imposing Consent: Electoralism vs. Democratization in El Salvador." In Paul W. Drake and Eduardo Silva, eds., *Elections and Democratization in Latin America, 1980–1985*. Center for Iberian and Latin American Studies. San Diego: University of California Press.

———. 1987. "Petroleum and Pacts: The Transition to Democracy in Venezuela." *Latin American Research Review* 22: 63–94.

———. 1997. *The Paradox of Plenty: Oil Booms and Petro-States*. Berkeley: University of California Press.

Keck, Margaret E. 1992. *The Workers' Party and Democratization in Brazil*. New Haven: Yale University Press.

Keck, Margaret E., and Kathryn Sikkink. 1998. *Activists beyond Borders: Advocacy Networks in International Politics*. Ithaca: Cornell University Press.

Key, V. O., Jr. 1949. *Southern Politics in State and Nation*. New York: Knopf.

———. 1955. "A Theory of Critical Elections." *Journal of Politics* 17: 3–18.

———. 1961. *Public Opinion and American Democracy*. New York: Knopf.

———, with the assistance of Milton C. Cummings Jr. 1966. *The Responsible Electorate: Rationality in Presidential Voting, 1936–1960*. Cambridge, Mass.: Belknap Press of Harvard University Press.

Kiewiet, D. Roderick. 1983. *Macroeconomics and Micropolitics: The Electoral Effects of Economic Issues*. Chicago: University of Chicago Press.

Kiewiet, D. Roderick, and Douglas Rivers. 1984. "A Retrospective on Retrospective Voting." *Political Behavior* 6: 369–93.

Kinder, Donald R., Gordon S. Adams, and Paul W. Gronke. 1989. "Economics and Politics in the 1984 Presidential Election." *American Journal of Political Science* 33: 491–515.

Kinder, Donald R., and D. Roderick Kiewiet. 1979. "Economic Discontent and Political Behavior: The Role of Personal Grievances and Collective Economic Judgments in Congressional Voting." *American Journal of Political Science* 23: 495–527.

———. 1981. "Sociotropic Politics." *British Journal of Political Science* 11: 129–61.

Klein, Ethel. 1984. *Gender Politics: From Consciousness to Mass Politics*. Cambridge, Mass.: Harvard University Press.

Kohn, Margaret. 1999. "Civic Republicanism versus Social Struggle: A Gramscian Approach to Associationalism in Italy." *Political Power and Social Theory* 13: 201–35.

Kramer, Gerald H. 1971. "Short-Term Fluctuations in U.S. Voting Behavior, 1896–1964." *American Political Science Review* 65: 131–43.

Kuklinski, James H., and Darrell M. West. 1981. "Economic Expectations and Voting Behavior in United States House and Senate Elections." *American Political Science Review* 75: 436–47.

Lane, Robert. 1959. *Political Life: Why People Get Involved in Politics*. Glencoe, Ill.: Free Press.

LaPalombara, Joseph, and Myron Weiner, eds. 1966. *Political Parties and Political Development*. Princeton: Princeton University Press.

Latin American Studies Association. 1984. *Electoral Process in Nicaragua: Domestic and International Influences: Report of the LASA Delegation to Observe the Nicaraguan General Election of November 4, 1984*. Austin, Tex.: LASA.

———. 1990. *Electoral Democracy under International Pressure: The Report of the Latin American Studies Association Commission to Observe the1990 Nicaraguan Election*. Pittsburgh: LASA.

Lazarsfeld, Paul, Bernard Berelson, and Hazel Gaudet. 1944. *The People's Choice: How the Voter Makes Up His Mind in a Presidential Campaign*. New York: Duell, Sloan, and Pearce.

LeDuc, Lawrence, Richard G. Niemi, and Pippa Norris, eds. 1996. *Comparing Democracies: Elections and Voting in Global Perspectives*. Thousand Oaks, Cal.: Sage.

———. 2002. *Comparing Democracies 2: New Challenges in the Study of Elections and Voting*. Thousand Oaks, Cal.: Sage.

LeoGrande, William M. 1985. "The United States and Nicaragua." In Thomas W. Walker, ed., *Nicaragua: The First Five Years*, 425–46. New York: Praeger.

———. 1998. *Our Own Backyard: The United States in Central America, 1977–1992*. Chapel Hill: University of North Carolina Press.

Lernoux, Penny. 1982. *Cry of the People: The Struggle for Human Rights in Latin America— the Catholic Church in Conflict with U.S. Policy*. New York: Penguin Books.

Levine, Daniel H. 1992. *Popular Voices in Latin American Catholicism*. Princeton: Princeton University Press.

Lewis-Beck, Michael S. 1988. *Economics and Elections: The Major Western Democracies*. Ann Arbor: University of Michigan Press.

Lijphart, Arend. 1971. *Class and Religious Voting in European Democracies: A Preliminary Report*. Glasgow: University of Strathclyde.

———. 1984. *Democracies: Patterns of Majoritarian and Consensus Government in Twenty-one Countries*. New Haven: Yale University Press.

———. 1994. *Electoral Systems and Party Systems: A Study of Twenty-seven Democracies, 1945–1990*. Oxford: Oxford University Press.

Lindberg, Staffan. 2002. "Problems in Measuring Democracy: Illustrations from Africa." In Ole Elgström and Goran Hyden, eds., *Development and Democracy: What Have We Learned and How?* New York: Routledge.

Linfield, Michael. 1991. "Human Rights." In Thomas W. Walker, ed., *Revolution and Counterrevolution in Nicaragua*, 275–94. Boulder, Colo.: Westview Press.

Linz, Juan. 1990. "The Perils of Presidentialism." *Journal of Democracy* 1: 51–69.

Linz, Juan, and Alfred Stepan. 1996. *Problems of Democratic Transition and Consolidation: Southern Europe, South America, and Post-Communist Europe*. Baltimore: Johns Hopkins University Press.

Lipset, Seymour Martin. 1959. "Some Social Requisites of Democracy: Economic Development and Political Legitimacy." *American Political Science Review* 53: 69–105.

———. 1960. *Political Man: The Social Bases of Politics*. Garden City, N.Y.: Doubleday.

———. 1963. *The First New Nation: The United States in Historical and Comparative Perspective*. New York: Basic Books, 1963.

Lipset, Seymour Martin, and Stein Rokkan. 1967. "Cleavage Structures, Party Systems, and Voter Alignments: An Introduction." In Seymour Martin Lipset and Stein Rokkan, eds., *Party Systems and Voter Alignments: Cross-national Perspectives*. New York: Free Press

Lodge, Milton, Kathleen M. McGraw, and Patrick Stroh. 1989. "An Impression-Driven Model of Candidate Evaluation." *American Political Science Review* 83: 399–419.

Lopez, Julio, Orlando Nuñez, Carlos Fernando Chamorro, and Pascual Serres. 1979. *La caida del somocismo y la lucha sandinista en Nicaragua*. San Jose, Costa Rica: EDUCA.

Lowery, David. 1985. "The Keynesian and Political Determinants of Unbalanced Budgets: U.S. Fiscal Policy from Eisenhower to Reagan." *American Journal of Political Science* 29: 428–60.

Luciak, Ilja A. 1995. *The Sandinista Legacy: Lessons from a Political Economy in Transition*. Gainesville: University of Florida Press.

———. 2001. *After the Revolution: Gender and Democracy in El Salvador, Nicaragua, and Guatemala*. Baltimore: Johns Hopkins University Press.

Lupia, Arthur, and Mathew McCubbins. 1998. *The Democratic Dilemma: Can Citizens Learn What They Really Need to Know?* Cambridge: Cambridge University Press.

MacCaulay, Neil. 1985. *The Sandino Affair*. Durham: Duke University Press. Orig. pub. 1967.

MacKuen, Michael B., Robert S. Erikson, and James A. Stimson. 1992. "Peasants or Bankers: The American Electorate and the U.S. Economy." *American Political Science Review* 86: 597–611.

MacRae, C. Duncan. 1977. "A Political Model of the Business Cycle." *Journal of Political Economy* 85: 239–63.

Magaloni, Beatriz, and Alejandro Poiré. 2004. "The Issues, the Vote, and the Mandate for Change." In Jorge Dominguez and Chappell Lawson, eds., *Mexico's Pivotal Democratic*

Election: Candidates, Voters, and the Presidential Campaign of 2000. Stanford: Stanford University Press.

Mainwaring, Scott. 1990. "Presidentialism in Latin America." *Latin American Research Review* 25 (1): 157–79.

———. 1999. *Rethinking Party Systems in the Third Wave of Democratization: The Case of Brazil.* Stanford: Stanford University Press.

Mainwaring, Scott, Guillermo O'Donnell, and Samuel Valenzuela, eds. 1992. *Issues in Democratic Consolidation: The New South American Democracies in Comparative Perspective.* Notre Dame, Ind.: University of Notre Dame Press.

Mainwaring, Scott, and Timothy R. Scully, eds. 1995. *Building Democratic Institutions: Party Systems in Latin America.* Stanford: Stanford University Press.

Mair, Peter. 1997. *Party System Change: Approaches and Interpretations.* Oxford: Clarendon Press.

Malbin, Michael. 1989. "Legislative-Executive Lessons from the Iran-Contra Affair." In Lawrence C. Dodd and Bruce I. Oppenheimer, eds., *Congress Reconsidered.* 4th ed. Washington, D.C.: Congressional Quarterly Press.

Malley, Nadia. 1985. "Relations with Western Europe and the Socialist International." In Thomas W. Walker, ed., *Nicaragua: The First Five Years,* 485–98. New York: Praeger.

Mann, E. Thomas, and Raymond E. Wolfinger. 1980. "Candidates and Parties in Congressional Elections." *American Political Science Review* 74: 617–32.

Marcus, George E., and Michael B. MacKuen. 1993. "Anxiety, Enthusiasm, and the Vote: The Emotional Underpinnings of Learning and Involvement during Presidential Campaigns." *American Political Science Review* 87: 672–85.

Marcus, George E., Russell Neuman, and Michael MacKuen. 2000. *Affective Intelligence and Political Judgment.* Chicago: University of Chicago Press.

Markus, Gregory B. 1982. "Political Attitudes during an Election Year: A Report on the 1980 NES Panel Study." *American Political Science Review* 76: 538–560.

———. 1986. "Stability and Change in Political Attitudes: Observed, Recalled, and 'Explained.' " *Political Behavior* 8: 21–44.

———. 1988. "The Impact of Personal and National Economic Conditions on the Presidential Vote: A Pooled Cross-Sectional Analysis." *American Journal of Political Science* 32: 137–54.

———. 1992. "The Impact of Personal and National Economic Conditions on Presidential Voting, 1956–1988." *American Journal of Political Science* 36: 829–35.

Markus, Gregory E., and Philip E. Converse. 1979. "A Dynamic Simultaneous Equation Model of Electoral Choice." *American Political Science Review* 73: 1055–70.

Mayhew, David R. 2002. "Electoral Realignments: A Critique of an American Genre." New Haven: Yale University Press.

McCann, James A., and Chappell Lawson. 2003. "An Electorate Adrift? Public Opinion and the Quality of Democracy in Mexico." *Latin American Research Review* 38 (3): 60–81.

McClintock, Cynthia. 1981. *Peasant Cooperatives and Political Change in Peru.* Princeton: Princeton University Press.

McConnell, Shelley A. 1997. "Institutional Development." In Thomas W. Walker, ed., *Nicaragua without Illusions: Regime Transition and Structural Adjustment in the 1990s,* 45–63. Wilmington, Del: Scholarly Resources.

McPherson, James M. 1990. *Abraham Lincoln and the Second American Revolution*. New York: Oxford University Press.

Michelat, Guy, and Michel Simon. 1975. "Catégories socio-professionelles en milieu ouvrier et comportement politique." *Revue Française de Science Politique* 25: 291–316.

———. 1977. *Classe, religion et comportement politique*. Paris: Presses de la Fondation nationale des sciences politiques et Éditions Sociales-Messidor.

Milbrath, Lester W., and M. L. Goel. 1977. *Political Participation: How and Why Do People Get Involved in Politics?* Chicago: Rand McNally.

Miller, Arthur H., William M. Reisinger, and Vicki L. Hesli, eds. 1993. *Public Opinion and Regime Change: The New Politics of Post-Soviet Societies*. Boulder, Colo.: Westview Press.

———. 1996. "Understanding Political Change in Post-Soviet Societies: A Further Commentary on Finifter and Mickiewicz." *American Political Science Review* 90: 153–66.

Miller, Arthur H., and Martin P. Wattenberg. 1985. "Throwing the Rascals Out: Policy and Performance Evaluations of Presidential Candidates, 1952–1980." *American Political Science Review* 79: 359–72.

Miller, Peter V. 1991. "The Polls—A Review: Which Side Are You On? The 1990 Nicaraguan Poll Debacle." *Public Opinion Quarterly* 55: 281–302.

Miller, Valerie. 1982. "The Nicaraguan Literacy Crusade." In Thomas W. Walker, ed., *Nicaragua in Revolution*, 241–58. New York: Praeger.

Miller, Warren E., and J. Merrill Shanks. 1982. "Policy Directions and Presidential Leadership: Alternative Interpretations of the 1980 Presidential Election." *British Journal of Political Science* 12: 299–356.

Milner, Henry. 2002. *Civic Literacy: How Informed Citizens Make Democracy Work*. Hanover, N.H.: University Press of New England.

Moore, Barrington, Jr. 1966. *Social Origins of Dictatorship and Democracy: Lord and Peasant in the Making of the Modern World*. Boston: Beacon Press.

Morales, Waltraud Queiser, and Harry E. Vanden. 1985. "Relations with the Nonaligned Movement." In Thomas W. Walker, ed., *Nicaragua: The First Five Years*, 467–84. New York: Praeger.

Morley, Morris H. 1994. *Washington, Somoza, and the Sandinistas: State and Regime in U.S. Policy toward Nicaragua, 1969–1981*. Cambridge: Cambridge University Press.

Muller, Edward N., Thomas O. Jukam, and Mitchell A. Seligson. 1982. "Diffuse Political Support and Antisystem Political Behavior: A Comparative Analysis." *American Journal of Political Science* 26 (2): 240–64.

Muller, Edward N., and Mitchell A. Seligson. 1994. "Civic Culture and Democracy: The Question of Causal Relationships." *American Political Science Review* 88: 635–52.

Mutz, Diana Carole. 1998. *Impersonal Influence: How Perceptions of Mass Collectives Affect Political Attitudes*. Cambridge: Cambridge University Press.

Nardulli, Peter F. 1995. "The Concept of a Critical Realignment, Electoral Behavior, and Political Change." *American Political Science Review* 89: 10–22.

Neuman, W. Russell, Marion R. Just, and Ann N Crigler. 1992. *Common Knowledge: News and the Construction of Political Meaning*. Chicago: University of Chicago Press.

Nie, Norman H., and Kristi Andersen. 1974. "Mass Belief Systems Revisited: Political Change and Attitude Structure." *Journal of Politics* 36: 540–91.

Nie, Norman H., Sidney Verba, and John R. Petrocik. 1976. *The Changing American Voter*. Cambridge, Mass.: Harvard University Press.

Nordhaus, William D. 1975. "The Political Business Cycle." *Review of Economic Studies* 42: 169–90.

Norsworthy, Kent W. 1997. "The Mass Media." In Thomas W. Walker, ed., *Nicaragua without Illusions: Regime Transition and Structural Adjustment in the 1990s*, 281–304. Wilmington, Del.: Scholarly Resources.

O'Donnell, Guillermo A. 1994. "Delegative Democracy." *Journal of Democracy* 5: 55–69.

O'Donnell, Guillermo A., and Philippe C. Schmitter. 1986. *Transitions from Authoritarian Rule: Tentative Conclusions about Uncertain Democracies*. Baltimore: Johns Hopkins University Press.

Oquist, Paul. 1992. "Sociopolitical Dynamics of the 1990 Nicaraguan Elections." In Vanessa Castro and Gary Prevost, eds., *The 1990 Elections in Nicaragua and Their Aftermath*. Lanham, Md.: Rowman and Littlefield.

Orozco, Manuel. 1999. "Freedom in One Country? The International Dimensions of Democracy in Nicaragua." Ph.D. diss., University of Texas.

Page, Benjamin I. 1978. *Choices and Echoes in Presidential Elections*. Chicago: University of Chicago Press.

Paige, Jeffery. 1997. *Coffee and Power: Revolution and the Rise of Democracy in Central America*. Cambridge, Mass.: Harvard University Press.

Perez-Stable, Marifeli. 1982. "The Working Class in the Nicaraguan Revolution." In Thomas W. Walker, ed., *Nicaragua in Revolution*, 133–45. New York: Praeger.

Pierce, John C., and Douglas D. Rose. 1974. "Nonattitudes and American Public Opinion: The Examination of a Thesis." *American Political Science Review* 68: 626–49.

Pitcher, M. Anne. 2002. *Transforming Mozambique: The Politics of Privatization, 1975–2000*. Cambridge: Cambridge University Press.

Polakoff, Erica, and Pierre La Ramee. 1997. "Grass-Roots Organizations." In Thomas W. Walker, ed., *Nicaragua without Illusions: Regime Transition and Structural Adjustment in the 1990s*, 185–201. Wilmington, Del: Scholarly Resources.

Polletta, Francesca. 2002. *Freedom Is an Endless Meeting: Democracy in American Social Movements*. Chicago: University of Chicago Press.

Pomper, Gerald M. 1975. *Voters' Choice: Varieties of American Electoral Behavior*. New York: Dodd, Mead.

Popkin, Samuel L. 1979. *The Rational Peasant: The Political Economy of Rural Society in Vietnam*. Berkeley: University of California Press.

———. 1991. *The Reasoning Voter: Communication and Persuasion in Presidential Campaigns*. Chicago: University of Chicago Press.

Powell, G. Bingham, Jr. 1982. *Contemporary Democracies: Participation, Stability, and Violence*. Cambridge, Mass.: Harvard University Press.

Powell, G. Bingham, Jr., and Guy D. Whitten. 1993. "A Cross-National Analysis of Economic Voting: Taking Account of the Political Context." *American Journal of Political Science* 37: 391–414.

Prevost, Gary. 1991. "The FSLN as Ruling Party." In Thomas W. Walker, ed., *Revolution and Counterrevolution in Nicaragua*, 101–15. Boulder, Colo.: Westview Press.

———. 1997. "The FSLN." In Thomas W. Walker, ed., *Nicaragua without Illusions: Regime Transition and Structural Adjustment in the 1990s,* 149–64. Wilmington, Del: Scholarly Resources.

Prevost, Gary, and Harry E. Vanden, eds. 1997. *The Undermining of the Sandinista Revolution.* New York: St Martin's Press.

Przeworski, Adam. 1991. *Democracy and the Market: Political and Economic Reforms in Eastern Europe and Latin America.* Cambridge: Cambridge University Press.

———. 1992. "The Games of Transition." In Scott Mainwaring, Guillermo O'Donnell, and J. Samuel Valenzuela, eds., *Issues in Democratic Consolidation: The New South American Democracies in Comparative Perspective.* Notre Dame, Ind.: University of Notre Dame Press.

Przeworski, Adam, and John Sprague. 1986. *Paper Stones: A History of Electoral Socialism.* Chicago: University of Chicago Press.

Puryear, Jeffrey M. 1994. *Thinking Politics: Intellectuals and Democracy in Chile, 1973–1988.* Baltimore: Johns Hopkins University Press.

Putnam, Robert O., with Robert Leonardi and Raffaella Y. Nanetti. 1993. *Making Democracy Work: Civic Traditions in Modern Italy.* Princeton: Princeton University Press.

———. 2000. *Bowling Alone: The Collapse and Revival of American Community.* New York: Simon and Schuster.

Rabinowitz, George, James Prothrow, and William Jacoby. 1982. "Salience as a Factor in the Impact of Issues on Candidate Evaluation." *Journal of Politics* 44: 41–63.

Rae, Douglas W., and Michael Taylor. 1970. *The Analysis of Political Cleavages.* New Haven: Yale University Press.

Rahn, Wendy M., John Brehm, and Neil Carlson. 1999. "National Elections as Institutions for Generating Social Capital." In Theda Skocpol and Morris P. Fiorina, eds., *Civic Engagement in American Democracy.* Washington, D.C.: Brookings Institution Press, and New York: Russell Sage Foundation.

Reding, Andrew A. 1991. "The Evolution of Governmental Institutions." In Thomas W. Walker, ed., *Revolution and Counterrevolution in Nicaragua,* 15–47. Boulder, Colo.: Westview Press.

Remmer, Karen L. 1985. "Redemocratization and the Impact of Authoritarian Rule in Latin America." *Comparative Politics* 17: 253–75.

———. 1991. "The Political Impact of Economic Crisis in Latin America in the 1980s." *American Political Science Review* 85: 777–800.

———. 1993. "The Political Economy of Elections in Latin America, 1980–1991." *American Political Science Review* 87: 393–407.

Ricciardi, Joseph. 1991. "Economic Policy." In Thomas W. Walker, ed., *Revolution and Counterrevolution in Nicaragua,* 247–73. Boulder, Colo.: Westview Press.

Robinson, William I. 1992. *A Faustian Bargain: U.S. Intervention in the Nicaraguan Elections and American Foreign Policy in the Post–Cold War Era.* Boulder, Colo.: Westview Press.

———. 1997. "Nicaragua and the World: A Globalization Perspective." In Thomas W. Walker, ed., *Nicaragua without Illusions: Regime Transition and Structural Adjustment in the 1990s,* 23–42. Wilmington, Del.: Scholarly Resources.

———. 2003. *Transnational Conflicts: Central America, Social Change, and Globalization*. New York: Verso.

Rokkan, Stein. 1967. "Geography, Religion, and Social Class: Crosscutting Cleavages in Norwegian Politics." In Seymour Martin Lipset and Stein Rokkan, eds., *Party Systems and Voter Alignments: Cross-national Perspectives*. New York: Free Press.

———, with Angus Campbell, Per Torsvik, and Henry Valen. 1970. *Citizens, Elections, Parties: Approaches to the Comparative Study of the Processes of Development*. New York: McKay.

Rose, Richard, William Mishler, and Christian Haerpfer. 1998. *Democracy and Its Alternatives: Understanding Post-communist Societies*. Cambridge: Polity Press of Blackwell Publishers.

Rose, Richard, and Derek Urwin. 1969. "Social Cohesion, Political Parties, and Strains in Regime." *Comparative Political Studies* 2: 7–67.

Rosenberg, Shawn, with Lisa Bohan, Patrick McCafferty, and Kevin Harris. 1986. "The Image and the Vote: The Effect of Candidate Presentation on Voter Preference." *American Journal of Political Science* 30: 108–27.

Rosenau, James N. 1997. *Along the Domestic-Foreign Frontier: Exploring Governance in a Turbulent World*. New York: Cambridge University Press.

Ross, Marc Howard. 1993. *The Culture of Conflict : Interpretations and Interests in Comparative Perspective*. New Haven: Yale University Press.

Ruchwarger, Gary. 1987. *People in Power: Forging a Grassroots Democracy in Nicaragua*. South Hadley, Mass.: Bergin and Garvey.

Sandino, Augusto César. 1980. *Ideario politico*. Compiled by Carlos Fonseca. Managua: Secretaria Nacionál de Propaganda y Educación Politica FSLN.

Sarlvik, Bo. 1969. "Socioeconomic Determinants of Voting Behavior in the Swedish Electorate." *Comparative Political Studies* 2: 99–135.

Sartori, Giovanni. 1976. *Parties and Party Systems: A Framework for Analysis*. Cambridge: Cambridge University Press.

Schaar, John H. 1981. *Legitimacy in the Modern State*. New Brunswick, N.J.: Transaction Books.

Schattsneider, E. E. 1960. *The Semisovereign People: A Realist's View of Democracy in America*. New York: Holt, Reinhard and Winston.

Schlozman, Kay Lehman. 2002. "Citizen Participation in America: What Do We Know? Why Do We Care?" In Ira Katznelson and Helen V. Milner, eds., *Political Science: The State of the Discipline*. New York: W. W. Norton. 433–61.

Schumpeter, Joseph. 1950. *Capitalism, Socialism, and Democracy*. New York: Harper and Row.

Schwab, Theodore, and Harold Sims. 1985. "Relations with the Communist States." In Thomas W. Walker, ed., *Nicaragua: The First Five Years*, 447–66. New York: Praeger.

Scott, James C. 1976. *The Moral Economy of the Peasant: Rebellion and Subsistence in Southeast Asia*. New Haven: Yale University Press.

———. 1985. *Weapons of the Weak: Everyday Forms of Peasant Resistance*. New Haven: Yale University Press.

Selbin, Eric. 1993. *Modern Latin American Revolutions*. Boulder, Colo.: Westview Press.

Seligson, Mitchell A., and John A. Booth. 1995. *Elections and Democracy in Central America, Revisited*. Chapel Hill: University of North Carolina Press.

Seligson, Mitchell A., and William J. Carroll III. 1982. "The Costa Rican Role in the Sandinista Victory." In Thomas W. Walker, ed., *Nicaragua in Revolution*. New York: Praeger.

Seligson, Mitchell A., and Edward N. Muller. 1987. "Democratic Stability and Economic Crisis: Costa Rica, 1978–1983." *International Studies Quarterly* 31 (3): 301–26.

Serra, Luis Hector. 1991. "The Grass-Roots Organizations." In Thomas W. Walker, ed., *Revolution and Counterrevolution in Nicaragua*, 49–75. Boulder, Colo.: Westview Press.

Shanks, Merrill, and Warren Miller. 1991. "Partisanship, Policy, and Performance: The Reagan Legacy in the 1988 Election." *British Journal of Political Science* 21: 129–97.

Shapiro, Ian. 1996. *Democracy's Place*. Ithaca: Cornell University Press.

———. 1999. *Democratic Justice*. New Haven: Yale University Press.

Shaw, Daron. 1999. "A Study of Presidential Campaign Event Effects from 1952–1992." *Journal of Politics* 61: 387–422.

Shively, W. Phillips. 1972. "Party Identification, Party Choice, and Voting Stability: The Weimar Case." *American Political Science Review* 66: 1203–25.

Skocpol, Theda. 1979. *States and Social Revolutions: A Comparative Analysis of France, Russia, and China*. London: Cambridge University Press.

Skocpol, Theda, with the assistance of Marshall Ganz, Ziad Munson, Bayliss Camp, Michele Swers, and Jennifer Oser. 1999. "How Americans Became Civic." In Theda Skocpol and Morris P. Fiorina, eds., *Civic Engagement in American Democracy*. Washington, D.C.: Brookings Institution Press, and New York: Russell Sage Foundation.

Skocpol, Theda, and Morris P. Fiorina. 1999. "Making Sense of the Civic Engagement Debate." In Theda Skocpol and Morris P. Fiorina, eds., *Civic Engagement in American Democracy*. Washington, D.C.: Brookings Institution Press, and New York: Russell Sage Foundation.

Sniderman, Paul M., Richard Brody, and Philip E. Tetlock. 1991. *Reasoning and Choice: Explorations in Political Psychology*. New York: Cambridge University Press.

Sniderman, Paul M., Michael Gray Hagen, Philip E. Tetlock, and Henry E. Brady. 1986. "Reasoning Chains: Causal Models of Policy Reasoning in Mass Publics." *British Journal of Political Science* 16: 405–30.

Spalding, Rose J. 1994. *Capitalists and Revolution in Nicaragua: Opposition and Accommodation, 1979–1993*. Chapel Hill: University of North Carolina Press.

Spoor, Max. 1994. "Neo-liberalism and Institutional Reform in Post-1990 Nicaragua: The Impact on Grain Markets." *Bulletin of Latin American Research* 13: 185–202.

Stahler-Scholk, Richard. 1995. "The Dog That Didn't Bark: Labor Autonomy and Economic Adjustment in Nicaragua under the Sandinista and UNO Governments." *Comparative Politics* 28: 77–102.

Statistical Abstract of Latin America. 2002. Vol. 38. Latin American Center. Los Angeles: University of California Press.

Stimson, James A. 1976. "Belief Systems: Constraint, Complexity, and the 1972 Election." In Richard G. Niemi and Herbert F. Weisberg, eds., *Controversies in American Voting Behavior*. San Francisco: W. H. Freeman.

———. 1999. *Public Opinion in America: Moods, Cycles, and Swings*. Boulder, Colo.: Westview Press.

Sundquist, James L. 1983. *Dynamics of the Party System: Alignment and Realignment of Political Parties in the United States*. Rev. ed. Washington, D.C.: Brookings Institution.

Swift, Elaine K. 1996. *The Making of an American Senate: Reconstitutive Change in Congress, 1787–1841*. Ann Arbor: University of Michigan Press.

Tarrow, Sidney. 1996. "Making Social Science Work across Space and Time: A Critical Reflection on Robert Putnam's *Making Democracy Work*." *American Political Science Review* 90: 389–97.

Téfel, Reinaldo Antonio. 1978. *El infierno de los pobres: diagnostico sociologico de los barrios marginales de Managua*. Managua: Distribuidora Cultural.

Thompson, E. P. 1966. *The Making of the English Working Class*. New York: Vintage Books.

———. 1971. "The Moral Economy of the English Crowd in the Eighteenth Century." *Past and Present* 50 (February): 76–136.

———. 1975. *Whigs and Hunters: The Origin of the Black Act*. 1st American ed. New York: Pantheon Books.

———. 1991. *Customs in Common*. London: Merlin.

Thorp, Rosemary. 1998. *Progress, Poverty, and Exclusion: An Economic History of Latin America in the Twentieth Century*. Baltimore: Johns Hopkins University Press/International Development Bank Publications.

Tichenor, P. J., G. A. Donohue, and C. N. Olien. 1970. "Mass Media Flow and Differential Growth in Knowledge." *Public Opinion Quarterly* 34: 159–70.

Tilly, Charles. 1995. *Popular Contention in Great Britain, 1758–1834*. Cambridge, Mass.: Harvard University Press.

———. 1997. *Roads from Past to Future*. Lanham, Md.: Rowman and Littlefield.

———. 1998. "Where Do Rights Come From?" In Theda Skocpol, ed., with the assistance of George Ross, Tony Smithard, and Judith Eisenberg Vishniac, *Democracy, Revolution, and History*. Ithaca: Cornell University Press.

Tocqueville, Alexis de. 1956. *The Old Regime and the Revolution*. New York: Harper & Brothers.

———. 1969. *Democracy in America*. Ed. J. P. Mayer. Garden City, N.Y.: Doubleday.

Tsing, Anna Lowenhaupt. 1993. *In the Realm of the Diamond Queen: Marginality in an Out of the Way Place*. Princeton: Princeton University Press.

Tufte, Edward R. 1978. *Political Control of the Economy*. Princeton: Princeton University Press.

Tyler, T. R., K. A. Rasinski, and K. M. McGraw. 1985. "The Influence of Perceived Injustice upon Support for the President, Political Authorities, and Government Institutions." *Journal of Applied Social Psychology* 15: 700–725.

Useem, Bert, and Michael Useem. 1979. "Government Legitimacy and Political Stability." *Social Forces* 57: 840–52.

Valenzuela, Arturo. 1978. *The Breakdown of Democratic Regimes: Chile*. Juan J. Linz and Alfred Stepan. Baltimore: Johns Hopkins University Press.

Vanden, Harry E. 1982. "The Ideology of the Insurrection." In Thomas Walker, ed., *Nicaragua in Revolution*. New York: Praeger.

———. 1991. "Foreign Policy." In Thomas W. Walker, ed., *Revolution and Counterrevolution in Nicaragua*. Boulder, Colo.: Westview Press.

Vanden, Harry, and Gary Prevost. 1993. *Democracy and Socialism in Sandinista Nicaragua.* Boulder, Colo.: Lynne Rienner.

Vanhanen, Tatu, ed. 1992. *Strategies of Democratization.* Washington, D.C.: Crane Russak.

———. 1997. *Prospects of Democracy: A Study of One Hundred Seventy-two Countries.* New York: Routledge.

Verba, Sidney, and Norman H. Nie. 1972. *Participation in America: Political Democracy and Social Equality.* New York: Harper & Row.

Verba, Sidney, Kay Lehman Schlozman, and Henry E. Brady. 1995. *Voice and Equality: Civic Volunteerism in American Politics.* Cambridge, Mass.: Harvard University Press.

Vilas, Carlos M. 1986. *The Sandinista Revolution: National Liberation and Social Transformation in Central America.* Trans. Judy Butler. New York: Monthly Review Press.

Von Mettenheim, Kurt. 1995. *The Brazilian Voter: Mass Politics in Democratic Transition, 1974–1986.* Pittsburgh: University of Pittsburgh Press.

Walker, Thomas W., ed. 1982. *Nicaragua in Revolution.* New York: Praeger.

———, ed. 1985. *Nicaragua: The First Five Years.* New York: Praeger.

———. 1991a. *Nicaragua: The Land of Sandino.* 3rd ed. Boulder, Colo.: Westview Press.

———, ed. 1991b. *Revolution and Counterrevolution in Nicaragua.* Boulder, Colo.: Westview Press.

———.1997a. "Introduction: Historical Setting and Important Issues." In Walker, ed., *Nicaragua without Illusions: Regime Transition and Structural Adjustment in the 1990s.* Wilmington, Del.: Scholarly Resources.

———, ed. 1997b. *Nicaragua without Illusions: Regime Transition and Structural Adjustment in the 1990s.* Wilmington, Del.: Scholarly Resources.

———, ed. 1997c. *Reagan versus the Sandinistas: The Undeclared War on Nicaragua.* Boulder, Colo.: Westview Press.

———. 1997d. "Reflections," in Walker, ed., *Nicaragua without Illusions: Regime Transition and Structural Adjustment in the 1990s.* Wilmington, Del.: Scholarly Resources.

Ware, Alan. 1996. *Political Parties and Party Systems.* Oxford: Oxford University Press.

Weatherford, M. Stephan. 1978. "Economic Conditions and Electoral Outcomes: Class Differences in the Political Response to Recession." *American Journal of Political Science* 22: 917–38.

Weaver, Eric, and William Barnes. 1991. "Opposition Parties and Coalitions." In Thomas W. Walker, ed., *Revolution and Counterrevolution in Nicaragua,* 117–42. Boulder, Colo.: Westview Press.

Wheelock. Jaime Roman. 1981. Raices indigenas de la lucha anticolonialista en Nicaragua: De Gil González a Joaquín Zavala, 1523 a 1881. Managua: Editorial Nueva Nicaragua.

Wickham-Crowley, Timothy P. 1992. *Guerrillas and Revolution in Latin America: A Comparative Study of Insurgents and Regimes since 1956.* Princeton: Princeton University Press.

Williams, John T. 1990. "The Political Manipulation of Macroeconomic Policy." *American Political Science Review* 84: 767–95.

Williams, Philip J. 1994. "Dual Transitions from Authoritarian Rule: Popular and Electoral Democracy in Nicaragua." *Comparative Politics* 26: 169–85.

Wolfinger, Raymond E., and Steven J. Rosenstone. 1980. *Who Votes?* New Haven: Yale University Press.

Wolin, Sheldon. 1994. "Fugitive Democracy." *Constellations* 1: 11–25

Woloch, Isser. 1994. *The New Regime: Transformations of the French Civic Order, 1789–1820s.* New York: W. W. Norton.

Wood, Gordon S. 1969. *The Creation of the American Republic, 1776–1787.* Chapel Hill: University of North Carolina Press.

———. 1974. *Revolution and the Political Integration of the Enslaved and Disenfranchised.* Washington, D.C.: American Enterprise Institute for Public Policy Research.

———. 1992. *The Radicalism of the American Revolution.* New York: Knopf.

Yashar, Deborah. 1997. *Demanding Democracy: Reform and Reaction in Costa Rica and Guatemala, 1870s–1950s.* Stanford: Stanford University Press.

Young, James Sterling. 1966. *The Washington Community, 1800–1826.* New York: Columbia University Press.

Zaller, John. 1992. *The Nature and Origins of Mass Opinion.* Cambridge: Cambridge University Press.

Zimmermann, Matilde. 2000. *Sandinista: Carlos Fonseca and the Nicaraguan Revolution.* Durham: Duke University Press.

Index

ABC News, electoral predictions of, 87, 97
affluence theory: democratic transition
and, 24–25, 33, 286–87; as limited
perspective, 306; resources for
democratic citizenship and, 286–87;
Sandinista revolution and, 57
Africa, elite pacting in, 27n45
age: assessments of governing competence
and, 158–59, 170–71; Contra War as
election issue and, 199; demographic
modeling of vote patterns and, 191–92,
197–99; U.S. voters and, 193n8; vote
intent in 1990 and, 193–94; vote intent
in 1996 and 2001 and, 260, 261, 271–72
Alemán, Arnoldo: authoritarianism of, 246,
278; Bolaños and, 236, 239; campaign
of 1996 and, 226–30; campaign of 2001
and, 239; candidate selection for 1996
and, 223; Catholic Church support for,
227; Chamorro endorsement of, 230,
241, 245, 247, 276; citizens' evaluation
of, 243–44, 245–46; civil liberties and,
236; class and vote patterns and,
269–71, 273, 317; conciliatory approach
of, 232; constitutional reform under,
233; corruption under, 235, 238, 246;
delegative presidency and, 233;
economic policy of, 233–34; elite class
interests and, 18; expectations of
administration of, 233; fraud, electoral,
suspicions and, 298; governing

competence of, 255–61; image of as
candidate, 251–54; imprisonment of,
67, 241, 276, 319; inflexibility of, 229;
international pressure on, 298;
landownership issues and, 211;
legislature as check on excesses of, 318;
Liberal Party and, 214, 227; "love
letter to Nicaragua" of, 230; as mayor
of Managua, 228, 231; Minimum
Agenda and, 229; moderate rule by,
232–33; Obanda y Bravo support for,
227, 247, 253; opposition to, 232;
Ortega and, 229, 232, 233, 234;
presidency of, 232–36; prosecution of,
240–41, 284, 318–19; prospective
strategy of, 229; reform efforts under
Sandinismo and, 62; resourcefulness
of common citizens and, 293;
retrospective strategy of, 228;
retrospective voting and, 21–22; social
policy of, 233–34, 236, 237, 278;
Somoza dictatorship and, 226, 228,
229–30; victory of, 230–31. *See also*
election of 1996
Alemán family, corruption prosecution
against, 241
Almond, Gabriel, 299
American Revolution, compared to
Sandinista revolution, 310–12, 314,
315
amnesty proposals, election of 1990 and, 82